FOR DUMMIES
BESTSELLING
BOOK SERIES

Catholicism For Dun

P9-BYT-796

Sheet

The Twelve Articles of Catholic Faith

The following articles mirror the Apostles' Creed, which lists what all Catholics believe:

- **Article 1: I believe in God the Father, almighty, maker of heaven and earth.** This affirms that God exists, that he's a Triune God (one God in three persons, known as the Holy Trinity), and that he created the known universe.

- **Article 2: And in Jesus Christ, his only Son, our Lord.** This attests that Jesus is the Son of God and that he's most certainly divine. The word *Lord* implies divinity, because the Greek *Kyrios* and the Hebrew *Adonai* both mean *lord* and are only ascribed to God. So the use of *Lord* with *Jesus* is meant to profess his divinity. The name *Jesus* comes from the Hebrew *Jeshua,* meaning *God saves.* So Catholics believe that Jesus is Savior.

- **Article 3: He was conceived by the power of the Holy Spirit.** This affirms the human nature of Christ, meaning he had a real, true human mother, and also affirms his divine nature, meaning he had no human father but by the power of the Holy Spirit was conceived in the womb of the Virgin Mary. He's therefore considered both God and man by Christians — fully divine and fully human.

- **Article 4: Jesus Christ suffered under Pontius Pilate, was crucified, died, and was buried.** The human nature of Christ could feel pain and actually die, and he did on Good Friday. The mention of Pontius Pilate by name wasn't meant so much to vilify him forever in history but to place the Crucifixion within human history. So reference is made to an actual historical person, the Roman governor of Judea, appointed by Caesar, to put the life and death of Jesus within a chronological and historical context. It also reminds the faithful that one can't blame all Jews for the death of Jesus, as some have erroneously done over the ages. Certain Jewish leaders conspired against Jesus, but the actual death sentence was given by a Roman and carried out by Roman

soldiers. So both Jew and Gentile alike shared in the spilling of innocent blood. Anti-Semitism based on the Crucifixion of Jesus is inaccurate, unjust, and erroneous.

- **Article 5: He descended into hell, on the third day he rose again.** The hell Jesus descended into wasn't the hell of the damned, where Jews and Christians believe the devil and his demons reside. Hell was merely a word that Jews and early Christians used to describe the place of the dead. This passage affirms that on the third day he *rose,* meaning Jesus came back from the dead of his own divine power. He wasn't just clinically dead for a few minutes, he was *dead* dead; then he rose from the dead. More than a resuscitated corpse, Jesus possessed a glorified and risen *body*.

- **Article 6: He ascended into heaven and is seated at the right hand of the Father.** The Ascension reminds the faithful that after the human and divine natures of Christ were united in the Incarnation, they could never be separated. In other words, after the saving death and Resurrection, Jesus didn't dump his human body as if he didn't need it anymore. Catholicism teaches that his human body will exist forever. Where Jesus went, body and soul, into heaven, the faithful hope one day to follow.

- **Article 7: From thence he will come again to judge the living and the dead.** This article affirms the Second Coming of Christ at the end of the world to be its judge. Judgment Day, Day of Reckoning, Doomsday — they're all metaphors for the end of time when what's known as the General Judgment will occur. Catholics believe that after the death of any human person, immediate private judgment occurs and the person goes directly to heaven, hell, or *purgatory* (an intermediate place in preparation for heaven).

Catholicism For Dummies®

- **Article 8: I believe in the Holy Spirit.** This part reminds the believer that God exists in three persons — the Holy Trinity — God the Father, God the Son, and God the Holy Spirit. What's referred to as *the Force* in the movie *Star Wars* isn't the same as the Holy Spirit, who is a distinct person equal to the other two — God the Father and God the Son.

- **Article 9: I believe in the holy Catholic Church.** Catholics believe that the Church is more than a mere institution and certainly not a necessary evil. It's an essential dimension and aspect of spiritual life. Christ explicitly uses the word *church* (*ekklesia* in Greek) in Matthew 16 when he says, "I will build My Church."

- **Article 10: I believe in the forgiveness of sins.** Christ came to save the world from sin. Belief in the forgiveness of sins is essential to Christianity. Catholicism believes sins are forgiven in Baptism and in the Sacrament of Penance. For more on the Sacrament of Penance, see Chapter 7.

- **Article 11: I believe in the resurrection of the body.** From the Catholic perspective, a human being is a union of body and soul, so death is just the momentary separation of body and soul until the end of the world, the Second Coming of Christ, the General Judgment, and the resurrection of the dead. The just go, body and soul, into heaven, and the damned go, body and soul, into hell.

- **Article 12: I believe in life everlasting.** As Christ Our Savior died, so, too, must mere mortals. As he rose, so shall all human beings. Death is the only way to cross from this life into the next. At the very moment of death, private judgment occurs; Christ judges the soul. If it's particularly holy and virtuous, it goes directly to heaven. If it's evil and wicked and dies in mortal sin, it's damned for eternity in hell. If a person lived a life not bad enough to warrant hell but not holy enough to go right to heaven, Catholics believe the person goes to *purgatory*, which is a middle ground between heaven and earth, a state where departed souls *want* to go to be cleansed of any attachments to sin before going through the pearly gates.

Common Catholic Prayers

- **Our Father:** Our Father, Who art in heaven, hallowed be Thy name; Thy kingdom come; Thy will be done on earth as it is in heaven. Give us this day our daily bread; and forgive us our trespasses as we forgive those who trespass against us; and lead us not into temptation, but deliver us from evil. Amen.

- **Hail Mary:** Hail Mary, full of grace. The Lord is with thee. Blessed art thou among women, and blessed is the fruit of thy womb, Jesus. Holy Mary, Mother of God, pray for us sinners, now and at the hour of our death. Amen.

- **Glory Be:** Glory be to the Father, to the Son, and to the Holy Spirit, as it was, is now, and ever shall be, world without end. Amen.

- **Act of Contrition:** O my God, I am heartily sorry for having offended Thee. I detest all my sins, not only because I fear the loss of Heaven and dread the pain of Hell, but most of all, because Thou art Thee my God, who art all good and deserving of all my love. O My God, I firmly resolve, with the help of Thy grace, to sin no more and to avoid the near occasion of sin. Amen.

Copyright © 2003 Wiley Publishing, Inc.
All rights reserved.

Item 5391-7.

For more information about Wiley Publishing, call 1-800-762-2974.

For Dummies: Bestselling Book Series for Beginners

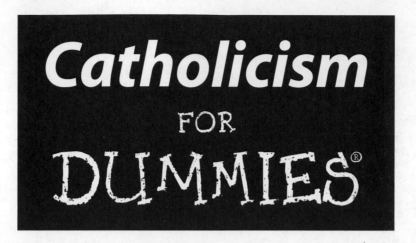

Catholicism FOR DUMMIES®

by Rev. John Trigilio Jr., PhD, ThD and
Rev. Kenneth Brighenti, PhD

Wiley Publishing, Inc.

Catholicism For Dummies®

Published by
Wiley Publishing, Inc.
111 River St.
Hoboken, NJ 07030-5774
www.wiley.com

Copyright © 2003 by Wiley Publishing, Inc., Indianapolis, Indiana

Published simultaneously in Canada

No part of this publication may be reproduced, stored in a retrieval system, or transmitted in any form or by any means, electronic, mechanical, photocopying, recording, scanning, or otherwise, except as permitted under Sections 107 or 108 of the 1976 United States Copyright Act, without either the prior written permission of the Publisher, or authorization through payment of the appropriate per-copy fee to the Copyright Clearance Center, 222 Rosewood Drive, Danvers, MA 01923, 978-750-8400, fax 978-646-8600. Requests to the Publisher for permission should be addressed to the Legal Department, Wiley Publishing, Inc., 10475 Crosspoint Blvd., Indianapolis, IN 46256, 317-572-3447, fax 317-572-4447, or e-mail permcoordinator@wiley.com

Trademarks: Wiley, the Wiley Publishing logo, For Dummies, the Dummies Man logo, A Reference for the Rest of Us!, The Dummies Way, Dummies Daily, The Fun and Easy Way, Dummies.com, and related trade dress are trademarks or registered trademarks of John Wiley & Sons, Inc. and/or its affiliates in the United States and other countries and may not be used without written permission. All other trademarks are the property of their respective owners. Wiley Publishing, Inc., is not associated with any product or vendor mentioned in this book.

For general information on our other products and services or to obtain technical support, please contact our Customer Care Department within the U.S. at 800-762-2974, outside the U.S. at 317-572-3993, or fax 317-572-4002.

Wiley also publishes its books in a variety of electronic formats. Some content that appears in print may not be available in electronic books.

Library of Congress Control Number: 2002114828

ISBN: 0-7645-5391-7

Manufactured in the United States of America

10 9 8 7 6 5 4 3

Nihil Obstat: Rev. Daniel J. Mahan, STB, STL
                 Censor Librorum

Imprimatur: Rev. Msgr. Joseph F. Schaedel
                 Vicar General/Moderator of the Curia

Indianapolis, Indiana
March 25, 2003
Feast of the Annunciation

About the Authors

Rev. John Trigilio, Jr., PhD, ThD, serves as the pastor of Our Lady of Good Counsel (Marysville, Pennsylvania) and St. Bernadette (Duncannon, Pennsylvania). He is the President of the Confraternity of Catholic Clergy and Executive Editor of its quarterly journal, *Sapientia* magazine. Father Trigilio is a co-host of two weekly TV series on the Eternal Word Television Network (EWTN): *Web of Faith* and *Council of Faith*. He also serves as a theological consultant and online spiritual advisor for EWTN. He's been listed in Who's Who in America in 1993 and Who's Who in Religion in 1999 and is a member of the Fellowship of Catholic Scholars. He was ordained a priest for the Diocese of Harrisburg (Pennsylvania) in 1988.

Rev. Kenneth Brighenti, PhD, serves as pastor of Saint Ann (Raritan, New Jersey). He is the Managing Editor of *Sapientia* magazine, member of the Board of Directors for the Confraternity of Catholic Clergy, and is co-host of *Council of Faith*, a weekly TV series on EWTN. Father Brighenti also served as a U.S. Naval Reserve Chaplain for ten years and was ordained a priest for the Diocese of Metuchen (New Jersey) in 1988.

Dedication

This book is dedicated to Our Lady, Queen of the Clergy, and Saint Joseph, Patron of the Universal Church.

And to His Holiness Pope John Paul II, the Bishop of Rome, Vicar of Christ, Supreme Head of the Catholic Church, and the Servant of the Servants of God. His life and priesthood and his pontificate have embraced the cross, have defended the orthodox teachings of the faith, and have inspired and encouraged Catholics all over the world to rejoice in their religion and to live it faithfully in service to God and to share it freely and openly in word and deed.

And to Reverend Mother Angelica, PCPA, founder of EWTN, who despite her many sufferings (injuries, strokes, surgeries, therapy, pain, and discomfort, as well as the cross of personal attack and persecution, insults and threats) has never stopped loving, hoping, and serving the Lord Jesus in His Holy Catholic Church by spreading the Word and teaching and defending the faith through electronic modern media and telecommunications.

We also dedicate this book to our loving parents, who gave us life and love and shared their Catholic faith:

John and Elizabeth Trigilio, Percy and Norma Brighenti

Finally, in loving memory of the following faithful departed:

John Trigilio, Sr. (1927–1998), father

Joseph P. Trigilio (1964–1997), brother

Michael S. Trigilio (1966–1992), brother

Mary Jo Trigilio (1960), sister

Authors' Acknowledgments

Father Brighenti and Father Trigilio are indebted to the following for their assistance, encouragement, opinions, guidance, advice, and input throughout this project: Rev. Fr. Robert J. Levis, PhD, Rev. Fr. Thomas Nicastro, Jr., Rev. Fr. Dennis G. Dalessandro, Louis and Sandy Falconeri & Family, Doctors Keith and Christina Burkhart & Family, Thomas McKenna, Jessica Faust, Sandy Blackthorn, Tracy Boggier, Tim Gallan, Esmeralda St. Clair, and a special note of thanks and gratitude to our parishioners at Our Lady of Good Counsel (Marysville, Pennsylvania), Saint Bernadette (Duncannon, Pennsylvania), and Saint Ann (Raritan, New Jersey) where we serve as pastors.

We are also grateful to the Poor Clare Nuns of Perpetual Adoration (Hanceville, Alabama), the Religious Teachers Filippini (New Jersey), the Discalced Carmelite Nuns (Erie, Pennsylvania), and the Dominican Nuns of the Perpetual Rosary (Lancaster, Pennsylvania) for their prayers and support throughout our seminary formation and sacred priesthood.

Publisher's Acknowledgments

We're proud of this book; please send us your comments through our Dummies online registration form located at www.dummies.com/register/.

Some of the people who helped bring this book to market include the following:

Acquisitions, Editorial, and Media Development

Senior Project Editor: Tim Gallan

Acquisitions Editor: Tracy Boggier

Consultant: Sandy Blackthorn

Copy Editor: Esmeralda St. Clair

Acquisitions Coordinator: Holly Grimes

Technical Editor: Rev. Dennis M. Duvelius

Editorial Manager: Christine Meloy Beck

Editorial Assistant: Melissa Bennett

Cover Photos: © Thierry Dosogne/ Getty Images/ The Image Book

Cartoons: Rich Tennant, www.the5thwave.com

Production

Project Coordinator: Dale White

Layout and Graphics: Seth Conley, Kelly Emkow, Carrie Foster, Michael Kruzil, Brent Savage, Jacque Schneider, Rashell Smith

Proofreaders: John Greenough, Andy Hollandbeck, Angel Perez, TECHBOOKS Production Services

Indexer: TECHBOOKS Production Services

Special Help: Joan Friedman

Publishing and Editorial for Consumer Dummies

    Diane Graves Steele, Vice President and Publisher, Consumer Dummies

    Joyce Pepple, Acquisitions Director, Consumer Dummies

    Kristin A. Cocks, Product Development Director, Consumer Dummies

    Michael Spring, Vice President and Publisher, Travel

    Brice Gosnell, Associate Publisher, Travel

    Suzanne Jannetta, Editorial Director, Travel

Publishing for Technology Dummies

    Andy Cummings, Vice President and Publisher, Dummies Technology/General User

Composition Services

    Gerry Fahey, Vice President of Production Services

    Debbie Stailey, Director of Composition Services

Contents at a Glance

Table of Contents

Introduction

· ·

*T*hree great religions trace their roots to the prophet Abraham: Judaism, Christianity, and Islam. And one of those great religions, Christianity, is expressed in three great traditions: Catholicism, Protestantism, and Eastern Orthodoxy. You may already know that. You may also already know that, currently, more than 1 billion Catholics occupy the earth. That's approximately one-fifth of the world's population.

Whether you're Catholic or not, you may be totally clueless or just unaware of some aspects of Catholic tradition, history, doctrine, worship, devotion, or culture. No sweat. Regardless of whether you're engaged, married, or related to a Catholic or your neighbor or co-worker is a Catholic or you're just curious about what Catholics really do believe, this book is for you.

Catholicism For Dummies realizes that you're smart and intelligent, but maybe you didn't attend Blessed Sacrament Grade School, St. Thomas Aquinas High School, or Catholic University of America. Then this book's goal is to give you a taste of Catholicism. It's not a catechism or religion textbook but a casual, down-to-earth introduction for non-Catholics and a reintroduction for Catholics. It gives common-sense explanations about what Catholics believe and do in plain English, with just enough why and how thrown in for it to make solid sense.

Although *Catholicism For Dummies* is no substitute for the official *Catechism of the Catholic Church,* our hope is that it'll wet your whistle. We don't cover everything about Catholicism, but we do discuss the basic stuff so that the next time you're invited to a Catholic wedding, Baptism, funeral, Confirmation, or First Communion, you won't be totally confused. And you may even have an edge on some of the other relatives who are even more clueless about Catholicism than you.

About This Book

This book covers plenty of material on Catholicism — from doctrine to morality and from worship and liturgy to devotions. But you don't need a degree in theology to understand what's in this book. Everything's presented in an informal, easy-to-understand way.

This book is also a reference, unlike the schoolbooks you had as a kid. You don't have to read the chapters in order, one after the other, from front cover to back cover. You can just pick the topic that interests you or find the page that addresses the specific question that you have. Or you can just indiscriminately open the book and pick a place to begin reading.

This book has six parts, and each part is broken down into chapters. Each chapter is further divided into sections, and each section contains info on some specific aspect of Catholicism.

Conventions Used in This Book

The Church is known to be among the top ten when it comes to keeping good records. In fact, the monks were the first to print the Bible, by hand, long before Gutenberg was able to mass-produce it on his printing press (1450). And if you were baptized or married in a Catholic church, you can always find a record of your Baptism in the parish where the Baptism or marriage took place — even if it was more than say, 60 years ago. So naturally, after 2,000 years of Baptisms, weddings, funerals, tribunals, annulments, Church councils, papal documents of one kind or another, *hagiographies* (biographies of the saints), investigations for canonization, and so on, the Church has its share of records and printed text, for sure. What's more, Latin is still the official language of the Church, so official documents are first written in Latin before being translated into English or some other language.

The upshot of the Church's penchant for carefully written and well-kept texts is that we couldn't avoid using Catholic-specific terms and some Latin in this book. However, we italicized difficult terms and then did our utmost to offer complete but easy-to-understand definitions and translations alongside those terms. If you'd like some help with the Latin, we suggest that you start with a copy of *Latin For Dummies* by Hull, Perkins, and Barr (Wiley).

Throughout this book, if you see the word *orthodox* with a small letter *o,* it means correct or right believer. However, if you see the capital letter *O,* then *Orthodox* refers to the eastern Orthodox Churches, such as the Greek, Russian, and Serbian Orthodox Churches.

Also, if you see the word *church* with a small letter *c,* it refers to a church building or parish, but *Church* with a capital *C* refers to the universal Catholic Church.

Foolish Assumptions

While writing this book, we made some assumptions about you:

✔ You have Catholic friends, neighbors, or relatives, and you're curious about Catholicism and want to know a little more about it.

✔ You've heard or read something about Catholics or Catholicism, and you have a question about Catholic belief or practice.

✔ You may or may not be Catholic. Perhaps you were baptized Catholic but not raised Catholic. Maybe you're committed to a different faith or still searching or have no faith to speak of. Regardless, you do want to know something about Catholics.

How This Book Is Organized

Two thousand years of history, theology, spirituality, prayer, devotion, worship, and morality can't be put into one small book. We've obviously left some stuff out. We've summarized plenty, too. Our goal is to give you the bottom line — the essential guts of Catholicism.

To make it easy for you to find the particular innards that you're interested in, we've divided this book into parts, each covering a particular topic. Each part contains chapters relating to that topic.

Part 1: Getting Familiar with the Basics

This part deals with fundamentals. It basically answers the question *who* — who is a Catholic and who runs the Catholic Church? We cover basics like Catholicism as a mainstream religion, Catholicism as an expression of Christianity (such as Protestantism and Orthodoxy), and the kinds and activities of Catholics. We also explain the power structure. From the pope to priests, we peek at the hierarchy of the Catholic Church — the chain of command, so to speak.

Part II: Understanding All Those Beliefs

This part deals with the content of faith — the principal and major doctrines and beliefs of Catholicism. It basically answers the question *what* — what do Catholics believe, what are their forms of worship, and what do they do at them? It also explains how the faith is nurtured, supported, cultivated, and enhanced through the Mass, the official worship of God, and through the seven sacraments: Baptism, Penance, Confirmation, Holy Eucharist, Matrimony, Holy Orders, and the Anointing of the Sick.

Part III: Behaving Like a Saint

This part deals with Catholic behavior — Catholic morality. It basically answers the question *how* — how do Catholics put their Christian faith into practice? How do they live their faith from day to day through what they say and do? We cover the moral laws of Catholicism as a natural extension of laws in general — rules or codes of conduct meant to protect members by promoting good behavior and discouraging bad. From the natural moral law to the Ten Commandments to the moral virtues and the seven deadly sins, we examine various boundaries of behavior.

Part IV: Practicing Catholicism through Devotions

This part of the book deals with Catholic devotions — special prayers and activities that Catholics say and do outside of the Mass and sacraments that continue and cultivate a personal relationship with God. The Church believes that the ultimate goal of all true devotion is promoting, supporting, enhancing, and encouraging a strong, healthy, and total love of God. So this part begins with devotions centering on God alone and then covers devotions to those that Catholics believe are God's faithful servants and friends — the saints. This part also explains that showing devotion to the Virgin Mary and other saints isn't considered worship; it's merely *honoring* special people.

Part V: The Part of Tens

Every *For Dummies* book has a Part of Tens. It's a trademark of the series. So in this book, we give you ten famous Catholics, ten popular saints, and ten popular Catholic places. These people and places put a face and scenic background to the doctrines, morals, and rituals discussed throughout the book.

Part VI: Appendixes

In the back of this book, you can find a couple of very useful Appendixes.

Appendix A contains a *very* condensed, abridged, summarized history of the Catholic Church from the ancient and medieval period, through the time of the Reformation and Counter-Reformation, through the Renaissance and Enlightenment, to the modern era.

All the popes, beginning with St. Peter, are listed in Appendix B, followed by a listing of the feast days, memorials, and solemnities in the liturgical calendar.

Icons Used in This Book

This book uses icons to point out various types of information:

The From the Bible Icon helps you to make the connection between Catholicism and Sacred Scripture. If you read the text that's next to this icon, you'll see how Catholicism — the Mass, the Rosary, the hierarchy of the Church, and so on — is rooted in Scripture.

Ummm, well, we can't remember what this icon's supposed to point out. Just kidding. This icon draws your attention to information that's worth remembering, because it's basic to Catholicism.

This icon alerts you to technical or historical background stuff that's not essential to know. Feel free to divert thine eyes whenever you see this icon.

This icon points out useful tidbits to help you make more sense out of something Catholic.

This icon points out caution areas of Catholicism, such as the obligation to attend Mass on Sunday or Saturday evening. Not doing so, without a legitimate excuse, such as illness or severe weather, is a grave sin.

Where to Go from Here

Catholicism For Dummies is sort of like Sunday dinner at an Italian grandmother's home. Nonna brings out everything to the table: bread, antipasto, cheese, olives, prosciutto and melon, tomatoes and mozzarella; then comes the pasta or macaroni, in marinara or meat sauce, with sausage and peppers, meatballs and veal; then comes the chicken, the pork, or the beef; followed by salad; and topped off with fruit and cheese, spumoni, gelato, ricotta pie, zabaglione, and an espresso with a splash of sambucca.

Likewise, in this book, we've brought out a little bit of everything on Catholicism: doctrine, morality, history, theology, canon law, spirituality, and liturgy. You can go to any section and discover Catholicism. You can pick and choose what interests you the most, get answers to specific questions on your mind, or just randomly open it anywhere and begin reading. On the other hand, you may want to start from the beginning and work your way to the end, going through each chapter one by one. We don't guarantee that you'll be full when you're finished, but we hope that you'll get a good taste of what Catholicism is really about.

Part I
Getting Familiar with the Basics

The 5th Wave   By Rich Tennant

"This is our family Bible. It's truly a lamp to my feet, a light for my path and a balance unto our bookshelf."

In this part . . .

What's a Broadway play, a Metropolitan opera, or a major-league baseball game without a program? Get'cha program here! This part helps you find out who all the players are in Catholicism, as well as who is and who isn't a Catholic.

In addition, this part gives you a peek at what Catholicism is all about. Get a glimpse into what Catholics believe and why. Find out whether Catholics really are Christian after all. And take a gander at the ecclesiastical chain of command — who's in charge of whom.

Chapter 1

What It Means to Be Catholic

In This Chapter

▶ Getting an idea of what Catholicism is all about

▶ Enjoying religious traditions and customs

▶ Belonging to a parish is a good thing

*B*eing Catholic means living a totally Christian life and having a Catholic perspective. To Catholics, all people are basically good, but sin is a spiritual disease that wounded humankind initially and can kill humankind spiritually if left unchecked. Divine grace is the only remedy for sin, and the best source of divine grace is from the *sacraments,* which are various rites that Catholics believe have been created by Jesus and entrusted by him to his Church.

What's the bottom line from the Catholic perspective?

✔ More than an intellectual assent to an idea, Catholicism involves a daily commitment to embrace the will of God — whatever it is and wherever it leads.

✔ Catholicism means cooperation with God on the part of the believer. God offers his divine grace, and the Catholic must accept it and then cooperate with it.

✔ Free will is sacred. God never forces you against your free will. Yet doing evil not only hurts you, it also hurts others, because a Catholic is never alone. Catholics are always part of a spiritual family called the *Church.*

✔ More than a place to go on the weekend to worship, the Church is a mother who feeds spiritually, shares doctrine, heals and comforts, and disciplines when needed.

In this chapter, you get a peek at what Catholicism is all about — the common buzzwords and beliefs — a big picture of the whole shebang. (The rest of this book gets into the nitty-gritty details.)

What Exactly Is Catholicism Anyway?

The cut-to-the-chase answer is that *Catholicism* is the practice of Roman Catholic Christianity. *Catholics* are members of the Roman Catholic Church, and they share various beliefs and ways of worship, as well as a distinct outlook on life.

The basic beliefs

Catholics are first and foremost *Christians*. Like Jews and Muslims, Catholics are *monotheistic,* which means that they believe in one God, but Catholics, like all Christians, believe that Jesus Christ is the Son of God, which is unique to Christianity. Catholics also believe that

- ✔ **The Bible** is the inspired, error-free, and revealed word of God. (See Chapter 3 for more on the Bible.)

- ✔ **Baptism,** the rite of becoming a Christian, is necessary for salvation — whether the Baptism occurs by water, blood, or desire. (See Chapter 6.)

- ✔ **God's Ten Commandments** provide a moral compass — an ethical standard to live by. (For more on the Ten Commandments, see Chapter 10.)

- ✔ **The Holy Trinity** — one God in three persons — is also part of Catholic belief. In other words, Catholics embrace the belief that God, the one Supreme Being, is made up of three persons: God the Father, God the Son, and God the Holy Spirit. (See Chapter 3.)

Catholics recognize the unity of body and soul for each human being. So the whole religion centers on the truth that humankind stands between the two worlds of matter and spirit. The physical world is considered part of God's creation and is, therefore, inherently good until an individual misuses it.

The *seven sacraments* — Baptism, Penance, Holy Eucharist, Confirmation, Matrimony, Holy Orders, and the Anointing of the Sick — are outward signs that Christ instituted to give grace. These Catholic rites marking the seven major stages of spiritual development are based on this same premise of the union of body and soul, matter and spirit, physical and spiritual. The seven sacraments involve a physical, tangible *symbol,* such as the *water* used in Baptism and the *oil* when anointing, to represent the invisible spiritual *reality,* the supernatural grace given in each sacrament. (For more on the seven sacraments, see Chapters 6 and 7.)

Symbols — from burning incense and candles to stained glass windows depicting the saints, from cruets of oil or water to unleavened bread and wine — are an important part of Catholic worship. The human body has five senses that connect to the physical world. Catholicism uses tangible symbols (see

Chapter 5) that the senses can recognize so to be reminded of an invisible reality — the delivery of *divine grace,* which is God's gift of unconditional love.

Grace is a totally free, unmerited gift from God. Grace is a sharing in the divine; it's God's help — the inspiration that's needed to do his will. It was grace that inspired the martyrs in the early days of Christianity to suffer death rather than deny Christ. It was grace that bolstered St. Bernadette Soubirous (see Chapter 18) enough to sustain the derision of the locals in reaction to her claims to have seen the Virgin Mary. You can't see, hear, feel, smell, or taste grace, because it's invisible. Catholic belief, however, maintains that grace is the life force of the soul. Like a spiritual megavitamin, grace inspires a person to selflessly conform to God's will, and like the battery in the mechanical bunny rabbit, grace keeps the soul going, going, going, and going. Granted purely out of God's love, grace is necessary for salvation. Catholicism says that grace is an undeserving and unmerited free gift from God that wasn't owed to his people. As a gift, however, a person can accept or reject it. If accepted, it then must be cooperated with. Grace is given so that the will of God may be done. Grace must be put into action through those who receive it.

The primary way of worship

Catholics belong to their own churches, called *parishes,* which are local places of worship. The Catholic daily and weekly church service is the *Holy Mass,* a reenactment of *Holy Thursday,* when Jesus celebrated the Last Supper, and *Good Friday,* when he died to purchase the rewards of eternal life in heaven for humankind. (See Chapter 8 for more on the Mass.)

Sunday attendance at a parish isn't just expected; it's a moral obligation. Not going to Sunday Mass without a worthy excuse, such as illness or bad weather, is considered a grave sin.

Many Christians attend church services on Sunday, but Catholics actually don't have to attend Mass on that particular day. They can go to Mass on Saturday evening instead.

The practice of attending what's called the *Vigil Mass,* the Saturday evening Mass, wasn't universally allowed until 1983. The rationale for this relatively new practice is that in the Jewish tradition *after sundown* means the next calendar day, so Mass celebrated after sundown on Saturday evening can count for a Sunday obligation.

Originally, the Saturday evening Mass was intended to offer a solution for Catholics who had to work on Sunday, while Mass was being celebrated. Sunday is still the preferred day of Christian worship, a day to go to Church as a family and spend time as a family. Nevertheless, the option of going to Mass Saturday evening isn't restricted anymore just to Catholics who work the next day. The obligation to refrain from unnecessary work, however, still remains on Sunday, because it's the *Day of the Lord* for Christians all over the world.

This night-before worship is somewhat unique to Catholicism. To accommodate the busy schedules that so many families have today, most parishes have Mass the evening before a holy day, too, and then some Masses on the morning of the holy day itself. (For more on the holy days of obligation, see Chapter 8.)

It may appear that Catholics can just go to Mass to fulfill a duty and obey a church law, but attending Mass is actually much more than just being physically present in Church. Catholic worship involves the whole person — body *and* soul. That's why Catholics use different postures, such as standing, sitting, kneeling, and bowing, and do plenty of listening, singing, and responding to phrases. For example, if the priest says, "The Lord be with you," Catholics respond, "And also with you" or "And with your spirit."

Unfortunately, some Catholics don't fully appreciate or accept God's grace nor do they practice what's preached. It's been said that one of the most dangerous places on earth is the Catholic parish parking lot! Some people — not out of necessity but mere convenience — always have to be the first one in the car and out on the road before Mass even ends. These are the same Catholics who hug the end of the pew nearest the door; they make others step over them to sit down. Most Catholics, however, show respect and stay until the end of the last hymn, after the priest and deacon leave the sanctuary.

The fundamental perspective

Catholicism offers a distinct perspective on the world and life. The Catholic perspective sees everything as being intrinsically created good but with the potential of being abused. It honors the individual intellect and well-formed conscience and encourages members to use their minds to think things through. In other words, instead of just giving a list of do's and don'ts, the Catholic Church educates its members to use their ability to reason and to apply laws of ethics and a natural moral law in many situations.

Catholicism doesn't see science or reason as enemies of faith but as cooperators in seeking the truth. Although Catholicism has an elaborate hierarchy to provide leadership in the Church, Catholicism also teaches individual responsibility and accountability. Education and the secular and sacred sciences are a high priority. Using logical and coherent arguments to explain and defend the Catholic faith is an important characteristic.

Catholicism isn't a one-day-a-week enterprise. It doesn't segregate religious and moral dimensions of life from political, economic, personal, and familial dimensions. Catholicism tries to integrate faith into everything.

The general Catholic perspective is that because God created everything, *nothing* is outside God's jurisdiction and that includes your every thought, word, and deed — morning, noon, and night, 24/7.

The General Ground Rules

The minimum requirements for being a Catholic are called the precepts of the Church:

- ✔ Attending Mass every Sunday and holy day of obligation.
- ✔ Going to confession annually if not more often or when needed.
- ✔ Receiving Holy Communion during Easter. Receiving weekly or daily is encouraged, though.
- ✔ Observing laws on fasting and abstinence: one full meal on Ash Wednesday and Good Friday; not eating meat on Fridays during Lent.
- ✔ Obeying the marriage laws of the Church.
- ✔ Supporting the Church financially and otherwise.

You can find out more about the precepts of the Church in Chapter 9. More generically, however, Catholics are basically required to live a Christian life, pray daily, participate in the sacraments, obey the moral law, and accept the teachings of Christ and his Church.

Knowing the faith is the first step to being Catholic, and it entails *catechesis,* the process of discovering the Catholic faith and *what* is to be believed and finding out all the important doctrines.

Accepting the faith is the second step, and it entails *trust.* The Catholic believer must trust that what's being taught is indeed the truth. After knowing *what* the Church believes, the Catholic is then asked *to believe* all that they have been told. It's the act of saying, "Yes," to the question "Do you believe?"

Practicing the faith is the third — and most difficult — step. Obeying the rules isn't just mindless compliance. It involves appreciating the wisdom and value of the various Catholic rules and laws. Believers are asked to put that belief into action, to practice what they believe. Catholics are taught that all men and women are made in the image and likeness of God and that all men and women have been saved by Christ and are adopted children of God. That belief, if truly believed, requires that the person act as if she really means it. Behaving like a racist or anti-Semite would contradict such a belief.

So are you a cradle Catholic or a convert?

Some Catholics remain close to their faith from the beginning of their lives to the present, and other Catholics may change their focus for a time, to return wholeheartedly later on. Still, some Catholics may have come from another religious background or were completely unfamiliar with religion until converting to Catholicism.

✔ **Cradle Catholics** are born, baptized, and raised in the Catholic faith.

✔ **Converts** previously belonged to another religion or no religion and came into the Catholic religion later on.

✔ **Reverts** are cradle Catholics who left the Church, perhaps joining another religion. Eventually, they return or *revert* back to their Catholic heritage later on.

Celebrating Year-Round

A really cool thing about Catholicism is that many days of the calendar year are a cause for celebration. The date may be reserved to honor a saint or commemorate a special passage in the life of Christ, such as the Feast of the Transfiguration when Christ transfigured himself before the apostles (Luke 9:28–36; Matthew 17:1–8; Mark 9:2–8). You may notice, as you continue reading, that many Catholic celebrations and customs involve their fair share of the priest blessing this and that. See the "Hey, Father Joe — bless this, will ya?" sidebar in this chapter, for more on priestly blessings.

✔ **January 6 is the traditional and universal Feast of the Epiphany.** Catholic parishes in the United States, however, that say the Mass in English, celebrate this feast on the first Sunday after New Year's Day. Epiphany commemorates the visit of the Magi, the three kings bearing gifts for the newborn Christ in the stable at Bethlehem.

A Catholic custom among Polish, Slovak, Russian, and German families is to have their pastor bless chalk on this day. Then, with the blessed chalk, they write over their door the numerals for the current year and, in the middle of the numerals, the initials CMB for the three wise men, Casper, Melchior, and Balthasar. So on Epiphany Sunday 2005, for example, the custom is to write "20 + C + M + B + 05" over your door with your blessed chalk. This custom merely reminds all in the home to ask the prayers of Casper, Melchior, and Balthasar during the calendar year 2005.

Besides being an abbreviation for the names of the three wise men, CMB is also the abbreviation for the Latin *Christus Mansionem Benedicat* (may Christ bless the home).

✔ **February 2 is the Feast of Candlemas.** Also known as the Presentation of the Christ (Luke 2:22–38), Candlemas is celebrated on the day before the Feast of St. Blaise when Catholics get their throats blessed. (For more on St. Blaise, see the "Hey, Father Joe — bless this, will ya?" sidebar, in this chapter.) White beeswax candles are blessed during or after Mass on February 2, and people take a few home with them. Then when Catholics pray in their home, asking for God's assistance especially during a time of anxiety, distress, calamity, war, dangerous weather, or illness — and when the priest is called to administer one of the seven sacraments — the Anointing of the Sick (formerly called *Extreme Unction*), these candles are lit before the Priest enters the house. Folks really pray up a storm at times like these.

Hey, Father Joe, bless this, will ya?

Catholics love to have priests or deacons bless them, as well as some of their personal belongings — their home, car, or dog. More often, however, Catholics ask priests to bless a personal and tangible religious item — their rosary, medal, statue, Bible, and so on. Any article of devotion or something integral to human life and activity can be blessed, but that doesn't mean it becomes a lucky charm. The priestly blessing is merely a way of showing gratitude to God for his divine grace and putting these blessed items under his watchful care.

For example, if you see an outdoor statue of Mary in the front or back yard of a Catholic home, chances are it's been blessed. It's not magic and does nothing to help the grass grow. It's just a gentle reminder of Mary, the Mother of God, and of Catholic affection for her.

Throats are blessed in church every year on February 3, the Feast of St. Blaise (see Chapter 16), a bishop and martyr who saved a choking boy. From that point on, candles blessed the day before (February 2) have been used to bless all throats of Catholics, asking St. Blaise's intercession from all ailments of the throat. Palm branches are blessed on Palm Sunday, the Sunday before Easter, and Catholics take them home and often weave them into crosses and place them on a wall crucifix. Last year's palms

are burned and used on Ash Wednesday to impose ashes on everyone's forehead to remind them of prayer, fasting, and penance.

Some Catholics who don't attend Mass regularly get the dubious title of PAT (palms, ashes, and throats) Catholics, meaning they only come to church when freebies are handed out. Thankfully, they're a small minority. The ashes, the throat blessing, or the palms aren't magical. They're merely tangible symbols of a spiritual life.

Anytime a priest or deacon blesses a religious article, such as a rosary, statue, or medal of one of the saints, he makes the sign of the cross with his right hand over the object(s) and sprinkles holy water on it after saying the prayers of blessing. The holy water reminds the owner that the blessed item is now reserved for sacred use (to enhance prayer life, for example) and shouldn't be used for profane (nonreligious) use.

So almost anything can be blessed, as long as the item will only be used for moral purposes and isn't going to be sold. Blessings aren't magical, but blessings do change an object into a *sacramental,* which means that it's a reminder of God's grace and generosity and, particularly when used in conjunction with prayer, invokes God's blessing on all who use it. (For more on sacramentals, see Chapter 16.)

✔ **March 17 is St. Patrick's Day.** Who doesn't know about the wearing o' the green to commemorate the Emerald Isle on the Patron Feast Day of Ireland? Morning Mass, parades, Irish soda bread, potato soup, green beer — all great customs. Because many Irish immigrants came to the United States during Ireland's potato famine, it's no wonder that more people celebrate St. Patrick's Day in United States than in Ireland.

St. Patrick was born in A.D. 387 at Kilpatrick, near Dumbarton, in Scotland and died on March 17th in the year 493. His father was an officer of the Roman Army. Irish pirates captured 16-year-old Patrick and sold him into slavery for six years in Ireland where he learned the Celtic language and combated the Druid religion. His *Confession* and his *Letter to Coroticus* are all that's officially known of St. Patrick. The *Confession* reveals his call by Pope St. Celestine I to convert the Irish, and Coroticus was a warlord with whom Patrick communicated. Pious tradition contends that he explained the Trinity — three persons in one God — by showing the converts a three-leaf shamrock.

✔ **March 19 marks the Solemnity of St. Joseph, the Husband of Mary and Patron of the Universal Church.** Even though Lent is a time of penance and mortification, some feast days are so special that the Church wants us to celebrate them with gusto even if they happen to fall during the penitential days of Lent. (For more on the Lenten season, see Chapter 8.) This was extremely important in the old days when many Catholics refrained from eating any meat or dairy products all 40 days of Lent and also only ate one full meal a day. You can imagine how weak and frail that could make many people. So to ease up on the penance done in Lent, the faithful were dispensed from fasting on special feasts called solemnities, such as St. Joseph on March 19 and the Annunciation on March 25, when the Archangel Gabriel announced to Mary that she was to be the mother of Jesus. Italians and Sicilians take full advantage of St. Joseph's Day being a Solemnity and really whoop it up by eating foods normally given up for Lent, erecting tables with a statue of the saint and asking a priest to bless breads and pastries. The breads are distributed to the poor, and family and friends consume the pastries. A favorite is *Zeppole,* a special cream puff made in honor of St. Joseph or as he is called in Italian, *San Giuseppe.*

✔ **May is a month dedicated to Mary, the mother of Jesus.** It's also the month of Mother's Day. Catholics traditionally have May Crownings — (see Chapter 14) crowns of roses adorn a statue of Mary, and boys and girls who just made their First Holy Communion wear the same outfits for the occasion. Catholics sing Marian hymns, and in some places, outdoor processions take place; a statue of Mary is carried through the streets.

✔ **June 13 is the Feast of St. Anthony of Padua.** Many local Italian communities celebrate the Feast of St. Anthony of Padua with special Masses and processions. Ironically, Anthony himself wasn't Italian but

Portuguese. Yet he did spend some time in Italy. St. Anthony, an eloquent preacher, came into this world in 1195, when St. Francis of Assisi (October 4), was 13 years old. Although they were contemporaries who both lived in Italy, history didn't leave any records to confirm that these two great saints actually ever met. St. Anthony is the patron saint of lost items and marriages.

What's your preference?

If you went to a Catholic parish on the west side of town for Sunday Mass last week and go to Mass on the other side of town next Sunday, you may notice a difference in the language that the priest says the mass in, or you may notice that a healing service takes place at the end of the Mass. Both services are Catholic, which means that both Masses are sanctioned by the pope in Rome, but each Mass is celebrated a little differently.

The **Latin (Western) Church** follows the ancient traditions of the Christian community in Rome since the time of St. Peter and St. Paul in the first century A.D. As the capital of the Roman Empire, the Latin language and Roman culture, from law to architecture, greatly influenced the Catholic Church in this region. It spread all over to embrace present-day Western Europe and Poland. Most of the parishes and dioceses in the United States and Canada and almost all the churches in Central and South America belong to the Latin Church. Even though the Mass and other sacraments are no longer exclusively said in the Latin language, the same gestures, prayers, vestments, and so on are used in all the churches of the West. The Mass after the Second Vatican Council is called the *Novus Ordo* (new order) Mass and is usually celebrated in the vernacular (common tongue), or it may still be said in Latin.

The **Eastern Catholic Church** is in full union with the Vatican and includes the Byzantine Church and other Eastern Orthodox Churches that were restored under the authority of the Bishop of Rome in the 17th century. The seven sacraments are valid, but the Eastern Mass is exactly like the Greek or Russian Eastern Orthodox Churches — the Churches of the Patriarchs of Constantinople and Moscow, respectively, which separated from the authority of Rome in the Schism of 1054 and follow the Liturgy of St. John Chrysostom. Eastern Catholics make up the other lung of the church, along with the Latin (Western) Roman Catholics, which most people in the United States and Western Europe are familiar with.

The Tridentine Mass is said only in the Latin language. Often attended by those Catholics who have a great love for the so-called *old* Mass, the Tridentine Mass was the only Mass used in Catholic parishes from the Council of Trent (16th century) to 1963. To celebrate the Tridentine Mass, the priest uses the Roman Missal of 1962, which contains all the necessary and essential prayers, Scripture readings and liturgical directions. The priest also celebrates the Tridentine Mass facing the altar. In 1988, Pope John Paul II granted permission for priests to celebrate the Tridentine Mass again in an encyclical called *Ecclesia Dei.*

Charismatic Masses aren't a separate type of Mass; rather, they are *Novus Ordo* Masses celebrated in the charismatic manner. *Charismatic* means sharing in the gifts of the Holy Spirit, such as healing or speaking in tongues. Folks who are unfamiliar with the Catholic Charismatic Movement often mistake Charismatic Masses for Pentecostal services. Similar to Pentecostal Protestants, Charismatic Renewal Catholics are devoted to the Holy Spirit and to the gifts of the Holy Spirit.

✔ **October 1 is the Feast of St. Thérèse of Lisieux (1873–1897), also known as the Little Flower.** Roses are traditionally blessed and given to the sick, infirm, elderly, and other special-needs parishioners on this date. This tradition is undoubtedly the result of the saint's promise, made while she was on earth, to spend her heaven sending "a shower of roses" to the faithful still on earth. (See Chapter 18 for more on St. Thérèse.)

✔ **December 12 is the Feast of Our Lady of Guadalupe.** Catholics, especially those of Hispanic heritage, celebrate this feast about two weeks before Christmas every year. In Mexico City, the Basilica of Guadalupe stands on Tepeyac Hill, the site where a dark-skinned Virgin Mary appeared to St. Juan Diego, a poor Indian peasant, nearly 500 years ago. The Virgin of Guadalupe left her image on Juan Diego's cloak. Today, a picture of the Virgin of Guadalupe decorates just about everything Hispanic, from storefronts to T-shirts and from cars to shrines; many Hispanics identify with and devote themselves to her. (To read more about this basilica, see Chapter 19.)

Understanding the Four Marks of the Church

Nearly 2,000 years, 265 popes, and more than 1 billion members in the Catholic Church means something is working to keep the thing going. One of the primary cornerstones of the Church is the *Four Marks of the Church.* The belief professed in the *Nicene Creed* (see Chapter 3), which is said at every Sunday Mass, expresses the Four Marks of the Church. The Creed professes belief "in one holy catholic and apostolic Church." The *Creed* is a summary of all the essential points of Christian doctrine formulated by Sacred Tradition (see Chapter 3), which the Church believes is part of the unwritten word of God.

One (unity)

The first characteristic of the Catholic Church is her unity. The office and person of the pope means that the Church has one supreme head. One *deposit of faith* means one set of doctrines for the entire Church now presented in the universal catechism. Catholics on all continents everywhere in the world believe the same articles of faith. One set of laws, known as *canon law* (see Chapter 9), governs the entire Church. The Code of Canon Law for the Western (Latin) Church is different from the Eastern (Byzantine) Church, yet both come from one and same source, the pope, the supreme lawgiver. Both sets of canon law overlap each other in the most significant areas, so continuity is kept. But whether you're Roman Catholic or Eastern Catholic, you're under the authority of one supreme court, one supreme legislator, and one supreme judge, the Roman pontiff, alias the pope. One set of Catholic rites, the *seven sacraments,* marking the seven stages of major development, and they're celebrated the same way everywhere. Worship services may be in different languages, but only bread and wine are used at every Mass; no one may substitute anything else, no matter what the culture is in that location.

This unity of liturgy, doctrine, and authority is a hallmark of Catholicism. Other religions are unified in belief and practice, but Catholicism is unique in that unity is personified in one single person, the pope, who ensures that the same seven sacraments are celebrated correctly all over the world, that the same set of doctrines are taught everywhere and that every member, religious, lay or clergy, accept the supreme authority of the bishop of Rome.

The Eastern Orthodox Church, for example, has the exact same seven sacraments all over the world and a body of laws to govern them, but the patriarch who governs their churches — the patriarch of Constantinople for the Greek Orthodox Church and the patriarch of Moscow for the Russian Orthodox Church — is on equal par with the other Eastern Orthodox patriarchs in Alexandria, Jerusalem, and Antioch. They have *Synods,* gatherings of bishops, but no one single person is supreme head of all Orthodox Christians all over the world. Preferential respect and honor is given the patriarch of Constantinople, because he predated the patriarchate of Moscow, yet the former can't interfere with the authority or ministry of the latter.

Before the Schism of 1054, the other patriarchs viewed the pope as the patriarch of the West; he was given the title *Primus inter Pares,* which is Latin for *first among equals.* Since the Schism, however, the Eastern Orthodox Church no longer recognizes the supreme authority of the pope, and each church is governed by its own spiritual leader (patriarch). Catholicism on the other hand, both the Western and Eastern branches, has one set of doctrines, one means of public worship, and one and the same supreme authority — the pope. Even though the seven sacraments are celebrated a little differently depending on whether you're in a Western or Eastern Catholic church, it's still the same seven sacraments.

Holy (sanctity)

The second characteristic of the Catholic Church is her holiness. Not all members, leaders included, are *de facto* holy. The scandals that riddle Catholic history prove that painfully enough. But the Church as a whole is holy, because she's considered the bride of Christ, and also, the Mystical Body of Christ. (For more on the Mystical Body of Christ, see Chapter 14.) Individually, members are capable of sinning, but as something founded by Christ himself to save souls, the Church as a whole can't sin. Her sanctity is expressed in her daily prayer.

All over the world, priests, deacons, sisters, brothers, seminarians, and laity pray the *Liturgy of the Hours,* otherwise known as the *Divine Office* or the *Breviary.* Mostly made up of the Psalms and including many other readings from the Bible, this ancient collection and manner of praying goes back to the early and ancient church.

The holiness of the Church is also experienced in the daily celebration of Mass. Somewhere in the world every hour on the hour a Mass is being celebrated. The Church is also the guardian of the sacraments so that they're properly, validly, and reverently celebrated all over the world and all the time. As vehicles of grace, the sacraments sanctify Catholics every time they're received.

Often, someone will name a corrupt pope, bishop, or priest from history or more recent vintage as an argument against the holiness of the Church. Just as you see individual examples of a bad husband or a bad wife here and there, the institution of marriage isn't bad just because some married people can't fulfill their vows and maintain a permanent, faithful, fruitful, and loving relationship. Likewise, you've heard of abusive fathers or mothers who abandon their children, yet the institution of family isn't tainted or tarnished by the minority who don't live up to the family values and commitments they ought. So, why should the Church be any different? As a whole, the Church, unlike a government, which is the creation of mere mortals, is like a family — the family of God. God is its founder, and as such, its core and structure are perfect, but individual Catholics are where the imperfections, flaws, faults and mistakes happen. Catholicism sees the Church as a divine institution that has had some sinful Catholics in its ranks, beginning with the pope in Rome to the layperson in the pew. Yet, it's more than the mere sum of its parts. The Church includes all the living baptized on earth and all the saints in heaven and all the departed souls in purgatory as well.

Catholic (universality)

The third characteristic is the *catholic* (universal) nature of the Church. Not limited to any nation, country, or culture, the Catholic Church maintains unity within diversity. Every spoken language on earth is used in some way, either in the translation of Scripture or in the Mass and sacraments. Although the head of the Church is also the bishop of Rome, it's not just an Italian church. A Polish pope proves that. His numerous pastoral visits all over the world remind people that it's a universal faith that transcends all boundaries. The fact that the Catholic Church incorporates both East and West (Byzantine and Latin traditions) is another example of universality.

On all the continents of the world, at least one priest celebrates Mass, teaches Catholic doctrine, and honors the authority of the pope. Spanning time and space, Catholicism seeks to spread the Gospel through missionary work. Whether it was Matteo Ricci bringing the Catholic faith to China in the 16th century, St. Peter in Rome during the first century, or Pope John Paul II visiting Africa, Asia, North and South America, and Europe in the 21st century, the point is that the Church belongs in all places all over the earth, and that's truly universal.

Watch the next Mass on television from the Vatican at Christmas or Easter, and see how many cultures and peoples are represented just among the cardinals and bishops who work in the Vatican, as well as all the pilgrims and visitors who come to Rome every day.

Apostolic (continuity)

The final characteristic is one of connection with the past, particularly the ability to trace origins back to the original *apostles,* the 12 men personally chosen by Jesus in addition to and separate from the 72 *disciples,* who also followed him, but from a distance. The word *apostle* comes from the Greek *apostello,* which means *to send forth* or *to dispatch,* and the word *disciple* comes from the Latin *discipulus* meaning *student.*

Jesus founded the Church on the apostles, and the need to maintain roots is more than mere nostalgia. Every ordained deacon, priest, or bishop can trace his orders back, ultimately, to one of the 12 apostles. That's how vital and crucial the link remains. Credibility and authority can be traced back to the original fishermen handpicked by Jesus to lead his Church. *Apostolic* means that the Church has distinct ties, roots, and connections to the original 12 apostles Jesus chose to begin his Church: Simon Peter, his brother Andrew, James and John, Philip, Thomas, Bartholomew or Nathaniel, Matthew, James the Less or the Younger, Simon the Zealot and Jude Thaddeus, and of course, the infamous Judas Iscariot who turned traitor. (For more on deacons, priests, bishops, and the hierarchy of the Church, see Chapter 2.)

Membership Has Its Privileges

Belonging to a parish and diocese isn't really optional in the Catholic Church. Not belonging is, well, not beneficial. Catholicism tries to balance the individual with the community. Communal public worship has its time and place, such as every Sunday at Mass; quiet solitude, such as private meditation, mental prayer, silent retreats, holy hours, and such, also have their time and place.

Catholics don't have a choice when it comes to worshipping both communally and personally. Catholics believe that human beings need both dimensions. This is why the cross is such a powerful symbol to Catholics: The vertical bar represents their personal relationship with the Lord, which only they can cultivate. The horizontal bar represents their obligation and duty to also belong to the faith family of the parish and diocese. When Catholics are registered in a parish, they get more than weekly envelopes to drop in the basket. They also get a spiritual family that wants to pray with and for them. When Catholics are asked to be a godfather or godmother for Baptism or a sponsor for Confirmation, only registered Catholics can get verification from the pastor that they're Catholics in good standing. When they're in the hospital for an appendectomy or any type of surgery or treatment, registered parishioners are often listed on the census as being Catholic. And who do you suppose the Catholic chaplain visits? Unregistered Catholics slip between the cracks, getting lost unintentionally.

Ever notice remarks in the newspaper and media that so-and-so is a "former" or a "fallen away" Catholic? You almost never read of former or fallen away Muslims, Jews, Presbyterians, Methodists, Episcopalians, Baptists, or Lutherans. They exist — just ask their pastors. The media, however, is always fascinated by *ex*-Catholics. The mystery and mystique are still a part of Catholicism even though the Mass isn't necessarily in Latin anymore. Celibacy, the male priesthood, vestments and incense, Mary and the saints, the Pope, nuns, and all other practices and paraphernalia that are uniquely Catholic always capture the curiosity of non-Catholics.

Not everyone agrees with what the Catholic Church teaches or likes how she prays or approves of all her policies, but like all well-established and ancient religions, she's here to stay. (And, yep, just as Harley Davidson owners call their motorcycles *her* and as sailors call their ships *her,* Catholics call their Church *her,* too.)

Chapter 2

Who's Who in the Catholic Church

Chain of command: Every structured environment has one — from governments to corporations to schools to sports programs. The Catholic Church is no exception. This chapter explains who's who in the Catholic Church and gives you a glimpse into the authority and duties of its various members.

Getting to Know the Pope

Best known throughout the world and among more than 1 billion Catholics as *the pope,* the bishop of Rome is the supreme and visible head of the Catholic Church. The word *pope* is actually an English translation of the Italian *il Papa,* meaning *father,* which leads you to another title for the pope — *Holy Father.* Just as a Catholic priest is called "Father" in a spiritual sense, so too, the pope is called "Holy Father" by Catholics all over the world.

He has a slew of other titles, too: Successor of St. Peter, Vicar of Christ, Patriarch of the West, Primate of Italy, Supreme Pontiff, Roman Pontiff, Sovereign of the Vatican City State, and Head of the College of Bishops. The most common and best-known titles, however, are pope, Holy Father, and Roman Pontiff.

Think you're under pressure at work? The pope has *two* big jobs: He's the bishop of Rome (see the section "Bishops, archbishops, and cardinals" for more about bishops) *and* the head of the entire Catholic Church.

How the pope gets his job

The *College of Cardinals* elects the pope. Nope, that's not a university where priests and bishops learn how to become cardinals. Unlike Notre Dame and Catholic University, the *College of Cardinals* merely refers to all the cardinals around the world, just as the *College of Bishops* is a way of describing all the world's Catholic bishops.

The pope handpicks bishops to become *cardinals,* and their primary function in life is to elect a new pope when the old pope dies or resigns. Because most modern popes live at least ten years or more in office (except Pope John Paul I, who lived only one month), cardinals do have other work to do instead of just waiting around for the boss to pass on. (For details about cardinals and their jobs, see the section "Bishops, archbishops, and cardinals," later in this chapter.)

Cardinals under the age of 80 are eligible to vote for the next pope. The limit of electors is set at 120, but Pope John Paul II appointed so many that the number of eligible voters has become 137. When you take into consideration, however, the number of cardinals who are approaching retirement age and those who are in bad health, it's reasonable to presume that the actual number of electors at the time of the next papal election will be lower than 120 as more retire or die over the next several months to a year or two. This will mean that more cardinals need to be named at that time.

They can vote for any other cardinal or any Catholic bishop, priest, deacon, or layman, anywhere in the world and of any liturgical rite, such as Latin, Byzantine, and so on. (See the "What's your preference?" sidebar in Chapter 1 for more on liturgical rites.) Although extremely rare, if a layman is elected, he needs to be ordained a deacon, then a priest, and then a bishop before being installed or crowned pope because the job of being pope is simultaneous with that of being the bishop of Rome. Normally, the cardinals select another cardinal, because they know each other better, and cardinals number 137 — a small number to pick from versus the nearly 3,500 bishops around the world and more than 400,000 priests. Should a layman be elected pope (as in the case of Benedict IX), he would first have to be ordained a deacon, then a priest, and then a bishop before he could function as pope, because the authority resides in his office as bishop of Rome. Should a priest be chosen, he would need to be ordained a bishop prior to being installed as pope.

Uh, Cardinal, sir? What's that mallet for?

When the pope dies, an ancient but simple ceremony is performed before the cardinals are called to Rome to elect a new pope. The most senior-ranking cardinal enters the room of the dead pontiff and gently strikes his forehead with a silver mallet, calling the pope by his baptismal name. If he doesn't answer by the third time, he's pronounced dead.

Today, however, the pope's personal physician is called in first, and he makes the medical determination that the man is dead before the senior-ranking cardinal is summoned to perform the ceremonial ritual with the mallet.

Then the pope's ring (the Fisherman's Ring) and his papal insignia are smashed so that no one can affix the seal on any documents until a new pope has been elected.

Are there pope primaries?

Unlike Western democracies, such as the United States, Canada, and Great Britain, the government of the Catholic Church, called the *hierarchy,* is more like a monarchy than a democracy. Catholicism is hierarchical in that one person, the pope, is supreme head over the universal Church. Yet bishops govern the local churches in what's called the *diocese* and pastors in turn represent the bishop in each local parish. Individual Catholics don't vote for the next pope or for their bishop or pastor. The Catholic hierarchy operates like a military chain of command as opposed to an elected, representative government. So nope — no local primaries, no election campaigns, no debates, no political ads, and no popular vote.

Other religions and Christian churches allow for lay participation in positions of authority from a little to a lot, but Catholicism has been predominantly monarchical since the appointment of St. Peter. (See Chapter 18 for more on St. Peter, the first pope.) Laypersons are encouraged to participate in other ways.

You may have heard the saying: He, who enters the conclave a pope, leaves a cardinal. The meaning? When a pope becomes sick or elderly or dies, rumors run rampant as to who will take the Chair of St. Peter. Often, the press names certain cardinals as the most likely candidates; they're called *papabile* (meaning *pope-able*) in Italian. But the *papabile* are usually the ones that the other cardinals *never* elect. So if a man enters the *conclave* — the private meeting of all the cardinals for the specific purpose of electing the pope — as a favorite, or worse yet, if he comes off as wanting the job, then he'll leave a cardinal, because his fellow cardinals will choose someone more humble.

Dimpled, pimpled, or hanging chads?

No sooner than 15 days and no later than 20 days after the death or resignation of the pope, all the cardinals are summoned to Rome for the secret conclave. *Conclave* comes from the Latin *cum clave*, meaning *with key*, because the cardinals are literally locked into the Sistine Chapel until they elect a new pope.

After the cardinals from around the world assemble inside the conclave, they begin discussions and deliberations. Almost like a sequestered jury, the cardinals are permitted no contact with the outside world during the conclave. Under pain of *excommunication* (see Chapter 9), no cardinal is ever allowed to discuss what transpires at these elections — to keep the element of politics and outside influence to a bare minimum.

A two-thirds majority decision is needed to elect a new pope. When voting for a new pope, each cardinal writes a name on a piece of paper, which is placed on a gold *paten* (plate). The paten is then turned upside down, so the ballot can fall into a *chalice* (cup) underneath. This symbolism is deep, because the chalice and paten are primarily used at the Catholic Mass to hold the wafer of bread and cup of wine that, when consecrated, becomes the body and blood of Christ during the Eucharistic Prayer. (See Chapter 8 for the scoop on the Mass and Eucharistic Prayer.)

If no one receives two-thirds of the votes or if the nominee declines the nomination, then wet straw is mixed with the paper ballots and burned in the chimney. The wet straw makes black smoke, which alerts the crowds gathered outside that a two-thirds majority decision hasn't yet been made. One vote occurs in the morning and one in the evening. The election continues twice a day, every day for 21 elections. If no one is elected by a two-thirds majority, then on the 22nd ballot, the man who receives a simple majority (50 percent plus one) is elected pope. If someone receives two-thirds of the votes and he accepts, the ballots are burned without the straw, which blows white smoke to alert the crowds.

Traditionally, the election of a new pope took place in one of three different forms:

- **Acclamation:** A name is presented, and everyone unanimously consents without the need of a secret ballot.

- **Compromise:** If no one achieves a two-thirds majority after several ballots, then the entire College of Cardinals may choose one or several electors to select a candidate, and the entire body is bound to accept that choice. A unanimous vote to employ compromise is necessary for it to be valid.

✔ **Scrutiny:** Each cardinal proposes a candidate and gives reasons for his qualifications before the individual cardinals cast their secret ballot. This is the only valid method currently permitted in papal conclaves.

After a cardinal has received a two-thirds majority vote, he's asked whether he accepts the nomination. If so, he's then asked, "By what name are you to be addressed?"

Pope John II (A.D. 533) was the first to change his name when he was elected pope, because he was born with the name Mercury after the pagan god. So he chose the Christian name John instead. But it was not until Sergius IV (1009) that all subsequent popes continued the tradition of changing their name at the time of election. So Pope Pius XII (1939) was originally Eugenio Pacelli, John XXIII (1958) was Angelo Roncalli, Paul VI (1963) was Giovanni Montini, John Paul I (1978) was Albino Luciani, and John Paul II (1978) was Karol Wojtyla.

Is he really infallible?

Catholicism maintains that the pope is *infallible,* incapable of error, when he teaches a doctrine on faith or morals to the universal Church in his unique office as supreme head. When the pope asserts his official authority in matters of faith and morals to the whole church, the Holy Spirit guards him from error. Papal infallibility doesn't mean that the pope can't make *any* mistakes. He's not infallible in scientific, historical, political, philosophical, geographic, or any other matters — just faith and morals. It boils down to trust. Catholics trust that the Holy Spirit protects *them* from being taught or forced to believe erroneous doctrines by preventing a pope from issuing them. Whether it's as subtle as getting him to change his mind to as drastic as striking him dead, in any event, Catholics firmly believe that God loves them and loves the truth so much that he would intervene and prevent a pope from imposing a false teaching upon the whole Church. It doesn't mean that personally and individually the pope is free from all error. He could privately be wrong just so long as he doesn't attempt to impose or teach that error to the universal Church, because the Holy Spirit would somehow stop him from doing so.

So what does infallibility mean?

Infallibility is widely misunderstood. It's *not* the same as the Catholic belief of *inspiration* or *impeccability:*

✔ **Inspiration** is a special gift of the Holy Spirit, which He gave to the *sacred authors,* those who wrote the Sacred Scripture (the Bible), so that only the things God wanted written down *were* written down — no more, no less. So the pope isn't inspired, but Matthew, Mark, Luke, and John were when they wrote their Gospels.

✔ **Impeccability** is the absence and inability to commit sin. Only Jesus Christ, being the Son of God, and His Blessed Mother had impeccability — via a special grace from God. Popes aren't impeccable, so they're capable of sin. Which, by the way, was visible in the case of the first pope, St. Peter, when he denied Christ three times just before the Crucifixion (Matthew 26:69–75).

Everything the sacred authors wrote in the Bible is inspired, but not everything every pope says or writes is infallible. *Infallibility* means that if the pope attempts to teach a false doctrine on faith or morals, the Holy Spirit prevents him (even by death) from imposing such an error on the faithful. So, for example, no pope can declare, "As of today, the number of commandments is nine instead of ten." Nor can he declare, "Jesus was not a man" or "Jesus was not the Son of God."

Infallibility also doesn't mean perfect. Infallible statements aren't perfect statements, so they can be improved so that subsequent popes can use better or more accurate language. Yet infallible statements can never be contradicted, rejected, or refuted.

So according to Catholicism, an immoral pope (you'll find several in Church history) can sin like any man and will answer to God for his evil deeds. However, as supreme head of the Church, the pope retains his infallibility on matters of faith and morals as long as he remains pope.

No pope in 2,000 years has formally and officially taught an error of faith or morals to the universal Church. Individually, some may have been poor or inadequate theologians or philosophers, and some may have had erroneous ideas about science. That has nothing to do with papal infallibility, however, because the main objective is to preserve the integrity of Catholic faith for all the members at all times and in all places.

The pope can exercise his papal infallibility in two ways. One is called the *Extraordinary Magisterium* and the other is called *Ordinary Magisterium.* The word *magisterium* is from the Latin word *magister* meaning *teacher,* so the *Magisterium* is the teaching authority of the Church, which resides with the pope alone and with the pope along with the bishops all over the world.

The Extraordinary Magisterium

Extraordinary means just that, out of the ordinary. When an Ecumenical (General) Council is convened, presided, and approved by the pope, and he issues definitive decrees, they're considered infallible, because they come from the Extraordinary Magisterium. The Church has held an all-time total of 21 councils. These are gatherings of the world's bishops and cardinals, and sometimes, priests, deacons, and laity are invited to observe, but only bishops and the pope can discuss and vote. Usually, these councils met to resolve theological controversies, such as the divinity and humanity of Christ, or to respond to a crisis, such as the Reformation. The culmination of these councils is a written letter that explains the faith, interprets Scripture, or settles disputed topics of faith and morals. They never contradict the Bible but apply biblical truths to contemporary concerns and problems as well as giving more understanding to essential core beliefs. The names and years of the councils throughout Church history are as follows:

1. Nicea (325)
2. First Constantinople (381)
3. Ephesus (431)
4. Chalcedon (451)
5. Second Constantinople (553)
6. Third Constantinople (680–81)
7. Second Nicea (787)
8. Fourth Constantinople (869–70)
9. First Lateran (1123)
10. Second Lateran (1139)
11. Third Lateran (1179)
12. Fourth Lateran (1215)
13. First Lyons (1245)
14. Second Lyons (1274)
15. Vienne (1311–12)
16. Constance (1414–18)
17. Basel-Ferrara-Florence (1431–45)
18. Fifth Lateran (1512–17)
19. Trent (1545–63)
20. First Vatican (1869–70)
21. Second Vatican (1962–65)

The Ecumenical Councils have defined doctrines such as: the divinity of Christ (Nicea), the title of Mary as the Mother of God (Ephesus), the two natures of Christ, human and divine, being united to the one divine person (Chalcedon), the term *transubstantiation* (see Chapter 8) to describe how the bread and wine are changed at Mass into the Body and Blood of Christ (Lateran IV), the seven sacraments, Sacred Scripture, and Sacred Tradition (see Chapter 3) and other responses to the Reformation (Trent), and papal infallibility (Vatican I). These conciliar decrees and ex cathedra papal pronouncements form the Extraordinary Magisterium.

Also considered infallible teachings, the *ex cathedra* (Latin for *from the chair*) pronouncements from the pope are also part of the Extraordinary Magisterium. The word *cathedral* comes from the Latin *cathedra,* because it's the church where the bishop's chair *(cathedra)* resides. The chair is symbolic of authority going back to Roman days when Caesar or his governors sat on a chair and made public decisions, pronouncements, or judgments. When the pope teaches *ex cathedra,* he's not physically sitting on a particular chair but exercising his universal authority as Supreme Teacher. Unlike those governments, which separate their executive, legislative, and judicial branches, in the Catholic Church, the pope is all three rolled into one. He's the chief judge, the chief lawmaker, and the commander in chief all at the same time. That's why the triple crown (also known as a *tiara* or *triregnum*) was used in papal coronations — to symbolize his three-fold authority and that he's higher in dignity and authority than a king (one crown) or even an emperor (double crown). (Pope Paul VI was the last pope to wear the tiara. It's a matter of personal choice and preference now, but in the past, it was considered custom and tradition.)

The Ordinary Magisterium

The second way that an infallible teaching is taught to Catholics is through the *Ordinary Magisterium,* which is the more common and typical manner, hence the reason why it's called *ordinary.* This is the consistent, constant, and universal teaching of the popes through their various documents, letters, papal encyclicals, decrees, and so on. It's never a new doctrine but one that has been taught *ubique, semper et ab omnibus* (Latin for *everywhere, always and by all*). In other words, when the pope reinforces, reiterates, or restates the consistent teaching of his predecessors and of the bishops united with him around the world, that's considered the Ordinary Magisterium and should be treated as infallible doctrine.

The word *papal* refers to anything that has to do with the pope, and when he writes papal documents, which is anything authored by the pope, the title that popes use to refer to themselves the most is *Servant of the Servants of God* (*Servus Servorum Dei* in Latin). St. Gregory the Great (590–604) was the first pope to use this title. But other people address him as *Your Holiness* or *Holy Father* and so on. Check out the different types of papal documents in the listing that follows:

- ✔ Papal Bulls
- ✔ Papal Encyclicals
- ✔ Papal Briefs
- ✔ Apostolic Exhortations
- ✔ Apostolic Constitutions
- ✔ Apostolic Letters
- ✔ Motu Proprios

Prior to the Second Vatican Council (1962–65), more commonly known as Vatican II, the type of papal document determined how much authority the pope intended to exercise. (See Chapter 8 for more on Vatican II.) For example, the lowest level was the *Motu Proprio,* which is a Latin phrase meaning *of his own initiative.* Somewhat like an international memo, it's a short papal letter granting a dispensation or making a modification applying to the whole world but on a disciplinary matter only, such as an issue that has nothing to do with doctrine. An example of Motu Proprio was when John Paul II granted permission to celebrate the Tridentine Mass. On the other hand, *Papal Bulls* were considered the highest authority. For example, the Dogma of the Immaculate Conception by Pius IX in 1854, which refers to Mary being given a special grace from God that preserved her from original sin, carries the full weight of papal authority. *Dogma* means doctrine — an official teaching on faith or morals that's divinely revealed. Catholics consider the Assumption of Mary and the Immaculate Conception infallible teachings, because they involve the solemn, full, and universal papal authority. (See Chapter 14 for more information on Mary, the Immaculate Conception, and the Assumption.)

Since Vatican II, however, the *content* and *context* of the document determines the degree of authority and not just the type of papal document. If the pope intends to definitively teach the universal Church on a matter of faith or morals, then that is his supreme authority as head of the Church being expressed. When John Paul II issued his Apostolic Letter *Ordinatio Sacerdotalis* in 1994, he officially declared that the Catholic Church has no power to ordain women. (See Chapter 12 for more on the role of women in the Church.) *Ordinatio Sacerdotalis* was *not* an ex cathedra papal statement, but it's part of the Ordinary Magisterium, and thus, according to the Prefect for the Sacred Congregation for the Doctrine of the Faith, the teaching is infallible.

Papal encyclicals are letters addressed to the world on contemporary issues and concerns. *Encyclical* comes from the Latin word for *circular,* because these documents are meant to circulate around the world. The name of each letter consists of the first two words of the letter in Latin, because every official document coming from the Vatican is still in the Latin language.

Encyclicals aren't *ex cathedra* pronouncements. The only two *ex cathedra* pronouncements in 2,000 years have been the dogmas of the Immaculate Conception (1854) and the Assumption (1950). They're examples of the Extraordinary Magisterium and an exercise in papal infallibility. (When the pope teaches *ex cathedra* — which is very, very rare — he's exercising his universal authority as Supreme Teacher of a doctrine on faith or morals, and he's incapable of error.)

Some examples of more notable encyclicals follow:

- ✔ **Pius XII** issued many letters, most notably 1943's *Mystici Corporis* on the nature of the Church and *Divino Afflante Spiritu* on promoting biblical studies.

- ✔ **Paul VI** wrote the encyclical *Humanae Vitae*, which presents the Church's teaching on abortion and artificial contraception. It's not an *ex cathedra* statement, but *Humanae Vitae* is a part of the constant, consistent, and universal teachings of the popes and bishops over the ages. (For more about the church's stand on artificial contraception, as well as other sticky issues, turn to Chapter 12.)

✔ **John Paul II** has written a significant number as well, with the most famous being *Laborem Exercens* in 1981 on human work, *Veritatis Splendor* in 1993 on the natural moral law, *Evangelium Vitae* in 1995 on the dignity, sanctity and inviolability of human life and the things that threaten it, such as abortion, euthanasia, and the death penalty, and *Fides et Ratio* in 1998 on the compatibility of faith and reason.

✔ **Leo XIII** wrote *Rerum Novarum* in 1891, which discusses capital and labor. It defends private property and business, as well as the right of workers to form trade unions and guilds.

✔ **John XXIII** wrote *Mater et Magistra* in 1961 on Christianity and social progress and *Pacem in Terris* in 1963 on establishing universal, global peace through truth, justice, charity, and liberty.

Encyclicals are the routine, day-to-day, consistent teaching of the Ordinary Magisterium, which is equally infallible when it concerns faith and morals and reiterates the constant, consistent and universal teaching of the popes and bishops. Their content requires religious submission of mind and will of faithful Catholics around the world. So-called dissent from papal teaching in encyclicals isn't part of Catholic belief. The Catholic faithful willfully conform to papal teaching and don't dispute it.

Now that's job security

Popes are elected for life unless they voluntarily — without pressure or coercion — resign from office. (Pope Pontian was the first one to abdicate from the office in A.D. 235. Pope St. Peter Celestine V was the most famous one to resign in 1294 to go back to monastic life. Pope Gregory XII was the last one to quit in 1415.) No one can depose a pope even if he becomes insane, sick, or corrupt. No ecumenical council has the authority to remove him from office. So when a bad pope gets in, and from time to time, a bad pope did get elected, the only course of action is to pray to St. Joseph for a happy death of the pope in question. (St. Joseph is the patron of a happy death, because he probably died of natural causes in the arms of Mary and Jesus.)

This is our two cents' worth: Of the 265 popes in history, only a dozen were real scoundrels and caused great scandal. Seventy-eight popes are recognized as holy saints (see Chapter 15), leaving 175 pretty good, all right guys. Better stats than for presidents, prime ministers, or monarchs around the world. See the listing in Appendix B for a look at all the popes through history.

The good, the bad, and the ugly

Catholicism regards St. Peter as the first pope, handpicked by Jesus Christ himself, according to the Gospel of St. Matthew (16:18), when Jesus said, "Thou art Peter and upon this rock I shall build my Church." If you count St. Peter as the first pope, then John Paul II is the 265th pope or the 264th Successor of St. Peter, depending on where you begin. And you thought that memorizing the names of all the world leaders was hard when you were 10 years old?

Some colorful characters are interspersed among the bunch of 265 popes. Seventy-eight of them are canonized saints, and ten more are beatified, which is one step short of sainthood, so approximately 32 percent of the papacy has been really good. Of all the rest, only twelve are actually considered morally evil and corrupt scoundrels.

Although even one bad pope is one too many, Jesus himself picked 12 imperfect sinners to be his apostles. The first pope, St. Peter, weakened and denied Christ three times, and Judas, one of the first bishops, betrayed him for 30 pieces of silver. One repented; the other hanged himself instead of seeking mercy.

Probably the worst pope ever, Alexander VI (1492–1503) was a Borgia. The name is infamous; the Borgias were a notorious yet influential Italian family during the Renaissance when no unified Kingdom of Italy existed, only small principalities, dukedoms, and city-states. Pope Alexander VI had several illegitimate children before and during his reign as pope, two of whom are noteworthy: Cesare Borgia and his sister Lucrezia Borgia. Cesare grew up to be a ruthless autocrat, and Lucrezia is reputed to have been the most famous poisoner. Alexander VI is the epitome of nepotism, bribery, deceit, debauchery, and anything else you can imagine. The Borgias were the Sopranos of their time. The list of Borgias included 11 cardinals, 2 popes, a queen of England, and a saint.

And Benedict IX (1032–1045) was a close second to the worst pope. Assuming the throne of St. Peter in his late teens or early twenties, this playboy pope incited a riot in Rome, because the people were so disgusted with his antics.

Lady pope? Hardly. The so-called Pope Joan never existed except in myth from the 13th to 17th centuries. French Protestant David Blondel (1590–1655) disproved the myth once and for all in a scholarly refutation, but the story is so bizarre that some still believe it despite the lack of any credible evidence. The legend goes that a woman named Joan impersonated a man so that she could enter the clerical life and rise through the ecclesiastical ranks of the hierarchy, which she allegedly did with ease. Supposedly, her short hair and manly dress fooled everyone until one day, while riding a horse, she gave birth to a child and was exposed as a fake — only to be stoned to death by the angry mob. And if you believe that, we'll tell you another one . . .

Where the pope hangs his hat

The pope's home is *Vatican City*, an independent nation since the Lateran Agreement of 1929, when Italy recognized its sovereignty. Vatican City covers only 0.2 square miles (108.7 acres), has fewer than a thousand inhabitants, and rests in the middle of Rome.

Papal trivia: Why does the pope wear white?

Because most popes were first cardinals before being elected bishop of Rome, they kept their scarlet clothing but embellished it with white ermine fur during the Middle Ages. Pope St. Pius V, elected in 1566, decided to keep his white Dominican habit, however, so he adapted the cassock, the full-length clerical gown, making it white. From then on, the pope wore a white cassock. Cardinals wear red, bishops wear purple, and priests wear black.

After 300 years of Roman persecution, the Emperor Constantine, born Flavius Valerius Constantinus, first legalized Christianity in A.D. 313 with the Edict of Milan and thus formally ended the state sponsored persecutions of the Christians. In A.D. 321, he donated the imperial property of the Lateran Palace to the Bishop of Rome, which began a trend of donating property in recompense for all the land and possessions that the Romans took from the early Christians during the pagan era. (For more on Emperor Constantine, see the "Dreaming of Jesus" sidebar in Appendix A.)

The donation of large estates stopped around A.D. 600, but 154 years later, King Pepin (the Short) of the Franks (who was also the father of Charlemagne) issued the Donation of A.D. 754: The pope would govern the territory of central Italy (16,000 square miles). From 754–1870, Vatican City was part of the Papal States, also known as *Patrimonium Sancti Petri* (the Patrimony of St. Peter). During the unification of Italy, Giuseppe Garibaldi and Count Camillo Benso di Cavour, the two men most responsible for creating the Kingdom and modern nation of Italy in 1870, seized the Papal States and, for all practical purposes, ended the secular rule of the popes. It wasn't so much that Pope Pius IX was opposed to a unified Italy nor was he enamored with ruling the Papal States, rather, he feared that the secular, anti-religious, anti-clerical politics of Garibaldi, Cavour, and King Victor Emmanuel would endanger the Catholic Church's autonomous control over her schools, hospitals, and churches, because in other countries, nationalism meant the seizing of property and businesses by hostile governments.

Today, Vatican City is the smallest independent nation in the world. Ironically, it also has the largest number of embassies and ambassadors around the globe. Marconi, the inventor of radio, built a radio for Pope Pius XI; thus Vatican Radio began in 1931. Now, in addition to a radio and short-wave antennae, the Vatican also has television and Internet programming.

The only real citizens of Vatican City, aside from the pope, are the full-time diplomats who work for the *Holy See* (the pope and the various offices of Church government in the Vatican). These diplomats, clergy and laity alike, come from countries all over the world and still retain their own nationality and citizenship but are given a Vatican passport while employed to represent the Vatican. Originally sent to Rome in 1506, about 107 Swiss guards protect the pope, decorating the *Piazza* (outdoor square where people gather) with their colorful costumes. In addition, plain-clothes Swiss guards, with electronic surveillance and sophisticated weapons, also keep a close eye on the Holy Father, especially since the attempted assassination in 1981.

Who's Next in the Ecclesiastical Scheme of Things

Because the Catholic Church has a billion-plus members, the pope depends on many helpers to govern the vast institution. The ranking system goes like this: The pope's at the helm, followed by cardinals, archbishops/bishops, vicar generals, monsignors, and priests. The rest of the Church is made up of deacons, monks, nuns, brothers, sisters, and laypersons. (The latter — lay men and lay women — make up 99.9 percent of the Church.)

Cardinals

Although the primary responsibility of the College of Cardinals is to elect a pope (see "How the pope gets his job" section, earlier in this chapter), cardinals have many other responsibilities as well. The *Roman Curia* is the whole group of administrators (Cardinal Prefects) that head up their departments (congregations, tribunals, and so on), working together as the right hand of the pope. The pope governs through the Roman Curia, something like cabinet members who assist the president or department ministers who assist the prime minister. For example, a Cardinal Secretary of State represents the Holy See to foreign governments, because Vatican City is the world's smallest independent country. And you can find a different cardinal heading up each congregation, such as the Congregation for

- Bishops
- Catholic Education
- Causes of the Saints
- Clergy
- Divine Worship and Discipline of the Sacraments
- Evangelization of Peoples

> ✔ Institutes of Consecrated Life and Societies of Apostolic Life
>
> ✔ Oriental Churches

A different cardinal also heads up each of several commissions and councils, as well as three high courts of the Catholic Church: the Apostolic Penitentiary, the Apostolic Signatura, and the Roman Rota, all of which deal with canon law (see Chapter 9) and its application and interpretation.

Cardinals who don't work in the Curia run an archdiocese, mostly functioning as an archbishop would — ordaining, confirming, and doing the day-to-day business of being chief shepherd of the archdiocese. These cardinals are also often the *metropolitans,* which means that they supervise the province of two to several dioceses, usually all in the same state or region. A metropolitan doesn't have immediate authority over neighboring bishops or their dioceses even though they're within the cardinal archbishop's province as metropolitan.

A metropolitan does report to Rome, however, if one of the bishops in his province is derelict in his duties, commits scandal or crime, and so on. Often, the *apostolic nuncio,* the papal ambassador to that country, consults with the cardinal when vacancies appear in his province as in the case of a bishop dying or retiring. For example, the Cardinal Archbishop of Philadelphia is the Metropolitan for Pennsylvania, which incorporates the eight dioceses of Philadelphia, Pittsburgh, Erie, Harrisburg, Scranton, Allentown, Greensburg, and Altoona-Johnstown.

Bishops and archbishops

Besides being the head of the Catholic Church, the pope is also the bishop of Rome. The pope isn't more a bishop than any other bishop, but his authority covers more territory. The pope has supreme, full, immediate, and universal jurisdiction all over the world, whereas a local bishop, who may also be an archbishop or a cardinal, possesses jurisdiction only in his *diocese,* which is the typical geographical designation in Catholic governance — an administrative territory.

Dioceses and archdioceses: The areas that they govern

Each individual bishop retains his own authority, which comes from episcopal ordination and consecration. *Episcopal* refers to anything that has to do with a bishop or bishops, and episcopal ordination and consecration is the sacrament by which a priest becomes a bishop. It's the third and fullest level of the Sacrament of Holy Orders. (The first level is the ordination of a deacon, and the second is the ordination of a priest.) Three bishops lay hands on the priest being ordained bishop, and his head is anointed with Chrism Oil.

The local bishop runs the diocese. He's not an ambassador of the pope but governs the local diocese as an authentic successor of the apostles, just as the pope governs the universal Church as the successor of St. Peter.

The pope appoints the bishops, and they must make a visit to the Holy Father every five years and give a report on their particular diocese. The rest of the time, the bishop goes around the diocese confirming adults and teenagers, ordaining men to the *diaconate,* the office of deacon, and to the priesthood once a year. Only bishops have the authority to administer the Sacrament of Holy Orders whereby men are ordained deacons, priests, or bishops. Bishops make pastoral visits to the parishes and chair numerous meetings with their staff. (See Chapter 6 for more on the Sacrament of Confirmation, and see Chapter 7 for more on the Sacrament of Holy Orders.) He's like a pastor of an extra-large parish. (See the section "The parish priest" for details about pastors.)

The local diocese is composed of a collection of local parishes, just like a state is a collection of counties and cities. Many dioceses are comprised of several state counties, and in a few places, the entire state makes up one diocese. New Jersey, for example, has five dioceses: Trenton, Patterson, Metuchen, Camden, and the Archdiocese of Newark.

In general, you can think of a local parish like a town or city, and the local pastor is like the mayor. The diocese is like a state or province, and the bishop is like the governor. (The pope is like the prime minister, governing the entire nation, except that he governs the universal Church all over the world.)

An archbishop runs a really large diocese, known as an *archdiocese.* For example, an archbishop is given authority in each of the following archdioceses: Newark, San Francisco, Denver, Hartford, Miami, St. Louis, and Omaha. Sometimes, though, the archbishop is also a cardinal, which is the case in Philadelphia, New York City, Washington, D.C., Boston, Chicago, Baltimore, Los Angeles, and Detroit. Cardinals rank right below the pope. When they're not electing a new pope (see the "How the pope gets his job" section, earlier in this chapter), cardinals spend most of their time working in their archdioceses or in the Vatican.

The bishops within an entire country or nation get together at least once a year in a gathering known as an *episcopal conference.* The American bishops belong to the United States Conference of Catholic Bishops (USCCB), the Canadian Bishops belong to the Canadian Conference of Catholic Bishops (CCCB), and in Australia, it's the Australian Catholic Bishops Conference (ACBC), and in Great Britain, it's the Catholic Bishops' Conference of England and Wales (CBCEW).

Cathedrals: The place where they hang out

The cathedral is to the local diocese what the Vatican is to the universal Church. The cathedral is the official church of the diocese where the bishop's chair resides, and his chair (*cathedra* in Latin) is a symbol of his authority as a successor to the apostles.

Ironically, St. Peter's Basilica in the Vatican, where the pope celebrates most of his Masses, isn't technically the pope's cathedral church. The cathedral for the diocese of Rome is actually St. John Lateran, where the popes originally lived before moving to the Vatican.

Bishops celebrate most Masses at the cathedral church. In addition, it's often the place where the Chrism Mass (also known as the *Mass of the Oils*) takes place — unless the bishop decides to have it elsewhere in the diocese. (See the sidebar, "Nope, the Mass of the Oils has nothing to do with your car's engine," in this chapter, for details about this special Mass.)

Cathedrals also have daily and weekly Mass like other parishes, as well as weddings, funerals, baptisms, and such. But the pride of the cathedral is in the ordinations to the episcopacy, priesthood, or diaconate, as well as the Chrism Mass. (For more on ordination and Holy Orders, see Chapter 7.)

Note: Only the bishop may sit in his *cathedra,* so any other priest celebrating Mass must use another chair.

Nope, the Mass of the Oils has nothing to do with your car's engine

The Chrism Mass takes place on Holy Thursday or some other day of Holy Week, and all the priests of the diocese are asked to be present if possible. At this Mass, the bishop formally blesses olive oil in enormous multi-gallon containers to be distributed to all the parishes and priests throughout the diocese. Three oils are blessed at this annual Mass:

✔ **The Oil of Catechumens** (*Oleum Catechumenorum)* is used to bless people prior to their Baptism and during enrollment as *catechumen,* students of the faith preparing for Baptism.

✔ **The Oil of the Sick** (*Oleum Infirmorum)* is appropriate when administering the Sacrament of the Anointing of the Sick, formerly known as Extreme Unction.

✔ **Chrism Oil** (*Sacrum Chrisma),* also called Sacred Chrism, is for newly baptized persons, and the bishop also uses Chrism Oil when administering the Sacraments of Confirmation or Holy Orders. Like Oil of the Sick and Oil of Catechumens, Chrism is made from olive oil but unlike the other two, balsam is added to make it more fragrant and appealing to the nose.

The vicar general

Vicars general aren't military leaders like Generals Montgomery, De Gaulle, and MacArthur. They're priests who are second in command in the diocese and appointed by the bishop to help him govern the local Church. Sometimes, episcopal vicars are also appointed to assist the bishop in certain areas, such as vocations, the marriage tribunal, clergy personnel, Hispanic, or minority ministries, and so on. In large dioceses, such as New York or London, vicars general are often auxiliary bishops, ordained bishops who assist the bishop of the diocese in the same way any other vicar general does, except that they can help the bishop ordain deacons and priests.

Often, these priests are given the honorary title of *monsignor*. This title has no extra authority, dignity, or salary. You can recognize a monsignor by the color of his *cassock* — a long, close-fitting garment worn by clerics. *Monsignor* is merely a title of honor given by the pope at the request of the local bishop. This honorary title may be bestowed in three different forms:

- **Papal Chamberlain:** Also known as *Chaplain of His Holiness,* this is the lowest ranking of the title of monsignor. They wear black cassocks with purple buttons and trim.

- **Domestic Prelate:** These monsignors are also known as *Honorary Prelates of His Holiness,* and they wear purple or black cassocks with red buttons and trim.

- **Prothonotary Apostolic:** This is the highest ranking of the title. It's designated by a purple *ferraiolone,* a silk cape worn over the cassock.

The parish priest

The *parish priest* (also known as a *pastor*) is next in the hierarchy after the vicar general. Pastors are appointed by the bishop and represent the bishop to the local *parish,* which is a collection of neighborhoods in one small region of the county within a given state.

The pastor is helped by a *parochial vicar* (formerly known as a *curate* or an *assistant pastor*) and/or sometimes by a permanent deacon, religious sister, or lay parishioners as a *pastoral associate*. The parish council and finance committee, which are made up of lay parishioners for the most part, advise and counsel the pastor but don't have administrative or executive authority.

Tough training

In the movie *Going My Way* (Paramount; 1944), Fr. O'Malley (portrayed by Bing Crosby) may have sung a few tunes and tangled with the nuns in the school, but the typical Catholic priest isn't what you see in that film. Priests are expected to obtain a graduate, post-graduate, or doctoral degree, and they often spend anywhere from 4 to 12 years in the *seminary,* which is the equivalent of Protestant divinity school. Most have at least a master's degree in divinity or theology, if not a higher academic degree on par with medical doctors and attorneys.

Besides scholastic training, seminarians also receive practical experience from *apostolates,* which are weekly or summertime assignments in parishes, hospitals, nursing homes, prisons, classrooms, and such, to unite pastoral education with theological and philosophical education.

Busy job

A parish priest celebrates daily Mass, hears confessions every week, gives marriage counseling, provides prenuptial counseling, gives spiritual direction, anoints and visits shut-ins and the sick in hospitals and nursing homes, teaches *catechism* (a book that contains the doctrines of Catholicism) to children and adults, baptizes, witnesses marriages, performs funerals and burials, attends numerous parish and diocesan meetings, prays privately every day, does spiritual and theological reading, and finds time to relax now and then with family and friends. And once a year, he's expected to make a five-day retreat in addition to doing his regular spiritual direction and daily prayer. Yeah, busy job.

With over a billion Catholics worldwide and only about 404,626 priests to minister to their spiritual needs, that leaves an average of about one priest per 2,517 Catholics. Some areas have as many as 2,500 to 6,000 or more people per priest.

The hub in the wheel: The parish church

The parish church is where the priest does his job and where most Catholics hang out on Saturday evening or Sunday morning to attend Mass.

The local Catholic parish is often named after a title of the Lord Jesus Christ, such as *Blessed Sacrament* or *Sacred Heart,* or a title of the Blessed Virgin Mary, such as *Our Lady of Good Counsel* or *Our Lady of Seven Sorrows,* or after one of the saints, such as *St. Ann, St. Bernadette,* or *St. Joseph.* The parish is the heart of the diocese because it's where most Catholics get baptized, go to confession, attend Mass, receive Holy Communion, are confirmed, get married, and are buried from.

A few American parishes still have a parochial school connected to them, and even fewer have a convent of nuns who staff the school, but you can still find them here and there. Catholic grade schools were once the bread and butter of vocations and often fed into Catholic high school and college. In other words, these parish schools encouraged boys and girls to consider becoming priests and nuns and most continued their Catholic education all the way through college even if they didn't have a religious vocation. But economics, demographics, and declining numbers of religious sisters and brothers have resulted in the consolidation and closing of many parish schools. Public schools in many places are well staffed, well funded, and more accessible. And an even more rare occurrence is the parish cemetery. Nowadays, the diocese has centralized schools and cemeteries, but a few old country parishes still have a graveyard in the back of the property.

Father, are you a diocesan or religious priest?

Catholic priests are *diocesan* (secular) or *religious* (regular). Diocesan priests belong to the diocese that they're located in, but religious order priests, such as Franciscan or Dominican, belong to that order.

Diocesan (secular) priests

Diocesan priests are called *secular* priests to distinguish them from the religious priests who belong to communities and orders. The typical parish priest is usually a diocesan priest. That means he belongs to the geographical area of the diocese, which often comprises several counties in one state. He makes a promise of obedience to the local bishop and a promise of celibacy.

A diocesan priest gets a modest monthly salary from the parish. In addition, the parish or diocese normally provides room and board (meals and lodging) and health insurance, but only a few dioceses also provide car insurance. Diocesan priests live in parishes alone or with another priest, but basically have their own living quarters inside the *rectory* — the house where the parish priests live. They do their own work and usually just share one meal together and then relax on their own as well.

Diocesan priests are responsible for buying and maintaining their own automobiles as well as personal property — clothing, books, computers, televisions, stereos, and so on. The individual diocesan priest pays his federal, state, and local taxes, including Social Security taxes. After making monthly car payments, insurance and possibly paying off banks loans from college, not much is left of the monthly salary, but the parish or diocese provide his necessities. Honoraria and gifts from baptisms, weddings, and funerals differ from parish to parish and from diocese to diocese, but it's *very important* to note that a priest never charges any fees for his services. Free will offerings are often made to him or to the parish, but it's sinful, sacrilegious, and rude for any cleric to ask for money while performing his sacred ministry.

Canon law (see Chapter 9) guarantees every priest one day off per seven-day week and one month (30 days) of vacation per year, not including the one-week annual retreat. Because many laity have two days off per week, that one-month vacation shrinks quickly in comparison.

Religious (regular) priests

Religious priests are referred to as *regular,* because they follow the *regula,* which is Latin for *rule,* the structured life of a religious community. The Rule refers to how a religious order trains, lives, governs itself, and practices. Religious priests are more commonly known as *order priests* after the religious *order* that they belong to, such as the Franciscans, Dominicans, Jesuits, Benedictines, and Augustinians. They wear particular *habits* (religious garb) and take solemn vows of poverty, chastity, and obedience. Because religious priests often take vows of poverty, they don't own their own cars or personal possessions. Many use community automobiles that everyone in the order shares. They own the clothes on their back and little else. They don't get salaries like diocesan priests but are given an extremely modest monthly allowance to buy toiletries and snacks, as well as to go out for dinner or a movie once in a while. If they need to buy something expensive or want to take time off for vacation, they must ask permission of the superior.

They normally live together with three or more (sometimes up to 10, 20, or more) members of the community in the same house, sharing everything. The entire community usually shares one television, stereo, computer, and so on. This encourages them to recreate together, because they must also live together, pray together, and work together. Unlike diocesan (secular) clergy who get small salaries and pay taxes, religious clergy own nothing. If they inherit anything whatsoever, it goes to the community or to the order, whereas a diocesan priest could get the family home if he's an only child, but he would also have to pay all the taxes and upkeep as well.

Deacons

Deacons are next in the hierarchy, right after priests. *Permanent deacons* are men ordained to an office in the Church who normally have no intention or desire of becoming priests. They can be single or married. If the latter, they must be married *before* being ordained a deacon. If their wife dies before them, they may be ordained a priest if the bishop permits and approves.

Transitional deacons are *seminarians,* students in training for the priesthood, at the last phase of their formation. After being a deacon for a year, they're ordained a priest by the bishop.

Deacons can baptize, witness marriages, perform funeral and burial services outside of Mass, distribute Holy Communion, preach the *homily,* which is the sermon given after the Gospel at Mass, and are obligated to pray the Divine

Office (Breviary) each day. *The Divine Office, Breviary,* or *Liturgy of the Hours* are all the same thing. These are the 150 Psalms and Scriptural readings from the Old and New Testament that every deacon, priest, and bishop must pray every day and a few times during each day. This way, in addition to the biblical readings at daily Mass, the cleric is also exposed to more Sacred Scripture each day of his life.

Permanent deacons, especially those who are married, have secular jobs to support their families and also help the local pastor by visiting the sick, teaching the faith, counseling couples and individuals, working on parish committees and councils, and giving advice to the pastor.

Deacons, priests, and bishops are considered *clerics,* members of the clergy, in the Catholic Church.

Monks and nuns, brothers and sisters

Technically speaking, monks and nuns live in *monasteries* (from the Greek *monazein,* meaning *to live alone*), which are buildings that have restricted access to the outside world and as much time as possible is spent in work and in prayer. Monasteries are places where only women as nuns reside or where only men as monks live. Few monasteries have guest accommodations, and the monks or nuns live a monastic type of spirituality, such that they all gather in the chapel to pray together and then all eat together and then all work somewhere in the monastery, cooking, cleaning, and so on.

Religious sisters, on the other hand, live in *convents,* a word that comes from the Latin *conventus* meaning *assembly*. Convents offer more open access inside and out to the secular world. Residents typically live and pray in the convent but work outside in schools, hospitals, and so on.

Friaries (from the Latin word *frater* meaning *brother*) are the male version of convents, a place where religious men called *brothers* live, work, and pray together, but work is done outside the friary. St. Dominic and St. Francis of Assisi both founded the first group of friars in the Church. Up to that time, a man's choice of religious vocation was limited to either becoming a diocesan-parish priest or a monk, living in the monastery. Friars bridged the gap between the urban parish and the monastery, and they aren't as cloistered or semi-cloistered as their monk and nun counterparts. How cloistered the group is depends on the religious order or community and the founder who started it.

You can find hundreds of different religious orders, communities, and congregations in the world today. Each community and order bases its spirituality on the founder of its congregation, such as St. Dominic, the founder of the Dominicans. By the way, St. Francis founded the Franciscans, St. Clare founded the Poor Clares, St. Lucy Filippini founded the Religious Sisters Filippini, and Mother Teresa founded the Missionaries of Charity. Some communities specialize in teaching and others in hospital work. Some engage in several active apostolates, and a few devote themselves to a cloistered life of contemplative prayer.

For example, the Sisters of St. Joseph, the Sisters of Mercy, Religious Sisters Filippini, Dominican Sisters, Daughters of Charity, and Sisters of Saints Cyril and Methodius often work in schools, hospitals, and nursing homes. But Carmelite, Dominican, Poor Clare, and other nuns stay in the monastery and pray, fast, and work for the sanctification of souls. You may have seen Mother Angelica and the other Poor Clare nuns on television from time to time and noticed that even while they're in the chapel, they're separated *(cloistered)* from the general public. A few nuns in the order are designated as externs, living outside the cloister, so they can go to the store and buy food and other necessities, because the nuns on the inside rarely leave the monastery except for illness or a death in the family. Cloistered nuns live and stay in the monastery whereas religious sisters work outside the *convent,* the house where they live.

In contrast, the sisters in parochial schools aren't nuns but religious sisters; they don't live in a cloistered monastery but in a convent, and they teach in the parish school.

You can tell the order of the monk, nun, sister, or friar by their *habit* (religious garb). Franciscans typically wear brown, the Dominicans wear white, the Benedictines wear black, and the Missionaries of Charity wear white with blue stripes. Some communities of women no longer wear a veil on their head but wear a pin that identifies them with their order instead. The style, size, and color of the women's veils also designate their community.

Religious brothers and sisters aren't members of the clergy, but they aren't members of the lay faithful, either. They're called *consecrated religious,* which means that they've taken sacred vows of poverty, chastity, and obedience. Religious brothers live in community with other brothers and religious women live in community with other sisters — not only do they share the same house, but also more of them are in it, anywhere from 3 to 30 in many cases. They share all meals together and try to work together, pray together, and recreate together. Because they take a vow of poverty, they don't own their own car (no insurance, loan payments, or gasoline to buy either), and they have no personal savings or checking account. The religious order that they belong to provides all this, and they must ask their superiors when they need or want something. This is where that vow of obedience kicks in.

Part II
Understanding All Those Beliefs

The 5th Wave   By Rich Tennant

"When did we stop giving an 'amen' and start giving the 'wave'?"

In this part . . .

You find out what Catholics teach and believe and how they worship. Discover that Catholicism is in fact a biblical religion. Find out how and why the Catholic Bible is different from the Protestant Bible. And read about who Jesus is to Catholics. Is he God? Man? Human? Divine?

This part also covers how Catholicism uses the whole person in Catholic worship — body and soul. See how the sacraments speak to both. Look at the connection between what's believed and how that belief affects the way that Catholics worship God.

Catholic ritual is mysterious, but in this part, you can take a peek behind the curtain and see what's going on. Find out about ancient ceremonies and traditional prayers that go back two millennia. Find out why there are seven sacraments, no more and no less, and what's holiest about Catholicism: the Mass.

Chapter 3

Ya Gotta Have Faith

Y ou may think that having faith is similar to believing in fantasies or fairy tales or accepting the existence of UFOs, ghosts, abominable snowmen, the Loch Ness monster or Bigfoot, but faith is something entirely different. In this chapter, we tell you what faith really is and explain what having it means to Catholics.

How Do You Know If You Have Faith?

It's plain and simple; you have *faith* if you trust the word of someone else. When you take what someone says on faith, you believe in what the other person is telling you even though you haven't personally witnessed it or maybe you don't understand it — even if it's difficult to believe. In other words, faith means agreeing with, believing in, *trusting* something — without hard, cold evidence — that you can't know or comprehend on your own.

So far, faith doesn't sound all that different from believing in Santa Claus or the Easter Bunny, but having faith is a bit more complicated. Having faith means being able to live with unanswered questions — sometimes, tough ones. For example, why does evil exist in the world? Why is it that people still go to war? And what about the existence of terrorism, disease, and crime? Faith doesn't answer these questions. (Some think that the answer, "It's God's will," suffices, but it doesn't.) Faith, however, gives you the courage to endure and survive without having the answers. Instead of providing a set of answers to painful and complicated enigmas, faith provides the means to persevere.

The *Catechism of the Catholic Church,* a book defining the official teachings of the Catholic Church, has this to say about faith:

- Faith is first of all a personal adherence of man to God. At the same time, and inseparably, it is a *free assent to the whole truth that God has revealed* (section 150).

- Faith is a personal act — the free response of the human person to the initiative of God who reveals himself. But faith isn't an isolated act. No one can believe alone, just as no one can live alone (section 166).

To Catholics, faith isn't something you find. It's a gift from God. He offers it freely to anyone and everyone, but it must be freely received as well. No one can be forced to have or accept faith. And when it's presented, each individual responds differently — at different levels, at different times, and in different ways. Some reject it, some ignore it, and some treat it casually. Others cherish their faith deeply. As the adage goes: For those who believe, no explanation is necessary, and for those who do not believe, no explanation is possible.

Having Faith in Revelations

Catholic faith involves more than just believing that God exists. It's about believing *in* God as well as *whatever* God has revealed. Objectively, you can look at faith as the sum total of revealed truths given by God, which is often called the *deposit of faith* — the doctrines of the Church. Subjectively, you can consider faith as your personal response *(assent)* to those revealed truths.

We hear ya: "But what do you mean by revealed truths? And, for that matter, just what *are* God's revealed truths?" By *revealed truths,* we mean a *revelation,* God's unveiling of supernatural truths necessary for human salvation. (The word *revelation* comes from the Latin *revelare,* meaning to *unveil.*) Some of these are truths that you could never know by science or philosophy; the human mind is incapable of knowing them without divine intervention, so God revealed them to mere mortals. For example, the revealed truth of the Holy Trinity is that there is only one God but Three Persons (but not three gods, however). This is something that the human intellect could never discover on its own. God had to tell that one himself. Other revelations, such as the existence of God or that it's immoral and sinful to steal, lie, and murder, can be known by using human reason alone, but God reveals these truths directly anyway, because not everyone understands them at the same time and in the same way. The essence of these revelations can and are presumed knowable to anyone with the use of reason, so someone can't claim they didn't know it was wrong to commit murder. But because of original sin (Chapter 6), some of the applications and distinctions of these basic truths require more reasoning and thinking. So to even out the playing field, God revealed some important truths so that even those people who aren't intelligent or quick minded won't be caught off guard.

As for what God's revealed truths are, the most concise answer is *his word. The Word of God* is the revelation of God to his people. What is the Word of God? Catholics believe that the Word of God comes in two forms:

- ✔ **The spoken word:** Also called *the unwritten word or Sacred Tradition.*
- ✔ **The written word:** Known also as *Scripture* or the *Bible.*

Both the spoken and the written word come from the same source and communicate the same message — the truth.

Catholics believe that his word reflects what's in the mind of God, and because God is all truth and all good, his word conveys truth and goodness. Catholics have deep respect for and devotion to the Word of God.

Faith in the written word: The Bible

Catholicism is a biblical religion. Like all Christian religions, it cherishes the Bible as the inspired, infallible, inerrant, and revealed Word of God.

That said, a couple of key differences exist between the Catholic and Protestant perspectives on the Bible:

- ✔ The belief in one or two channels of revelation
- ✔ The interpretation of the biblical text

Forms of revelation

Protestant Christianity regards the Bible, the *written word,* as the only source of divine revelation whereas Catholic Christianity and Eastern Orthodox Christianity considers both the *written word* and the *unwritten word* (also known as the *spoken word* or *Sacred Tradition*) as coming from one and same source — God himself. Another way of looking at it is to think of some Christians as seeing only one channel of revelation — *sola scriptura,* which is Latin for *Scripture alone* — and other Christians as seeing two channels of revelation: Sacred Scripture *and* Sacred Tradition — the written word of God and the unwritten or spoken word of God. (Just divert thine eyes to the "Faith in the spoken word: Sacred Tradition" section, later in this chapter, for an explanation of what the unwritten word is.)

It isn't that Catholics believe only in tradition, Protestants believe only in the Bible, and never the twain shall meet. Christians of all denominations cherish the Word of God as being divinely inspired and revealed. But Catholics don't limit the Word of God to the Bible. Is the Word of God strictly the written word of the Bible or is it both the written word and the unwritten or spoken word as well? The debate continues and both religions seek to establish mutual respect for one another and promote further dialogue.

The interpretation of the text

Since the time of the Reformation, opinion on the interpretation of the sacred text has differed significantly. Some Christians hold for a literal interpretation of every word and phrase of Scripture; other Christians hold for a faithful interpretation, which is sometimes literal and sometimes not. Catholic Christianity along with all Christians consider God to be the Author of Sacred Scripture and therefore the Bible is indeed the Word of God, but as mentioned before, Catholicism sees the Bible as the written word and considers Sacred Tradition as the unwritten or spoken Word of God. Catholicism uses that second half of the equation in her interpretation of the biblical texts. Catholics regard the Bible as the inspired and revealed word of God, but it's also seen as a collection of sacred literature. Rather than just looking at the Bible as one big book, Catholicism treats the Bible as a collection of smaller books under one cover: The Word of God written by men yet inspired by God.

The Bible tells of salvation history, but it's much more than a history book. It contains the Psalms of David — songs that the King wrote in honor of God, yet the Bible is much more than a hymnal. It contains poetry, prose, history, theology, imagery, metaphor, analogy, irony, hyperbole, and so on. Because it's not exclusively one form of literature, as you would have in a science textbook, one needs to know and appreciate the various literary forms in the Bible in order to interpret it as the author intended. For example, when Jesus says in the Gospel (Mark 9:43), "And if your hand causes you to sin, cut it off," the Catholic Church has interpreted that to be a *figure of speech* rather than something to be taken *literally.* Yet in some cultures of the world, the hands of thieves are cut off. At the same time, Catholicism interprets literally the passage of John 6:55 — "For my flesh is real food and my blood real drink." Because individuals can disagree on what should be interpreted literally and what isn't, Catholicism resorts to one final authority to definitively interpret for all Catholics what the biblical text means for the Catholic faith. That ultimate authority is called the *Magisterium* (from the Latin word *magister* meaning *teacher*), which is the authority of the pope and the bishops around the world in union with him to instruct the faithful. (For more on the Magisterium, see Chapter 2.)

Catholics believe that Christ founded the Church, a necessary institution, to safeguard and protect revelation by authentically interpreting the biblical texts. It's not that Sacred Scripture and Sacred Tradition are in competition with one another or that it's a question of either/or. Rather, it's seen as a mutual partnership. Whenever and wherever the Bible is silent on an issue or where the meaning is ambiguous or disputed, then Sacred Tradition steps in to clarify the matter. The Church, founded by Christ ("I will build my Church" — Matthew 16:18) is not superior to Scripture, but she's the steward and guardian as well as interpreter of the inspired and revealed Word of God. The Church assumes the role of authentic interpreter not on her own but by the authority given her by Christ: "He who hears you, hears Me." (Luke 10:16) Also, "In truth I tell you, whatever you bind on earth shall be bound in heaven." (Matthew 18:18) The Church makes an authentic interpretation and an authoritative decision regarding those issues that aren't explicitly addressed in Sacred Scripture, but only because Christ has entrusted her to do so.

The history behind the Bible

What follows is a snapshot of how the Bible was created and how different versions evolved — the Catholic versions and the Protestant versions. If you're eager for more information on the Bible, however, check out *The Bible For Dummies* by Jeffrey Geoghegan and Michael Homan (Wiley).

To understand the history of the Bible, you really have to go back to 1800 B.C. when the oral tradition of the Hebrew people started, because Abraham and his tribes were nomadic people and didn't have a written language of their own. Mothers and fathers verbally *(oral)* handed down (the Latin word *traditio* means to hand down and it's the root of the English word for *tradition*) the stories of the Old Testament about Adam and Eve, Cain and Abel, the Tower of Babel, Noah and the Ark, and so on. Bibles weren't available back then, and folks didn't even have any written parchments either. It was all told by word of mouth, which we call *oral tradition*.

Bible trivia

Want a few interesting Bible tidbits? You got it:

The word *bible* isn't even in the Bible. Do a word search on your computer, and you'll see that nowhere from Genesis to the Apocalypse is the word *bible* ever mentioned. But the word *Scripture* appears 53 times in the King James Version of the Bible, and the phrase *Word of God* appears 55 times.

So if the word itself isn't in the Bible, why call it the Bible? The word comes from the Greek *biblia,* meaning a collection of books, and the origin goes back even farther to the word *biblos,* meaning papyrus. In ancient times, the paper from trees to write on didn't exist — only stone or papyrus. Imagine — stone books.

The Catholic Church gave the name *Bible* to the Bible — to the collection of inspired books known as the Old and New Testaments. The Church also decided which books belonged in the Bible and which were left out, because nowhere from Genesis to Apocalypse can you find a list of which documents belong and which don't. Modern-day Bible publishers and editors have added the table of contents, but the contents weren't disclosed in the sacred text itself. Why does the Bible contain four Gospels? Who decided that Matthew should come before Mark? Why isn't the Gospel of Thomas or the Gospel of Peter in the Bible? Who says that the New Testament contains only 27 books? What happened to the Apocalypse of Moses and the Apocalypse of Adam? The Bible doesn't tell you what books belong in it, so the Church had to use her authority and make that decision.

Moses appeared in 1250 B.C. when the Hebrew people were delivered from the bondage of slavery in Egypt and entered the Promised Land. The era of Moses opened the road to some of the written word, because Moses was raised in the court of Pharaoh, and so he learned how to read and write. But the predominant bulk of revelation was still the oral tradition, handed down from generation to generation, because the rest of the Hebrews were slaves and most were unable to read or write at that time. According to *pious tradition,* Moses composed the first five books of the Hebrew Bible, what Christians call the Old Testament, namely, Genesis, Exodus, Leviticus, Numbers and Deuteronomy. The proof that he really did write them, however, is inconclusive. *Pious tradition* refers to belief without documented proof, but Sacred Tradition, on the other hand, is considered revealed, accurate, and true, because the belief came from God.

Substantial writings weren't saved until 950 B.C., during the reign of King Solomon. But after the death of King Solomon, his kingdom was divided between the northern (Israel) and the southern (Judah) kingdoms.

The Assyrians conquered Israel in 721 B.C. and initiated the first *diaspora,* the dispersion of many Jews, so they wouldn't be centrally located in one area as they had been in their own kingdom of the North. When the Babylonians conquered the South in 587 B.C., they, too, dispersed more Jews to thin out the territory and prevent a restoration of a Jewish kingdom. During the time of the Babylonian captivity and exile, the Jews of the *diaspora* were spread all over the known world. Some retained their Hebrew language, but most lost it and adopted the common language — Greek. (If you could read and write at this time in history, you were reading and writing Greek.)

Consequently, in the year 250 B.C., an effort was underway to translate all Jewish Scripture into the Greek language. The thing is, more Jews lived outside of Palestine than in. In the third century B.C., nearly two-fifths of the population in Egypt alone, especially in Alexandria, was Jewish and yet unable to read and write in Hebrew. These Greek-speaking Jews were known as *Hellenistic Jews.*

According to pious tradition, 70 scholars gathered together to begin the daunting task of translation, hence the term *Septuagint* from the number 70 in Greek for this version of the Bible. However, no parallel effort was afoot at this time to compile a strictly Hebrew collection of the Old Testament books. Because most of the world's Jews were no longer speaking Hebrew but speaking Greek, the need for an all-Greek version of Jewish Scripture was obvious. The smaller community of Hebrew-speaking Jews in the Holy Land wasn't as plentiful, influential, or interested at that time to compile a strictly Hebrew version. The Septuagint Version of the Bible (sometimes abbreviated by the Roman numerals LXX for 70) contained 46 books and became the standard collection of Jewish Scripture, at least for the Hellenistic Jews, and even the Jews in Palestine accepted this collection of books.

Seven of the 46 books were never composed or written originally in the Hebrew language but were regarded as inspired texts nonetheless. These seven books — the Books of Baruch, Maccabees I and II, Tobit, Judith, Ecclesiasticus (also known as *Sirach*), and Wisdom — were known and used by Jews even in the Holy Land, including Jesus and his disciples. The early Christians likewise accepted the inspired status of these seven books, because no one had refuted them during the time of Christ. Because they were later additions to the more ancient Hebrew writings, however, these seven books were called the *Deuterocanonical Books* (meaning *second canon*); the 39 Hebrew books were known as the *Canonical Books.*

Jewish authorities in Jerusalem had no explicit objection to these seven books until the year A.D. 100, well after the Christians had split from formal Judaism and formed their own separate religion. The Temple of Jerusalem was destroyed in A.D. 70, and in the year A.D. 100, Jewish leaders at the Council of Jamnia sought to purify Judaism of all foreign and Gentile influence, which meant removing anything not purely Hebrew. Because the seven Deuterocanonical Books were never written in Hebrew, they got pitched.

By now, though, Christianity was totally separate from Judaism and didn't doubt the authenticity of the seven books, because these books were always considered equal to the other 39. That is, at least until Martin Luther initiated the Protestant Reformation in 1517 and chose to adopt the Hebrew canon (39 books) rather than the Greek canon (46 books) of the old Septuagint (LXX).

So in the listing of the Old Testament, a discrepancy exists between the Catholic and the Protestant Bibles. Catholic Bibles list 46 books and Protestant Bibles list 39. Recently, though, many publishers have added the seven books in Protestant Bibles, such as the King James Version, but they're carefully placed in the back, after the end of the canonical texts, and they're identified as being part of the *Apocrypha,* which is from the Greek word *apokryphos* meaning *hidden.*

So what the Catholic Church considers Deuterocanonical, Protestant theologians consider Apocrypha. And what the Catholic Church considers Apocrypha, Protestants call *Pseudepigrapha* (meaning *false writings*), which are the alleged and so-called Lost Books of the Bible. These Lost Books were never considered as being inspired by the Church, so they were never included as part of any Bible, Catholic or Protestant. Such books as the Assumption of Moses, the Apocalypse of Abraham, the Ascension of Isaiah, the Gospel of Thomas, the Gospel of Peter, the Acts of St. John, and others, were all considered uninspired and therefore never made it into the Bible.

Interestingly enough, Catholics and Protestants have never seriously disputed the list of the New Testament books, and both the Catholic and the Protestant Bibles have the exact same names and number (27) of books in the New Testament. (For more info about the New Testament, see Chapter 4.)

Faith in the spoken word: Sacred Tradition

God's word is more than letters on a page or sounds to the ear. His word is *creative.* When God speaks the word, it happens. For example, the book of Genesis in the Bible tells us that God created merely by saying the word: "God said, 'let there be light,' and there was light."

Catholics believe that the Word of God is found not only in the Bible but also in the unwritten or spoken word — *Sacred Tradition.* In this section, we show you what Sacred Tradition is and introduce you to the single-most important part of that tradition, the Creed, as well as other sources for the tradition, including letters written by the popes.

Before the word was written, it was first spoken. God first said, "Let there be light," and later on, the sacred author wrote those words on paper. Jesus first spoke the word when he preached his Sermon on the Mount. He didn't dictate to Matthew as he was preaching. Matthew rather wrote things down much later, well after Jesus died, rose, and ascended into heaven. None of the Gospels were written during Jesus' life on earth. He died in A.D. 33, and the earliest Gospel manuscript, which is the Aramaic version of Matthew, alluded to by ancient sources goes back between A.D. 40 and 50. The other three Gospels — Mark, Luke, and John — were written between A.D. 53 and 100. Matthew and John, who wrote the first and the last Gospels, were two of the original 12 apostles, so they personally heard what Jesus said and saw with their own eyes what he did. Mark and Luke weren't apostles but disciples, and most of their information on what Jesus said and did wasn't a first-hand eyewitness account but information handed down (remember that the word *tradition* means *to hand down*) to them by others who were witnesses. The unwritten or spoken Gospel was told by word of mouth by the apostles well before the *evangelists,* the Gospel writers, ever wrote one letter let alone a word. Luke received much of his data from Jesus' mother, the Virgin Mary, and Mark received plenty of info from Peter, the one Jesus left in charge.

If it took some time between what Jesus actually said and did from when the Gospel writer put it on paper (actually on parchment), what took place during that period? Before the written word was the unwritten or spoken word. Just as in the Old Testament, things happened and were said long before they were written down, so, too, in the New Testament, Jesus preached his sermons and worked his miracles, died on the Cross, rose from the dead, and ascended into heaven long before anyone wrote it down. No one took notes while he preached. No letters were written between Jesus and the apostles. Sacred Tradition predates and precedes Sacred Scripture, but both come from the same source — God.

The New Testament is totally silent on whether Jesus ever married or had children. The Bible says nothing about his marital status, yet Christians believe he had no wife and no kids. Sacred Tradition tells that he never married just as Sacred Tradition says that the Gospels number only four. Without a written list, how and who decides if the Old Testament contains 39 or 45 books and the New Testament has 27? If it's only the written word, then an answer doesn't exist. If another avenue exists, say the unwritten word, then we can go by that. Catholicism carefully distinguishes between mere human tradition and divinely inspired Sacred Tradition:

- ✔ **Human traditions** are man-made laws that can be changed. An example of a human tradition is Catholics not eating meat on Fridays during Lent. Celibacy for priests of the Latin Church is another human tradition, which any Pope could dispense, modify, or continue.

- ✔ **Sacred Traditions** are considered part of the unwritten Word of God, because it's been believed for centuries, since the time of the Apostolic Church, which refers to that period of time in Church history from the first to the second century A.D. It's called *Apostolic,* because the apostles lived at that time. An example of a Sacred Tradition is the *dogma* of the Assumption of Mary. A *dogma* is a revealed truth that's solemnly defined by the Church — a formal doctrine that the faithful are obligated to believe. Although it's not explicit in Sacred Scripture, the Assumption of Mary means that Mary was assumed, body and soul, into heaven by her divine Son. Even though it wasn't solemnly defined until 1950 by Pope Pius XII, it's been believed (and never doubted) by Catholic Christians since the time of the apostles. Other examples of Sacred Tradition can be found in the doctrines defined by the 21 General or Ecumenical Councils of the Church, from Nicea (A.D. 325) to Vatican II (1962–1965). (See Chapter 2 for more on the councils.)

The Creed

The most crucial and influential part of Sacred Tradition is the Creed. The word comes from the Latin *credo,* meaning "I believe." A Creed is a statement or profession of what members of a particular church or religion believe as being essential and necessary. The two most ancient and most important creeds are the *Apostles' Creed* and the *Nicene Creed,* which is recited or sung every Sunday and holy day of obligation at Catholic Masses all over the world. (Like Sundays, *holy days of obligation* are specific days in the calendar year on which Catholics are required to go to Mass. See Chapter 8 for more on holy days.) The *Nicene Creed* was the fruit of the Council of Nicea, which convened in A.D. 325 to condemn the heresy of Arianism (see Chapter 4) and to affirm the doctrine of the divinity of Christ. The oldest creed, however, is the Apostles' Creed. Although it's doubtful that the 12 apostles themselves wrote it, the origin of this creed comes from the first century A.D.

A sophisticated development of the *Apostles' Creed,* which is a Christian statement of belief attributed to the 12 apostles, the Nicene Creed reflects one's loyalty and allegiance to the truths contained in it. The *Catechism of the Catholic Church* explains that the Creed is one of the four pillars of faith, along with the Ten Commandments, the seven sacraments, and the Our Father. The text of the Apostles' Creed and the Nicene Creed, which follows, succinctly summarizes all that Catholicism regards as divinely revealed truth:

- **The Apostles' Creed:** I believe in God, the Father Almighty, the Creator of heaven and earth, and in Jesus Christ, His only Son, our Lord: Who was conceived of the Holy Spirit, born of the Virgin Mary, suffered under Pontius Pilate, was crucified, died, and was buried. He descended into hell. The third day He arose again from the dead. He ascended into heaven and sits at the right hand of God the Father Almighty, from thence He shall come to judge the living and the dead. I believe in the Holy Spirit, the holy Catholic Church, the communion of saints, the forgiveness of sins, the resurrection of the body, and life everlasting. Amen.

- **The Nicene Creed:** We believe in one God, the Father, the Almighty, maker of heaven and earth, of all that is, seen and unseen. We believe in one Lord, Jesus Christ, the only Son of God, eternally begotten of the Father, God from God, Light from Light, true God from true God, begotten, not made, of one Being with the Father. Through him all things were made. For us men and for our salvation, he came down from heaven: by the power of the Holy Spirit he was born of the Virgin Mary, and became man. For our sake he was crucified under Pontius Pilate; he suffered, died and was buried. On the third day he rose again in fulfillment of the Scriptures; he ascended into heaven and is seated at the right hand of the Father. He will come again in glory to judge the living and the dead, and his kingdom will have no end. We believe in the Holy Spirit, the Lord, the giver of life, who proceeds from the Father and the Son. With the Father and the Son he is worshipped and glorified. He has spoken through the Prophets. We believe in one holy catholic and apostolic Church. We acknowledge one baptism for the forgiveness of sins. We look for the resurrection of the dead, and the life of the world to come. Amen.

The following sections explain the Apostles' Creed in detail, so you can get a better understanding of this Sacred Tradition and the Catholic belief system. (It's divided into 12 articles for easier digestion.)

If you're Catholic, you gotta go public

When you profess the faith, that is.

At the Baptism of an infant, the parents and godparents are asked, "Do you renounce Satan, and all his works and all his empty promises?" (If the person being baptized is at the age of reason, 7 or older, he is asked the question directly.) If the answer is yes, then the priest or deacon proceeds with, "Do you believe in God, the Father Almighty, Creator of Heaven and Earth?" And so on.

After Baptism, Christians — when they're at the age of reason — are expected to publicly profess the faith by reciting or singing the Nicene Creed at Mass with the entire congregation.

✔ **Article 1: I believe in God the Father, almighty, creator of heaven and earth.** This affirms that God exists, that he's one God in three persons, known as the Holy Trinity, and that he created the known universe.

Creation is understood as making something from nothing. The created world includes all inanimate matter, as well as plant, animal, human, and angelic life.

✔ **Article 2: And in Jesus Christ, his only Son, our Lord.** This attests that Jesus is the Son of God and that he's most certainly divine. The word *Lord* implies divinity, because the Greek word *Kyrios* and the Hebrew word *Adonai* both mean *Lord* and are only ascribed to God. So the use of *Lord* with *Jesus* is meant to profess his divinity. The name *Jesus* comes from the Hebrew word *Jeshua,* meaning *God saves.* So Catholics believe that Jesus is Savior.

Jesus' last name wasn't Christ. So even if mailboxes existed back in his time, a mailbox wouldn't have listed the names Jesus, Mary, and Joseph Christ. *Christ* is a title meaning *anointed* from the Greek word *christos.* The Hebrew word *Messiah* also means *anointed.*

✔ **Article 3: Who was conceived of the Holy Spirit.** This affirms the human nature of Christ, meaning that he had a real, true human mother, and it also affirms his divine nature, meaning that he had no human father, but by the power of the Holy Spirit he was conceived in the womb of the Virgin Mary. Therefore, he's considered both God and man by Christians — fully divine and fully human.

The union of the two natures in the one divine person of Christ is called the *Incarnation* from the Latin word *caro* meaning *flesh.* The Latin word *Incarnatio* or *Incarnation* in English translates to *becoming flesh.*

✔ **Article 4: He suffered under Pontius Pilate, was crucified, died and was buried.** The human nature of Christ could feel pain and actually die, and he did on Good Friday. The mention of Pontius Pilate by name wasn't meant so much to vilify him forever in history but to place the Crucifixion within human history. So reference is made to an actual historical person, the Roman governor of Judea, appointed by Caesar to put the life and death of Jesus within a chronological and historical context. It also reminds the faithful that one can't blame all Jews for the death of Jesus, as some have erroneously done over the ages. Certain Jewish leaders conspired against Jesus, but a Roman gave the actual death sentence, and Roman soldiers carried it out. So both Jew and Gentile alike shared in the spilling of innocent blood. Anti-Semitism based on the Crucifixion of Jesus is inaccurate, unjust, and erroneous.

✔ **Article 5: He descended into hell, the third day He rose again from the dead.** The *hell* Jesus descended into wasn't the hell of the damned, where Christians believe that the devil and his demons reside. *Hell* was also a word that Jews and ancient Christians used to describe the place of the dead, both the good and the bad. Before salvation and redemption, the souls of Adam and Eve, Abraham, Isaac, Jacob, David, Solomon,

Esther, Ruth, and so on, all had to wait in the abode of the dead, until the Redeemer could open the gates of heaven once more. They weren't paroled from hell for good behavior.

This passage affirms that on the third day he *rose,* meaning Jesus came back from the dead of his own divine power. He wasn't just clinically dead for a few minutes, he was *dead* dead; then he rose from the dead. More than a resuscitated corpse, Jesus possessed a glorified and risen *body.*

✔ **Article 6: He ascended into heaven and sits at the right hand of God the Father almighty.** The Ascension reminds the faithful that after the human and divine natures of Christ were united in the Incarnation, they could never be separated. In other words, after the saving death and Resurrection, Jesus didn't dump his human body as if he didn't need it anymore. Catholicism teaches that his human body will exist forever. Where Jesus went, body and soul, into heaven, the faithful hope one day to follow.

✔ **Article 7: From thence he shall come again to judge the living and the dead.** This article affirms the Second Coming of Christ at the end of the world to be its judge. Judgment Day, Day of Reckoning, Doomsday — they're all metaphors for the end of time when what's known as the General Judgment will occur. Catholics believe that after the death of any human person, immediate private judgment occurs, and the person goes directly to heaven, hell, or *purgatory* — an intermediate place in preparation for heaven. (For more on purgatory, see Chapter 15.) At the end of time, when General Judgment happens, all the private judgments will be revealed, so everyone knows who's in heaven or hell and why. Private judgment is the one that Catholics are concerned about most, because immediately after death, a person is judged by their faith or lack of it and how they practiced that faith — how they acted and behaved as believers. General Judgment is merely God's disclosure of everyone's private judgment. It's *not* an appeal of prior judgment nor is it a second chance.

Satan's jealousy

A Catholic belief is that angels were created before humankind and that their angelic will, unlike yours, is incapable of changing once a decision has been made. Angels have one irrevocable act of will, and they know this. So when the angel Lucifer and his colleagues conspired to go against the will of God, they sinned and could never seek forgiveness or redemption due to their essence and nature. Humans, on the other hand, are capable of changing their minds — of repenting and seeking forgiveness. So the Catholic perspective is that Satan hates human beings, because humans have a second chance that he'll never have. The fact that the Second Person of the Holy Trinity became man by taking a human nature further infuriated him, because God never became an angel but did become man in the person of Jesus Christ.

✔ **Article 8: I believe in the Holy Spirit.** This part reminds the believer that God exists in three persons — the Holy Trinity — God the Father, God the Son, and God the Holy Spirit. What's referred to as *the Force* in the movie *Star Wars* isn't the same as the Holy Spirit, who is a distinct person equal to the other two — God the Father and God the Son.

✔ **Article 9: (I believe in) the holy Catholic Church, the communion of saints.** Catholics believe that the Church is more than a mere institution and certainly not a necessary evil. It's an essential dimension and aspect of spiritual life. Christ explicitly uses the word *church* (*ekklesia* in Greek) in Matthew 16 when he says, "I will build My Church."

The role of the Church is seen as a continuation of the three-fold mission Christ had while he walked the earth — to *teach, sanctify,* and *govern* — just as he was simultaneously *prophet, priest,* and *king.* The Catholic Church continues his *prophetic* mission of *teaching* through the *Magisterium* (see Chapter 2), the teaching authority of the Church. She continues his *priestly* mission of *sanctification* through the celebration of the seven sacraments. And the Church continues his *kingly* mission of being shepherd and pastor through the *hierarchy.* The phrase *communion of saints* means that the Church includes not just all the living baptized persons on earth but also the saints in heaven and the souls in purgatory as well. (See Chapters 6 and 7 for an overview of the seven sacraments; See Chapter 2 for more on Church hierarchy; for more on the communion of saints, see Chapter 15.)

✔ **Article 10: (I believe in) the forgiveness of sins.** Christ came to save the world from sin. Belief in the forgiveness of sins is essential to Christianity. Catholicism believes sins are forgiven in Baptism and in the Sacrament of Penance and Reconciliation, which is also known as *confession.* (For more on the Sacrament of Penance, see Chapter 7.) Mother Teresa of Calcutta said that, "It is not that God is calling us to be successful, rather he is calling us to be faithful." In other words, Catholicism acknowledges that all are sinners and all men and women are in need of God's mercy and forgiveness. Religion and the Church are not for perfect people who never sin (perfect people don't exist anyway), but they're for sinners who need the help that religion and the Church provide.

✔ **Article 11: (I believe in) the resurrection of the body.** From the Catholic perspective, a human being is a union of body and soul, so death is just the momentary separation of body and soul until the world ends and all the dead are resurrected. The just will go, body and soul, into heaven, and the damned will go, body and soul, into hell.

Belief in the Resurrection leaves no room for reincarnation or past-life experiences. Catholics believe that you're unique, body and soul, and neither part of you can or will be duplicated even if human cloning is perfected someday. This is why Christians believe that death isn't the last chapter in anyone's life. For the believer, death is a doorway for the soul. The body and soul will eventually get back together again because the body participated in the good that the soul performed or the evil it committed. So the body as well as the soul must be rewarded or punished for all eternity.

Death isn't the saddest day for the Christian or for a Christian's loved ones, because Christians firmly believe that being made in the image and likeness of God means that the ultimate destiny is in the next life. St. Augustine (A.D. 354–430) said that human beings were created not for this world but for the next.

St. Augustine was born a pagan but his mother, St. Monica, became a Christian and prayed for more than 20 years that her son would also embrace the faith and become baptized. Before doing so, however, Augustine lived a playboy life. His conversion has become an inspiration for many. He would later become a bishop and finally be named a saint despite his wild past. (See Chapter 6 for more on St. Augustine.)

✔ **Article 12: (I believe in) life everlasting.** As Christ died, so, too, must mere mortals. As he rose, so shall all human beings.

Death is the only way to cross from this life into the next. At the very moment of death, private judgment occurs; Christ judges the soul. If a person was particularly holy and virtuous on earth, the soul goes directly to heaven. If an individual was evil and wicked and dies in the state of mortal sin, that soul is damned for eternity in hell.

But what if a person lived a life not bad enough to warrant hell but not holy enough to go right to heaven? Catholics believe that *purgatory* is a middle ground between heaven and earth. It's a place of *purgation,* hence the name *purgatory*. (For more on purgatory, see Chapter 15.)

Seeking the Truth

In the 13th century, St. Thomas Aquinas (see Chapter 18), a philosopher, explained how the human mind seeks different kinds of truth. He said that

✔ **Scientific truth** (also known as *empirical truth*) is known by observation and experimentation. So, for example, you know that fire is hot by burning your finger with a lit match.

✔ **Philosophical truth** is known by using human reason. You know that two plus two equals four, for example. So if two chairs are in a room and someone says, "I'll get two more," you know by using reason that the total will be four chairs. You don't need to count the chairs after they arrive.

✔ **Theological truth,** known only by faith, is the final and highest level of truth. It can't be observed, and it can't be reasoned; it must be believed by faith — taken on God's word, because he revealed it.

The First Vatican Council (1869–70) taught that by using human reason, certain truths, like the existence of God, are attainable on your own power but that you also need the intervention of supernatural revelation to know all you need to know to be saved.

St. Thomas Aquinas also delineated five proofs for the existence of God in a monumental work called the *Summa Theologica*. Since Vatican I taught that the human mind can know some things of religion on its own without having to depend on divine revelation, it's good to see the example given by St. Thomas. Aquinas reasoned that humans can prove the existence of God through motion, causality, necessity, gradation, and governance. Granted, you may not be able to persuade an atheist to become a missionary priest this way, but these proofs are still pretty compelling.

Through motion

Before you were conceived in your mother's womb, you were merely a *potential* being. You didn't become real, or actual, until the occurrence of the act that created a new human life.

Likewise, at one time, everything now in existence was merely potential, because everything has a beginning. In other words, to get to the actual here and now, you first must have an actual beginning — a start. So at some point, all human beings — and all things — never were.

Some force had to start the motion from potential existence to actual existence. And that force could never have been potential itself; it always was, is, and shall be. Otherwise, that force would've had to be started by some other force, which would've had to be started by some other force, and so on. This means that an actual beginning would never have been. And, again, the here and now must have an actual beginning.

Before the Big Bang, when the universe was only potential, what force started the motion for it to become actual and real? St. Thomas said that the force is God, the Prime Mover — moving the potential universe into becoming the actual one.

Through causality

My mom and dad caused me to be born, just as yours did. Our grandparents caused our parents to be born. And so on. So every cause was first an effect of a previous cause. So if you go all the way back to the beginning of everything, something or someone had to be the cause of all causes.

Just as the force that started the motion from potential existence to actual existence could never have been potential itself, the cause of all causes could never have been the effect of a previous cause. In other words, the cause of all causes was never an effect but always a cause — or, as philosophers put it, an uncaused cause. St. Thomas said that uncaused cause is God. He caused everything to be by starting Creation in the first place.

Through necessity

The universe would not blow up or crash to a screeching halt if you had never been born. This is a real ego-popper.

No one individual is necessary. Everything in the universe is basically contingent on — dependent on — something else to exist. Think of it this way: If you turn off a light switch, the flow of electricity to the light bulb is cut off. Without the electricity, you don't have light. If God removed his Being from sustaining you, you'd be like a turned-off light bulb.

One being must be necessary in order to keep the contingent (unnecessary) beings in existence. Otherwise, nothing would exist at all. Thomas said the necessary being is God.

Through gradation

Existence and being have different levels:

Look at inanimate matter, like rocks. They represent a basic level of existence. They're just there.

The next level is plant or vegetative life — simple but able to reproduce.

Farther up is animal life. It can reproduce and grow like plant life, but it also has *sense* knowledge. Animals can detect information from their eyes, ears, nose, mouth, and so on.

Next is human life, which can do all the stuff animal life can, as well as reason rationally. And human life has a free will.

Moving along the hierarchy of being is angelic life — pure spirits with no body. Angels are superior to men and women in that their minds have all the knowledge they will ever have all at one time and their minds are much more powerful than the minds of mere mortals, too, because they're not distracted by having a body. Without bodies, they never get sick, never feel pain, and never need food or sleep or shelter. They're immortal and as pure spirits have power over the material world.

The final and ultimate level of existence is a Supreme Pure Being who has no beginning and no end. St. Thomas said that this Supreme Being is God. Like angels, God has no mortal body but is pure spirit, but unlike angels, he has no beginning whereas he created the angels. Unlike angels, who have limited knowledge and power, God has infinite power, which means that he's *omnipotent;* he has infinite knowledge, which means that he's *omniscient;* and he's everywhere — he's *omnipresent.*

Through governance

Ever wonder why the earth is just the right distance from the sun and has just the right balance of gases to maintain an atmosphere that supports life? The balance is delicate, much like the ecosystem in which plants produce oxygen and animals produce carbon dioxide that keeps their machines running.

The planets rotate and orbit at fixed rates instead of crashing into one another. The fundamental laws of physics, chemistry, and biology must be followed; otherwise, life wouldn't exist. These facts point to a higher intelligence — a being that made these physical laws, because they didn't just happen on their own.

Nature tends to go from order to chaos. Who put things in order to begin with? A higher intelligence is indicated when you study how human DNA is so intricate and orderly and consistent. Rather than being mere chance, life on earth is no mistake, and it follows a plan. St. Thomas said that the Great Governor is God.

These five proofs can't convince an atheist or agnostic, but they might get their minds clicking. The bottom line is that the existence of God is reasonable and that faith doesn't contradict or oppose reason. Rather, it complements it.

Chapter 4

Believing in Jesus

Every Catholic is taught the Apostles' Creed from childhood. The second line, "I believe in Jesus Christ, His Only Son, Our Lord," is the basis for understanding who Jesus is, where he came from, what he did, and why he did it.

The more elaborate and developed Nicene Creed (A.D. 325) is recited or sung in parishes at Sunday Mass. Yet the Apostles' Creed can be said at children's Masses, because it's shorter and easier to comprehend. The Nicene Creed, a *very* theological profession of faith, takes that short phrase about Jesus from the Apostles' Creed and expands it into a detailed article of Catholic doctrine. (You can compare the Apostles' Creed with the Nicene Creed for yourself; Chapter 3 contains both.)

Granted, that detailed article is a mouthful, but it says volumes about what the Catholic Church believes about the person called Jesus. This chapter doesn't say volumes, but it does tell you the need-to-know points for understanding Catholicism's perspective on Jesus.

Understanding Jesus, the God-Man

Like all Christians, Catholics share the core belief that Jesus of Nazareth is Lord and Savior. The term *Lord* is used, because Christians believe Jesus is *divine* — the Son of God. The term *Savior* is used, because Christians believe that Jesus saved all humankind by dying for our sins.

The Old Testament usually uses the word *Lord* (*Adonai* in Hebrew) in connection with the word *God* (*Elohim* in Hebrew). An example is the phrase "Hear, O Israel, the Lord our God is one" in Deuteronomy 6:4. But the New Testament asserts through the Epistle of St. Paul to the Philippians (2:11) "that Jesus Christ is Lord."

Catholics also believe that Jesus was human as well as divine. So "true God" and "became man" are key phrases in the Nicene Creed, which highlights the fundamental doctrine of Jesus as the God-Man:

- ✔ As God, Jesus possessed a fully divine nature, so he was able to perform miracles, such as changing water into wine, curing sickness, disease, and disability, and raising the dead. His greatest act of divinity was to rise from the dead himself.

- ✔ As man, Jesus had a human mother, Mary, who gave birth to him and nursed him. He lived and grew up like any other man. He taught, preached, suffered, and died. So Jesus had a fully human nature as well.

Jesus, the God-Man, having a fully divine nature and a fully human nature in one divine person, is the core and center of Catholic belief.

Some people may think that Catholicism considers Jesus a hybrid — half human and half divine. That's not the case at all. Catholicism doesn't see Jesus as having a split personality or as a spiritual Frankenstein, partly human and partly divine. He's regarded as fully human and fully divine — true man and true God. He's considered one divine person with two equal natures, human and divine. This is the cornerstone of all Christian mysteries. It can't be explained completely but must be believed on faith. (See Chapter 3 for the scoop on what faith really means.)

The human nature of Jesus

Jesus had a physical body with all the usual parts: two eyes, two ears, two legs, a heart, a brain, a stomach, and so on. Because he had a physical body, he also had five senses. So he could experience physical pain and pleasure. He also possessed a human intellect (mind) and will (heart) and experienced human emotions, such as joy and sorrow. The Gospel According to John, for example, says that Jesus cried at the death of his friend Lazarus.

Jesus wasn't born with the ability to speak. He had to learn how to walk and talk — how to be, act, and think as a human being.

Jesus did *not* share sin with human beings. Being human doesn't mean being capable of sinning. And it doesn't mean that you've sinned somewhere along the line. Being human means having a free will and rational intellect joined to a physical body. Humans can choose to do good or choose to do evil.

Catholics believe that human beings don't determine what's good or evil, because that's intrinsic to the thing itself. Whether something is good or evil is independent of personal opinion. Murder is evil in and of itself. Someone may personally think an action is good, but if it's intrinsically evil, they're only fooling themselves and will eventually regret it. Jesus in his humanity always chose to do good, but that didn't make him any less human. Even though he never got drunk, swore, told a dirty joke, or had a dirty thought, he was still human.

The Catholic Church graphically reminds her members of the human nature of Jesus by conspicuously placing a crucifix in every church. A *crucifix* is a cross with the crucified figure of Jesus attached to it. It's a reminder to Catholics that Jesus didn't pretend to be human. The nails in his hands and feet, the crown of thorns on his head, and the wound in his side where a soldier thrust a lance into his heart all poignantly remind the faithful that Jesus' suffering, which is known as his *Passion,* was real. He felt real pain, and he really died. He was really human. Were he only a god pretending to be human, then his pain and death would've been faked. A crucifix graphically reminds Catholics that those wounds and that gruesome death was real and so was the pain and suffering associated with it. (In case you were wondering, the letters INRI often seen on crucifixes is an abbreviation for the Latin words put there by Pontius Pilate: *Iesus Nazarenus Rex Iudaeorum, or Jesus of Nazareth, King of the Jews.)*

It's important to keep in mind that Catholicism doesn't depend *exclusively* on the Bible for what's known about Jesus. *Sacred Tradition* (see Chapter 3) fills in some of the gaps when the Bible is silent or ambiguous on certain points, such as whether Jesus ever married or had any siblings.

Did Jesus have a wife and kids?

The last verse of the Gospel According to John (21:25) says, "There are also many other things Jesus did but if these were to be described individually, I do not think the whole world would contain the books that would be written."

The Bible is silent in some areas. Was Jesus ever married? Did he have a wife and children? The Bible doesn't say either way. You could presume he was unmarried, because a wife is never mentioned. (The Bible does mention Peter's *mother-in-law* being cured, but the Bible never classifies the other disciples and apostles as married or single.)

No Christian denomination or religion has ever believed that Jesus was married, even though the Bible never categorically states that he remained unmarried. The reason? Tradition. Christianity has maintained the tradition that Jesus was celibate and never married even though the Bible at best implies it by never mentioning a wife or children.

Even Jesus got some downtime

Jesus wasn't a workaholic. He got some rest and recreation while visiting his friends Martha, Mary, and Lazarus (John 12:2), and he attended the wedding feast of Cana with his mother (John 2:1–2). Jesus took a nap in a boat while the apostles stayed awake on deck (8:22–23) and went to an out-of-the-way place to pray (Matthew 14:23). So, too, God the Father rested after creating the whole world (Genesis 2:1–3).

Whenever the Bible is silent or ambiguous, Sacred Tradition fills in the gaps. So to Catholics, a written record in the Bible is that he was a man, his name was Jesus, and his mother was Mary, and a revealed truth of Sacred Tradition is that he never married.

Did Jesus have any brothers or sisters?

Some Christians believe Mary had other children after she had Jesus, but the Catholic Church officially teaches that Mary always remained a virgin — before, during, and after the birth of Jesus. She had one son, and that son was Jesus.

Another belief among some Christians is that Joseph had children from a prior marriage, and after he became a widower and married the mother of Jesus, those children became stepbrothers and stepsisters of Jesus. Those who believe that Jesus had siblings invoke Mark 6:3 and Matthew 13:55: "Is this not the carpenter's son, the son of Mary and the brother of James and Joseph and Simon and Jude? Are not his sisters here with us?" And Matthew 12:47 says, "Your mother and your brothers are standing outside."

So who were these brothers and sisters mentioned in the Gospel, if they weren't actual siblings of Jesus? The Catholic Church reminds its members that the original four Gospels were written in the Greek language, not the Queen's English that's in the King James Version of the Bible. The Greek word used in all three occasions is *adelphoi,* (plural of *adelphos*) which can be translated as *brothers*. But that same Greek word can also mean *cousins* or *relatives,* as in an uncle or a nephew.

An example is shown in the Old Testament. Genesis 11:27 says that Abram and Haran were brothers, sons of Terah. Lot was the son of Haran and thus the nephew of Abram, who was later called Abraham by God. Ironically, Genesis 14:14 and 14:16 in the King James Version of the Bible refer to Lot as the *brother* of Abraham. The Greek word used in the Septuagint version of the Old Testament is again *adelphos*. Obviously, a word that denoted a nephew-uncle relationship was unavailable in ancient Hebrew or Greek. So an alternative use of *brother* (*adelphos* in Greek) is used in those passages, because Lot was actually Abraham's nephew.

The Catholic Church reasons that if the Bible uses *brother* to refer to a nephew in one instance, then why not another? Why can't the *adelphoi* (brothers) of Jesus be his relatives — cousins or other family members? Why must that word be used in a restrictive way in the Gospel when it's used broadly in the Old Testament?

The Church uses other reasoning as well. If these *brothers* were siblings, where were they during the Crucifixion and death of their brother? Mary and a few other women were there, but the only man mentioned in the Gospel at the event (Calvary) was the Apostle John, and he was in no way related to Jesus, by blood or marriage. No other male relatives or even friends are mentioned. And before Jesus died on the cross, he told John, "Behold your mother" (John 19:27). Why entrust his mother to John if other adult children could've taken care of her? Only if Mary were alone would Jesus worry about her enough to say what he did to John.

And the Church asks this: If Jesus had blood brothers, or even half-brothers or stepbrothers, why didn't they assume roles of leadership after his death? Why allow Peter and the other apostles to run the Church and make decisions if immediate family members were around? Yet if the only living relatives were distant cousins, nieces, nephews, and such, then it all makes sense.

The debate will continue for centuries to come. The bottom line is the authoritative decision of the Church. Catholicism doesn't place the Church above Scripture but sees her as the one and only authentic guardian and interpreter of the written word and the unwritten or spoken word, which is also called *Sacred Tradition*.

The divine nature of Jesus

Catholics believe that Jesus performed miracles, such as walking on water, expelling demons, rising from the dead himself and raising the dead, such as Lazarus in Chapter 11 of the Gospel of St. John, and saving all humankind, becoming the Redeemer, Savior, Messiah. He founded the Catholic Church and instituted, explicitly or implicitly, all seven sacraments. (The *seven sacraments* are Catholic rituals marking seven stages of spiritual development. See Chapters 6 and 7 for more on the seven sacraments.)

Jesus is the second person of the Holy Trinity — God the Son. And God the Son (Jesus) is as much God as God the Father and God the Holy Spirit.

Although Christians, Jews, and Muslims all believe in one God, Christians believe in a *Triune God,* one God in three persons — God the Father, God the Son, and God the Holy Spirit — also known as the *Holy Trinity.* The mystery of the Holy Trinity is how you can have three divine persons but not three gods. Catholics don't perceive the Holy Trinity as three gods but as three distinct but not separate persons in one God.

The obedient Son of God

Catholicism regards Jesus as the eternal Son of the Father and teaches that the relationship between Father and Son is one of profound love. It's not stoic or Victorian, but painful and real.

The belief that the relationship between Father and Son is so close, intense, and perfect led St. Thomas Aquinas to say that the third person of the Holy Trinity — the Holy Spirit — is the living, personified fruit of that mutual love.

Hey now, don't take it to extremes!

The Catholic Church tries to avoid two extremes.

One is seeing Jesus as merely the best human being who ever lived. Catholicism teaches that Jesus was not adopted as Son, because he always was, is, and shall be Son. I'm an adopted child of God by Baptism. Catholics are created human and then adopted as sons and daughters into God's family through Baptism, but Jesus always was divine and always was the Son from all eternity. His human nature had a beginning in time like yours, from the moment he was conceived at the *Annunciation,* when the angel Gabriel announced that Mary was to have a son (Luke 1:26-38). His divine nature, on the other hand, has no beginning and no end.

The other extreme is seeing Jesus as a hero. Some scholars try to portray Jesus as the hero of humankind. Heroes are people who do it first

so others can follow. Albert Einstein, for example, didn't have to be the first one to discover the theory of relativity any more than Columbus had to be the first one to discover the New World. Someone else could have done it, and the discoveries have been repeated more than once.

Catholicism teaches that Jesus wasn't a hero: What he did (save the entire human race) no one else could ever duplicate, repeat, or replace. What he did couldn't have been done by anyone else. Only the God-Man Jesus could save humankind, because he was both human *and* divine.

To the Catholic Church, overemphasizing Jesus' humanity to the exclusion of his divinity is as bad as ignoring or downplaying his humanity to exalt his divinity.

Deep thoughts about Father and Son

To the Catholic Church, the relationship between God the Father and God the Son (Jesus) isn't the same as the relationship between human parents and children.

Human fathers aren't fathers before their sons or daughters are born. If you were an only child, for example, could your dad ever have been called a father before you existed? No. Until a son or daughter is born, no man is a father.

So if you think in those terms, you may think that God the Father didn't exist before the Son (Jesus) was born. But the Church says that God the Father has always been the Father. So if the Father has always been the Father, then the Son (Jesus) has always been, too. Jesus is

the eternal Son of the Father. The Father didn't exist without the Son for even one instant, one second or microsecond, because the Father was always Father and the Son was always Son. Unlike our human experience, God the Father doesn't exist *before* the Son, both exist at the same time. The two words depend on each other and the two Persons of God the Father and God the Son have always existed together simultaneously.

The Church teaches that God doesn't exist in time and space, as people know it, so nobody needs to get worried that the Father didn't exist prior to the Son. It's not like the chicken and the egg paradox of which came first.

Obedience is a sign of love and respect, and Catholics believe that Jesus obeyed the will of the Father. To Catholics, "Thy will be done" is more than just a phrase of the *Our Father*. It's the motto of Jesus Christ, Son of God.

And Catholic belief maintains that God the Father's will was for Jesus to

✔ Reveal God as a community of Three Persons *(Father, Son,* and *Holy Spirit)* united in divine love

✔ Show God's love for all humankind

✔ Be humankind's Redeemer and Savior

Looking At the Gospel Truth

The New Testament contains four Gospels, which tell the life and words of Jesus. The four evangelists, Matthew, Mark, Luke, and John, each wrote one of the four Gospels.

The four Gospels aren't four *separate* Gospels but four *versions* of one Gospel. That's why each one is called *The Gospel According to Matthew* or *The Gospel According to Mark,* for example, and not *Matthew's Gospel* or *Mark's Gospel.* That being the case, the Catholic Church emphasizes that it's imperative to consider the four Gospels as actually forming one whole unit. No one single account gives the entire picture, but like facets on a diamond, all sides form to make one beautiful reality. The faithful need all four versions to appreciate the full depth and impact of Jesus. Catholicism cherishes each different perspective but stresses that all four together, in conjunction with the other inspired writings of the New and Old Testaments, give a better portrait of Jesus.

Catholic beliefs about the Gospel

Even though a different man wrote each of the four Gospels, the same Holy Spirit inspired each man. *Inspiration* is a special gift of the Holy Spirit given to the *sacred authors* (those who wrote the Bible) so that only the words that God wanted written down *were* written down.

Both the Holy Spirit and the author, inspired by the Holy Spirit, intended to use or not use the same words and to present or not present the same ideas and images based on the particular author's distinct audience. This concept is clear in the Gospel According to Matthew. He was addressing potential converts from Judaism. He himself was a Jew and wanted to assure his fellow Jews that Jesus was the Messiah promised in the Old Testament. So he made subtle comparisons between Jesus and Moses, who was the Deliverer in the Old Testament. Just as Moses led the Chosen People from the slavery of Egypt into the freedom of the Promised Land, Jesus would deliver all humankind from the slavery of sin into the Promised Land of Paradise.

Even though each Gospel writer had a separate audience, each of the four Gospels has relevance today, because the Holy Spirit inspired all four authors. To the Church, inspired texts have many meanings; they transcend time and space; and unlike many historical documents, they're not confined to one group, one place, or one era. This belief is why the Catholic Church painstakingly tries to incorporate all four Gospels at the Sunday Mass over a period of every three years. (See Chapter 8 for more on Scripture readings at Mass.)

Figure 4-1 shows how Matthew, Mark, Luke, and John are often depicted in art from Revelation (Apocalypse) 4:7. According to St. Ambrose, a man with wings symbolizes Matthew, because he begins his Gospel account with the human origins and birth of Christ. Mark starts his account with the regal power of Christ, the reign of God, and is therefore, symbolized by a lion with wings, which was held in high esteem by the Romans. Luke begins his account with the father of John the Baptist, Zachary, the priest, and is symbolized by an ox with wings, because the priests of the temple often sacrificed oxen on the altar. John is shown as an eagle, because he soars to heaven in his introduction to the Gospel with the pre-existence of Christ as the Word (*logos* in Greek).

Figure 4-1:
The writers
of the four
Gospels
are often
depicted
like this
from
Revelation
(Apoca-
lypse) 4:7.

 Matthew, The Man

 Mark, The Lion

 Luke, The Ox

 John, The Eagle

How the Gospels came to be

Were Matthew, Mark, Luke, and John standing on the sidelines taking notes as Jesus preached or performed miracles? No. In fact, only two of the four, Matthew and John, were actual apostles and eyewitnesses, so you can't think of Matthew, Mark, Luke, and John as, say, reporters covering a story for the media.

Before the Gospels were written, the words and deeds of Jesus were told by word of mouth. In other words, the Gospels were preached before they were written. The spoken word preceded the written word. And after it was written, because the papyrus on which the scrolls were written was so fragile, expensive, and rare, most people didn't read the Word, but heard it as it was spoken in church during Mass. The Church calls it the three-level development of the Gospel: First, the actual sayings and teachings of Christ; second, the oral tradition where the apostles preached to the people what they saw and heard; third, the writing by the sacred authors to ensure that the message wouldn't be altered.

The New Testament was written between A.D. 35 and 100. St Irenaeus in A.D. 188 was the first person to mention the *Tetramorph* — the four Gospels. But it wasn't until the Council of Carthage in A.D. 397 that the final and official judgment of the Church came out and explicitly listed the 27 books in the New Testament, including the four Gospels. St. Jerome was the first one to combine both the Old and New Testaments into one volume and to translate all the books from Hebrew, Aramaic, and Greek into Latin, which was the common tongue of his time. It took him from A.D. 382 to 405 to finish this monumental task, but he was the first one to coordinate the first complete and whole Christian Bible.

Comparing Gospels

The Catholic Church regards the entire Bible as the inspired and inerrant Word of God, so the Gospels in particular are crucial, because they accurately relate what Jesus said and did while on earth. As we discuss in Chapter 3, the Catholic Church believes that the Bible is sacred literature, but as literature, some parts of it should be interpreted literally, and other parts are intended to be read figuratively; the Gospels are among the books that are primarily interpreted literally insofar as to what Jesus said and did.

Matthew and Luke

Matthew opens his Gospel with a long genealogy of Jesus, beginning with Abraham and tracing it all the way down to Joseph, the husband of Mary, "of whom Jesus was born, who is called the Messiah."

Matthew was addressing potential converts from Judaism. A Jewish audience was probably interested in hearing this family tree, because the Hebrew people are often called the Children of Abraham. That's why Matthew began with Abraham and connected him to Jesus to open his Gospel.

Luke offers a similar genealogy to Matthew's but not until Chapter 3 of his Gospel, and he works backward from Jesus to Adam, 20 generations before Abraham. Luke was a Gentile physician, and his audience was Gentile, not Jewish. Neither Matthew nor Luke used editorial fiction, but each carefully selected what to say to his respective audience through the inspiration of the Holy Spirit. A Gentile audience wasn't as concerned with a connection to Abraham as a Jewish audience. Gentiles were interested in a connection between Jesus and the first man, Adam, because Gentiles were big into Greek philosophy. Plato, Socrates and Aristotle, just to mention a few famous Greek thinkers who lived before Christ, philosophized about the origins of humanity, and thus, making a link between Jesus and the first man would have greatly appealed to them. For example, take a look at St. Paul's Epistle. The *Epistles* are letters, by the way, and are another part of the New Testament. St. Paul's Epistle capitalized on the connection to Adam when he remarked that Christ is the New Adam, because in the first Adam, all died, and in the new (last) Adam, who is Christ, all are reborn to new life. (1 Corinthians 15:22–45.) A Gentile audience, influenced by Greek philosophy, would be more interested in seeing a connection between Jesus Christ and the first human being whereas a Jewish audience is keen on seeing the continuity from Abraham to Jesus.

In the Sermon on the Mount, Matthew mentions that prior to giving the sermon, Jesus "went up the mountain" (Matthew 5:1), but Luke describes Jesus giving a Sermon on the Plain, "a stretch of level ground" (Luke 6:17). Both men quote the teachings from these sermons, called the *Beatitudes*. See the following version from Matthew 5:

Seeing the crowds, he went up on the mountain, and when he sat down his disciples came to him. And he opened his mouth and taught them, saying:
"Blessed are the poor in spirit, for theirs is the kingdom of heaven.
"Blessed are those who mourn, for they shall be comforted.
"Blessed are the meek, for they shall inherit the earth.
"Blessed are those who hunger and thirst for righteousness, for they shall be satisfied.
"Blessed are the merciful, for they shall obtain mercy.
"Blessed are the pure in heart, for they shall see God.
"Blessed are the peacemakers, for they shall be called sons of God.
"Blessed are those who are persecuted for righteousness' sake, for theirs is the kingdom of heaven.
"Blessed are you when men revile you and persecute you and utter all kinds of evil against you falsely on my account. Rejoice and be glad, for your reward is great in heaven, for so men persecuted the prophets who were before you.

Now contrast the Sermon on the Mount in the Gospel of Matthew with Luke 6:17–23 that follows:

And he came down with them and stood on a level place, with a great crowd of his disciples and a great multitude of people from all Judea and Jerusalem and the seacoast of Tyre and Sidon, who came to hear him and to be healed of their diseases; and those who were troubled with unclean spirits were cured. And the entire crowd sought to touch him, for power came forth from him and healed them all. And he lifted up his eyes on his disciples, and said:
"Blessed are you poor, for yours is the kingdom of God.
"Blessed are you that hunger now, for you shall be satisfied.
"Blessed are you that weep now, for you shall laugh.
"Blessed are you when men hate you, and when they exclude you and revile you, and cast out your name as evil, on account of the Son of man! Rejoice in that day, and leap for joy, for behold, your reward is great in heaven; for so their fathers did to the prophets.

So why the difference in location for these sermons — mount and plain?

Any good preacher knows that when you have a good sermon, you can use it more than once, especially if you're preaching in another place to a different crowd. It's not unreasonable to presume that Jesus preached his Beatitudes more than once, because he moved around quite a bit and, aside from the apostles, no one in the crowd would have heard the message before.

Matthew mentions the occasion of the Sermon on the Mount, because his Jewish audience would've been keen on such a detail. The reason? Moses was given the Law, the Ten Commandments, on Mount Sinai. So Jesus was giving the law of blessedness, alias the *Beatitudes,* also from a mount. Matthew also makes sure to quote Jesus, saying that he had "not come to abolish the Law, but to fulfill it," (Matthew 5:17) also appealing to a Jewish listener. Moses gave the Ten Commandments that came from God to the Hebrew people, and now Jesus was going to fulfill that Law.

Luke, on the other hand, mentions the time that the sermon was given on a plain. Why mention the obscure detail of a level ground? Luke was writing for a Gentile audience. Unlike the Jewish audience of Matthew, who was used to the Law being given from God to Moses on Mount Sinai, the Gentiles were accustomed to giving and listening to philosophical debates in the Greek tradition. Philosophers such as Plato, Socrates, and Aristotle debated one another on level ground, standing shoulder-to-shoulder, eye-to-eye, instead of lecturing from an elevated podium, so to give a sense of fairness and equality to the discussion. Because a Gentile audience would've been more interested in a speech given by Jesus in similar fashion, Luke retold such an occurrence.

Even a slight difference can be detected in some of the wording of Luke's account versus that of Matthew, as well as an addition of "woe to you" given by Jesus to correspond with each "blessed are you," which isn't found in Matthew. Again, a preacher often adapts an older sermon by adding, subtracting, or modifying his original work, depending on his second audience. The Catholic Church maintains that the discrepancy comes from a change Jesus made, because neither sacred author would feel free to alter anything Jesus said or did on his own human authority.

Mark

Mark is the shortest of the four Gospels, due to the fact that his audience was mainly Roman. When you belong to an imperial police state, you're not as concerned about making intricate connections to a Hebrew past, and you're not interested in lengthy philosophical dialogues. You want action. That's why the Gospel According to Mark has fewer sermons and more movement. It's fast-paced, nonstop, continuous narrative, like an excited person telling the events "a mile a minute." Romans would've been far more attentive to Gospel According to Mark than to those of Matthew, Luke, or John.

Mark explicitly describes the Roman Centurion, a military commander of a hundred soldiers, at the Crucifixion as making the proclamation, "Truly, this man was the Son of God." (Mark 15:39) His Roman audience would've certainly perked up when that was said, because it was an act of faith from one of their own kind.

Like Luke, Mark wasn't one of the original 12 apostles. Matthew and John were apostles, but Luke and Mark were 2 of the 72 disciples. The *apostles* were there in person to witness all that Jesus said and did. The *disciples* often had to resort to second-hand information, told to them by other sources. Luke most likely received much of his information from Mary, the mother of Jesus, and Mark undoubtedly used his friend Peter, the chief apostle, as his source.

John

John was the last one to write a Gospel, and his is the most theological of the four. The other three are so similar in content, style, and sequence that they're often called the *Synoptic Gospels,* from the Greek word *sunoptikos,* meaning *summary* or *general view.*

John, who wrote his Gospel much later than the others, was writing for a Christian audience. He presumed that people had already heard the basic facts, and he provided advanced information to complement the Jesus 101 material covered in Matthew, Mark, and Luke. In other words, The Gospel According to John is like college calculus, and the Synoptic Gospels are like advanced high school algebra.

John sets the tone by opening his Gospel with a philosophical concept of pre-existence: Before Jesus became man by being conceived and born of the Virgin Mary, he existed from all eternity in his divinity, because he's the second person of the Holy Trinity. Take a look at the first line from the Gospel According to John: "In the beginning was the Word, and the Word was with God and the Word was God."

This is a very philosophical and theological concept. John wanted his audience to see Jesus as being the Word of God: As he says, "The Word became flesh and dwelt among us" (John 1:14). He was saying that Jesus was the incarnate Word — the Word taking on flesh.

The first book of the Bible, Genesis, starts with the same phrase John uses in the opening of his Gospel: "In the beginning." According to Genesis 1:3, God said, "Let there be light, and there was light." In other words, by merely speaking the word, God *created.* John built on that in his Gospel, saying that Jesus *was* the Word. The Word of God wasn't a thing but a person. The Word was creative and powerful. Just as God said the word and light was created, Jesus spoke the word and the blind received their sight, the lame walked, and the dead came back to life.

Dealing with Heresy and Some Other $10 Words

Christians were violently and lethally persecuted for the first 300 years after the death of Jesus — from the time of Emperor Nero and the burning of Rome, which he blamed on the Christians. So for the first 300 years, Christianity remained underground. Through word of mouth, Christians learned about Jesus of Nazareth and his preaching, suffering, death, Resurrection, and Ascension.

It wasn't until A.D. 313, when Emperor Constantine legalized Christianity in his Edict of Milan, that Christians were even allowed to publicly admit their religious affiliation. But once Christianity became legal, it soon became predominant and even became the state religion.

Leaving the catacombs and entering the public arena, Christians began devoting themselves to theological questions that the Bible didn't specifically address. For example, Scripture teaches that Jesus was God and man, human and divine. Yet *how* was he both? How were the human and divine natures of Jesus connected? So the second 300 years after Jesus' death, the fourth to seventh centuries, became a Pandora's box of theological debate.

To the Catholic Church, *heresy* is the denial of a revealed truth or the distortion of one so that others are deceived into believing a theological error. After Christianity was legalized, the *Christological heresies* that referred to the nature of Christ became rampant. Debates often degenerated into violent arguments, and the civil authorities, such as the Roman Emperor, often intervened, urging or even demanding that the religious leaders, such as the pope, patriarchs, and bishops, cease the unrest by settling the issues once and for all.

This section explains some of the heresies, or false rumors, that plagued the Church during early Christianity.

Gnosticism and Docetism

Gnosticism comes from the Greek work *gnosis,* for *knowledge.* During the first century B.C. to the fifth century A.D., Gnostics believed in secret knowledge, whereas the Judeo-Christians were free and public about disclosing the truth divinely revealed by God. Gnostics believed that the material world was evil and the only way to salvation was through discovering the "secrets" of the universe. This belief flew in the face of the Hebrew and Christian religions, which believed that God created the world (Genesis) and that it was good, not evil. Keeping revelation secret wasn't meant to be; rather, it should be shared openly with others.

Docetism comes from the Greek word *dokesis,* meaning *appearance.* Docetists, a spin-off from Gnosticism, first and second centuries A.D., asserted that Jesus Christ only appeared to be human. They considered the material world, including the human body, so evil and corrupt that God, who is all good, couldn't have assumed a real human body and human nature. He must have pretended.

The Gnostic antagonism between the spiritual and the material worlds led Docetists to deny that Jesus was true man. They had no problem with his divinity, only with believing in his real humanity. So if that part was an illusion, then the horrible and immense suffering and death of Jesus on the cross means nothing. If his human nature was a parlor trick, then his Passion also was an illusion.

The core of Christianity, and of Catholic Christianity, is that Jesus died for the sins of all humankind. Only a real human nature can feel pain and actually die. Docetism and Gnosticism were considered hostile to *authentic Christianity,* or more accurately, *orthodox Christianity.* (The word *orthodox* with a small letter *o* means correct or right believer. However, if you see the capital letter *O,* then *Orthodox* refers to the eastern Orthodox Churches, such as the Greek, Russian, and Serbian Orthodox Churches.)

Note that, even today, remnants of neo-Gnosticism are in some modern ideologies and theories of religion. New Age spirituality and Dianetics, which is the Church of Scientology, propose to reveal secrets and unlock secret powers of human nature. Docetism seems to have died out pretty much, however.

Arianism

Arianism was the most dangerous and prolific of the heresies in the early Church. (By the way, the Arianism that we're referring to isn't about modern-day skinheads with swastikas and anti-Semitic prejudices.) *Arianism* comes from a cleric named Arius in the fourth century (A.D. 250–336), who denied the divinity of Jesus. Whereas Docetism denied his humanity, Arianism denied that Jesus had a truly divine nature equal to God the Father.

Arius proposed that Jesus was created and wasn't of the same substance as God — he was considered higher than any man or angel, because he possessed a similar substance, or essence, but he was never equal to God. His Son-ship was one of adoption. In Arianism, Jesus *became* the Son, whereas in orthodox Christianity, he was, is, and will always be the Son, with no beginning and no end.

Arianism caught on like wildfire, because it appealed to people's knowledge that only one God existed, and if Jesus was also God, it could appear as if two gods existed instead of only one.

Emperor Constantine, living in the Eastern Empire, was afraid that the religious discord would endanger the security of the realm. He saw how animate and aggressive the argument became and ordered that a council of all the bishops, the patriarchs, and the pope convene to settle the issue once and for all. The imperial city of Nicea was chosen to guarantee safety. In Nicea, the world's bishops decided to compose a creed that every believer was to learn and profess as being the substance of Christian faith. That same creed is now recited every Sunday and Holy Day at Catholic Masses all over the world. It's known as the Nicene Creed, because it came from the Council of Nicea in A.D. 325.

The punch line that ended the Arianism controversy was the phrase "one in being with the Father" in the Nicene Creed. The more accurate English translation of the Greek and Latin, however, is *consubstantial* or *of the same substance as the Father.* This line boldly defied the Arian proposition that Jesus was only similar but not equal in substance to the Father in terms of his divinity.

Nestorianism

Another heresy was Nestorianism, named after its founder, Nestorius. This doctrine maintained that Christ had two *hypostases* (persons) — one divine and one human. Nestorius condemned the use of the word *Theotokos,* which was Greek for *bearer* or *mother of God.* If Jesus had two persons, the most that could be said of Mary was that she gave birth to the human person of Jesus and not to the divine.

Another Ecumenical Council was convened, this time in the town of Ephesus in A.D. 431, where the participants ironed out the doctrine that Jesus had one person, not two, but that two natures were present — one human and one divine nature. Because Christ was only one person, then Mary could rightly be called the Mother of God, because she gave birth to only one person.

In other words, Jesus didn't come in parts on Christmas day for Mary and Joseph to put together. He was born whole and intact, one person, two natures. The Church says that because Mary gave birth to Jesus, the Church could use the title Mother of God, realizing that she didn't give Jesus his divinity. (This concept is similar to the belief that your mother gave you a human body, but only God created your immortal soul. Still, you call her *mother.*)

Monophystism

The last significant heresy about Jesus was known as *Monophystism.* This idea centered on a notion that the human nature of Jesus was absorbed into the divine nature. Say, for example, that a drop of oil represents the humanity of Jesus and the ocean represents the divinity of Jesus. If you put the drop of oil into the vast waters of the ocean, the drop of oil, representing his humanity, would literally be overwhelmed and absorbed by the enormous waters of the ocean — his divinity.

The Ecumenical Council of Chalcedon in A.D. 451 condemned Monophystism. A simple teaching was formulated that one divine person with two distinct, full, and true natures, one human and one divine, existed in Jesus. These two natures were *hypostatically* (from the Greek *hypostasis,* for *person*) united to the one divine person. Thus the *Hypostatic Union,* the name of the doctrine, explained these things about Jesus:

✔ **In his human nature,** Jesus had a human mind just like you. It had to learn like yours. Therefore, the baby Jesus in the stable at Bethlehem didn't speak to the shepherds on Christmas Eve. He had to be taught how to speak, walk, and so on. Likewise, his human will, like yours, was free, so he had to freely choose to embrace the will of God.

In other words, in his humanity, Jesus knew what he learned. And he had to freely choose to conform his will to the divine will. (*Sin* is when your will is opposed to the will of God.) Any human knowledge not gained by regular learning was infused into his human intellect by his divine intellect. Jesus knew that fire is hot just as you've learned this fact. He also knew what only God could know, because he is a divine person with a human and a divine nature. The human mind of Christ is limited, but the divine is infinite. His divinity revealed some divine truths to his human intellect, so he would know who he is, who his Father is, and why he came to earth.

✔ **The divine nature** of Jesus had the same divine intellect and will as that of God the Father and God the Holy Spirit. As God, he knew and willed the same things that the other two persons of the Trinity knew and willed.

In other words, in his divinity, Jesus knew everything, and what he willed, happened.

✔ **As both God and man,** Jesus could bridge the gap between humanity and divinity. He could actually save humankind by becoming one of us, and yet, because he never lost his divinity, his death had eternal and infinite merit and value. If he were only a man, his death would have no supernatural effect. His death, because it was united to his divine personhood, actually atoned for sin and caused redemption to take place.

It's a mouthful to be sure, but the bottom line in Catholic theology is that the faithful fully and solemnly believe that Jesus was one divine person with a fully human nature and a fully divine nature. Each nature had its own intellect and will. So the divine nature of Jesus had a divine intellect and will, and the human nature of Jesus had a human intellect and will.

Nobody knows the time

When asked about the time and date of the end of the world, the apparent ignorance in Mark 13:32 "of that day or of that hour, no one knows, not even the angels in heaven, nor the Son, only the Father," is proof that the human intellect of Christ was not privy to all that the divine intellect of Christ knew. The divine mind of Jesus was infinite, because he had the mind of God; the human mind of Jesus was, like the human mind, limited. It could only know so much and only what God the Father wanted his mind to know.

Some modern scholars have proposed that Jesus didn't know that he was divine even if only in his human intellect would be this ignorance. But the Catholic Church points to Luke 2:42–50, which says that when Jesus' parents found the 12-year-old Jesus preaching in the Temple, the young Jesus responded that he was in his Father's house and that he was about to do the work of the Father. So even the young Jesus knew that he was divine. To the Church, "The Father and I are one" (John 10:30) and "before Abraham came to be, I AM" (John 8:58) dispel any identity crisis in Jesus. He knew that he was divine, because only one person was in Jesus at all times and that person was the second person of the Holy Trinity.

Chapter 5

Worshipping Catholic Style

*O*ne of the most familiar and yet mysterious aspects of Catholicism is its way of worship, chock-full of ancient rites and rituals. Catholic worship is based on the principle that humankind stands between the worlds of matter and spirit. In other words, human beings belong to both the material world, which the body interacts with, especially through the five senses, and the spiritual world, which the soul interacts with by divine grace.

So the way that Catholics worship — from kneeling to burning incense, to using physical, tangible symbols in their ceremonies — centers on the dynamic relationship between the material and spiritual worlds. This chapter shows you what worshipping Catholic style is all about.

Getting Body and Soul into the Act

Christians believe that a human being is made of a body and a soul, both of which are created by God and are, therefore, good. In addition, because Jesus, the Son of God, had a human body and a human soul *united* to his divine nature, the connection between the two is a necessary one.

Catholic worship capitalizes on the dynamic relationship between body and soul — between the material world and the spiritual world. That's why the entire human person is engaged in Catholic rites and rituals.

> ✔ **Rites:** The necessary words, actions, and gestures of a religious ceremony. For example, the Rite of Baptism or the Rite of Christian Marriage is the precise words spoken and the actions performed for these two sacraments.

✔ **Rituals:** The established forms for the rites — the detailed order of the words and actions to use and how to properly celebrate the rites. For example, the Roman Ritual is the book used by priests and deacons when they celebrate the rites. It tells them what materials are needed, details the sequence of events, and states in print what the required words and actions are. The Roman Ritual used to be one volume but now is printed in individual volumes for each sacrament — a ritual volume for performing weddings, one for funerals, one for Baptisms, and so on.

During a Catholic Mass, words are spoken, heard, or read. Bodies sit, stand, or kneel. Tangible symbols — the water used for baptizing, for example, or the oil used for anointing — exist outside the body and are perceived by one or more of the five senses. These outward symbols remind the faithful of the internal action of invisible divine grace entering the human soul.

Understanding Some Symbols and Gestures

Kneeling and praying with beads, crosses depicting a crucified Jesus, and sprinkling holy water on this and that are telltale Catholic practices. And we tell you the meaning behind them as it relates to the body and soul — the dynamic between the material and spiritual worlds.

The sign of the cross

The most common Catholic gesture is the sign of the cross. Latin (Western) Catholics make the *sign of the cross* by using their right hand to touch the forehead, then the middle of the breast, then the left shoulder, and finally the right shoulder. As they do this, they say, "In the name of the Father and of the Son and of the Holy Spirit, Amen." This one complete gesture makes a cross — an intersection of a vertical line from forehead to breast and a horizontal line from left to right shoulder.

Byzantine Catholics make a similar sign of the cross but go to the right shoulder first and then to the left. Byzantine Catholics are former Eastern Orthodox Christians who split from Rome in 1054 and who came back into full communion in the 17th century by accepting the authority of the bishop of Rome as pope and head of the Church. They include the Ruthenian, Ukrainian, Greek Catholic, Melkite, Romanian, and Italo-Albanian Byzantine Churches.

In addition to the Byzantine, Eastern Catholics also include Maronite, Coptic or Chaldean Catholic Churches, which are in union with Rome as well.

Most importantly, the sign of the cross symbolically reaffirms for Catholics two essential Christian doctrines: The Holy Trinity — Father, Son, and Holy Spirit — and humankind's salvation through the cross of Christ.

The genuflection

Another telltale sign of a Catholic is *genuflection,* which is touching the right knee to the floor while bending the left knee. The sign of the cross is made simultaneously with this gesture. Catholics only genuflect in front of the Holy Eucharist. The Holy Eucharist *is* the real body and blood of Jesus, so Catholics show the ultimate form of respect by genuflecting or kneeling before him. The Holy Eucharist is kept in a large metal container or vault called a *tabernacle,* or sometimes, the Eucharist is displayed behind glass in a gold container called a *monstrance.* (See Chapters 7 and 8 for more on the Eucharist, and Chapter 16 for more on the tabernacle and monstrance.)

The crucifix

The *crucifix* is a typically Catholic symbol, a cross bearing an image of Jesus being crucified. Protestant Christians typically have crosses with no *corpus* (that's Latin for *body*) of Jesus attached. The graphic symbol of the crucifix became predominant in the Western Church to remind Catholics that Jesus was true man as well as true God and that his suffering and death were very real and painful. The crucifix reminds Catholics of the high price paid for humankind's sins and inspires believers to repent of their sins and be grateful for the salvation obtained by Jesus' death on the cross.

Holy water

Holy water is a *sacramental* — a religious object or action created by the Catholic Church as opposed to those instituted by Jesus himself. (To find out more about sacramentals, see Chapter 16.) Helpful and beneficial but totally optional, sacramentals are inferior and subordinate to the seven sacraments, which are necessary in order to live a life made holy by the gift of grace from God. Sacraments give the recipient a special grace necessary to fulfill the mission of that particular sacrament, but sacramentals offer a different and subordinate grace depending on the spiritual demeanor of the recipient. In other words, sacraments give grace independent of the spiritual state of the recipient. For example, a groom who is in the state of mortal sin when he gets married is still validly married. On the other hand, a groom who has a mortal sin on his soul gets no grace from the blessing the priest gives to the newly married couple after they pronounce their vows. (Later in this chapter and in Chapters 6 and 7, we provide more detail about each of these sacraments.)

Sacraments are like food for the soul, and sacramentals are like supplemental vitamins.

Holy water, which is water blessed by a priest, bishop, or deacon, is the most widely used sacramental. Non-Catholics may think of holy water as the stuff that burned the face of the possessed 12-year-old in the movie *The Exorcist.* Holy water can be used to drive out demons (see Chapter 16); so on rare occasions the Church uses it for that purpose. But more regularly, holy water is used as a symbolic reminder of Baptism. On entering or leaving a church, Catholics dip their right hand, usually with two fingers, into a *font,* a cup of holy water that's on a wall near the doors of the church. Then they make the sign of the cross, wetting their forehead, breast, and shoulders. They're visibly reminding themselves that they're entering the House of God, the Holy of Holies, and blessing with holy water is good preparation for worship.

Holy water is sprinkled on the congregation at Mass whenever the priest chooses to do so in place of the Penitential Rite, which would have taken place at that time. (See Chapter 8 for what's what at the Mass.) Catholics also take small quantities of holy water home with them to fill fonts on their walls and bless themselves whenever leaving home, because the home is the *domestic Church* for Catholics. Home is where the family lives, and it's from the family that the Church grows and lives. Priests, deacons and bishops must come from families, and families need to attend church and support them.

Anytime a priest or deacon blesses a religious article, such as rosary beads, a statue, or a medal of one of the saints, he sprinkles holy water on the object after saying the prayers of blessing. The holy water reminds the owner that the object is now reserved for sacred use — to enhance prayer life, for example, and shouldn't be used for profane (nonreligious) use. Likewise, a blessed cup, called a *chalice,* used at Mass to hold the wine that the priest consecrates, can't be used for any other purpose. It can't be used to drink wine or juice at the dinner table, for example. (See the "Hey, Father Joe — bless this, will ya?" sidebar in Chapter 1 for more about blessings.)

In case you were wondering, holy water is blessed when Baptisms are celebrated in the church, particularly at the Easter Vigil, which means Holy Saturday night, the evening before Easter Sunday, or it can be blessed anytime during the year when the quantity runs out or evaporates.

Sensing God

The five senses — sight, touch, smell, hearing, and taste — are all used in Catholic worship. Catholics believe that the internal action of divine grace entering the human soul can't be seen, felt, smelled, heard, or tasted. But because external symbols *can* be perceived by the senses, Catholics use many external symbols for the human body to perceive, while the soul receives the divine grace.

Through sight

More information is gathered by the sense of sight than any other. From the words you read to the pictures and images that you look at, the ability to see is important to human knowledge.

Depicting God

Catholicism teaches that God the Father has no human body. He's pure spirit, and that means totally invisible.

But because of the importance of the human sense of sight, people have felt the need to represent God visually somehow — to create a visible symbol of the invisible God. One problem has been that the First Commandment forbids *graven images,* which are objects of worship — idols.

The pagans, such as the ancient Babylonians, Egyptians, Persians, Greeks, and Romans, had many gods and goddesses, which were represented in stone or metal and worshipped. The Hebrew people, on the other hand, were one of the few ancient cultures to have a *monotheistic* religion, *mono* meaning *one* and *theos* meaning *god.* Although their pagan counterparts had plenty of idols to worship, the Hebrews were forbidden from making an image or idol of God.

From Abraham until Moses, no one even knew the name *God.* He was the *nameless One.* This invisible, imageless, and nameless deity was different than pagan gods, because according to the ancient way of thinking, after you knew the name of the god or of the evil spirit or demon, for that matter, you could control it somehow. Invoking the name and having an image of the god gave the believer some influence over that being. But the one true God had no name and couldn't be depicted by any image.

After paganism died out in Western culture and the Roman Empire embraced Christianity, the danger of distorting the nature of the one true God evaporated. After God the Son took on a human nature in the person of Jesus, who had a real and true human body, fear about symbolically representing God the Father or God the Holy Spirit in Christian art disappeared.

God the Father, Jesus, and the Holy Spirit are most often represented in visible form as follows:

- ✔ **God the Father** is usually depicted as on old man with a long flowing beard, an image that came from the early Europeans. In modern and contemporary Christian art, however, God the Father is also represented with Asian or African features, for example. The modern reasoning is that if God is a spirit, why portray him just as a Caucasian man?

- ✔ **Jesus** had a face, but with no pictures of him to draw from, artists have used their own creativity to depict the Savior.

- ✔ **God the Holy Spirit** is almost always portrayed as a dove, because the Bible speaks of a dove descending on Jesus at his Baptism by John the Baptist.

Today, you can see God portrayed in paintings on walls and canvases, as well as in stained glass. Michelangelo's *Creation of Adam* remains a masterpiece to this day.

Conveying meaning through colors and symbols

When you walk into St. Patrick's Cathedral in New York City or into the Cathedral of Notre Dame in Paris (not the football shrine), you're overwhelmed by the colors shining through the magnificent stained glass windows. Originally, stained glass windows were meant to teach the Catholic faith to illiterate peasants. Unable to read, they could look at the pictures depicted in the stained glass and learn all about salvation history. Stories from the Bible, Church history, and symbols of the seven sacraments, for example, have been shown in stained glass.

Depending on the occasion, priests and deacons wear different-colored liturgical *vestments,* garments for worship services, for Mass — green, white, red, purple, black, or gold. Vestments often have symbols on them, such as a cross; the first and last letters of the Greek alphabet, the *alpha* and *omega,* representing Jesus, who is the beginning and the end; you may also see the letter *M* for Mary, the Mother of Jesus.

Marble altars and floors are often engraved with symbols, such as the two keys for St. Peter. The symbolism is taken from the Gospel According to Matthew, which describes Jesus entrusting the keys of the kingdom to Peter. So, too, an eagle is the symbol for St. John the Evangelist (see Chapter 4), and a pelican pecking her own heart to feed her young with her blood represents Christ, who feeds Catholics with his blood in Holy Communion.

In addition, Catholic architecture and art uses visual symbols to enhance the faith. For example, the gothic cathedrals spiral up toward heaven to remind the faithful of their destiny in the next world — and not to get too comfortable in this earthly one. To literally see the beauty of Catholic worship, you can visit the Shrine of the Most Blessed Sacrament in Hanceville, Alabama. (See Chapter 19.) The marble, the gold, the stained glass, the light, the altar, the tabernacle, and especially the seven-foot-tall monstrance surrounded by gold and jewels all attract the human eye and inspire the human soul to aspire to heaven. These things, which are attractive to the five senses, also help the soul to transcend the material world into the spiritual realm.

Through touch

Just as no one has seen God, because he's invisible, no one has touched him either. Yet everyone knows how vital the sense of touch is to human beings from the moment they're born. Being held by a parent and feeling tender, loving hands offer a sense of security.

Just like the sense of sight, the sense of touch is also used in Catholic worship. Getting baptized, people literally feel the water being poured over their head. When getting anointed, they feel the Oil of the Sick being applied to their forehead and the palms of their hands. During the Sacrament of Matrimony, the bride and groom join right hands before pronouncing their vows. At Confirmation, those being confirmed feel the Chrism Oil being put on their foreheads. In addition, when being ordained a priest, a man can feel the two hands of the bishop being imposed on the top of his head. (An overview of these sacraments — Baptism, Anointing of the Sick, marriage, Confirmation, and Holy Orders — is provided later in this chapter, and Chapters 6 and 7 provide the nitty-gritty details about each.)

Catholics praying the Rosary (see Chapter 13) can feel the beads as they pray the Hail Marys and meditate on the mysteries of Jesus and Mary. On Ash Wednesday, Catholics can feel the ashes of burnt palms (from last year's Palm Sunday) being imposed on their forehead. On the Feast of St. Blaise (see Chapter 16), February 3, two crossed candles can be felt on their throat, while the priest blesses their throats. In addition, holy-water fonts are at every entrance and exit of Catholic churches, so believers can touch the holy water with their right hands and bless themselves.

Through smell

The sense of smell is as much a part of human beings as the other four senses; so Catholic worship uses what it can to appeal to this function of the body.

Burning incense

The most obvious appeal to the nose in Catholic worship involves burning *incense,* which is made from aromatic resins of certain trees that are dried to a powder or crystalline form. When placed on burning charcoal, incense produces a visible smoke and a recognizable aroma that fills the church. The smoke represents prayers going up to heaven, and the sweet aroma reminds people of the sweetness of God's divine mercy.

Incense has been used in worship since pagan times. In the Old Testament, Psalm 141 speaks of prayers rising up to heaven "like burning incense." Moses was commanded by God to burn incense on the altar before the Ark of the Covenant, which held the Ten Commandments.

On a more practical level, incense was burned in the Middle Ages when churches didn't have decent air circulation, and parishioners didn't wear deodorant. On a hot summer Sunday, the smell in the church became quite potent unless *plenty* of incense was burned and thoroughly swung through-out the entire congregation. Yep, in pre-Lysol days, incense was the best thing going. By the way, this practical application of incense didn't take away from its symbolic significance.

Incense remains an integral part of Catholic worship today. Eastern Orthodox Catholics use incense every day and every week during liturgical worship. Latin (Western) Catholics may use it on special holy days, maybe once a week at Sunday Mass, and almost always at Catholic funerals.

At funerals, incense is burned at the coffin as well as the altar, because the body had been a temple of the Holy Spirit when the soul lived inside. The body will be resurrected by Jesus and reunited with its soul at the Resurrection of the dead.

Anointing with oil

Another familiar smell to Catholics is *Chrism Oil* or sometimes called *Oil of Chrism,* which is olive oil that's been blessed by the local diocesan bishop. This oil is used to consecrate bishops, anoint the hands of priests, confirm Catholics, baptize Catholics, bless bells, and consecrate altars and churches. It produces a distinctive aroma that the sense of smell can detect quite easily. The strong but pleasant odor comes from *balsam,* an aromatic perfume that's added to the Chrism Oil.

The local bishop blesses three oils during Holy Week, the week before Easter, at a special Mass called the *Chrism Mass,* or *Mass of the Oils.* At this special Mass, the bishop blesses Chrism Oil, the Oil of the Sick, and the Oil of Catechumens. All three are olive oils, blessed in huge multi-gallon containers. Then the oil is distributed to the priests and deacons of the diocese. Chrism oil is the only one of the three, however, to have balsam added to it.

Through sound

It goes without saying that the most obvious way a believer hears God is by listening to his word. Catholicism is a biblical religion. The words of the Bible are read aloud at every Catholic Mass, be it Sunday or daily Mass. Readings are taken only from the Bible. Catholics believe that no other poetry or prose can replace the inspired Word of God. The readings are from both the Old and New Testaments. In every parish on the weekend, after the Old Testament reading and before the New Testament Epistle reading, a Psalm is normally sung. After the Epistle, a passage from one of the four Gospels is read. And many Catholic hymns are based on scriptural citations.

Listening to the words of Scripture is the primary way that the sense of hearing is employed, but the prayers of the priest and congregation are also considered important, so the congregation is asked to pay attention and respond at the appropriate time. Hearing the *homily,* a sermon given at Mass immediately after the Gospel by a priest, deacon, or bishop, the pastoral explanation and application of the Gospel, is a vital part of the Liturgy of the Word, the first half of the Catholic Mass.

The Catholic Church also uses plenty of music, especially organ music and choirs, and *Gregorian Chant,* Latin chant named after Pope St. Gregory the Great, A.D. 590–604. The reasoning is that the beautiful sounds of the pipe organ and delicate tones of the human voice are also reminders of God.

Through taste

Catholicism even employs the sense of taste in its worship. The Holy Eucharist is the most important, sacred, and pivotal aspect of Catholic worship, because it's regarded as the real, true, and substantial body and blood, soul and divinity of Christ — under the *appearances* of bread and wine. Those appearances appeal to and are perceived by the sense of taste.

At Communion time, the believer receives the Holy Eucharist, but it still tastes like unleavened bread and grape wine. (The Latin Church uses unleavened bread, but the Eastern Church uses leavened bread.) The sense of taste doesn't perceive the change of substance, hence the term *transubstantiation* (see Chapter 8), from bread and wine into the body and blood of Christ. This makes participating in Communion possible, because if the Holy Eucharist tasted like flesh and blood, no one could stomach it.

The central mystery and dogma of Catholic faith is that the substances of bread and wine are really changed into the substances of the body and blood, soul and divinity of Christ by the priest when he says the words of consecration at Mass. Yet the appearances of bread and wine remain to enable the faithful to eat his body and drink his blood. These appearances are sometimes called the *accidents,* but they have nothing to do with mishaps or car crashes. The philosophical term *accident* is used in Catholic theology to distinguish outward appearances from the invisible but underlying essence.

The Seven Sacraments

The most sacred and ancient Catholic rites of worship are the seven sacraments. The word *sacrament* comes from the Latin *sacramentum,* meaning an *oath* or *obligation,* because early Christians saw these seven special ceremonies as being able to bind the believer to God and his Church.

The *Catechism of the Catholic Church* defines the seven sacraments as "efficacious signs of grace, instituted by Christ and entrusted to the church, by which divine life is dispensed to us." (1131). The key words in this definition are *signs* and *grace.* Grace is invisible — a supernatural gift from God that makes people holy, enabling and empowering human beings to do good. Being invisible, however, grace is difficult to recognize and remember. That's where the seven sacraments come in. They're religious ceremonies that use visible signs to symbolize invisible grace given by God.

Why do Catholics have seven sacraments? Why not more or less? The easy answer is that Jesus instituted all seven. In the 13th century, however, philosopher St. Thomas Aquinas (see Chapters 3 and 18) pointed out that seven stages of human development occur in the realm of nature, so it makes sense that God created the sacraments to correspond with each of those events. It's not that God *had* to make seven sacraments, Aquinas said, but it's *reasonable* to have seven:

- ✔ We are born: Baptism
- ✔ We are fed: Holy Eucharist
- ✔ We grow: Confirmation
- ✔ We need healing: Penance
- ✔ We recover: Anointing of the Sick
- ✔ We need family: Matrimony
- ✔ We need leaders: Holy Orders

The Sacraments of Initiation — Baptism, Holy Eucharist, and Confirmation — are discussed in Chapter 6. The Sacraments of Mercy — Penance and Anointing of the Sick — and the Sacraments of Community — Matrimony and Holy Orders — are discussed in Chapter 7.

Chapter 6

The Sacraments of Initiation

Three of the seven sacraments — Baptism, Confirmation, and Holy Eucharist — are classified as *Sacraments of Initiation*. Through Baptism, people enter (are *initiated* into) the Catholic Church. Through Confirmation, they're considered personally responsible for their faith. Through Holy Eucharist, which is also called *Holy Communion*, they express their unity with the Church — all her doctrines, laws, and practices.

The Byzantine (Eastern) Catholic Church administers all three Sacraments of Initiation at the same time — at infancy. This has been the Church's practice throughout history. The Latin (Western) Catholic Church separates the three sacraments into completely different celebrations at different ages. Normally, *infants* are baptized, *children* receive Holy Eucharist at the age of discretion (around 7 years of age), and *adolescents* or *young adults* are confirmed anywhere from 7 to 16 years old, but most Catholics in the U.S. are confirmed at around 14 years old. This chapter explains the Sacraments of Initiation and offers insight into the ceremonies of Baptism, Confirmation, and First Communion. (Chapter 7 explains the rest of the seven sacraments.)

Come On in — the Water's Fine

Baptism is the first of the seven sacraments. It's the one sacrament that all Christian denominations share in common, even though each religion baptizes at different ages and some only in one way, such as immersion. A few Christian denominations only baptize by completely immersing or dunking the person head to toe in the water, but most allow immersion or infusion such as the pouring of water over the head of the new Christian. Like the

Sacrament of Confirmation and the Sacrament of Holy Orders, you're only baptized once. These three sacraments confer an indelible mark on the soul, which can never be repeated nor is it ever removed. So, no one can ever be un-baptized or re-baptized.

In the eyes of the Catholic Church, any Baptism that uses water and the invocation of the Holy Trinity as well as the intention to do what the Church does, that is, "I baptize you in the name of the Father and of the Son and of the Holy Spirit," is a valid sacrament. So Catholicism regards Episcopalian, Anglican, Lutheran, Methodist, Presbyterian, Baptist, United Church of Christ, Assembly of God, Church of the Nazarene, Church of the Brethren, Amish, Church of God, Disciples of Christ, Adventist, and Evangelical Baptisms to be valid. And if a follower of one of these Christian churches wants to become Catholic, he doesn't have to be re-baptized.

That said, Catholicism doubts the Baptisms in the following faith communities to be a valid sacrament: Christian Scientists, Quakers, Salvation Army, Jehovah Witnesses, Unitarians, and Mormons (Church of Jesus Christ of Latter Day Saints). The reason has nothing to do with the religions themselves or their members, because all espouse a true love of God and neighbor. The reason merely has to do with what Catholicism considers to be a valid sacrament.

Becoming Christ's kith and kin

Your first birth from your mother's womb made you a member of the family established by your parents and their respective families. You have an immediate family of parents and siblings and an extended family of grandparents, aunts, uncles, cousins, in-laws, and such.

Just as natural birth ushers people into blood and marriage relationships, Baptism — as a supernatural birth — establishes ties to spiritual families. By being baptized, *born again* of water and the Spirit, new Christians become children of God by adoption. In other words, they're adopted into the family of God; they can't be born into that family, because they're human, and God is divine. Jesus Christ, God and man, divine and yet human, becomes their brother. Mary, the Mother of Jesus, becomes their spiritual mother because siblings share a relationship with the parents. If Jesus is their brother by adoption, then his mother, Mary, becomes their mother by adoption.

So through Catholic Baptism, a Christian's immediate spiritual family is God the Father, Jesus, God's son and a brother to all, and Mary, the Mother of Jesus and a mother to all. And every one who was, is, or ever will be baptized becomes their extended spiritual family. Catholics believe that Baptism makes all people brothers and sisters in Christ, whether they're Catholic, Protestant, or Orthodox.

Baptism also connects the new Catholic to the Church. The title *Father* is given to the priest, because he typically does the baptizing. That is, the Holy *Mother* Church, the Catholic Church, gives birth to the new Christian from the spiritual womb of the baptismal font. The water of the baptismal font has been likened to the waters that surrounded the baby in the womb — thus the reason it's called the *spiritual womb*. A person is reborn through the waters of Baptism with the assistance of the priest doing the baptizing. It's only an analogy, but it's endured for 2,000 years.

Since the restoration of the *permanent diaconate* at the Second Vatican Council (1962–65), deacons can now baptize as can priests and bishops. The *permanent diaconate* refers to those deacons who are usually married and don't become priests. *Transitional deacons,* however, are unmarried seminarians who intend to become priests a year after being ordained a deacon. (See Chapter 2 for more on deacons.)

At the moment of Baptism, a new Catholic also joins the local parish and diocese as well. The *parish* is the faith community of a neighborhood, composed of Catholic families in that area; the *diocese* is the faith family of many parish communities in one geographic region of the state. So, if you were baptized at Notre-Dame de Paris in France, for example, you'd be a member of the Roman Catholic Church at large, a member of the Archdiocese of Paris and a member of the Notre-Dame Cathedral Parish, all at the same time.

Washing away original sin

More than make connections and relationships, Baptism also washes away *original sin,* the sin of the original parents of the whole human race: Adam and Eve. The Book of Genesis (1:26–27) says that God created man in his own image and likeness, male and female. The first man was called Adam, and the first woman, the wife of Adam, was called Eve. They were the prototype man and woman, and their sin affected all men and women after them. And the Bible says that their sin was disobedience.

Even secular science today uses the name Eve to refer to the first human woman — the first *homo sapien.* We want to mention that avowed atheist scientists from Oxford University in England have identified seven ancestral matriarchal groups from which all Europeans appear to have descended. Every European, according to the study, can trace his evolutionary history back to the seven ancestral mother groups, also referred to as the *Seven Daughters of Eve.* This corroborates the discovery of biochemists Allan Wilson and Vincent Sarich of the University of California at Berkley who've shown that every man and woman on earth, past, present, and future, can be traced genetically to one human woman.

Biology has shown that you inherit many physical characteristics from your natural parents — eye and hair color, facial features, body shape, and so on. Good and bad traits and some diseases are handed down from generation to generation. Likewise, original sin is transmitted from generation to generation by birth.

Original sin doesn't mean that a baby in the womb somehow commits a sin before being born. If Junior kicks too much inside, he's not being a bad boy, for example. Mom just may have had too much spicy Italian sausage. To the Catholic Church, original sin isn't a personal sin of the unborn, but a sin transmitted from generation to generation by birth. All men and women are born with original sin, and only Baptism can wash it away.

Catholicism sees original sin differently from *actual sin*, which is what a rational person does when she consciously, deliberately, and willingly disobeys God. Original sin is the natural inclination to sin.

For example, nobody is born with polio, measles, or chicken pox, but folks aren't born with any immunity to these diseases, either. A baby needs to be vaccinated, so the human body can produce its own antibodies and fight these diseases when it's exposed to them. Likewise, you can think of original sin as being born without any immunity or ability to internally fight sin. On the spiritual level, human beings, born without any resistance to sin, need a spiritual vaccination.

Baptism is to original sin what the polio vaccination is to the poliovirus. Baptism restores what should have been — a spiritual resistance or immunity to sin and temptation. The first sin of the first parents, Adam and Eve, wounded human nature, and every one inherited that wounded nature from them. Baptism washes it away.

Nuff said? Not quite. We want to take this analogy a bit farther. Vaccinations only prevent some diseases by helping the human body become resistant to them. But getting shots as an infant doesn't guarantee that you'll never get other diseases, such as cancer. Using common sense and good health habits can help prevent other diseases. And just as vaccinations are but a first step for a healthy physical life, Baptism is but a first step for a healthy spiritual life. Cultivating a good, healthy spiritual life means avoiding what's bad for your soul, such as sin and evil, and doing what's good for your soul — prayer and works of mercy motivated by divine grace.

In addition to getting rid of original sin, Baptism also imparts or infuses *sanctifying grace,* a special free gift from God. Sanctifying grace makes the new Christian a child of God and applies the merits of Jesus Christ, his suffering and death for sins, to the new Christian personally, because the person being baptized is mentioned by name. Catholicism believes that sanctifying grace allows human beings to enter heaven. It justifies them in the eyes of God by uniting them with the Savior and Redeemer, Jesus Christ. Without sanctifying grace, one can't stand before the utter holiness of God who is sanctity personified. Normally, you receive this special grace only through the sacraments, but God does provide some means to make sure all men and women have the potential and possibility of salvation.

Baptizing with water

The most common form of Baptism is by water. The Gospels say that one must be born again of water and the Holy Spirit (John 1:33). The early Christians and their successors have been baptizing with water for almost two millennia but with some slight differences:

- **Immersion:** Some Christian denominations fully immerse a person in water three times while saying the invocation of the Holy Trinity, also known as the *Trinitarian formula,* "I baptize you in the name of the Father and of the Son and of the Holy Spirit."

- **Aspersion:** Other Christians sprinkle water on the forehead of the one being baptized and then invoke the Trinitarian formula.

- **Infusion:** Catholics (mostly Latin) baptize by pouring water over the head of the one being baptized while the Trinitarian formula is pronounced.

All three methods use water and the invocation of the Holy Trinity. Only water can be used — no other substance. But immersion or infusion are preferred.

Many ask why Catholics baptize infants whereas other Christians wait until the individual is old enough to decide for himself if he wants to be baptized. Fair question. Think of it this way:

- Birth allowed you to enter and join the family you were born into. Your mom and dad picked out a name to call you, and your family name was given to you. You had no choice as to what your first or last name would be; yet you entered a family with a name. Likewise, Baptism is the believer's entrance and membership into the family of faith. Believers become children of God and members of the Church by Baptism.

- Just as being born made you a member of your family, it also made you a member of the civil community. A birth certificate establishes that you're a citizen of a specific country by birth. You were born in the United States or Canada, for example, and that makes you a citizen of the country merely by being born on its soil. You had no choice as to what nationality you would be and yet you were born a citizen of a nation that accepts you as a member. Likewise, Baptism makes you a member of God's family and the family of faith called the Church.

It's just like the United States giving citizenship to babies when they're born. All the rights and privileges of citizenship are bestowed on newborn infants even though they're too young to know or realize it. Similarly, baptized infants don't know or realize that they're Catholic Christians any more than they know that they're Americans, but the infants have an identity and share in the rights and privileges that only members can enjoy. And just as U.S. citizens can renounce their citizenship after they turn 18, Catholic Christians can renounce their religion when they become adults. When they're old enough, they can consciously choose to continue or reject their religion. No mother or father would delay naming their son until he was old enough to decide for himself what name he wanted, nor would they allow their daughter to renounce her citizenship until she was old enough to vote and choose for herself what nation she would belong to. Likewise, Catholic parents baptize their children, so they receive a faith, a name, and a nationality — without their consent but for their own good nonetheless.

In the past, infant mortality was so high that many babies didn't survive birth or early childhood, so Baptism as an infant insured that their souls wouldn't perish. Today, with modern medicine and progress, it's not the fear of death but hope for great potential and wonderful possibilities that encourages Catholic parents to baptize their children. It gives them an identity and a spiritual beginning. Anyway, the New Testament affirms that *entire households* were baptized, which meant the parents and children as well. So infant Baptisms have occurred from the very beginning.

Shedding blood for Christ

From A.D. 60 to the end of the 3rd century, the Romans violently persecuted the early Christian Church. Christianity wasn't even legal until after Emperor Constantine's Edict of Milan in A.D. 313. During those first 300 years of Roman persecution, many who believed in Christ as the Son of God weren't yet baptized with water. These unbaptized believers were called *catechumens,* which meant that they were preparing for Baptism by study and prayer but were not yet baptized. After all, people coming from a decadent pagan lifestyle needed time to clean up their act before being baptized, and some took several weeks, months, or even a year or two to prepare for their Baptism. After Baptism, they renounced their pagan ways and did no more dabbling in the idolatry and immorality of their secular contemporaries.

These catechumens and students of Christianity, otherwise known as the pre-baptized, were treated just as if they were full-fledged baptized Christians. The Roman gladiators and animals in the arena didn't distinguish between baptized Christians and those preparing for Baptism. Both were violently persecuted.

The notion of being baptized by shedding your own blood for Christ and/or his Church grew up during the Roman persecutions. And the Catholic Church has always revered these unbaptized *martyrs* — people who die for their faith — maintaining that the divine mercy of God wouldn't penalize them or ignore their sacrifice merely because they died before their Baptism by water.

In addition, Herod killed many infants (Matthew 2:16) in an failed effort to kill the newborn Christ. Those infants, known as the *Holy Innocents,* are martyrs, too, because they shed their blood, so Christ could live. So Baptism by blood is as valid as Baptism by water. The following quote from the *Catechism of the Catholic Church* shows what the Church has to say about Baptism by blood:

> The Church has always held the firm conviction that those who suffer death for the sake of the faith without having received Baptism are baptized by their death for and with Christ. This *Baptism of blood,* like the *desire for Baptism,* brings about the fruits of Baptism without being a sacrament. (1258)

Having the will but not the way

Part of Catholic theology is the *Universal Salvific Will of God,* which is just a fancy way of saying that God basically would like for everyone, all men and women, to join him in heaven. Men and women have free will, though, so he *offers* the gift of grace, but men and women must freely accept and then cooperate with it.

The whole truth and nothing but the truth

The late Archbishop Fulton J. Sheen said that few people reject Christ or even hate the Catholic Church, but many reject and hate false notions and erroneous ideas about Christ, Christianity, and Catholicism. (See Chapter 17 for more on Archbishop Sheen.)

The Catholic Church doesn't see itself as being right and all other religions as being wrong, but Catholicism does firmly believe that Jesus Christ himself founded the Catholic Church, and therefore, the Church possesses all the truths and graces necessary for salvation, whereas other faiths possess only some (partial) truth and grace. You can think of it like this: Catholicism sees itself more like someone who knows everything about mathematics versus someone who knows only algebra, geometry, or trigonometry. The Church believes that all religions know some truth, but it knows more. She doesn't claim perfect or total knowledge of science, philosophy, or other disciplines, but in the area of faith and theology, the Church believes that she has been given the fullness of truth and the mission to teach it to all nations.

Hollywood Baptism

Even non-Catholics know the term *godfather,* thanks to the series of movies carrying that name. The movies, however, use the term to indicate a Mafia boss, not a godparent. During the baptismal scene in *The Godfather* (1972; Paramount), Michael Corleone, one of the Mafia characters in the movie, assumes the role of sacramental godfather and is asked the question, "Do you renounce Satan?" At the very moment that he responds, "I do," the viewer sees that Michael's henchmen are killing another character somewhere else. The scene is not only ironic but also *sacrilegious* — something holy is desecrated. In the eyes of the Church, being a godparent is an honor, privilege, duty, and responsibility. A real godfather is someone who seriously practices his religion 24/7 and not just because it's the ethnic or cultural thing to do. Being a godparent means that a person is willing and able to be a spiritual role model for the baptized.

St. Augustine (A.D. 354–430) taught that God offers everyone *sufficient* grace to be saved, but it only becomes *efficacious* (successful) for those who freely accept and cooperate with that grace. In other words, God gives every human being the chance and possibility of going to heaven. Whether they get beyond the pearly gates, however, depends on the individual person. (For more on St. Augustine, see Chapter 15.)

That said, history, geography, economics, politics, language, culture, and other circumstances can create barriers that prevent everyone from knowing and believing the same thing in the same way. The Catholic Church maintains that no one is denied heaven merely because they live at the wrong time and/or in the wrong place. In other words, many people would be baptized by water if given a chance. People who've never heard of Christ or the Catholic Church may have an implicit desire to accept whatever God reveals, teaches, and commands without knowing exactly what that entails through no fault of their own.

People who lack any knowledge of Christ and his teachings are sometimes called *anonymous Christians,* and they don't consciously, deliberately, and willingly reject Christ and his Catholic Church, so they aren't responsible for not knowing the whole truth. Therefore, the Church believes in Baptism by desire, which allows salvation for non-Christians who, through no fault of their own, haven't yet accepted Christ explicitly but nonetheless live good, moral lives as if already Christian. Only those who consciously, deliberately, and willingly reject Christ are considered liable.

If people in their heart of hearts are sincerely disposed to God's will but, through no fault of their own, don't know about Jesus Christ — or they've never been shown by word and good example — then the Church presumes that they possess an implicit desire to be baptized. If someone had told them and given good example, they would've freely and willingly embraced Christianity and asked for Baptism by water.

The *Catechism of the Catholic Church* has this to say about Baptism by desire:

> Since Christ died for all, . . . we must hold that the Holy Spirit offers to all the possibility. . . . Every man who is ignorant of the Gospel of Christ and of his Church, but seeks the truth and does the will of God . . . can be saved. It may be supposed that such persons would have *desired Baptism explicitly* if they had known its necessity. (1260)

Recognizing the role of godparents

Every person being baptized, whether child or adult, must have a sponsor. The sponsors in Baptism have traditionally been called *godparents*. The minimum requirement is one sponsor, but usually when infants are baptized, they get two, one of each gender.

Canon law permits only one godparent of each gender — a godmother and godfather. For an adult or a child being baptized, these sponsors

 ✔ Can't be the parents of the one being baptized

 ✔ Must be 16 years or older

 ✔ Must be practicing Catholics, going to Mass every week

 ✔ Be already confirmed

If someone can't find two practicing Catholics to be the godfather and godmother, then one sponsor can be Catholic and the other a Christian witness if that person is a baptized Protestant Christian in good standing.

Prior to the medical advances of the 20th century, when people died at an earlier age because of illness, such as tuberculosis and the plague, godparents were the practical choice to raise a child if both parents died before the son or daughter grew up. Babies had two godparents in case one would not be able to fulfill the job of raising the child. If the parents died prematurely, then at least one of the godparents could do it. This is why many godparents come from both sides of the family. Today, being a godparent carries with it no legal right or ecclesiastical authority to the custody of children. Custody is a strictly legal matter that parents must decide with their attorney. Being a godparent, besides giving Christmas and birthday gifts every year, really means actively giving good Christian witness and example and being a role model and support by regularly and faithfully practicing the religion.

What goes on at a Baptism?

Baptisms in the Catholic Church usually take place on Sundays, during the parish Mass or in the early afternoon after all the Masses are over. It all depends on the parish, the pastor, and the parents. By the way, adults who were never baptized are highly encouraged to be baptized with other adults on Holy Saturday evening, during a service known as the Easter Vigil, because it's held on the night before Easter Sunday. Children, however, are baptized once a month or every Sunday, depending on the diocese and parish.

The person being baptized is asked to dress in white to symbolize purity of faith and cleansing of Baptism. Some parishes put a small white garment on the child, especially if she isn't already dressed in white. When adults are baptized, they typically put on a full-length white gown known as an *alb,* from the Latin word for *white*.

The white garment symbolizes the white garments that Jesus wore when he was placed in the tomb after his death on Good Friday. When the women and disciples returned on Easter day, they found the tomb empty except for the white robes. So it represents the promise of the Resurrection, made at Baptism. The promise is that the baptized body will one day die, like Christ's did, but it'll be raised from the dead someday by Christ.

The priest or deacon is usually the minister of Baptism, but anyone can baptize in an emergency, such as in a hospital or whenever someone's life is in danger.

1. During the Baptism of an infant, the priest or deacon asks the parents, "What name do you give your child?"

   He doesn't ask this question because he's too senile to remember or too blind to read the child's name on the card that he has in front of him, but because that person becomes a child of God by name and Jesus becomes her brother by name as soon as the person is baptized. The parents respond aloud, hopefully, with a Christian name, such as one of the saints or heroes of the Bible.

2. The priest or deacon asks, "What do you ask of God's church for your child?" The parents respond, "Baptism." If an adult is being baptized, answers the same.

3. The priest or deacon then asks the parents and the godparents whether they're willing and able to fulfill their duties to bring up this child in the Christian faith.

4. As a symbolic gesture, the priest or deacon makes the sign of the cross with his thumb gently on the forehead of the child or adult to show that the cross of Christ has saved her. The parents and godparents do likewise.

5. A particular passage from the Bible is read, usually from the New Testament, where Baptism is mentioned or alluded to.

6. After some other prayers, the first anointing takes place, and the infant's white garb is pulled slightly beneath the neck so the priest or deacon can smear a little *Oil of Catechumens* on the infant's neck with his thumb.

   The local bishop blesses this olive oil once a year during Holy Week and distributes it to all the parishes. It symbolizes that the person, born into the world, is now being set apart from the world by the anointing. She is soon to be baptized and therefore belongs not to the world but to God and heaven.

7. The priest or deacon blesses the water of Baptism. The prayer recalls how water has played an important role in salvation history as recorded throughout the Bible: It represents a sign of new life, the washing of sin, deliverance from slavery, and a new beginning.

8. The baptismal promises are made. Because the infant can't speak for herself, mom, dad, and the godparents answer for her. Adults who are being baptized, however, answer for themselves, of course. Later, probably when she's 14 years old, she answers those same questions on her own before the bishop on her own. The questions are easy — no one needs a lifeline or poll of the audience. The priest or deacon asks, "Do you renounce Satan? And all his works? And all his empty promises?" If things go well, everyone says "I do." If not, you have to check for devil worshippers among the crowd.

9. After the renunciation of evil, the *Apostles' Creed* is put in question form: "Do you believe in God, the Father Almighty, creator of heaven and earth?" Again, the hoped-for response is "I do." Then the other two persons of the Trinity are mentioned: "Do you believe in Jesus Christ . . ." and "Do you believe in the Holy Spirit . . . " and so on.

10. Finally comes the actual Baptism. The immediate family gathers around the baptismal font (see Figure 6-1), and the child is held over the basin while the priest or deacon pours water three times over the child's head and says, "I baptize you (the first and middle names are said aloud) in the name of the Father and of the Son and of the Holy Spirit. Amen." Usually, the baby cries, because the water tends to be a little cool.

11. The priest or deacon anoints the top of the new Christian's head with *Chrism Oil.*

    Like the Oil of Catechumens, the local bishop blesses the Chrism Oil during Holy Week, but this olive oil has balsam added to it to make it smell nice. The anointing symbolizes that the newly baptized Christian is now exactly that — a *Christ*ian. The word *Christ* means *anointed,* and a *Christian* is someone who's anointed in Jesus Christ. This anointing also means the person is now to share in the three-fold mission of Christ — to sanctify, proclaim, and give Christian leadership and example to the world.

12. A Baptismal candle is lit from the burning Easter Candle, which is present throughout the ceremony. It symbolizes that the new Christian is a light to the world. Then the *Our Father* is said and a blessing is given for mom, dad, and the family, and everyone celebrates.

For an adult who is being baptized, parents aren't involved, but a sponsor (godparent) is still necessary. During Baptism, the adult answers all the questions, receives all the anointings, and gets to hold the lit candle.

If you're invited to a Baptism

- You don't need to be Catholic or even a Christian to attend. Your presence is a sign of love, support, and friendship for the parents and for the baptized.

- If you're a Christian, you may want to join in the renewal of baptismal promises when they're asked.

- If you're the godfather, it's unwritten and unofficial tradition that you give the priest or deacon a token of appreciation in the form of a modest donation. Some parishes and dioceses allow the one doing the Baptism to keep it; others require that he give it to the parish; still others divide it up among the priests and deacons of the parish. It's not really a tip but an honorarium, and it's never required or expected. Yet in the United States, it's become customary for the godfather to make this offering, usually anywhere from $20 to $100.

Figure 6-1:
A baptismal
font.

The Holy Eucharist

The Holy Eucharist refers to Christ's body and blood present in the consecrated host on the altar. Eucharist refers to one of three aspects of Christ's body and blood — as *sacrifice* during the Consecration of the Mass, as Holy *Communion,* and as *Blessed Sacrament.* These three aspects form the core of Catholic belief on the Holy Eucharist.

In Chapter 8, we discuss the parts of the Mass in detail and the Holy Eucharist as a sacrifice, but this section just focuses on the sacred meal of Communion and the Blessed Sacrament.

Of all seven sacraments, the Holy Eucharist is the most central and important to Catholicism, because of the staunch belief that the consecrated bread and wine are actually, really, truly, and substantially the body and blood, soul and divinity of Christ. For Catholics, the presence of Christ in the Holy Eucharist is not just symbolic, allegorical, metaphorical, or merely spiritual. It's real. That's why it's also called the *Real Presence* — because Christ *really is present.* (For more on consecrated bread and wine and the Real Presence, see the Chapter 8.)

Some of the basic facts about the Holy Eucharist follow:

- ✔ The word *Eucharist* comes from the Greek *eucharistein,* meaning "thanksgiving." Catholics are grateful and give thanks to God for providing the bread from heaven, the Holy Eucharist, to feed and nourish the soul.

- ✔ The word *Communion* comes from Latin: *Co* means "with" and *unio* means "union." *Communio* means "union with." Catholics believe that Communion allows the believer to be united with Christ by sharing his body and blood.

- ✔ Only wheat bread and grape wine can be used. The moment the priest or bishop says the words of consecration — the words of Christ at the Last Supper, "This is My body" and "This is My blood," (Matthew 26:26–29). Catholics believe that the bread and wine become the body and blood, soul and divinity of Christ.

- ✔ In the Latin (Western) Church, unleavened bread is used, which is made from wheat flour and water — no other ingredients — much like the unleavened bread used by Christ at the Last Supper.

- ✔ In the Byzantine (Eastern) Church, leavened bread is used to symbolize the Resurrection, but no other ingredients are added.

✔ On the natural level, whatever we eat becomes part of us. That is, until there's too much of us, and then we must go on a diet. On the supernatural plane, when Catholics eat the body and blood of Christ, they're supposed to become more like Christ in his obedience to the Father, humility, and love for neighbor.

✔ Like Baptism, Holy Eucharist is also considered a *Sacrament of Initiation,* because new members are encouraged to participate regularly and often in Holy Communion.

To Catholics, the physical act of eating the consecrated host or drinking the consecrated wine from the *chalice,* a blessed cup (see Figure 6-2), is secondary to the underlying invisible reality that the human soul is being fed by the very body and blood, soul and divinity of Christ. The body merely consumes the *appearances* of bread and wine while the soul receives Christ personally and totally.

Figure 6-2:
A chalice from which Catholics drink consecrated wine.

Receiving Holy Communion

Later in the course of the Mass, after consecrating the host and wine, finishing the Eucharistic prayer, the *Our Father,* and so on (see Chapter 8 for more on the Mass), the priest and deacon, sometimes with the assistance of *extraordinary ministers* (nonclerics who have been given the authority to assist the priest), distribute Holy Communion to the faithful. Because this is really and truly the body and blood, soul and divinity of Christ, receiving Holy Communion, God's intimate visit with his faithful souls, is most sacred.

When believers receive Holy Communion, they're intimately united with their Lord and Savior, Jesus Christ. However, Communion isn't limited to the *communicant* (the one receiving Holy Communion) and Jesus Christ. By taking Holy Communion, the Catholic is also expressing her union with all Catholics around the world and at all times who believe the same doctrines, obey the same laws, and follow the same leaders. This is why Catholics (and Eastern Orthodox Christians) have a strict law that only people who are *in communion* with the Church can receive Holy Communion. In other words, only those who are united in the same beliefs — the seven sacraments, the authority of the pope, and the teachings in the *Catechism of the Catholic Church* — are allowed to receive Holy Communion.

In the Protestant tradition, Communion is often seen as a means of building unity among various denominations, and many have open Communion, meaning that any baptized Christian can take Communion in their services. Catholics and Eastern Orthodox Christians, on the other hand, see Communion not as the means but as the final fruit of unity. So only those in Communion can receive Holy Communion. It has nothing to do with who's worthy.

Think of it this way: If a Canadian citizen moves to the United States, lives in Erie, Pennsylvania, works in Erie, and has a family in Erie, he can do so indefinitely. Citizens from other nations can live their entire lives in the United States, but they can't run for public office or vote in an American election unless and until becoming U.S. citizens.

Does being or not being a citizen make you a good or bad person? Of course not. If citizens from other countries want to vote, they must give up their own citizenship and become U.S. citizens. Otherwise, they can live, work, eat, and die in the United States, but until they change citizenship, they remain citizens of their original place.

Likewise, non-Catholics can come to as many Catholic Masses as they want; they can marry Catholics and raise their children in the Catholic faith, but they can't receive Holy Communion in the Catholic Church until they become Catholic. Becoming Catholic is how a person gets united with and experiences union with the whole Catholic Church. Those in union can then receive Holy Communion.

Similarly, Catholics who don't follow the Church's laws on divorce and remarriage, or who obstinately reject Church teaching, such as the inherent evil of abortion, shouldn't go to Communion, because they're no longer in communion. It's not a judgment on their moral or spiritual state, because only God can know that. But receiving Holy Communion is a public act, and therefore, it's an ecclesiastical action requiring those who do it to be united with all that the Church teaches and commands and with all the ways that the Church prays.

The Holy Eucharist is food for the soul, so it's given and eaten during Holy Communion at the Mass. However, the form and manner of distribution bear slight differences, depending on whether you attend a Latin (Western) Rite Mass or a Byzantine (Eastern) Rite Mass:

✔ **Latin (Western) Rite:** Holy Communion is in the form of consecrated unleavened hosts made from wheat flour and water, just like the unleavened bread used by Jesus at the Last Supper. The host is flat and the size of a quarter or half-dollar. Latin Catholics may receive the host on their tongue or in their hand if the local bishop and the national conference of bishops permit.

✔ **Byzantine (Eastern) Rite:** Catholics receive consecrated leavened bread (the yeast or leaven symbolizes the Resurrection), which is placed inside the chalice (cup) of consecrated wine. The priest takes a spoon and gingerly places a cut cube of consecrated bread soaked in the consecrated wine inside the mouths of the communicants without ever touching their lips or tongue.

First Holy Communion

When boys and girls (usually in second grade) make their First Holy Communion, it's a big occasion for Catholic families. Like their Baptism, the day of First Communion is one filled with family, friends, and feasting after the sacred event has taken place in church.

Girls typically wear white gowns and veils and often look like little brides, and boys wear their Sunday best or new suits and ties just bought for the occasion. Some parishes have the entire class make their First Communion together at a Sunday or Saturday Mass, but other parishes allow each child to go on a different weekend.

The children are generally too young to appreciate all the theological refinements of *transubstantiation,* the act of changing the substances of bread and wine into the substances of the Body and Blood of Christ, but as long as they know and believe that it's not bread or wine they're receiving but the real Body and Blood of Jesus Christ, then they are old enough to take Holy Communion. (For more on transubstantiation, see Chapter 8.)

Like Penance and the Anointing of the Sick, Holy Eucharist can be received more than once. However, Baptism, Confirmation, and Holy Orders can't be repeated.

First Penance (see Chapter 7), which is going to confession for the first time, *must come before* First Communion.

Coming of Age: Confirmation

Soon after the kids are born and get fed, they start to grow. Growth is as vital to human life as nourishment. The body and mind must grow to stay alive. Catholics believe that the soul also needs to grow in the life of grace. Just as the human body must grow through childhood, adolescence, and then adulthood, the human soul needs to grow into maturity. Catholics believe that Confirmation is the supernatural equivalent of the growth process on the natural level. It builds on what was begun in Baptism and what was nourished in Holy Eucharist. It completes the process of initiation into the Christian community, and it matures the soul for the work ahead. The Byzantine Church confirms (chrismates) at Baptism and gives Holy Eucharist as well, thus initiating the new Christian all at the same time.

Too often Confirmation is the bribe to get Catholic kids who go to public school to attend CCD (Confraternity of Christian Doctrine), also known as religious education classes. As long as they attend eight years of CCD, they're eligible for Confirmation. But Confirmation is more than a carrot on a stick to keep kids in CCD classes. This Sacrament of Initiation means that they become young adults in the Catholic faith. Confirmation is the supernatural equivalent of the growth process on the natural level. Along with the Holy Eucharist, it builds on what was begun in Baptism and nourished in Holy Eucharist. It completes the process of initiation into the Christian community, and it matures the soul for the work ahead. During an infant's Baptism, parents and godparents make promises to renounce Satan and believe in God and the Church on behalf of the child. At Confirmation, before the bishop, the young adult renews those same promises, this time in her own words.

Does this mean that confirmed kids go to Mass on Sundays and CCD classes more faithfully and with less coercion? Don't bet on it. It's an unfortunate fact that after some are confirmed, they never come back for high school religious education. Human nature is such that some parental guidance, authority, and sometimes force are needed to get Johnny or Susie to fulfill their Sunday obligation. Confirmation doesn't change the person but builds on what's already there. Good habits start early, which is why regular *catechesis* (the process of learning the faith), prayer, study, and attending Sunday Mass must follow Baptism all the way through First Communion to Confirmation. A good foundation is confirmed and continues to flourish.

So what occurs during Confirmation? The Holy Spirit is first introduced to a Catholic the day that she's baptized, because the entire Holy Trinity — Father, Son, and Holy Spirit — are invoked at the ceremony. During Confirmation, God the Holy Spirit comes upon the person, accompanied by God the Father and God the Son, just as he did at *Pentecost*. The Feast of Pentecost commemorates the descent of the Holy Spirit from heaven to earth upon the 12 apostles and the Virgin Mary, occurring 50 days after Easter and 10 days after Jesus' Ascension (Acts 2:1–4).

Confirmation couldn't happen at a more appropriate time

About the age that young Roman Catholics are confirmed, usually between 12 and 16 years of age (though canon law allows as early as 7), many young men and women have just gone through puberty. This is a crucial time for them, because they're being tempted to give in to every whim of the flesh, from both the hormonal changes that are going on inside and the peer pressure from the outside. So, too, the effects of original sin have left the whole human race vulnerable and afflicted with *concupiscence,* the tendency to sin. Culturally, drugs, pornography, and illicit sex are present in many forms, creating even more pressure for teenagers to take drugs and lose their virginity. Although resisting the temptation to experiment with drugs and abstaining from pornography, masturbation, and sexual intercourse is difficult, it's made easier with the supernatural grace of Confirmation. Of course, it's not infallible, because free will is always present.

This sacrament is called *Confirmation,* because the faith given in Baptism is now confirmed and made strong. Sometimes, those who benefit from Confirmation are referred to as *soldiers of Christ*. This isn't a military designation but a spiritual duty to fight the war between good and evil, light and darkness — a war between the human race and all the powers of hell.

Confirmation means accepting responsibility for your faith and destiny. Childhood is a time when you're told what to do, and you react positively to reward and negatively to punishment. Adulthood, even young adulthood, means that you must do what's right on your own, not for the recognition or reward but merely because it's the right thing to do. Doing what's right can be satisfying, too. The focus is on the Holy Spirit, who confirmed the apostles on Pentecost (Acts 2:1–4) and gave them courage to practice their faith. Catholics believe that the same Holy Spirit confirms Catholics during the Sacrament of Confirmation and gives them the same gifts and fruits.

Traditionally, the twelve fruits of the Holy Spirit are charity, joy, peace, patience, benignity, goodness, long-suffering, mildness, faith, modesty, continency and chastity. These are human qualities that can be activated by the Holy Spirit. The seven gifts of the Holy Spirit are wisdom, understanding, counsel, fortitude, knowledge, piety, and fear of the Lord. These gifts are supernatural graces given to the soul.

The following occurs during the Sacrament of Confirmation:

   ✔ The ceremony may take place at Mass or outside of Mass, and the bishop wears red vestments to symbolize the red tongues of fire seen hovering over the heads of the apostles at Pentecost.

✔ Each individual to be confirmed comes forward with his sponsor. The same canonical requirements for being a godparent in Baptism apply for sponsors at Confirmation. At Baptism, Junior's mom and dad picked his godfather and godmother; for Confirmation, he picks his own sponsor. The sponsor can be the godmother or godfather if they're still practicing Catholics, or he may choose someone else (other than his parents) who's over the age of 16, already confirmed, and in good standing with the Church. One sponsor is chosen for Confirmation. (Most people have two sponsors, one godparent of each gender, for Baptism.)

✔ Each Catholic selects his own Confirmation name. At Baptism, the name was chosen without the child's consent because the child was too little to make the selection alone. Now, in Confirmation, another name — in addition to the first and middle names — can be added, or the original baptismal name may be used. It must be a Christian name, though, such as one of the canonized saints of the Church or a hero from the Bible. You wouldn't want to pick a name like Cain, Judas, or Herod, for example, and no secular names would be appropriate.

✔ The Catholic being confirmed stands or kneels before the bishop, and the sponsor lays one hand on the shoulder of the one being confirmed. The Confirmation name is spoken, and the bishop puts Chrism Oil on the person's forehead, says his name aloud, and then says, "Be sealed with the gift of the Holy Spirit." The person responds, "Amen." The bishop then says, "Peace be with you." And the person responds, "And with your spirit" or "And also with you."

Normally, only the bishop confirms the Catholics in his diocese. However, priests can be delegated to confirm adult converts from other religions when they're brought into full communion with the Roman Catholic Church at the Easter Vigil and they've attended the Rite of Christian Initiation of Adults (RCIA) program in the parish. Non-Catholics who are interested in the Catholic faith and converting to Catholicism attend RCIA classes.

Many Latin (Western) Catholics are baptized as infants, receive First Communion as children, and are confirmed as adolescents, but the Sacraments of Initiation are for any age. Adult converts who've never been baptized are baptized when they become Catholic; they're confirmed and receive their First Communion at the same Mass when they're baptized or if they were baptized in a Protestant Church, they make a Profession of Faith, are confirmed, and receive Holy Eucharist at the Easter Vigil Mass — the night before Easter.

Chapter 7

The Sacraments of Community and Mercy

In This Chapter

▶ Making marriage vows that'll stick

▶ Caring for the Church community through Holy Orders

▶ Spilling your guts in the confessional

▶ Strengthening the spirit through the Anointing of the Sick

The seven sacraments are the most sacred and ancient Catholic rites of worship. Three of the seven sacraments — Baptism, Confirmation, and Holy Eucharist — are classified as Sacraments of Initiation. They're all about being initiated into the Catholic Church, becoming personally responsible for faith, and expressing unity with the Church. (See Chapter 6 for more on the Sacraments of Initiation.)

In this chapter, we discuss the other four sacraments. Two of them — Matrimony and Holy Orders — are Sacraments of Community. They're all about uniting and ministering. The other two — Penance and the Anointing of the Sick — are Sacraments of Mercy. They're all about healing and strengthening.

The Sacraments of Community

Just as three sacraments are for the sake of initiation (see Chapter 6), two sacraments are for the sake of social development. The Sacrament of Matrimony takes care of the family, and the Sacrament of Holy Orders takes care of the society of the Church.

Marriage — Catholic style

The Catholic Church distinguishes between a legal marriage and the Sacrament of Matrimony. Marriage is regulated by the civil government, which has certain rules that must be followed to make a marriage legal. Being legally married in the eyes of the government, however, doesn't necessarily mean that two people have necessarily participated in the Sacrament of Matrimony. The Sacrament of Matrimony means becoming husband and wife through a sacred covenant with God and each other. But a legal marriage is a union that's recognized by the state alone, which may or may not simultaneously be the sacrament. In this section, we explain what must occur for the marriage to also be a valid sacrament in the eyes of the Church.

A Catholic marriage involves two baptized people, one or both of whom are Catholic. Their union isn't just an occasion for a good party; Catholic marriage is a *vocation,* a calling from God, from the Latin *vocare* meaning *to call.* Just as priests, deacons, religious sisters and brothers, nuns, and monks have a calling from God, so do married people, as well as unmarried people.

Being a good husband or wife — then a good father or mother — is as much a sacred calling from God as the call to enter a convent and become a Poor Clare, Dominican, or Carmelite nun. Married people are to be sanctified as much as clergy and religious brothers and sisters.

Because marriage is a vocation *and* a sacrament, marriage imparts a special grace that gives the recipients the strength and ability to assume and fulfill all the duties and responsibilities of Christian marriage. Three elements are required for a marital union to be a valid sacrament: The participants must enter the Sacrament of Matrimony with the intention that their union will be

- ✔ **Permanent:** Unto death
- ✔ **Faithful:** No adultery
- ✔ **Fruitful:** Open to the possibility of children if God wills it

The Sacrament of Matrimony must give to the bride and groom the necessary graces to bring those vows to fruition. However, getting married in the Catholic Church isn't as complicated as some may think. At least one person must be Catholic, but the other person can be any other religion. If the non-Catholic was baptized in a non-Catholic church, the non-Catholic needs documentation verifying Baptism. If the non-Catholic is unbaptized, unchurched, or of a non-Christian religion, a special dispensation from the local bishop is needed. The priest or deacon doing the ceremony can obtain it.

Like the Sacraments of Baptism, Confirmation, and Holy Orders, the Sacrament of Matrimony can only take place once between the same two people, unless one spouse dies. So due to the lifelong commitment that's required for the Sacrament of Matrimony, Catholics can only marry someone who's widowed or wasn't married before. If a person was previously married and the spouse is alive, it must be demonstrated that the marriage was invalid, so the previous union can be declared null and void through an annulment. (See Chapter 9 for more on annulments.) If that happens, both parties are free to marry someone else — the Church hopes *validly* this time. Are you wondering how it can be demonstrated that the Sacrament of Matrimony never occurred? If one or both spouses didn't *intend* to enter a permanent, faithful, and/or fruitful union, that deficiency renders the marriage invalid.

Keep in mind that Church annulments are *not* a form of divorce and have no affect whatsoever on the legitimacy of children, because that's a purely legal matter. Annulments *don't* make the children born of that union illegitimate. *Annulments* declare that a marriage was never a valid sacrament in the first place even if both parties entered into it with good faith and intentions. (For more details on annulments, see Chapter 9.)

A valid Sacrament of Matrimony requires the presence of a priest or deacon, a bride and groom (no same-sex marriages), and two witnesses of any religion. All the other stuff is icing on the cake — the ushers, bridesmaids, groomsmen, parents, grandparents, photographer, videographer, caterer, ring bearer, flower girl, organist, and soloist. (See the sidebar "Food, flowers, and faith" for our opinion on prioritizing wedding preparations.)

The bride and groom are the real ministers of the sacrament, because their "I do," makes them husband and wife. The priest or deacon is just an official witness for the Church — necessary, yes, but just a witness.

Only Scripture readings from the Bible can be read and only approved vows recited during the ceremony. Secular or other writings from other faiths can be read at the wedding reception before grace is prayed and the toast given, but they don't belong in church.

In most dioceses, Catholics who want to marry are asked to meet with a priest or deacon at least 9 to 12 months before the wedding. This period is called *Pre-Cana* after the name of the town, Cana, where Jesus and his mother, Mary, went to a wedding feast, and Jesus changed water into wine. During the Pre-Cana period, the priest or deacon offers practical financial and emotional advice to the couple, as well as instructions on the spiritual nature of marriage and Natural Family Planning (NFP), which, by the way, is not the old, forsaken Rhythm Method. Because the Catholic Church forbids artificial contraception, regulating birth and planning the size of a family must be based on morally allowable means, such as NFP. Chapter 12 has the scoop on NFP, if you're interested.

Why is so much time spent in preparation? Why can't weddings be spontaneous? Because the Sacrament of Matrimony is a vocation for life. The Catholic Church wants to prevent impulsive, shotgun weddings, or anything done in haste, rashness, or imprudence.

Three types of Catholic wedding ceremonies are available. The first is a wedding at Mass; the second is a wedding without a Mass; and the third is a *convalidation* ceremony, in which a couple who was previously married invalidly in the eyes of the Church (perhaps by a Justice of the Peace or Protestant minister) now seeks to have that marriage recognized by the Church or, as the canon lawyers call it, *convalidated.*

Getting the full treatment

A *Nuptial Mass,* the Sacrament of Matrimony with a Mass, normally occurs on Saturday and rarely on Sunday unless special permission has been obtained from the bishop, but they may also occur on weekdays. The Nuptial Mass is highly recommended and encouraged when *both* the bride and groom are Catholic, because two sacraments are received at this ceremony: the Sacrament of Matrimony and the Sacrament of the Holy Eucharist. Participating in two sacraments is a great way to start the marriage.

Just like a Sunday parish Mass, the wedding Mass has four Scripture readings: one from the Old Testament read by a friend or relative, a Psalm that's sung, one from the New Testament Epistles read by a friend or relative, and one from the Gospels read by the priest or deacon. Then the priest or deacon gives the sermon and proceeds to witness the vows.

Food, flowers, and faith

Brides often call the caterer first and the priest last to set the date for the wedding, but it should be the other way around. Granted, caterers book up 12 to 18 months ahead of time, and photographers, florists, and other folks in the wedding business require months of advance notice to start making preparations. But the food, photos, and flowers aren't the required elements of the Sacrament of Matrimony, so it makes perfect sense to contact the Catholic Church and the priest or deacon *first* — before making any other wedding plans. Besides, most dioceses ask Catholics to meet with a priest or deacon beginning up to a year before the wedding. So if you're getting ready to walk down the aisle, make sure that you give your faith at least as much consideration as the decision to serve chicken or beef.

Just before the formal vows, the priest or deacon asks the couple three important questions:

1. Have you come here freely and without reservation to give yourselves to each other in marriage?

2. Will you love and honor each other as husband and wife for the rest of your lives?

3. Will you accept children lovingly from God and bring them up according to the law of Christ and his Church?

Hopefully, both say, "Yes!" to all three questions, and the priest or deacon can proceed to the marriage vows.

The vows may be stated by the priest or deacon and repeated by the bride and groom, or the vows may be addressed as a question, to which the bride and groom merely respond, "I do." Following are examples of the two accepted versions:

> I, Concetta, take you Salvatore, to be my husband. I promise to be true to you in good times and in bad, in sickness and in health. I will love you and honor you all the days of my life.

Or:

> Do you, Salvatore, take Concetta, for your lawful wife, to have and to hold, from this day forward, for better, for worse, for richer, for poorer, in sickness and in health, until death do you part?

After the vows, the rings are blessed. Then the groom places one ring on the bride's finger and says, "Take this ring as a sign of my love and my fidelity, in the name of the Father and of the Son and of the Holy Spirit. Amen." The bride takes the other ring and places it on the groom's finger and says the same words.

The couple becomes husband and wife at the moment they exchange consent, not rings. Rings are merely a symbol.

After the exchange of rings, the prayers of the faithful are said, just like at Sunday Mass, followed by an offertory hymn and the preparation of the gifts on the altar. A relative or friend may bring up the bread and wine. And Mass proceeds as normal. (See Chapter 8 for a detailed look at the Mass.) After the *Our Father,* the new husband and wife kneel, while the priest gives a special nuptial blessing to the couple. Then they stand, give a sign of peace (hug or kiss) to their respective parents and return to the sanctuary. Communion proceeds as usual.

Dos and don'ts at Catholic weddings

Want some tips about what to do — and not to do — at a Catholic wedding?

Do arrive early, and dress as you would for any religious ceremony. Show good taste and modesty. Limit all food, beverages, and party activity to the reception. Keep the couple in your prayers, and be aware that traditionally, the bride's side of the church is on your left as you face the altar and sanctuary, and the groom's side is on the right. (This has nothing to do with canon law. Just Emily Post, we guess.) Weddings and funerals are the few exceptions when no collection baskets are passed at Mass, but *do* give the newlyweds a gift.

Don't come late, especially after her dad has already walked the bride down the aisle. It's rude

to the bride and groom, and it's disrespectful to the Church and God because the wedding is taking place in his house. Don't wear jeans, sweats, tank tops, or anything too provocative, like you belong in a singles' bar.

Don't chew gum. It looks atrocious, and it's disrespectful to chew gum, eat snacks, or drink any beverages in church. Don't smoke or consume any alcohol on church property, either. Don't feel awkward or embarrassed if this is your first time in a Catholic Church.

Don't feel that it's necessary to keep up with all the Catholic gymnastics; if you don't feel comfortable kneeling, stay seated.

Often, after Communion and the final prayer, the bride and groom walk to a statue of Mary. They place some flowers before the statue, while a soloist sings *Ave Maria,* the *Hail Mary* sung in Latin — a traditional Catholic hymn. (See Chapter 13 for details on the *Hail Mary.*) This custom arose from a pious practice of newlyweds asking for Mary's prayers, because Mary's intercession at the wedding feast of Cana prompted her son, Jesus, to change water into wine. So, too, the new husband and wife ask Mary, the Mother of Jesus, to pray to Jesus for them as well.

Finally comes the big announcement: The priest or deacon introduces "Mr. and Mrs. Petruzzi." Then they smooch and exit down the main aisle.

A wedding without a Mass

The Catholic wedding ceremony without a Mass is often celebrated when the bride or groom isn't of the Catholic faith. Without a Mass, Communion doesn't take place. If Communion took place, the non-Catholic wouldn't be able to receive it, because you must be Catholic to receive Communion. (See Chapter 6 for more on Communion.) So to spare any embarrassment, misunderstandings, or hurt feelings, the Church usually suggests a wedding ceremony without Mass for a Catholic and non-Catholic.

The ceremony is the same as the Nuptial Mass (see the preceding "Getting the full treatment" section) in that selections from the Old Testament and New Testament are read, along with a Psalm and a Gospel. The priest or deacon preaches a sermon after proclaiming the Gospel and then the wedding vows are pronounced, followed by the exchange of rings. Some prayers are offered on behalf of the new husband and wife, followed by the *Our Father,* after which the priest or deacon gives the nuptial blessing to the couple. Then comes the sign of peace (a hug and/or kiss), a final prayer, and the big announcement. The difference between the two ceremonies is that in the Nuptial Mass, right after the vows are pronounced and rings exchanged, the Mass continues.

Making it Catholic

A *convalidation ceremony* is needed when a Catholic couple gets married in a civil or non-Catholic ceremony, which makes it an invalid marriage in the eyes of the Church. Even if only one of them is Catholic, it's an invalid sacrament, because Catholics must always follow Church law. If two baptized but non-Catholic Christians get married, however, in a civil ceremony or in any religious denomination, the Catholic Church does recognize that as being valid as long as it's the first marriage for both of them.

After six months or more, if the couple decides to have their civil marriage recognized (sometimes erroneously called having it *blessed*) by the Catholic Church, then a *convalidation* is in order. This is a simple and private ceremony involving the couple, two witnesses, and the priest or deacon. The vows are pronounced, and the rings may be exchanged. If the rings can't be taken off, then they're simply blessed. It's not a renewal of vows but a making of the vows for the first time in the eyes of the Church. The convalidation makes a merely civil marriage a Sacrament of Matrimony.

Convalidations are a way to remedy a hasty decision to marry too soon. If a couple marries in haste but later realizes that, yes, they will remain together, the couple can have the union recognized by God and the Church through convalidation. It's not considered an option but a remedy to an unfortunate situation, because the Church prefers couples to marry validly the first time. Sadly, some couples run off and get married civilly or in a modest non-Catholic ceremony just to avoid a large, elaborate, and expensive Catholic wedding. The Church *never* demands or even suggests *big* weddings with huge bridal parties, stretch limousines, and country club receptions. Brides are allowed that, but if a couple wants a modest, simple, dignified, and reverent ceremony with a few family and friends and without all the high-priced, big-ticket items that often cost thousands of dollars, they can opt for that in the Catholic Church. The Nuptial Mass or the Rite of Marriage Outside of Mass is appropriate in either situation: elaborate or modest, expensive or economical. The choice is that of the bride and groom. What the Church cares about is the spiritual dimension that this is a sacrament and that marriage is a lifelong vocation. Society often places more emphasis on the wedding and less importance on the entire marriage.

If a Catholic gets married by a Justice of the Peace, a captain on a ship, a mayor, or a Protestant minister, and hasn't obtained a dispensation from the local Catholic bishop, then that marriage is invalid, and the Catholic isn't allowed to receive Holy Communion until that union is sanctioned by the Church in a convalidation. This situation often happens when a nonpracticing Catholic doesn't realize that a non-Catholic minister can still marry the couple in a non-Catholic ceremony with the Catholic Church's blessing as long as the couple meets with a priest or deacon and still fulfills all the same Pre-Cana preparations as everyone else. A dispensation from the local bishop is possible and can allow a Catholic bride or groom to be validly married in the eyes of the Church, by a non-Catholic minister, and in a non-Catholic church of the non-Catholic spouse, but the Catholic priest or deacon must fill out the necessary forms, and the couple still has to make the same preparations as other Catholic couples.

Occasionally, a Catholic goes against the advice and laws of the Church and marries a divorced person who hasn't obtained an annulment. This marriage takes place in a civil ceremony or by a non-Catholic minister, but it's not considered valid in the eyes of the Catholic Church. If an annulment is granted later on, and the couple wants to have their union recognized and sanctioned as a valid sacrament, then a convalidation is the appropriate and only remedy.

Because annulments aren't guaranteed, Catholics shouldn't *presume* that they'll get a convalidation after marrying in invalid civil ceremony.

A token of appreciation

If you're asked to be the best man at a Catholic wedding, chances are you'll have a special responsibility. Traditionally, the best man gives a modest honorarium to the priest or deacon on behalf of the bride and groom. That doesn't mean the best man is stuck with the check. Often, the groom and/or bride and/or parents of the groom and/or bride give an envelope with a check to the best man to give to the priest or deacon. (It's a free will offering, depending on personal preference, usually between $100 and $250.) Nowadays, many brides and grooms just handle the honorarium the night before at rehearsal, the same time that they take care of the organist and soloist.

And, while we're on the subject, if altar servers are present, it's also customary for the groom or best man to give each one $10 to $20.

The celibacy issue

Celibacy has been normative for the Latin (Western) Church since the 4th century and mandatory since the 11th. Married clergy, however, always existed in the Byzantine (Eastern) churches. The Latin Church has allowed some married clergy from other Christian denominations to get ordained to the Catholic priesthood if they convert to Catholicism, but typically, Catholic priests of the Latin (Western) Church are celibate.

A man may be ordained when he's single or married if he's Eastern Catholic, but after ordination, a single cleric can't marry, and a married cleric can't remarry if his wife dies, unless they have small children and he receives a dispensation from Rome. Marriage must precede ordination according to Eastern tradition, or it can never be received. This is the ancient tradition of both the Catholic and the Orthodox churches. So even if celibacy were made optional in the Latin Church, it wouldn't affect those who were unmarried at the time of their ordination.

Some Anglican, Episcopalian, and certain Lutheran ministers who are married and wish to convert to become Catholic priests have been allowed to enter the sacred ministry, because their marriage occurred *prior* to their ordination as Catholic clergy. But celibacy has been so much a part of the Western Catholic Church that even scandal won't erode its role and importance.

Holy Orders

Sacred ministers, those who serve the spiritual needs of others, in the Catholic Church are ordained by a bishop and by means of a special sacrament called *Holy Orders,* which creates the hierarchy of deacon, priest, and bishop.

This sacrament can be received only once, just like Baptism and Confirmation, but a man may also be ordained to a higher order up to the third degree. A man must first be ordained a deacon before being ordained a priest, and he must be ordained a deacon and then a priest before being ordained a bishop. So every priest and every bishop has experienced the Sacrament of Holy Orders more than once, yet he can never be re-ordained a deacon, priest or bishop, because it's for life.

Only baptized men can receive the Sacrament of Holy Orders. (For an explanation of why the priesthood is exclusively male, see Chapter 12.)

 Jesus Christ instituted the Sacrament of Holy Orders at the Last Supper simultaneously with his institution of the Sacrament of Holy Eucharist. In order to be able to change bread and wine into the body and blood, soul, and divinity of Christ, you need priests who've been given this power by virtue of their ordination. (See Chapter 6 for a discussion of the Holy Eucharist.)

Bishops receive the highest level of Holy Orders, and it's often said in the Church that bishops have the "fullness of the priesthood," because they alone have the authority to offer all seven sacraments — Baptism, Penance, Holy Eucharist, Matrimony, Anointing of the Sick, Holy Orders, and Confirmation. Priests only have the power and authority (also known as *faculties*) to celebrate five — Baptism, Penance, Holy Eucharist (Mass), Matrimony, and Anointing of the Sick. Deacons can only celebrate two, Baptism and Matrimony, provided that it's a wedding without a Nuptial Mass. In extreme necessities, some sacraments can be performed by a layperson, such as Baptism if an individual's life is in danger or Matrimony in mission countries if clergy aren't available on a regular basis. Normally, though, deacons, priests, and bishops celebrate the sacraments, because one of their primary functions is to administer the sacred rites of the Church to God's people.

Deacons, priests, and bishops receive plenty of pastoral and theological training. Catholic clergy candidates attend *seminary,* the Catholic equivalent to Protestant divinity school. A college degree, however, is a prerequisite for seminary, and then most *seminarians,* students who attend a seminary, start work on a master's degree — Master of Divinity (MDiv) or Master of Arts (MA) — in Theology. Post-college studies can range from four to eight years, depending on the candidate and the diocese he's studying for. Now and then, a few students go farther and earn a Doctorate in philosophy (PhD), theology (STD or ThD), or canon law (JCD).

Having a similar academic background as physicians, lawyers, and Protestant ministers gives the Catholic clergy a good foundation, but the academic background must also be complemented with solid prayer life. Seminarians must also receive *pastoral formation,* which is learning how to listen to people, counsel them, work with others, especially the sick and the needy, and so on, so he can function as a good pastor as well as an adequate theologian.

The Sacrament of Holy Orders doesn't make a man a Church aristocrat, but it does confer the dignity of the sacrament, and that entails the obligation to obey the pope and be of service to the people of God. In previous ages, though, some opportunistic and ambitious men rose through the clerical ranks and used their office of deacon, priest, or bishop to abuse ecclesiastical authority and satisfy personal needs. Nevertheless, the original purpose of Holy Orders was not to create an upper class but to provide spiritual leadership. Pastors are to see their role as shepherds who love and know their sheep instead of seeing their people as servants and peasants.

A leader can retire from the active ministry or be forced to leave if he misbehaves, but no deacon, priest, or bishop can ever have his Holy Orders taken away from him. A *defrocked* or *laicized* cleric can't wear clerical garb, and he can't licitly practice his ordained ministry. Being *defrocked* is involuntary and is imposed as a punishment for committing crime or scandal. *Laicization,* however, is at the request of the cleric who has not done anything immoral but wishes to be relieved of his obligations of celibacy and no longer wants to celebrate his sacred ministry. Both have the same effect: Defrocked and laicized priests can't wear the Roman collar, be called "Father," or publicly celebrate the sacraments. All requests for laicization must go to Rome, and only the Vatican can approve them. A defrocked or laicized cleric isn't given a salary or housing or insurance. He can marry, but he can never celebrate any of the sacraments publicly. The only exception is if a defrocked or laicized priest or bishop runs across a dying Catholic in danger of death *and* no other priest is available. Then the defrocked or laicized priest or bishop can anoint and hear the last confession. Otherwise, though, he's forbidden to ever practice his ordained ministry in public.

Chapter 2 provides detailed information about the rank and file of the Catholic Church and the specific duties of deacons, priests, and bishops.

The Sacraments of Mercy

In addition to the Sacraments of Initiation (Baptism, Holy Eucharist, and Confirmation) and the Sacraments of Community (Matrimony and Holy Orders), the two Sacraments of Mercy are Penance and the Anointing of the Sick.

Penance

Catholics believe that the Holy Mother Church gives birth in the Sacrament of Baptism, nourishes in Holy Eucharist, helps Catholics grow in Confirmation, and heals in the *Sacrament of Penance*.

Medicine and therapy can heal a wounded body, but Catholics believe that only God's grace can heal a wounded soul. That's why Jesus left the Sacrament of Penance to heal our spiritual wounds, which we call *sin*.

Often, people think of sin only as breaking God's laws. Sure, stealing, lying, and murdering break some of the Ten Commandments and are considered sinful. But Catholics believe that God said, "Thou shalt not," because he knew these sinful actions would wound spiritually.

Catholics think of sin is like a bacteria or virus to the soul. When a person lies, cheats, steals, or murders, it's like being infected with millions of deadly germs. The longer the infection is left untreated, the more it spreads and worsens. It wounds and can even kill the life of grace that enables entry into heaven.

Just as tumors are benign or malignant, Catholics believe that sins are venial or mortal. In other words, some sins aren't considered as serious as others and merely inflict a slight wound to the soul, but others are so intrinsically evil that they're considered deadly. They're called *mortal sins,* because they can kill grace. (For more on mortal sin, see Chapter 11.)

The *Sacrament of Penance* (also known as the *Sacrament of Reconciliation* or *Confession*) is for spiritual healing. According to the Gospels, after the Resurrection, Jesus appeared to the apostles, breathed on them, and said, "Receive the Holy Spirit. Whose sins you shall forgive, they are forgiven them; whose sins you shall retain, they are retained," (John 20:22–23).

Because Jesus gave the apostles the power to forgive sins, he must have wanted them to use it. So the Sacrament of Penance has been the very will of Christ from day one.

In the early Church, sins were confessed publicly before the local bishop and the entire community. But because Christians were only clustered into small groups at first, everyone knew what everyone else did anyway. But as Christianity's status changed from persecuted religion to the state religion, more and more members filled the ranks, and admitting faults before a large crowd became more embarrassing and delicate.

In Christianity's beginning, an *Order of Penitents,* public sinners performed public acts of penance. For example, those who denied their Christian faith in court to be spared from death in the arena under the Roman persecution period might perform public act of penance. So, too, a perhaps a person found guilty of stealing or murder, in which case, he'd serve a sentence in prison for his crime, but upon his release, he still needs to be reconciled with the church for his sins. But as more sins became private and less public, such as sins that aren't civil crimes or publicly known matters, the need for private confession arose. Regardless, whether a sin was public or private, only a priest (or bishop) had the power and authority to absolve sin in the name of Jesus Christ.

The Irish monks of the sixth and seventh centuries began the practice of private confessions, which became the norm for the rest of the Church. The manner in which this sacrament is done has developed over time, but the basics have always remained: confession, contrition, penance, and absolution.

Just like the Sacrament of the Holy Eucharist, the Sacrament of Penance may be received many times throughout a person's life. However, the first time that a young Catholic confesses his sins is before his First Communion, which in the Western Church is around the age of reason — 7 years old.

Offering his life in defense of the Seal

The patron of confessors, St. John Nepomucene (1340–93), known as the Martyr of the Confessional, was put to death for his unwillingness to reveal a woman's sins. Around 1393, King Wenceslaus IV, apparently one of those jealous types, demanded that St. John tell the king what the queen had revealed in the confessional. But St. John, honoring the Seal of Confession, wouldn't say a word about it. The king had him tortured, but still, St. John wouldn't reveal the queen's sins. Then the king commanded that St. John be drowned in the river.

You gotta confess

Catholics must confess all known mortal sins to a priest.

To receive the Holy Eucharist without having gone to confession and without receiving absolution for mortal sins makes matters worse. Receiving the Eucharist with mortal sin on your soul is a *sacrilege,* which means using something sacred for an unworthy purpose. It's disrespect for the sacrament and another mortal sin.

If you're seeking God's forgiveness, you can make a perfect act of contrition if you're in danger of death and no priest is available. A *perfect act of contrition* means that the sinner is sorry for his sins out of love for God and remorse for offending him rather than just a fear of punishment in the afterlife, and the sinner must have the absolute intention of going to confession to a priest or bishop as soon as possible if she survives. In situations where no threat to a person's life exists, however, the Church believes that mortal sins can't be forgiven and the soul damns itself to hell without absolution from a priest. The following is a common *Act of Contrition,* a prayer that's often said in the confessional to express the penitent's remorse and desire to avoid sinfulness in the future:

> O my God, I am heartily sorry for having offended Thee. I detest all my sins, because I dread the loss of heaven and fear the pain of hell, but most of all, because I have offended Thee, my God, who art all good and deserving of all my love. I firmly resolve, with the help of Thy grace, to sin no more and to avoid the near occasion of sin. Amen.

Telling sins to a priest isn't as scary as people think. Most people tell sensitive, delicate, and confidential information to their physicians and attorneys, so why not to their pastor? The priest is bound by the most absolute secrecy and confidentiality known to humankind. Not even the pope can get a priest to tell who went to him for confession or what was confessed. The priest must be willing to endure prison, torture, and death before violating the *Seal of Confession,* the secrecy of the sacrament. (See the "Offering his life in defense of the Seal" sidebar in this chapter.)

Over 2,000 years, many bad, immoral, unethical, and unscrupulous priests have existed, and many of them left or were thrown out of the priesthood. But none have ever revealed the secrets they knew from hearing confessions. The fact that even the bad or mediocre ones throughout all of history haven't done so — even after they've left the active ministry or the Catholic religion — is, to Catholics, a great sign of the power of the Holy Spirit protecting the dignity and sanctity of the Sacrament of Penance.

C'mon, priests *never* blab about what they hear in confession? Nope. Never. What's ironic is that some people who say they wouldn't or couldn't ever confess their sins to a human being, priest or not, have no trouble whatsoever going on national television and telling millions of people their deepest, darkest family secrets. Go figure. To see one of the finest and classic portrayals of the priesthood and the Seal of Confession on film, see Alfred Hitchcock's *I Confess* (1953; Warner Bros.) with Montgomery Clift and Anne Baxter.

The confidentiality of the sacrament is so strict and sacred that even enemies of the Church are often in awe of its endurance. The absolute secrecy ensures that anything can be confessed without fear of any retaliation, reaction, or response. Knowing that the priest can never tell anyone anything he hears gives penitents the strength and courage to confess everything.

If a priest does violate the seal of secrecy of the Sacrament of Penance, he's automatically excommunicated, and only the pope can give him absolution for such a crime. (For more on excommunication, see Chapter 9.)

Confession may take place in one of three different ways:

- ✔ **Private confession** is the most common form of confession. The *penitent* (person telling his sins) goes into a Catholic church and enters a *confessional,* also known as a *reconciliation room* or *penance room.* One is shown in Figure 7-1.

  Although some older confessionals don't allow the penitent the option of seeing the priest and confessing face-to-face, the newer penance rooms give the penitent the choice of kneeling behind a screen, just like in the older confessionals, and maintaining anonymity, or confessing face-to-face, thus revealing the penitent's identity (if only by face) to the priest.

  The person confesses all known and remembered mortal sins since the last confession. Venial sins may be and are encouraged to be confessed, but all mortal sins must be. If a person has no mortal sins or simply wants to include their venial sins with the mortal sins they need to confess, then telling the priest all your sins is a helpful thing, like telling the doctor about your minor aches and pains as well as the serious injuries. The best part is that any forgotten sins are also forgiven. Only the ones intentionally withheld make the sacrament invalid. The priest then gives a penance to be done by the penitent and gives absolution.

This form of confession happens almost every Saturday afternoon or evening in every parish around the world. A priest sits in a confessional every week, waiting for parishioners to confess. St. John Vianney (1786–1859), the patron saint of parish priests, heard confessions for nearly 20 straight hours, but most priests hear confessions for about 30 to 90 minutes straight every weekend.

But Catholics don't have to wait just for Saturday to go to confession. They can ask the priest to hear their confession anytime it's convenient. It's just easier and more practical for people to take advantage of the "man in the box" whenever possible.

✔ **Parish Penance services** are the second form of confession. Usually during Advent (before Christmas) and Lent (before Easter), parishes get several priests to visit as *confessors* — priests hearing the confessions. The whole congregation sings a hymn, listens to a Scripture reading, hears a brief sermon, and then everyone prays the *Act of Contrition* together as a group. Next, people individually go to a priest of their choosing, verbally confess *at least* all mortal sins in confidence, get a penance, and receive absolution.

Figure 7-1: Confessional in St. Peter's Basilica in Rome.

© Michael S. Yamashita/CORBIS

This form of confession is helpful, because often before Christmas and Easter — times of year when faith is foremost on people's minds — the lines for confessions on Saturdays are longer than the check-out lines in the stores.

✔ **General confession and absolution** is the third and most rare form. In a time of war, natural disaster, or when lives are in danger, if a large number of sinners can't logistically get to confession, because only one priest is available to hear the confessions of a couple hundred penitents, and it's too difficult for the people to come back next week, the priest can ask the bishop for permission to give general absolution without individual confession.

Simply having a large crowd and one priest isn't a serious enough reason to give general absolution. It's not like a spiritual car wash. General absolution without individual confession is valid only if the local bishop gives permission *and* for a grave and serious reason, such as when Three Mile Island nuclear power plant incident occurred in 1979. And the proviso is stated that all persons taking advantage of general absolution make a private confession as soon as possible — first chance they get if they survive — and confess at least all their mortal sins, including those that they had on their souls when they had the general confession.

Soldiers and sailors going off to battle are often given general absolution by the Catholic chaplain. If they survive, they must make a private confession as soon as possible.

Are you really, truly sorry?

Confessing all known mortal sins is the first step in this sacrament. Being truly sorry for them should go without saying, but we want to say it anyway: The contrition (sorrow) for sins must be genuine. The priest gives everyone the benefit of the doubt, but no one can fool God. If a man confesses the sin of adultery but isn't sorry — just sorry that his wife caught him — then none of his sins are absolved (forgiven), venial or mortal, because he made a bad confession. Verbal confession must coincide with interior contrition for the sin.

It's absolutely necessary for the Catholic to confess all known and previously unconfessed mortal sins. Any and all venial sins committed since the last confession may be and are encouraged to be confessed as well.

Perfect contrition is being sorry for your sins merely, because God is good and sin offends him. *Imperfect contrition* is being sorry, because you fear the pains of hell. The church believes that either will do, but perfect is obviously better. Still, when you're in a weak moment, those images of fire and brimstone can help keep you on the straight and narrow.

Spiritual ER

When you go to the doctor's office for a visit, you must tell the physician what's wrong before she can diagnose the problem and prescribe the remedy. Confession is like a spiritual checkup. The *penitent,* the person telling her sins, must tell the *confessor,* the priest hearing Confession, what her sins (symptoms) are, so the confessor can offer the proper advice and prescription. A confessor isn't a spiritual attorney or lawyer, but a spiritual physician. He does judge an appropriate penance, but only God judges whether the person is truly sorry for their sins. Someone can fake it and lie to the confessor and merely claim to be sorry (have contrition) for their sins, but they only fool the priest and not God. Without real sorrow, the sacrament doesn't work.

Withholding info from the confessor is as dangerous as withholding info from your doctor. Sin is a disease to the soul, and confession is like the ER; the spiritual physician (your confessor) needs to hear your problems and give treatment (absolution). The prescription is your penance.

So after you list your sins, the priest asks you to say an *Act of Contrition,* but you have to really mean what you're saying. Just as the responsibility for receiving the Holy Eucharist without being in the state of mortal sin rests with the conscience of the individual, the validity of the penitent's confession rests with the penitent and his own conscience. The priest doesn't know whether you're in the state of mortal sin, whether you're telling all your sins, whether you're really sorry, or whether you really intend not to avoid committing sin again, but you do. So only you and God know the exact state of your soul.

Doing penance

After you confess your sins, the priest gives you a penance to perform. In olden days, the penance was often to make a pilgrimage to the Holy Land and visit the shrines where Jesus lived, preached, suffered, and died. Later, when the trip became too dangerous, expensive, and impractical, smaller penances were created.

Nowadays, a penance may be to do something nice for your enemy every day for a week or every week for a month. It may be to visit a nursing home or hospital one day a week for a month. It may be to donate time to a soup kitchen or clothing bank. It may involve any one of the corporal or spiritual works of mercy (see Chapter 11). On the other hand, quite often, the penance is a set of prayers, such as saying the *Our Father* or the *Hail Mary* (see Chapter 13) five to ten times.

Whatever the penance, it's merely a token, because Catholics believe that the sacrifice of Christ on the cross is what made atonement for our sins. Your penance is for your benefit — to remind yourself that God comes first and you come last.

Absolving the sinner

Before you do the penance but after you're told what it is and you agree to do it (if you really can't perform the penance the priest assigns, tell him and he'll give you a different one), then the priest gives his sacramental absolution:

> God the Father of mercies through the death and resurrection of his Son has reconciled the world to himself and sent the Holy Spirit among us for the forgiveness of sins. Through the ministry of the Church may God give you pardon and peace, and I absolve you from all your sins, in the name of the Father, and of the Son and of the Holy Spirit. Amen.

If the person shows no sorrow or no firm purpose of amendment, then the priest can't give absolution. For example, if a man confesses to being in an adulterous relationship but refuses to end it and go back to his wife, the priest can't give absolution, because the man not only fails to feel sorrow but he intends to continue committing this sin — he has no firm purpose of amending his life. Also, if the person fakes out the priest by only pretending to be sorry, the absolution is invalid, because you can't fool God.

Only a priest or bishop (which includes cardinals and popes) can give absolution. Deacons don't have the power to celebrate this sacrament.

Anointing of the Sick

This sacrament was called *Extreme Unction* (last anointing), not because it was the last sacrament you received before checking out of this life but because it was the last anointing a person received. Baptism and Confirmation were the first two times a person would've been anointed. It was commonly called *Last Rites,* because before antibiotics and penicillin, more people died than recovered from disease and injury.

Modern medicine has given folks tremendous hope for recovery and remission from diseases, and many surgeries are now quite successful, unlike the days before blood transfusions, sterile instruments, and anesthesia. Back then, when sickness and injury usually resulted in death, Catholics called for the priest to anoint based on St. James' Epistle: "Are there any sick among you? Then let them send for the priests and let the priest pray over them, anointing them with oil." (James 4:14).

When the sick and injured weren't expected to survive, Extreme Unction was the sign that no more could be done, so the sick and injured were spiritually preparing for death. That's why even today, many of the elderly freak out when the Catholic hospital chaplain brings his purple stole and oils. They presume the worse and only see the sacrament as the beginning of the end.

In reality, the Anointing of the Sick is to offer prayers for possible recovery, but the more important intention is to give strength to the soul of the sick person. Often, when people are sick, they get discouraged, depressed, angry, annoyed, and afraid. The Church believes that the sacrament offers a special grace to calm the spirit. If physical recovery is God's will, so be it. If not, then the person needs the grace, strength, and encouragement to bear the illness with dignity. The Sacrament of Anointing of the Sick also remits (absolves) all sins the person is sorry for but did not previously confess in the Sacrament of Penance. On occasion, there isn't time for the person to make a confession, or the person is unconscious or not lucid enough to make a confession, so the anointing compensates by forgiving sins, which the person would've confessed were he able to do so. Because of this aspect of absolving sins, deacons can't anoint, but priests and bishops can.

The Anointing of the Sick involves using Oil of the Sick *(oleum infirmorum)* — olive oil blessed by the bishop during Holy Week. Anointing with oil is not a magical or good-luck gesture but a sincere sign of supernatural assistance to coincide with the physical medicine and treatment already being given. Those suffering are reminded of St. Paul's words: "Now I rejoice in my sufferings for your sake, and in my flesh I am filling up what is lacking in the afflictions of Christ on behalf of his body, which is the Church," (Colossians 1:24), and "For as Christ's sufferings overflow to us, so through Christ does our encouragement also overflow," (2 Corinthians 1:5). Catholic Christians firmly believe in *redemptive suffering,* whereby a person willingly offers up their personal aches and pains, trials and tribulations with Christ on the Cross.

The Catholic notion of redemptive suffering, that is, uniting your own suffering with the crucified Jesus gives a person's unavoidable suffering meaning and purpose. This notion is explicitly and implicitly expressed in the Sacrament of the Anointing of the Sick. Most of the time, it's the innocent who suffer, and guilty sinners seem to escape pain and misery. So instead of seeing suffering as a punishment, Catholics are asked to see suffering as (in the words of Mother Teresa of Calcutta) being personally kissed and embraced by the Crucified Lord. He holds us so close and so tight; we can feel the nails and thorns in our own body (analogously, of course).

Because many sick and injured people recover nowadays, or at least go into remission, Catholics are able to receive the Sacrament of Anointing of the Sick more than once — as many times as needed. The elderly, people with many ailments, and those with a deadly or serious disease, chronic pain and suffering, or recurring illness, can and should be anointed often.

Some Catholics see Anointing of the Sick as a spiritual oil change, and feel that every three months (or 3,000 miles) is a good time to anoint the bedridden, people in nursing homes, and others with chronic and pathological conditions. The following is a side note from one of us, Father Trigilio:

When my brother Michael was alive and suffering from muscular dystrophy, and when my dad was alive and endured his leukemia, I often anointed them whenever I came home to visit, which was often every three months or so.

Some parishes have a Mass of Anointing once or twice a year for the sick of the parish. (That's not people who're sick of the parish. It's parishioners who are sick.) The only caveat is that often, people with minor illnesses, aches, and pains and those suffering from nonphysical conditions that aren't life threatening want to be anointed, but the sacrament is for those in danger of death or in serious and critical condition medically speaking. In minor cases, a prayer for healing is appropriate. The sacrament shouldn't be overused or trivialized for every upset stomach and toe ache.

Many older Catholics have a "sick call set" crucifix hanging on the wall. This special crucifix opens up in preparation for the priest to make a *sick call*, a visit to the sick to anoint them, and inside are two white beeswax candles, a bottle of holy water, and a white cloth. The cloth is placed on a table near the sick person before the priest arrives to anoint him. The crucifix is laid on top of the cloth, and the two candles are put in their holders and lit, unless the patient is on oxygen, in which case, *no candles*. A family member greets the priest and escorts him to the sick person's room, which is *quiet*. In other words, the television isn't blaring *Who Wants To Be A Millionaire* or *Wheel of Fortune*. The priest anoints the sick person, and if able, the person receives Holy Communion, too. Holy Communion given to a dying person is called *viaticum*, which is Latin for *something for the journey*. The person and room are sprinkled with holy water.

The Catholic Church suggests that a dying person have a crucifix nearby to meditate on, a rosary, a Bible, holy water, and candles, if safe to use. These items make the setting sacred because the suffering person is going through his own form of Calvary and literally walking with the Lord as he approaches the place where Jesus was crucified.

The priest sticks his finger in the oil stock, which often has cotton squished inside to absorb the oil and keep it from spilling and going bad. He dabs some on his thumb and then anoints the head, saying, "Through this holy anointing may the Lord in his love and mercy help you with the grace of the Holy Spirit." Then, if possible, he anoints the palms of the person, saying, "May the Lord Who frees you from your sins, save you and raise you up." If it's an emergency, such as a patient in the trauma center, the priest can anoint any part of the body that's available if the doctors and nurses are working on the head and hands of the injured person.

Priests and bishops aren't anointed on the palms when given the Sacrament of the Anointing of the Sick, because their hands were already anointed at their ordination. Priests and bishops are anointed on the back of the hands instead.

Chapter 8

Celebrating the Catholic Mass

- -

In This Chapter

▶ Re-presenting Christ's sacrifice

▶ Discovering the various parts of the Mass

▶ Knowing when to stand, sit, or kneel

▶ Following the Church calendar

- -

*T*he *Mass,* or more precisely, the *Holy Sacrifice of the Mass,* is the most important, central, and sacred act of worship in Catholicism. This is because the Holy Eucharist is "the source and summit of Christian Life" (*Lumen Gentium;* 1964). Catholics believe that during the Mass, the priest changes the bread and wine into the Body and Blood of Christ, called the *Holy Eucharist,* which describes the liturgical act of worship itself or the end result or fruit of it.

Catholics profess that the Holy Eucharist can only happen by means of the Mass, and they give the same respect and adoration to the Holy Eucharist that's due to God. So it only makes sense that the Mass is central to Catholicism. It's not the only thing that they do or believe, but it's the center of their belief as they firmly maintain that Jesus Christ is really, truly, and substantially present in the Holy Eucharist. It's no wonder then that the Mass is sometimes referred to as the *Eucharistic Liturgy.* The word *Eucharist* comes from the Greek *eucharistein* meaning *thanksgiving,* and the word *liturgy* comes from the Greek word *leitourgia* meaning *public worship.* Several terms describe this essential and vital part of Catholic worship and belief:

- ✔ Breaking of the Bread

- ✔ Divine Liturgy

- ✔ Eucharistic Liturgy

- ✔ Holy Eucharist

- ✔ Holy Mass

- ✔ Holy Sacrifice of the Mass

- ✔ Lord's Supper

The phrase *Sacrifice of the Mass* may appear as though Catholics are trying to add to the one sacrifice of Christ on the cross on the original Good Friday, but the Sacrifice of the Mass isn't separate from the sacrifice that Christ offered on Calvary in A.D. 33. It's the same sacrifice reenacted in an unbloody manner.

Being God, Jesus' sacrifice on the cross isn't limited to space and time as it would be if he were only human. His divinity made his sacrifice eternal. It's not that his sacrifice 2,000 years ago wasn't good enough. Rather, it was so perfect and powerful that it can never be ended or repeated. It's eternal, because sins are still being forgiven even two millennia after his death.

The Church maintains that without all the blood and gore of the physical Crucifixion, the Sacrifice of the Mass re-presents (*not* represents) the same

- ✔ **Offering:** Jesus is the *Victim* at the Mass
- ✔ **Person making the offering:** Jesus is the *Priest* at the Mass
- ✔ **Effect:** The remission of sins

Jesus actually offers himself through the priest, making the offering on behalf of the people to God the Father. As victim, he's also the one being sacrificed. The Mass is the primary worship ceremony celebrated all over the world, in exactly the same way, every day of the week. The Mass embodies all that Catholics believe, all that they do, and how they do it. The Mass sums up all the doctrines of the Church, expresses how Catholics should live, and gives them the means to do it. To understand the Mass is to understand Catholicism. In this chapter, we help you do just that.

What Exactly Is the Mass?

The *Mass* is the sacred rite — the formal, official worship service of Catholicism. It incorporates the Bible (Sacred Scripture), prayer, sacrifice, hymns, symbols, gestures, sacred food for the soul, and directions on how to live a Catholic life — all this in one ceremony.

In the English language, the word *mass* describes a large group of people or a scientific characteristic of matter. But the word means something completely different in the context of the Holy Sacrifice of the Mass. To explain it, we need to briefly explain some language. This may seem a bit technical, but it won't take long — promise.

Honoring the Sabbath publicly

Mass, being the supreme act of worship, is the only way that a Catholic can fulfill the Third Commandment to keep holy the Sabbath day. On the seventh day of creation (Genesis 2:3), God established the *Sabbath* as a day of rest and the Day of the Lord. (See Chapter 10 for more on the Ten Commandments.) Even though the Jewish Sabbath is Saturday, the Last Supper took place on Holy Thursday, and Jesus died on Good Friday, the main focus of Christianity is that Christ rose from the dead on the first Easter Sunday. Therefore, Sunday is the Christian Sabbath. It's the day that Catholic Christians go to church to participate in the Mass.

You can pray anywhere and anytime and read the Bible alone or with others whenever and wherever you want, but you must go to church to attend Mass. Catholics can't just get together and hold Mass at home or someplace that's mutually convenient. Only an ordained priest can say the Mass. It can only occur through the exercised authority of an ordained priest, bishop, or pope. Attending Mass is important, because it connects the Catholic believer to other believers and to the universal, as well as local, Church. Missing Mass on Sunday or on a holy day of obligation is a mortal sin, unless bad weather, illness, or a real emergency prevents it. (For more on mortal sin, see Chapter 7.)

The Church professes that at the Mass, three levels of the Church converge and are united with one another, which is what the word *communion* means. The *Apostles' Creed* (see Chapters 3 and 13) uses the term *the communion of saints*, which refers to the three levels of the Church: the saints in heaven, the believers on earth, and the souls in purgatory. All three levels of the Church render worship and adoration to God. All those in heaven, on earth, and in purgatory unite at Mass so that all God's servants join in prayer. This social dimension is central to Catholicism. It's definitely not a religion of individualism but one of community. (See Chapter 15 for more information about the communion of saints.)

The cross has been a symbol of Christianity since the Crucifixion of Jesus on Good Friday. A cross itself is an intersection of a vertical line and a horizontal line, which can also symbolize the personal relationship that the believer has with God (vertical) and the social relationship that the believer has with his neighbor (horizontal). The Mass focuses on the cross and therefore stresses both relationships — the one with the Lord and the one with others.

Participating fully

Catholicism asks for more than the mere physical attendance of the congregation at Mass. The full, conscious, and active participation of the faithful is required by singing, praying, speaking, sitting, kneeling, and so on. The priest is the leader of the prayers during Mass, but the prayers of the people join his. His and their prayers are different at times and the same at other times. If the priest is standing and the people are kneeling, such as during the Eucharistic Prayer, both the priest and the congregation are participating through their own gestures and responses. Full, active, and conscious participation isn't limited to location or action. The people are kneeling in the pews, and the priest is near the altar, and still both can participate fully.

In addition to participation through verbal responses and physical gestures, interior participation, which counts more than anything else, also occurs. Every person should be communicating with God at Mass. Being disposed to, cooperative with, and willing to accept the supernatural divine graces being bestowed at the Mass should be the goal of all present. The music may be a little flat, the singing slightly off key, and the preaching sometimes boring, but the bottom line is that which can't be seen or heard — the spiritual benefits to the soul.

Uniting past, present, and future

The Catholic Church professes that the Mass isn't just a reenactment of the Last Supper, when Jesus took bread and wine and said the words, "This is My body," and "This is My blood," (Matthew 26:26–29). More than a ceremonial reenactment of an ancient ritual, the Mass combines past, present, and future at the same time:

- ✔ **Past:** The exact words and elements that Jesus used at the Last Supper on Holy Thursday are used faithfully and precisely.

- ✔ **Present:** The Mass brings grace, nourishment, and instruction for the people who are present.

- ✔ **Future:** It foreshadows the sacred banquet in heaven. Jesus often spoke of a heavenly banquet or wedding feast where guests would be well fed, lasting for eternity and surviving well after the world ends.

The Mass is pivotal, because it transports the participants back in time to Christ's Last Supper with his apostles, Christ's Passion and death on the cross, and his Resurrection and the empty tomb on the first Easter Sunday. The same words that Jesus spoke at the Last Supper are used to consecrate the same things that Jesus used back then — bread and wine — during the Sacrament of Holy Eucharist. The same sacrifice is offered — namely, the Son is sacrificed to the Father on behalf of all humankind. The same *risen* Christ comes to enter the soul of each person at Holy Communion when the congregation eat and drink his *living* (risen, not dead) flesh and blood.

St. Thomas Aquinas (see Chapters 9 and 18), a 13th century Dominican theologian, said that the Holy Eucharist, particularly at Mass, reminds the faithful of what Jesus did for humankind in the *past,* makes him *present* in the *Real Presence,* the consecrated bread and wine, and promises the faithful the *future* glory of heaven by giving food for eternal life. Therefore, Catholics see the Mass as the summit and zenith of all Christian worship. To Catholics, the

Mass incorporates the inspired Word of God in Scripture, and it makes present the word made flesh in the Holy Eucharist. (See the section, "Saying the Eucharistic Prayer," later in this chapter, for more details.)

If you keep on reading, you'll see that the Mass also gives directions through the readings and prayers said at Mass on how to live a Christian life:

- Being willing to sacrifice for others, as Jesus did
- Being obedient to the will of God
- Listening to his word
- Putting his word into practice

The Two Parts of the Mass

The first part of the Mass in the Western (Latin) Church is the *Liturgy of the Word,* and its main focus is on Bible readings as an integral part of daily and weekly worship. The second part is the *Liturgy of the Eucharist,* and its main focus is the holiest and most sacred part of the Mass — Holy Eucharist.

Eastern Catholics call their Mass the *Divine Liturgy,* but it's essentially the same. The Eastern Divine Liturgy is divided into four parts:

1. Preparation of the Gifts
2. Office of Antiphons
3. Service of the Word
4. Eucharistic Service

But Eastern Catholics also use the two-fold division of: *Liturgy of the Catechumens* and *Liturgy of the Faithful,* which coincide with the *Liturgy of the Word* and the *Liturgy of the Eucharist.* The differences are merely from the fact that in the West, the Mass follows the tradition of the Roman liturgy, but in the East, it's the liturgical tradition of Constantinople. We'll look more closely at the Western liturgy, because it's the most common, keeping in mind that both are full and equal rites in the Catholic Church.

The Liturgy of the Word

To signal the beginning of the Mass, the congregation, often led by an organist and choir, stand and sing an entrance hymn, while the priest, deacon, reader, servers, and if needed, the *extraordinary ministers* (laypersons who help the priest distribute Holy Communion) march down the aisle from the back of the church to the altar area in front. An opening song sets the proper mood and perspective for sacred worship. If the tabernacle (see Chapter 16) is in the center of the sanctuary, the priest and anyone passing in front of it genuflects as a sign of respect and recognition that Christ is truly present in the Holy Eucharist. Then the priest kisses the altar, and the priest and deacon bow before it, because it represents Christ. The belief is that the Holy Eucharist *is* Christ, and the altar only *represents* Christ. Then the priest, deacon, and servers go to their respective seats in the sanctuary but stay standing, while the sign of the cross officially begins the Mass.

Catholics begin and end every prayer and sacrament with the sign of the cross. It's one of the trademarks of Catholicism.

Acknowledging sin

The priest gives a short greeting, and then the *Penitential Rite* takes place. This isn't a general confession or general absolution. It doesn't replace the Sacrament of Penance, and it doesn't count as going to confession. (See Chapter 7 for details about the Sacrament of Penance.) The Penitential Rite is merely a public acknowledgement that everyone is a sinner and has sinned to some degree during the week, be it big or small. Usually, the rite starts with everyone saying the *Confiteor,* which is Latin for *I confess:*

> I confess to almighty God, and to you, my brothers and sisters, that I have sinned through my own fault, in my thoughts and in my words, in what I have done, and in what I have failed to do; and I ask blessed Mary, ever virgin, all the angels and saints, and you, my brothers and sisters, to pray for me to the Lord our God.

The Confiteor is followed by the *kyrie,* which is Greek for *Lord* as in *Kyrie eleison* or *Lord have mercy* and also *Christe eleison* or *Christ have mercy.* The rite expresses public guilt and shame for any sins against God, because committing sin is also an offense and a wound to the faith community.

St. Paul the Apostle described the Church as the body of Christ (1 Corinthians 12:12–13, 27) and the believers as the individual parts of that body. Catholics believe that just as the body is one and has many parts, and all the parts of the body, though many, are part of one body, so it is with Christ. For one Spirit baptized all into one body — Jews or Greeks, slaves or free — and all were made to drink of one Spirit.

If one or more parts are damaged or diseased, the whole body hurts. If one person sins, it affects all those present, because everyone is interconnected. That's the reason for the need to apologize to God and to neighbor. In the Parable of the Prodigal (Luke 15:11–32), the wayward boy comes home and seeks forgiveness of his father, but the father also patiently waits for the son to come home where he belongs. In terms of the Penitential Rite, the congregation is like the wayward boy. The Church is home. And God is the patient father. Likewise, the Penitential Rite symbolizes that everyone is a sinner to some degree and that everyone owns up to it before God and before each other. It expresses regret for sins committed and *sins of omission* (what you should've done but chose not to do), and asks that we pray for each other.

Praying the Gloria and an opening prayer

After the Penitential Rite comes the *Gloria* if the Mass is held on Sunday or a holy day of obligation. This ancient hymn recalls the singing angels at Christmas in Bethlehem who sang at Christ's birth, "Glory to God in the highest, and peace on earth to men of good will. . . ." (Luke 2:13–14) (See the section "Dressing for the Occasion," later in this chapter, for more on the holy days of obligation.)

> Glory to God in the highest, and peace to his people on earth. Lord God, heavenly King, almighty God and Father, we worship you, we give you thanks, we praise you for your glory. Lord Jesus Christ, only Son of the Father, Lord God, Lamb of God, you take away the sin of the world: have mercy on us; you are seated at the right hand of the Father: receive our prayer. For you alone are the Holy One, you alone are the Lord, you alone are the Most High, Jesus Christ, with the Holy spirit, in the glory of God the Father. Amen.

Traditionally, Catholicism has four kinds of prayer:

- ✔ **Adoration:** Praising God
- ✔ **Contrition:** Asking for God's forgiveness
- ✔ **Petition:** Asking God for a favor
- ✔ **Thanksgiving:** Showing God gratitude

The Church believes that the Mass is the highest and supreme form of prayer, so it has all four elements in it. The Gloria is the adoration part of prayer, whereas the Confiteor and Penitential Rite are the contrition part. Later in the Mass, after the homily (sermon) and the Nicene Creed, comes the Prayer of the Faithful, also known as the General Intercessions, which is a prayer of petition. The thanksgiving part comes after Holy Communion, when gratitude is shown for all the graces given at Mass.

After the Gloria, an opening prayer addresses all three persons of the Holy Trinity (Father, Son, and Holy Spirit) and usually sets the tone for the rest of the prayers and Bible readings at Mass. In a sense, it provides a theme for that Mass. Every Sunday, holy day, and feast day (honoring a saint) has its own unique prayers and readings, depending on the time of year or priority of the feast. (See the section, "Spiritual Seasons of the Year," later in the chapter.)

During each element of the Liturgy of the Word that we've described so far, the priest, deacon, and congregation stand throughout.

Reading Scripture

Any qualified *lector,* a layperson trained for the task of reading at Mass, can read the Old and New Testament. Lectors prepare each day or week to read Sacred Scripture at Mass. Everyone sits during the readings, while the lector stands in front near the altar and reads aloud. On Sundays, a selection from the Old Testament is read, as well as a Psalm, which is usually set to music and sung, and then a selection from one of the New Testament Epistles or from the Acts of the Apostles is read. The Acts of the Apostles is the book immediately after the Gospels and before the Epistles, and the Epistles are the letters of Saints Paul, James, Jude and John.

Usually, a musical arrangement of the word *Alleluia* is sung just before the reading of the Gospel, a passage from the New Testament Gospels of Matthew, Mark, Luke, or John. *Alleluia* is the Latin version of the Greek word *allelouia,* an expression of praise and joy that, in turn, comes from the Hebrew *hallelu-jah* for *praise the Lord.* This is the high point of the Bible readings, and it's the cue to stand. (Or the cue is when the priest or deacon stands up.) This change from sitting to standing shows the preeminence of the Gospels in their relationship to the other books of the Bible. The entire Bible is inspired, but the Gospels are special, because they contain the very words and deeds of Christ. So, Catholics stand when the Gospels are read, but remain seated, while the other parts of the Bible are read at Mass.

Only a deacon, priest, or bishop can read the Gospel at Mass. Sometimes, the Gospel book is also *incensed,* meaning that incense is burned in a container (called a *thurible* or *censor*) over the pages of the Gospel about to be read. Incense is a symbol of prayer rising up to heaven and recognition of the presence of divinity. The Gospels are incensed, because Christ is present whenever his words are read from the Bible.

The Bible plays an important role in daily Catholic prayer. The words of the Mass aren't just made-up mumbo jumbo; they're carefully selected from the Bible. The Gloria, Psalm, Old and New Testament readings, and so on, are all straight out of Scripture, which is also read during each of the seven sacraments.

The Church chooses the sacred texts to be read during a specific Mass; it isn't up to the priest or deacon. Each Sunday, the readings follow a three-year cycle (A, B, and C); the Gospels of Matthew, Mark, and Luke take precedence, with the Gospel of John sprinkled in here and there. After three years, if you go to Mass every Sunday, you'll have heard and been exposed to all four Gospels as well as most of the New Testament writings and Epistles. But the readings at the weekday Mass (Monday through Saturday morning) work a little differently. The weekday Mass uses a two-year cycle (I and II), because only two readings are done during the week — versus the three on the weekend. (See Table 8-1 in this chapter for more on the cyclical nature of the readings at Mass.) All even numbered years (2004, 2006, and so on) are Year II for daily biblical readings.

Because, on any given day, the readings are the same in every Catholic Church all over the world and also to prevent having Bible pages flipped all over the place, the Catholic Church uses a book called the *Lectionary.* This book, usually bound with a red cover, contains only readings from Sacred Scripture — nothing else. If it's not a book in the Bible, it's not in the Lectionary. The difference between the Lectionary and the Bible is merely the order and sequence of the writings. Lectionary readings are usually excerpts (*pericopes* or *cuttings*) not necessarily complete whole chapters. (See the "As easy as A, B, C" sidebar, in this chapter, for more on the Lectionary.)

The option exists to use a Book of the Gospels, which is exactly that, a book just containing the Gospels (Matthew, Mark, Luke and John). The Lectionary is still used in this case for the Old Testament, Psalm, and New Testament Epistle, but the priest or deacon would read from the Gospel Book rather than the Lectionary. This is to give more solemnity to the very special part of the Bible for Christians, which is the Gospel, because it contains what Jesus said and did. The Book of the Gospels is carried in the procession at the beginning of Mass and may be incensed by the priest or deacon before it's read.

As easy as A, B, C

At Mass, the congregation doesn't need to bring a Bible and follow along, because the priest, deacon, and lector read aloud from the *Lectionary* — a book that meets the specific needs of the Catholic Mass. The Lectionary only contains biblical readings, but they're arranged in a different order than the Bible. The Bible begins with Genesis and ends with Revelation (Apocalypse). The lectionary, however, begins with the Scripture readings for the first Sunday of the year and ends with those for the last Sunday. The Lectionary lists the readings for the first Sunday of Year A — an Old Testament reading, a Psalm, a New Testament Epistle, and a Gospel — followed by the readings for the first Sunday of liturgical Year B, and then Year C. The readings for the second Sunday of Year A, B, and C then follow the readings for the first Sunday, and so on.

The Lectionary is nothing more than Bible selections put together in such a way so that the person reading the Sacred Scriptures only has to read one or two pages side by side instead of going back and forth from one end of the Bible to the other, trying to find the chapter and verse needed. The Lectionary conveniently organizes the Scripture readings Sunday-by-Sunday and weekday-by-weekday.

One major drawback of the Lectionary is that although most Catholics know their Scripture readings from Mass, when asked to find the same readings in the Bible, they sometimes can't, because the Bible is arranged one way and the Lectionary another.

Because, as we discuss in Chapter 3, Catholicism is a religion based on the complete written and unwritten Word of God, more emphasis is placed on the Word as it is *proclaimed* (read aloud) rather than as *read* by people in their pews. Yet, to help those who can't hear too well and for those who want to read along — many Catholic parishes have a people's version of the altar *missal* (books containing all the prayers and Scripture readings used at Mass) or abridged seasonal versions in the pews to help the congregation follow the prayers and Scripture readings, including those of the priest.

The Roman Missal is the official book the priest uses at Mass, containing all the prayers that he must say as well as telling him what to do and how to do it. In some countries it's also known as a *Sacramentary* to distinguish it from the Lectionary, the book containing the Scripture readings.

 Whether you attend Mass or not, you can go online to see what the readings are for any day of the month at the United States Conference of Catholic Bishops Web site (www.usccb.org). You may notice that even though the selected readings for a particular day are from different parts of the Bible, they share a common theme. Several places on the Internet allow you to see and hear the Mass online as well.

Hearing the homily

After standing for the Gospel, the congregation sits and listens to the homily, which is different than a sermon.

- **Sermon:** Any explanation and reflection on the Word of God.
- **Homily:** A sermon that's preached at Mass after the Gospel is read and only by clergy — deacons, priests, or bishops. According to canon law, the local bishop may allow laity and religious brothers and sisters to preach a sermon under certain conditions, but they're never allowed to preach the homily itself.

The priest or deacon connects the Scripture readings to the daily lives of the people, the teachings of the Church, or the particular celebration at hand, such as a wedding or funeral.

Reciting the Creed

On Sundays and holy days, the homily is followed by the *Creed* (Profession of Faith), which is ordinarily the ancient Nicene Creed of A.D. 325. The Apostles' Creed, an ancient symbol of Baptism, *may* be used during Lent and Easter time and occasionally at Masses for children. The entire congregation stands to sing or recite the Creed. At the words *by the power of the Holy Spirit . . . became man,* all make a profound bow to show respect for the *Incarnation,* from the Latin word *caro* for flesh. The *Incarnation* refers to Jesus' taking on human flesh — being conceived in the womb of his mother. On Solemnities of the Annunciation (March 25) and Christmas (December 25), all kneel instead of just bowing.

The Creed succinctly sums up all that the *Magisterium* (the teaching authority of the Church; see Chapter 2) has taught for the past 2,000 years. See Chapter 3 for more information on the Creed.

Like the Boy Scout oath or the Hippocratic oaths that medical professionals recite, the Creed is a Christian oath, stating what Catholics believe as revealed to them by God through Sacred Scripture and Sacred Tradition.

Praying the General Intercessions

After the Creed, the *General Intercessions* (Prayer of the Faithful) takes place. The lector or deacon reads several petitions aloud, and the people respond to each one with "Lord, hear our prayer" or "Hear us, O Lord." The petitions are for the pope, the Church, the civil authorities, current concerns, and so on. For example, you may hear the lector say, "For Pope John Paul and all religious leaders, that they may preach the Word of God and teach the truths of our faith with fidelity and courage, let us pray to the Lord."

The Liturgy of the Eucharist

The second half of the Mass focuses on offering: the collection offering, the offering of the bread and wine to be consecrated, the sacrifice itself, the Consecration by the priest, and the Holy Communion of the faithful.

Gathering the offerings

As the Liturgy of the Eucharist begins, everyone sits down for the collection of offerings. Sometimes, a basket is passed from one end of the pew to the next, person by person. Traditionally, however, ushers pass the basket: Starting in front of the church and moving pew by pew to the back, the ushers extend a collection basket with a very long handle in front of each person. Either way is acceptable.

If there is an Offertory Procession (usually just on weekends or holy days of obligation in most parishes) while the collection is being taken, a few parishioners often go to the back of church where a cruet of plain drinking water, a cruet of grape wine, and a container of unconsecrated hosts (unleavened bread made from wheat flour and water) have been placed. Usually, two to four people bring the bread and wine (called *gifts*), along with the collection, in an offertory procession up to the altar area. The organist and choir lead the congregation in an offertory hymn.

Preparing the gifts on the altar

The priest, deacon, and servers meet the procession at the foot of the altar and receive the gifts. The deacon (or, if none is present, the priest) prepares the gifts on the altar in an action called, suitably enough, *the preparation of the gifts.* The deacon or priest pours wine into the *chalice* (the gold or silver cup that holds the wine that will become Christ's body and blood) and adds a few drops of water to symbolize the union of the divinity and humanity of Christ. The priest lifts the hosts of bread above the altar and says, "Blessed are you, Lord, God of all creation. Through your goodness we have this bread to offer, which earth has given and human hands have made. It will become for us the Bread of Life." The people respond, "Blessed be God forever."

Then the priest lifts the wine-filled chalice above the altar and says, "Blessed are you, Lord God of all creation. Through your goodness we have this wine to offer, fruit of the vine and work of human hands. It will become our spiritual drink." The people again respond, "Blessed be God forever."

Washing hands

The priest may incense the gifts and then washes his hands with water at the side of the altar. The washing is a ceremonial relic of the Jewish tradition present at the time of Jesus. At that time, the high priest washed his hands before making the sacrifice of killing an unblemished, spotless lamb in the Temple of Jerusalem on the day of Passover. So, too, celebrating Mass today, the priest prepares to offer up the Lamb of God (Jesus Christ) to God the Father, so he ceremonially washes his hands to offer a spotless sacrifice.

Some observers associate the priest's hand washing with the hand-washing act by *Pontius Pilate* (the Roman Governor of Judea who condemned Christ to death on the Cross) before the Crucifixion and death of Jesus on Good Friday. But the Church views that scene as a symbolic gesture in which Pilate claims that he's washing his hands of the death of an innocent man (Jesus). The hand washing of the priest isn't a connection with Pilate but a ritual purification, such as a connection with the high priest who made a symbolic sacrifice in the Temple of Jerusalem. The Catholic priest reenacts the real sacrifice of Jesus on the altar.

Praying on behalf of the people

Next, the people stand, and the priest says more prayers, addressing God on behalf of the people. Prayers are said over the gifts and then the people and the choir normally sing the words of the *Sanctus* (Latin for *Holy*): "Holy, Holy, Holy Lord, God of Power and Might. Heaven and Earth are full of Your Glory, Hosanna in the Highest. Blessed is He Who comes in the name of the Lord, Hosanna in the Highest." These words are taken from Isaiah 6:3 and Revelation 4:8 as well as Mark 11:9–10.

Saying the Eucharistic Prayer

After the *Sanctus,* the congregation kneels for the first time. Now comes the holiest part of the Mass.

The *Eucharistic Prayer,* which only the priest can say, recalls what happened at the Last Supper. The sequence of events is retold until the part where Jesus takes the bread. Then the priest changes from third person to first person and speaks as if Christ himself were standing on-site holding the host. The priest acts in the person of Christ *(in persona Christi)* as an *other Christ (alter-Christus)*. The priest doesn't say, "This is Christ's body" or "This is Jesus' blood." He uses the same pronoun, *My,* because at the moment of consecration, the priest *is* Jesus.

The priest uses the exact same words that Jesus used at the Last Supper (Matthew 26:26–29) at the Consecration: "This is My body, which will be given up for you." He elevates the Host above the altar for everyone to see. The priest genuflects, takes the chalice of wine, and goes again from the third person to the first, speaking as Christ: "This is the cup of My blood, the blood of the new and everlasting covenant. It shall be shed for you and for all so that sins may be forgiven. Do this in memory of Me." He elevates the chalice, and he genuflects.

The ringing of bells at the Consecration signifies the holiest moment of the Mass, an appropriate symbol of reverent rejoicing. In the Middle Ages, before stereo audio-microphones, people way in the back of a Gothic cathedral could barely hear anything that the priest was saying, so they needed a signal that the Consecration was happening. That signal was the ringing of bells. Often, bells are still rung today when the priest elevates the Host, and again, when the priest elevates the chalice.

Catholicism professes that during the *Consecration,* a miracle occurs — the priest *consecrates* the bread and wine: Just as Jesus did at the Last Supper, the priest takes the bread in the form of a Host and says, "This is My body." Then he elevates the Host for the congregation to see, bells are rung, and he genuflects. Then he takes the chalice (cup) of wine, saying "This is the cup of My Blood," elevates the chalice, and genuflects. Now it's the body and blood of Christ; it still looks, feels, and tastes like bread and wine, but it's not. This change of bread and wine into the real Body and Blood of Christ is called *transubstantiation.*

The Bible says that God *created* merely by speaking: "God said, 'Let there be light' and there was light." (Genesis 1:3) Likewise, by merely speaking the words of Christ over the bread and wine during Holy Communion, the priest changes them into the body and blood, soul and divinity of Christ through the authority given to him by the Sacrament of Holy Orders. Only an ordained priest has the authority to say Mass and consecrate the bread and wine.

Catholics kneel before the consecrated Host — the Eucharist — because it's not a piece of bread anymore — it truly is Christ. If the Holy Eucharist were just a symbol — such as bread and wine — then kneeling down and adoring it would be considered idolatry, but the Catholic Church has staunchly asserted for 2,000 years that the Holy Eucharist isn't a symbol. The Holy Eucharist is his body and blood. Therefore, the Holy Eucharist is Christ himself present in the consecrated Host, whether on the altar or in the *tabernacle,* a locked metal receptacle usually on an altar or table. (To see what a tabernacle looks like, go to Chapter 16.)

Eastern Catholics, such as the Byzantine, don't kneel because standing is their normal posture for reverence, but in the Latin (Western) Church, kneeling is the most profound sign of reverence. In the United States, Catholics kneel throughout the Eucharistic Prayer, but in Europe and elsewhere, they're only obligated to kneel during the Consecration.

Even when non-Catholics admit that they can't believe in the Eucharist, they do accept that if they believed what Catholics believe, they would have to show the same reverence, worship, and love for the Holy Eucharist as Catholics.

The consecrated bread and wine, called the *Eucharist,* has other names, too:

- ✔ Holy Eucharist
- ✔ Communion and Holy Communion
- ✔ Sacrament and Blessed Sacrament
- ✔ Sacrifice and Holy Sacrifice
- ✔ True Presence and Real Presence

The miraculous changing of what was bread and wine into the body and blood of Christ that occurs during the Consecration at each and every Mass is called *transubstantiation.* It refers to the changing of substances, in this case, the substances of bread and wine into the substances of the Body and Blood of Jesus. Catholicism bases this belief in the transubstantiation on two points:

- ✔ In the Gospels of Matthew, Mark, and Luke, each writer uses the same phrase to describe the Last Supper on Holy Thursday, the day before Jesus was crucified. Jesus took the bread, blessed it, broke it, and gave it to his disciples and said, "This is My Body" (*touto estin to soma mou* in Greek; *hoc est corpus meum* in Latin). The verb *to be* is used such that an equality exists between *This* (which refers to the bread) and *My Body.* So the bread becomes the body of Christ. Because all three Gospels (Matthew 26:26, Mark 14:22, and Luke 22:19) meticulously repeat the exact same phrase, as does St. Paul (1 Corinthians 11:24), these sacred words must be taken literally.

- ✔ The words of the Last Supper spoken by Christ over the bread and wine are consistent with the New Testament: Jesus explicitly and graphically commanded, "Eat My flesh and drink My Blood," more than a few times. He also said, "My flesh is real food and my blood real drink." Some in the crowd said, "How can this man give us his flesh to eat?" (John 6:52), and he responded, "Unless you eat the flesh of the Son of man and drink his blood, you have no life in you," (John: 6:53). "After this, many of his disciples drew back and no longer went about with him," (John: 6:66). The Church reasons that if Jesus had meant this to be symbolic, why would he allow so many of his followers to leave with a serious misunderstanding?

The bottom line is that Catholics believe that the Eucharist is always simultaneously an object of adoration and worship, being the Real Presence; it's the same Holy Sacrifice of God the Son to God the Father for the remission of sins; and it's sacred food to nourish the soul. In a sense, the Holy Eucharist is the Last Supper, his death on the cross on Good Friday, and his Resurrection on Easter Sunday all rolled into one.

- **Holy Thursday:** Jesus gave the sacrament of Holy Eucharist at the Last Supper.

- **Good Friday:** He sacrificed his life to save humankind from our sins.

- **Easter Sunday:** Christ reunited his body and blood, rose from the dead, and established the promise of eternal life.

All these events are exemplified in the Holy Eucharist.

Note: Just as Christ did at the Last Supper, the priest consecrates the bread and wine separately. He doesn't combine the two into one action by taking the bread and wine together and saying, "This is My body *and* My blood." He separates bread and wine, body and blood.

The reason? When a person's body is separated from his blood, what happens? Death. A person bleeds to death. The separate consecration of the bread and wine re-presents the separation of body from blood that happened on the cross on the first Good Friday. He died.

But Catholics don't receive dead flesh and blood in Holy Communion for Christ rose from the dead. Parishioners receive his living and risen flesh and blood in Holy Communion, because after Good Friday came Easter Sunday. After death came Resurrection. Going back to the Mass then, immediately after commemorating his death (the separation of body and blood) through the separate consecrations, the Memorial Acclamation of the Mass is said or sung: "Christ has died, Christ is risen, Christ will come again." So at Mass, body and blood are reunited as at the Resurrection. After the Consecration, both the body and blood of Christ are in the one Host, and Christ's body and blood are both also in every drop of consecrated wine. Being risen, Christ's body and blood are reunited. Latin (Western) Catholics have usually only received the Host instead of receiving from the cup, too. This practice reaffirms the belief that in one is really both — the consecrated Host is both the body and blood of Christ. The faithful are allowed and encouraged to receive Holy Communion under both forms from time to time whenever their bishop and pastor have it, but it's not necessary for them to do so.

The rest of the Eucharistic Prayer follows and the priest concludes with: "Through Him, with Him and in Him, in the unity of the Holy Spirit, all glory and power are Yours, Almighty Father, forever and ever." The people sing or say, "Amen," then stand and say the *Our Father,* and then the priest or deacon *may* say "Let us offer each other a sign of peace," and each parishioner gives those standing next to and near to him a simple handshake to show solidarity as one family of faith before the real and most intimate sign of unity — Holy Communion. The Church has never officially recognized the practice of holding hands as a sign of unity during the *Our Father,* because it originates from non-Catholic tradition. For Catholics, holding hands to *symbolize* unity is unnecessary, because at Holy Communion the unity is *real.* The word *communion* comes from the Latin *cum + unio* meaning *united with.* The sign of unity is the act of taking Communion, because it signifies that the person is *in union* with all that the Catholic Church teaches, does, and prays.

The *Agnus Dei* (Lamb of God) is said or sung: "Lamb of God, you take away the sins of the world: have mercy on us. Lamb of God, you take away the sins of the world: have mercy on us. Lamb of God, you take away the sins of the world: grant us peace," and then the people kneel. This comes from the words of St. John the Baptist (John 1:29).

Receiving Holy Communion

The priest first consumes the consecrated Host and then drinks the consecrated wine from the chalice. If a deacon is present, the priest gives him a consecrated Host and then the chalice to drink from.

Sometimes, Catholics refer to the chalice as only containing *the wine.* This is wrong, disrespectful, and sacrilegious, because it's no longer wine but the precious blood of Christ. After the priest speaks the words of Consecration, the priest changes the bread and wine into the body and blood, soul and divinity of Christ. Bread and wine are no longer present on the altar — only the appearances (also called *accidents*) of bread and wine — the substances have been changed via transubstantiation into Jesus' body and blood. (For more on transubstantiation, see the "Saying the Eucharistic Prayer" section, earlier in this chapter.)

While going in line to receive Holy Communion, Catholics in the congregation who are properly disposed approach the priest, deacon or extraordinary minister and are first given a consecrated Host. Sometimes, they may be offered the option of also taking a sip of the Precious Blood (the consecrated wine) from the cup. Before actually receiving, however, some sign of reverence for the Real Presence is required, be it a bow of the head, the sign of the cross, a genuflection, kneeling, and so on. The local bishop and the national conference of bishops for each nation give guidelines on which posture they prefer or suggest. In the United States, for example, standing is the norm, but with a bow of the head; however, it is forbidden to refuse Communion to someone who is kneeling. If the church or chapel has a Communion or altar rail, a short gate-like structure surrounding the sanctuary where people can kneel during Holy Communion, and people kneel at this, then no other sign of reverence is required, because kneeling is a sign of reverence.

When the person is first presented the consecrated Host, the priest, deacon or extraordinary minister says "the Body of Christ" to which he replies "Amen," signifying, "Yes, I do believe it is Jesus." Then if the Precious Blood is offered, he may choose to go to the person holding it who says, "the Blood of Christ," and he replies again, "Amen." Then he takes the cup (called a *chalice*) from her and drinks a few sips of the consecrated wine and hands the cup back. Catholics aren't allowed to *self-communicate,* which means going up to the altar and picking up the chalice for themselves. An authorized minister (priest, deacon or extraordinary minister) must give them Holy Communion.

Then after receiving Holy Communion, the faithful go back to their respective pew and pray silently for a few minutes before sitting down.

The whole and entire Christ is in one consecrated Host or in one part of the Host or in one drop of the consecrated wine. Both elements of Communion aren't necessary for the faithful to consume. If only consecrated Hosts are given, the people aren't being ripped off or cheated. Sometimes, Catholics are given the opportunity to receive both the Host *and* chalice, but those who receive both elements shouldn't think that they *must* have both elements in order to fully receive Communion.

Catholics can participate in Holy Communion if they're *properly disposed,* which means they

- Are unaware of any mortal sins that aren't yet confessed and absolved. (See Chapter 7 for a discussion of the Sacrament of Penance.)
- Don't publicly dissent from Church teaching, such as the Church's views on abortion.
- Fasted (not eating or drinking anything but water) for one full hour before receiving Holy Communion. The fast is one hour before Communion, not before the beginning of Mass.

The Church asks that the following people *not* take Communion:

- Non-Catholics
- Catholics in an invalid marriage. (See Chapter 7.)
- Catholics who've broken the one-hour fast (unless they're on medication, sick, elderly, or in the hospital)
- Catholics who haven't made their first confession (see Chapter 7) and First Communion. (See Chapter 6.)

You must be in communion to receive Communion. Being *in communion* means being united with *all* that the Church teaches, prays, and does. Non-Catholics, for example, obviously aren't in full or complete union; otherwise, they'd be Catholics.

Unlike the airport, no one checks your ID at Communion time to make sure you're Catholic. Sometimes, at weddings and funerals, the priest makes an announcement before Communion that only Catholics who are in full communion with the Church and who are in the state of grace (no mortal sins on their soul) should come forward. Even if this isn't said, it's implied and written in the back or front cover of many Catholic hymnals and missals. Unless someone displays obvious confusion regarding the procedure of receiving Holy Communion, normally no questions are asked. If somebody appears clueless ("What do I do with the Host?") as practicing Catholics know to open their mouth and extend their tongue or to open their hand and allow the Host to be placed on it, then the priest, deacon or minister might ask, "Are you Catholic?" It's not meant to be intrusive or insulting. If a Catholic is divorced and remarried outside the Church or not in the state of grace, because he didn't go to confession to have a mortal sin absolved, then he shouldn't take Holy Communion. Should you receive the Eucharist while you're in the state of mortal sin, you're quadrupling the negative effect of the mortal sin on your soul by committing *sacrilege* — using something sacred for an unworthy purpose.

Catholicism insists on a prior union of the person with the Church before the person is able to enjoy the fruit of that union — Holy Communion. So Catholics see Communion as the result of unity. Catholics are allowed to take Communion, but they also must obey the pope, come to Mass every weekend, accept all the teachings of the Church, and so on.

Putting the Word of God into practice

After the Roman Empire embraced Christianity, and especially during the era of the Holy Roman Empire of Charlemagne (the ninth century A.D.), the official language for the Western Church was Latin. (The Byzantine/Eastern Church used Greek.)

When Mass is celebrated in Latin today, the last words that the priest or deacon says is "Ite missa est." This has been grossly mistranslated as, "Go, the Mass is ended." The literal translation is "Go, the [congregation] is sent." *Missa,* which is usually translated as the noun *mass,* is actually a verb. *Missa est* comes from the verb *mitto/mittere*, which means *to send.* It doesn't mean that *Mass is ended,* but rather, that someone or something *is sent.*

Therefore, when the Mass comes to a conclusion, the priest or deacon isn't literally saying, "The Mass is ended." Instead, what *is* being said is, "Now that you have heard the word of Scripture and shared in the word made flesh by receiving Holy Communion, the congregation is now sent into the world to spread that Word of God and put it into practice." The conclusion of Mass is a commencement, not a finale. It's not something that's done over and over, but something that needs to be done over and over. Obeying the will of God and putting your faith into practice never stops until you're six feet under.

Vatican II and Latin

Commonly known as Vatican II, the Second Vatican Council (1962–65) was opened by Pope John XXIII and closed by Pope Paul VI. The Sixteen Documents of Vatican II were responses of the Catholic Church to reiterate the traditional teachings of the Church and to address contemporary concerns. The Sacred Liturgy, Revelation, Ecumenism, the Church, the World, the Laity, the Priesthood, the Diaconate, Revelation, Social Communication, and so on were all discussed. Presenting and explaining a 2,000-year-old religion to a modern world in contemporary terms was the primary goal of the council. Part of that was the renewal of the sacraments, especially the Holy Mass. Since the Council of Trent 400 years beforehand (1545–63), the universal norm for the Western Church was Latin. No new dogmas or doctrines were proclaimed or defined, but the old ones were merely restated and re-emphasized with modern vocabulary and context. The *content* of Faith was not changed but the *context* in which it was explained and the manner in which it was communicated was adapted for the modern era. Previous councils sought to define theological doctrine and resolve conflicts, but the Second Vatican Council was primarily a pastoral one in that it sought to promote greater spirituality while still defending the traditional teachings and practices of Catholicism.

Vatican II also allowed the introduction of the *vernacular* (native tongue) into the public worship of the Church, though preserving the rich Latin language and tradition. Now, Mass is said in the native language of the local place. Before Vatican II, Mass in the Latin Catholic Church was always in Latin. Having the Mass in one language anywhere and everywhere all over the world made it easy for Catholics to travel and feel truly *catholic* (from the Latin word *catholicus* and the Greek *katholikos* meaning *universal*). But Latin wasn't universally taught in the schools like it used to be, so many people didn't know any Latin at all. That's why the Church allowed for the native language — to promote a full, conscious, and active participation of the faithful in all the prayers, hymns, and responses of the Mass all over the world. Since Vatican II, Catholics have been asked — and are strongly encouraged — to participate *fully* in the Mass, not just to physically attend.

Even though the Mass was only celebrated in Latin before and during the papacy of Pope Pius XII (1939–58), and most Catholics were no longer fluent in Latin, Pope Pius XII didn't want the faithful to just sit in the pews as if spectators at Mass. He wanted the people to see that they had a role to play in the Mass — as active participants. So Pius XII challenged Catholics to restore the original purpose of the congregation — to unite themselves with the priest instead of saying private prayers and practicing their own personal devotions during Mass.

But when the worship service was in a language that the congregation didn't speak fluently, how could that happen? In either of the following two ways:

- ✔ **Missals:** Not to be confused with nuclear *missiles,* these are books containing all the prayers and Scripture readings used at Mass. The missals at a Latin Mass provide an additional English translation alongside the Latin, so the congregation can figure out what's being said. Reading the translation at a Latin Mass is something like reading a libretto to follow along at an Italian opera.

- ✔ **Repetition:** Many parts of the Mass, particularly those that require a response to the priest, are repeated so often that most people know them by heart. For example, the priest says, "Dominus vobiscum" (The Lord be with you), and the people respond automatically, "Et cum spiritu tuo" (And with your spirit), even though they aren't fluent in Latin.

Latin is still the official language of the Catholic Church, so anything coming from the Vatican and applying to the universal Church is written in Latin. For example, papal encyclicals and ecumenical council decrees (Chapter 2), the Code of Canon Law (Chapter 9) and so on are first written in Latin. Then the original Latin version becomes the typical edition on which all translations must be based. This applies to all official documents concerning doctrine, worship, and law.

The Church never intended to drop Latin completely. The Church still asks that Latin be used to preserve the Catholic heritage, much like Hebrew, Greek, Old Slavonic, and Arabic are used by other religions even today.

Just as Hebrew is still used by American Jews and Greek by American Eastern Orthodox Christians, Latin is the official and traditional language of Roman Catholics. Vatican II and the latest rules from Rome still encourage that some Latin be retained as part of Catholic heritage, especially parts of the Mass to which everyone knows the responses by heart — the *Gloria,* the *Sanctus* (Holy, Holy), the *Pater Noster* (Our Father), and the *Agnus Dei* (Lamb of God). (The *Kyrie* is actually a Greek version of the *Lord Have Mercy,* not Latin.)

In addition to allowing the priest to say the Mass in the native language of the congregation, Vatican II also made some other changes to the Mass:

- ✔ The first half of the Mass is now called the *Liturgy of the Word* to emphasize the Scripture readings that take place during this part. Prior to Vatican II, however, the first half of the Mass used to be called the Mass of the Catechumens. Studying and preparing for their Baptism, *Catechumens* were allowed to stay in church until the first half of Mass was over, but they were ceremoniously escorted out before the second half, known as the Mass of the Faithful. Not having made their First Holy Communion, they weren't yet allowed to receive Holy Communion. Parishes that have an annual RCIA (Rite of Christian Initiation of Adults) program or Catholic convert class will often dismiss *catechumens* (unbaptized non-Catholics studying to enter the Church; baptized non-Catholic Christians are called *candidates*) during Lent after the Liturgy of Word as was done long ago when it was called the Mass of the Catechumens. They leave the main church and have a class while the rest of the congregation continues with Mass, because the non-Catholic students can't receive Communion yet.

✔ Since Vatican II, Catholics attending Mass in the Latin (Western) Rite have been allowed the occasional option to receive both forms of Holy Communion — both the consecrated bread *and* the consecrated wine. However, it's *not necessary or mandatory* that the faithful receive both, because in the consecrated Host is both the Body and Blood, the Soul and Divinity of Christ.

Dressing for the Occasion

Yep, the Mass has some variety. The main focus of each Mass is the same, but slight differences exist depending on the occasion. This section gives you some background, so you know what to expect from a particular Mass.

Weekday and Sunday

The basic difference between Masses is weekday (also known as *daily Mass*) and Sunday. Weekday Mass obviously takes place Monday through Friday but also includes Mass on Saturday morning. Sunday Mass can be held Saturday evening and at any time on Sunday.

Saturday evening counts as Sunday using the ancient Hebrew practice of considering the new day to occur at sundown rather than sunrise. So as soon as the sun sets on Saturday evening, liturgically speaking, it's Sunday.

Sunday (or Saturday evening) Mass is obligatory for all Catholics, but weekday Mass is optional.

Sunday Mass is the parish Mass, meaning the whole parish is expected to participate. Sunday Masses include two readings, one from the Old Testament, and one from the New Testament, a Psalm, and the Gospel. At the weekday Mass, however, only one selection is read from the Old Testament or the New Testament, along with a Psalm, and a Gospel reading.

Usually, Sunday Mass includes an organ and a choir, but weekday Mass doesn't. Sunday Mass normally takes an hour. Weekday Mass typically takes about a half-hour.

Holy days of obligation

Holy days of obligation are days of the year when Catholics must attend Mass in addition to the normal Sunday Mass. The United States has six holy days of obligation:

- ✔ **January 1:** The Feast of Mary, the Mother of God
- ✔ **40 days after Easter Sunday:** Ascension Thursday
- ✔ **August 15:** Assumption of Mary into heaven
- ✔ **November 1:** All Saints' Day
- ✔ **December 8:** The Feast of the Immaculate Conception
- ✔ **December 25:** Christmas, the Nativity of Our Lord

It gets confusing sometimes. If certain holy days fall on a Saturday or Monday, they *aren't* considered holy days of obligation, because they're back-to-back with Sunday. The concern is that it would be burdensome to many Catholics to have to go to Church two days in a row.

In the United States, however, Christmas Day (December 25) and the Immaculate Conception (December 8) are always days of obligation even when they fall on Saturday or Monday. The reason is that Christmas and Easter are the highest-ranking holy days, and the Immaculate Conception is the patronal feast for the United States. But if All Saints' Day or the Assumption falls on a Saturday or a Monday, the obligation to attend Mass is lifted. If either of those days falls on a Tuesday, Wednesday, Thursday, or Friday, though, attending Mass is obligatory. Believe us, Catholics get confused with this formula — including the priests. And to make it even more perplexing, some parts of the United States have moved holy days, such as the Ascension from Thursday to the closest Sunday. If in doubt, it's best to call the local Catholic parish or just go to Mass anyway. Attending Mass is never a waste of time, even if it ends up not being a holy day of obligation.

Note that Europe has four more holy days: January 6 (Epiphany), March 19 (St. Joseph), Corpus Christi (Thursday after Trinity Sunday, which is the Sunday after Pentecost, which is 50 days after Easter), and the Solemnity of St. Peter and St. Paul (June 29).

Holy days are like Sundays in that Catholics must attend Mass, and if possible, refrain from unnecessary servile work. Some Catholic countries, such as Italy, Spain, and Ireland, give legal holiday status to some of these holy days, so people can attend Mass and be with family instead of at work.

Simple and solemn celebrations

Catholics believe that Mass can be celebrated in both simple and solemn ways. Simple celebrations, such as weekday Mass, usually have little or no music and singing. They're fairly low-key occasions that attract smaller numbers of *parishioners* (members of the parish) than solemn celebrations.

Solemn celebrations use singing and music, such as Sunday and holy day Mass. Solemn celebrations may also include the use of incense at different parts of the Mass, the use of gold vestments, the presence of the bishop, or a procession with the Gospel book. This solemnity is given to holy days not declared a holy day of obligation. For example, the feast day of the saint in whose name the parish is taken (St. Ann or St. Bernadette for example), isn't a day Catholics that must attend Mass on, even if they're from that parish. However, the Mass of that feast day can be celebrated with solemnity.

Weddings, funerals, ordinations, first Masses of priests, anniversary Masses honoring the years of marriage (silver and gold) or the years of priesthood, and feasts of the patron saint of the parish (such as St. Anne on July 26 or St. Bernadette on April 16 or Our Lady of Good Counsel on April 26) are reasons for more solemnity. During these types of celebrations, the Gospel and the Our Father may be chanted, to add to the solemnity

Some feasts of Jesus and Mary — such as the Feast of the Sacred Heart of Jesus (Third Friday after Pentecost) and the Feast of the Annunciation (March 25) — aren't holy days of obligation but *are* solemnities, which means that the Gloria and the Creed are said at Mass even if it's on a weekday.

Spiritual Seasons of the Year

The *liturgical year* (Church calendar) is as different from the calendar year as the fiscal year is for most people. The Church calendar begins on a different day than the civil year, but it still contains the same 12 months and 365 days. The liturgical year begins on the first Sunday of Advent, which is four Sundays before Christmas. The last Sunday of the year, the Feast of Christ the King, is the Sunday before the first Sunday of Advent.

To help the faithful with their public worship, the Church uses a seasonal year and calendar that go back two millennia — back to a time when most of the world was agrarian (farming). Farmers were very dependent on the seasons of the year to plant and harvest. Pagans as well as Jewish, Christian, and Muslim religions recognize the impact of the seasons of the year on people; they tied feasts and celebrations to the growing and cultivating of crops and livestock.

The Catholic liturgical year revolves around two feasts: Christmas and Easter. They're high holy days because they commemorate the birth and Resurrection of the Church's founder, Jesus Christ. The first half of the liturgical year focuses on the theme *Christ Our Light,* and it's epitomized by Christmas. The second half focuses on the theme *Christ Our Life,* epitomized by Easter.

Christ Our Light: The first half of the liturgical year

According to the Catholic Church calendar, Advent, Christmas, Epiphany, and the Baptism of the Lord all form the Christ Our Light theme. *Advent,* the season before Christmas, and Christmas itself occur in the winter when, in the Northern Hemisphere, the days are short and light is often longed for. Candles decorate the Advent wreath — a wreath of evergreen with four candles, three purple or violet and one rose or pink. Each week of Advent, a candle is lit until the fourth week when all four are ablaze. The colors correspond to the vestments the priest and deacon wear on the Sundays of Advent. Advent wreaths are used in Churches and private homes just to remind people to spiritually prepare for Christmas, to give light during these days of less daylight, and to remind the faithful that Jesus is the Light of the World.

Advent is a time for the faithful to prepare for Christmas spiritually, in the midst of all the shopping, decorating, baking, and parties. Advent tones down the festivity for Catholics so the real celebration can take place on the birthday of Jesus, Christmas Day. During Advent:

- ✔ Catholics typically go to confession to prepare for Christmas.
- ✔ Some attend weekday Mass.
- ✔ Most try to pray more and practice patience and tolerance — while the rest of the world often goes crazy having Christmas sales in October and bringing out Santa before Halloween.

Usually, by December 25, people have been saturated with Christmas music, Christmas parties, and Christmas carols. In Catholic parishes, though, no Christmas hymns or music are sung or played until December 25. Then they're sung all the way to New Year's, Epiphany (January 6 — when the Wise Men or Magi came to worship the Christ-child) and ending on the Baptism of the Lord (the Sunday after Epiphany — when John the Baptist baptized Jesus at the River Jordan).

By the way, no one knows the exact day of Jesus' birth. No one has found any greeting cards from Mary and Joseph to Jesus, showing that his birthday was December 25. No one has found any Roman record of his exact date of birth, despite the census of Caesar Augustus (Luke 2:1–5). So how did the Church come up with December 25 as the birthday of Jesus? Some have claimed it was an attempt to coincide a Christian feast with an established pagan festival, the day of the conquering sun. St. Augustine (354–430) said that Christmas falls on December 25 for the following reasons:

✔ Jesus said, "I am the *light* of the world." (John 8:12) If Jesus was the light of the world, what time of year does the light begin to increase? After the shortest day of the year, the *winter solstice,* daylight increases, second by second, minute by minute, until we have the longest day of the year, the *summer solstice.* After that, the amount of daylight begins to decrease, little by little, bit by bit, until we again reach the shortest day. So the light increases after the winter solstice, which is December 21.

✔ St. John the Baptist, the cousin of Jesus and the one who was a witness for Christ, "I must decrease, so He may increase." (John 3:30) If John said he must decrease, so Jesus can increase, when does daylight begin to decrease? After the summer solstice, which is June 21.

Since the calendar was changed from the Julius Caesar calendar to the Pope Gregory one, a few days have been moved around here and there. In any event, the Church picked December 25 (close to the winter solstice and after the shortest day of the year) to celebrate the birth of Jesus, the light of the world, by using a calendar date that coincides with the increase of daylight. The birthday of St. John the Baptist ("I must decrease") is celebrated on June 24, shortly after the summer solstice and after the longest day of the year, when daylight begins to decrease.

Christ Our Life: The second half of the liturgical year

According to the Church calendar, Lent, Easter, Ascension (40 days after Easter when Jesus ascended into heaven, body and soul), and Pentecost (50 days after Easter when the Holy Spirit came upon the 12 Apostles and the BVM in the Upper Room) form the Christ Our Life theme in the liturgical year. *Lent,* the season before Easter, occurs in the spring when new *life* appears after the death of winter. Easter takes place the first Sunday after the first full moon after the equinox, which means Easter floats every calendar year (as the Jewish Passover does).

Lent is a more penitential time than Advent, but both seasons prepare the faithful for a big feast. Lent begins with Ash Wednesday and lasts for 40 days. Catholics are asked to do modest mortifications and acts of penance during Lent for the purification of the body and soul. Lent is a time of confession, fasting, abstinence, more prayer, more Bible and spiritual reading, and more spiritual and corporal works of mercy. It culminates at Easter when Christ rose triumphant from the dead.

Other tidbits about the liturgical year

Besides Advent and Christmas, Lent and Easter, the Church calendar also includes what's known as *ordinary time* — Sundays and weekdays in between the Christmas season and Easter season, which of course includes the seasons of Advent and Lent that precede them. Ordinary doesn't mean unimportant, dull, boring or bland. Simply, ordinary time is anytime outside the liturgical seasons of Advent and Christmas, Lent and Easter. That's why this season is called *ordinary,* because it has no special name like the others do.

Solemnities, feasts, and memorials also occur during Advent and Lent, the Christmas season and the Easter season — throughout the liturgical year. See Appendix B in the back of this book for a listing of the solemnities, feasts, and memorials as they occur throughout the calendar year. But keep on reading if you'd like to get a glimpse of what these are all about:

- ✔ **Solemnities,** such as the Annunciation (March 25) or St. Joseph (March 19), are the highest-ranking days and are often holy days of obligation. (Even when they're not, the Gloria is usually included at Mass, and maybe the Nicene Creed.)

- ✔ **Feasts,** the next-highest ranking days, are celebrations that honor Jesus, Mary and the saints. The Mass held on a feast day includes specific Scripture readings and prayers. For example, the weekday readings at Mass may be continuous selections from Luke or Mark, but on the Feast of St. Matthew (September 21) the Gospel of Matthew is used, especially the part where Jesus calls him (Matthew 9:9).

  The main feasts in the Church year honor Jesus Christ and Mary. Lesser feasts honor the saints, from Peter and Paul, to Mark and Luke, and so on. A saint's feast day is usually the day that the saint died. That's the day that the saint left this earth and entered heaven, so the saint's death day on earth is his birthday in heaven.

  Not all the saints have verifiable or known death dates, and some have death dates that are already being used on the calendar. So some saints just get the next available day on the calendar. (We don't think they mind.)

- ✔ **Memorials** are the lowest-ranking days on the Church calendar. These are celebrations of all the rest of recognized saints who don't have full-fledged feast days. St. Denis (October 9) or St. Thomas Aquinas (January 28) have memorials. No specific Bible readings are assigned to each memorial. It's not that they're less important saints than those who have feasts as opposed to memorials. The difference doesn't lie so much in the saint himself as much as to where the celebration occurs and to what degree. Feasts are mandatory celebrations all over the world and with some extra solemnity either because of the theme (such as the Annunciation) or because the saint has been honored all over the world. Memorials are often optional, but even when not, they're usually lesser-known saints or ones who have not had universal devotion.

The sense of sight plays an important role in Catholic worship; the colors of a priest's vestments help the faithful know that certain celebrations are at hand.

- **Green:** The color of vestments used during ordinary time

- **Purple or violet:** Used during Advent and Lent (along with white and black, may also be used at Funeral Masses)

- **White and gold:** Most appropriate for Christmas and Easter

- **Red:** For on feasts of the Passion of Jesus and for the Holy Spirit, representing red tongues of fire, in addition to being worn for the feasts of *martyred saints,* who shed their red blood for Christ

- **Rose:** On the Third Sunday of Advent and the Fourth Sunday of Lent, the color rose may be worn as a sign of anticipated joy. Real men don't wear pink; we wear rose. If you take the somber color of purple or violet and brighten it with some white, it changes into rose, hence the notion of using this color as a visible sign that Christmas or Easter is soon to come. The Third Sunday of Advent also has the name *Gaudete* (Latin for *rejoice*) Sunday and the Fourth Sunday of Lent is also called *Laetare* (another Latin word for *rejoice*) Sunday. The easiest way to remember which is which? Laetare begins with the letter *L* as does Lent, so Gaudete must be in Advent.

Table 8-1 offers an at-a-glance look at the three-year Bible reading cycle (A, B, and C) for the weekend Mass and the two-year cycle (I and II) for the weekday Mass. Gotta love it if you're a priest or type-A personality.

Table 8-1	Liturgical Calendar (2003–08)					
Year	*2003*	*2004*	*2005*	*2006*	*2007*	*2008*
Sunday Cycle	B	C	A	B	C	A
Weekday Cycle	1	2	1	2	1	2
Ash Wednesday	5 Mar	25 Feb	9 Feb	1 Mar	21 Feb	6 Feb
Easter	20 Apr	11 Apr	27 Mar	16 Apr	8 Apr	23 Mar
Ascension Thursday	29 May	20 May	5 May	25 May	17 May	1 May
Pentecost	8 Jun	30 May	15 May	4 Jun	27 May	11 May
Corpus Christi	22 Jun	13 Jun	29 May	18 Jun	10 Jun	25 May
1st Sunday of Advent	30 Nov	28 Nov	27 Nov	3 Dec	2 Dec	30 Nov

Part III
Behaving Like a Saint

The 5th Wave
By Rich Tennant

@RICHTENNANT

...OR ELSE!

"I always speak to the kids in a quiet and respectful way, but occasionally I wear this to add a little punctuation."

In this part . . .

Y ou find out that Catholics are law-abiding people. They believe in and follow God's laws — the natural moral law, as well as Church law.

See how Catholics make sense of and interpret the Ten Commandments, which isn't just a bunch of no-nos and dos and don'ts. Read why Catholics believe that being good is more than just avoiding evil and obeying the Ten Commandments. Examine the seven deadly sins and the four moral virtues. You can take a look at some controversial issues, too. The Catholic Church may seem like Don Quixote in comparison to the rest of the world, but the Church does so out of commitment to its convictions.

Chapter 9

Catholic Law 101

● ●

In This Chapter

▶ Defining the different types of laws

▶ Thumbing through canon law

▶ Laying down the law with a few house rules

● ●

*L*aws aren't just arbitrary rules made by those in authority. Most people think it's obligatory that those responsible for the welfare of others should issue and enforce rules that protect and defend. Not to do so would be negligent.

Governments, clubs, organizations, families, and religions have rules and laws for the common good of their members. Whether for professional baseball or a friendly game of basketball in someone's driveway, an Elks meeting or a session of Congress, all groups have rules of behavior to protect their members from possible abuse or neglect, as well as to preserve the unity and integrity of the whole group.

In addition, families — even the smallest of them — have their own laws to live by. Johnny must be home by 10 p.m. on school nights, for example, or Susie must always ask for mom's or dad's permission before going to a friend's house for dinner.

The Church is considered the family of God, and rules exist to protect that family as a whole as well as the individual members. Specifically, Catholics are obligated to follow all the divine laws of God, the natural moral law, Church law (also known as *canon law*), and all the legitimate and ethical civil laws of their city, state, and nation as long as they don't contradict the laws of God or the Church. In short, a Catholic is expected to be a law-abiding citizen. This viewpoint is reinforced by what Christ said: "Render to Caesar what is Caesar's and to God what is God's," (Mark 12:17).

That said, people aren't expected to obey an irrational law any more than they can be expected to follow a law that hasn't been made public. For example, if a town, city, state, or province created a law that made it illegal for anyone to sneeze in public, that law would be irrational and couldn't be enforced or obeyed. (Of course, there oughta be a law that forbids waiters from sneezing on your dinner!) The goal of every good law is the common good — the mutual benefit of all or at least the most members.

So every real and binding law must make sense, be known, and be of benefit to people. This chapter covers such laws — as applied to the Catholic Church.

Following the Eternal Law of God

In the 13th century, Philosopher and theologian St. Thomas Aquinas (see Chapters 3 and 18) defined *law* as "a command of reason promulgated by a competent authority for the common good," and he divided it into the three categories that follow under the main title *the eternal law of God*.

- Divine positive
- Natural moral
- Human positive
  - Civil (also known as *secular law*)
  - Ecclesiastical (also known as *canon law*)

Note that human positive law also comprises civil and ecclesiastical law. But first, we want to explain what *eternal law* means. From all eternity, God has willed that all things act according to their nature. Created things must obey the laws of nature (physics, mathematics, chemistry, gravity, and so on), animals must obey their instincts, and humans must act according to their nature, which is rational. Being rational creatures, humans must also obey authentic laws that conform to reason, are made known, and exist for the common good. So the eternal law is nothing more than the combination of all laws that conform to reason and exist for the common good of everyone.

Besides scientific and physical laws, only intelligent, rational beings can know philosophical, theological, and moral laws — so only intelligent, rational beings are obligated to obey them. Catholics regard these laws like chemists regard formulas, cooks regard recipes, and pharmacists regard prescriptions: If you follow the rules, the results are guaranteed. If you fudge the figures or disregard the directions, the end product is in danger. The soul needs God's laws to find eternal happiness and obeying them is as crucial for Catholics as following the correct formula is for scientists.

The divine positive law

According to Exodus in the Old Testament, God issued his own set of laws, known as the *Ten Commandments,* which were given to Moses on Mount Sinai. God didn't give Moses ten suggestions or ten proposals but Ten Commandments. These laws aren't negotiable, and they apply to every human being who's at least 7 years old (the age of reason).

The first three commandments deal with your personal relationship with God: Love but one God, honor his name, and honor his day. The last seven deal with interpersonal relationships: Honor your parents and honor other people's lives, property, spouses, and their right to know the truth. Chapter 10 spells out all the details concerning the Ten Commandments.

Because God himself revealed the Ten Commandments, they're considered *divine* law. And because they were spelled out specifically with no room for ambiguity, they're also *positive* law. Hence the term *divine positive law.* For many people, the Ten Commandments — whether or not they're classified under the term *divine positive law* — are still treated as rules and regulations.

When you were a teenager, if your dad said that you had to be home by 10:30 one night and 11:00 p.m. another night, you probably thought the rule was arbitrary. After all, there's nothing sacred about 10:30 or 11:00 p.m. The reality is that parents who love their child establish parameters and boundaries, precisely because they love their son or daughter. A mother or father exercising their parental authority by setting curfews determines what's a safe time to be home. It's not the child who has the age, wisdom, and experience to know what's a good hour and what's an imprudent one.

But the divine positive law isn't abstract or arbitrary. It's simple and explicit: Thou shall not kill; Thou shall not commit adultery; Thou shall not steal; and so on. The Ten Commandments are all simple and clear. Although the last seven of the ten can be known by reason alone via the natural moral law (see "The natural moral law" section, coming up next), God chose to reinforce and equalize the playing field by divinely revealing them, too, instead of just leaving them for people to figure out on their own.

For example, the Bible shows that Cain knew that murdering his brother Abel (Genesis 4:8–9) was evil and immoral well before Moses ever received the Ten Commandments, the fifth of which says, "Thou shall not kill," (Exodus 20:13). Yet God chose to reveal even the commandments anyway. He did so to emphasize that he himself had personally and directly issued them and to balance the scales between the intellectually quick and those who aren't.

Think of it like the sticker on a hair dryer that says, "Do not immerse in water while plugged into outlet." Even though most people know via common sense not to do so, some people don't know that it's dangerous and lethal to let a plugged-in hair dryer fall into water. That's the reason for the stickers. Common sense should also tell folks to honor their parents, not to take an innocent life, not to cheat on their spouses, not to lie, not to steal, and so on. But for some people, common sense doesn't do it. So in his divine mercy, God revealed his divine positive law to remove all doubt and ambiguity.

The natural moral law

The Bible tells the story of Cain murdering his brother Abel centuries before Moses ever received the Ten Commandments, which included the injunction "Thou shall not kill." So if he'd had a good lawyer, such as *Rumpole of the Bailey* or the Dream Team — F. Lee Bailey, Johnny Cochran, and Barry Scheck — could Cain have had his day in court and been acquitted, because the law hadn't been promulgated until *after* the alleged crime took place?

> But your Divinity, my client is innocent of murder because he didn't have access to a Bible, and there's no way he could've known about the Fifth Commandment, because it wasn't written down by You and given to Moses until centuries after my client allegedly committed the deed.

Case closed? Not.

The Bible explains that because Cain *knew* he did something wrong, immoral, and sinful, he hid from the Lord. And Moses broke the same commandment (Exodus 2:12) before he got the Ten Commandments. After killing an Egyptian, Moses fled into the desert, because he *knew* he did wrong — even though he didn't get the Fifth Commandment for another 18 chapters.

So how did both Cain and Moses know it was wrong to murder an innocent person? And why did other civilizations, such as the Egyptians, Persians, Assyrians, Babylonians, Greeks, and Romans, all have laws forbidding murder, stealing, adultery, perjury, and so on, if they didn't have the revealed Word of God like the Hebrews did? How could Nazi soldiers and officers be condemned at the Nuremburg War Trials for crimes of genocide if they and their government had no religion and no belief in God, let alone any respect for his chosen people? Can all men and women be aware of an unwritten law merely by the use of reason? Does this naturally knowable law apply to all human beings at every time and in every place?

A century before Christ, the Roman stoic philosopher Cicero wrote:

> There is truly a law, which is right reason, fitted to our nature, proclaimed to all men, constant, everlasting. It calls to duty by commanding and

deters from wrong by forbidding, neither commanding nor forbidding the good man in vain when it fails to move the wicked. It can neither be evaded nor amended nor wholly abolished. No decree of Senate or people can free us from it. No explainer or interpreter of it need be sought but itself. There will not be found one law at Rome and another at Athens, one now and another later, but one law, everlasting and unchangeable, extending to all nations and all times. (*De Republica*, III, xxii, 33)

And St. Paul the Apostle said:

For when the Gentiles who don't have the law by nature observe the prescriptions of the law, they are a law for themselves even though they do not have the law. They show that the demands of the law are written in their hearts. (Romans 2:14–15)

Natural moral law is unwritten but is known by all men and women who have the use of reason. It uses basic common sense, prudence, and justice. Because it's known by reason, not written in stone or on paper, like the Commandments or the Bible, the moral law is *natural*. It's *moral* because it applies only to moral acts — actions of human beings that involve a free act of the will. (It doesn't apply to animals, because they don't have the use of reason.)

Because of the natural moral law, Cain and Moses knew it was wrong to commit murder before the Fifth Commandment ever came along. And because of the natural moral law, trials for war crimes can be conducted against anyone who commits genocide or mass murder regardless of the person's religion or lack of it. A Nazi couldn't have used the defense that he didn't recognize the authority of the Bible, because even the most evil of Nazis still had the use of reason, and reason is what discovers the natural moral law for each and every man and woman. Just obeying orders or following the civil law won't cut it either. An immoral act violates the natural moral law even if it conforms to the local civil law. Slavery was immoral and contrary to natural moral law even though the U.S. Supreme Court (1857) upheld it until it was overturned by the 14th Amendment (1868) after the Civil War. The Nuremburg Laws of Nazi Germany (1935) also violated the natural moral law, because they deprived Jews of their citizenship and paved the way for confiscation of personal property, deportation, incarceration, and doomed many to the concentration camps. Apartheid is another example of where the legalized racial segregation in South Africa from 1948 to 1991 defied the natural moral law. In all these cases, the civil law endorsed, tolerated, or promoted horrible injustices, precisely because the natural moral law was being violated. A government, a constitution, a law, or an amendment doesn't grant personhood. It comes from human nature made in the image and likeness of God. Jew and Christian, born and unborn; the natural moral law exists despite what political parties and civil authorities legislate to the contrary.

Banishing backstairs influence

Natural moral law is why the U. S. Senate Judicial Committee grilled the U.S. Supreme Court Justice Clarence Thomas, a Catholic, for his views at his nomination hearings before he took his Supreme Court seat in 1991. According to the Catholic Church, natural moral law logically leads to the conclusion that abortion is immoral, just as did it with the issue of slavery and women's suffrage, regardless of what the Supreme Court or Constitution says. Morality is not legislated, but good legislation can protect and promote good morality, because *that* promotes the common good. Immoral legislation must be eradicated, because it violates the natural moral law and further perpetuates injustice. Well before the Anita Hill allegations arose, Justice Thomas was being interrogated about his use of the term and his legal application of natural moral law in previous decisions, legal briefs, and opinions that he published. Senators Biden, Kennedy, and others feared that a Supreme Court Justice who felt subservient to the natural moral law rather than making the Constitution the ultimate authority would, therefore, be likely to overturn *Roe v. Wade,* the 1973 Supreme Court decision legalizing abortion on demand across the United States. Just as abolitionists used the natural moral law to combat legalized slavery and eventually pass the 14th amendment, pro-life anti-abortionists use the natural moral law argument to oppose the *Roe v. Wade* decision and push for another amendment protecting the life of the unborn fetus.

The human positive law

People create *human laws* — not God or nature. The Church maintains that natural and divine laws are immutable and eternal, because they come from God. However, human laws — whether they come from the Church or the government — are conditioned by contemporary circumstances, such as time, place, and culture. They're *positive* in that they're clearly written and promulgated.

Speed limits of 15 mph in a school zone, income tax laws, and the Patriot Act are all human laws. They're not perfect and can always be improved, changed, interpreted, dissolved, or re-created.

Human laws apply to humans, obviously, so when an animal does damage to property or people, the owners are often responsible. Also, human laws aren't meant to restrict activity and behavior but to protect and defend the inalienable rights of life and liberty of all people. So even though one of the Commandments is "Thou shall not steal," and the natural moral law tells people with reason that taking something that doesn't belong to them is unethical and wrong, civil laws also make theft a crime — a punishable one.

Human positive law comprises both civil law and canon (Church) law.

Civil law

Civil laws are all the laws written and enforced by cities, states, nations, and international communities, such as the United Nations (UN) and the North Atlantic Treaty Organization (NATO). Calgary, Alberta, has laws that apply only to residents of the municipality, but Alberta has laws that apply to all the cities and towns in the province. The Canadian Parliament, for example, makes laws that are binding in all its provinces, because the Canadian government has care of the whole country.

Some civil laws apply only to residents of the area, and other laws apply to anyone who works at or visits that place, too. For example, speed-limit laws are for everyone, regardless of where you live, vote, or have citizenship, but laws for where and when you vote depend on exactly where you live. Because civil laws (being human laws) aren't perfect, they can and must be interpreted and applied by a recognized authority.

Most Americans are familiar with English Common law, which defends the rights of individuals — especially the right of the accused to a fair trial and the right of being presumed innocent until proven guilty in a court of law. Roman law, however, is much older. This system seeks the discovery of truth as the primary directive, whereas English law seeks to protect the innocent as the pinnacle of justice. Both are good approaches but use different perspectives. The English system — on which American jurisprudence is based — uses a jury of peers to determine innocence or guilt. The Roman system uses testimony and evidence given to a judge or tribunal of judges to get to the truth of the matter. The early Church grew out of the ashes of the Roman Empire, so the Roman Empire and its culture influenced the Catholic Church, and the laws of the Church are based on Roman law rather than the American civil courts, which are based on English law.

Canon (Church) law

Canon law is the supreme law of the Church, and it specifies the universal norms and regulations for the entire Church. The actual application and implementation of these universal laws, however, are also contained in local law known as *Diocesan Statutes* (rules made by the local bishop for the parishes of his diocese) and others are spelled out in *liturgical rubrics* (details on how to celebrate the sacraments) as found in the *Roman Ritual,* books that contain the necessary prayers and the requirements for valid and licit celebration of the sacraments.

The Catholic Church is a religion and an institution. With more than 1 billion members worldwide and thousands of cardinals, bishops, priests, and deacons to govern the Church, it's both a necessity and a matter of justice to have laws pertaining to activities and people in the Church.

The word *canon* comes from the Greek *kanon,* which means *rule* and refers to decrees that are binding on all persons. *Canon law* refers to the laws that apply to all members of the Catholic faith. The Roman Church has 1,752 canons and 1,546 canons are in the Eastern Catholic Church. That's quite a bit more than the Ten Commandments, eh? It could be worse — the number of Roman Catholic canons actually decreased in 1983; 2,414 canons filled the Code from 1917 to 1982! The *Code of Canon Law* is the book containing the laws for the Catholic Church. The edition for the Western (Latin) Church is separate from the Eastern (Byzantine) Church edition.

It was the desire of Pope John XXIII to revise the 1917 Code of Canon Law that precipitated the Second Vatican Council (commonly referred to as Vatican II) in 1962. (To find out more about Vatican II, see Chapter 8.) Many Church laws had become arcane and obsolete after almost 50 years; so updating the universal rules of the Church was seen as a good thing. (You might ask why did it take so long? Remember that the Catholic Church is nearly 2,000 years old, and she takes a long time to make decisions that would affect more than 1 billion people around the world.) Before updating the laws, though, the ecumenical council convened to discuss how to better explain and liturgically celebrate the Catholic faith in the 20th century. The council closed in 1965, but the Code of Canon Law wasn't revised until 1983. And the *Catechism of the Catholic Church* wasn't revised until 1992.

The Code of Canon Law is patterned according to the Vatican II document *Lumen Gentium* (Dogmatic Constitution on the Church), which describes the Catholic Church as the living and continuing presence of Christ on earth — his mystical body and spotless bride. The Church that Christ himself founded continues his three-fold mission as priest, prophet, and king — to sanctify, teach, and govern. (See Chapter 3 for a discussion of the three-fold mission of Christ.) So, to cover all the bases of the Church's three-fold mission, the Code of Canon Law is divided into seven books as follows:

- ✔ **Book I** shares elementary legal terms and ideas and then defines laws that protect and defend the three-fold mission of the Church.

- ✔ **Book II** describes the people of God and the hierarchical structure of the Church;

- ✔ **Book III** explains the teaching office of the Church;

- ✔ **Book IV** discusses the sanctifying office;

- ✔ **Books V through VII** get into temporal goods, sanctions, and judicial procedures, respectively.

The biggest and most obvious change between the 1917 Code of Canon Law and 1983 Code is that the new and revised version is loaded with theology and biblical references. The same is true of the 1992 *Catechism of the Catholic Church*. Because both books are available to everyone — in print, online, and on CD-ROM — the Church realizes that more than canon lawyers and academic theologians are going to read the texts. Previously, legal and catechetical texts were only or primarily read by experts. Now, with electronic media making anything available, the Church painstakingly wants the layperson and nonexpert to see the connection between faith as taught by Sacred Scripture and Sacred Tradition and between the practices of that faith as contained in Church law. So, we get the theology and biblical foundation for the supreme authority of the pope as bishop of Rome and not just the legal facts of what power he exercises but also why. The legal necessities of a licit (legal) Baptism are also couched by the theological explanation. Canon 849 defines Baptism:

> [is] the gateway to the sacraments, is necessary for salvation, either by actual reception or at least by desire. By it people are freed from sins, are born again as children of God and, made like to Christ by an indelible character, are incorporated into the Church.

See how Baptism is connected to the other sacraments and how the effects of Baptism are told? This is more than just the legal requirement of water and the words, "I baptize you in the name of the Father and of the Son and of the Holy Spirit." Hopefully, if Catholics understand that canon law is more than just dos and don'ts, but that they're prudent, reasonable, and beneficial rules to protect the individual believer, the whole Church, and the content of faith, then following the laws of the Church will be more meaningful.

All the canons are useless unless they're seen in the context of assisting the institutional Church's mandate to continue the three-fold mission of Christ on earth today.

To get a glimpse of each canon law book, keep on reading.

Taking it to the top

Because the pope possesses full, supreme, immediate, and universal ordinary power (authority) to govern the Catholic Church (Canon 331), no member of the Church or its clergy can appeal a papal decision (Canon 333), and even an attempt to appeal to an ecumenical council is forbidden (Canon 1372). Even though no higher authority exists on earth than the *Holy See* (the term used to describe the pope and his staff), every single baptized Catholic has the right to appeal directly to Rome and to the pope (Canon 1417). This appeal is sometimes called *the appeal to Caesar* based on the ancient right of every Roman citizen to plead his case before

the emperor. Obviously, if a parishioner has a conflict with their pastor, normally it's handled at the next level, which is the diocesan bishop. The pope rarely interferes with lower authorities unless it's necessary, but the right of appeal to Rome remains intact with every Catholic at every stage of the game. If your pastor refuses to let you have a 10 a.m. wedding when the parish only advertises 11:00 a.m. and 2:00 p.m., for example, it would be too difficult, costly, and disproportionate to appeal to the pope to overrule that policy. However, if someone feels that justice hasn't been served, they can and ought to go to the next higher level, as it is their right.

Book I: The origins of canon law

Some of canon law is based on the divine positive law revealed by God, some on the natural moral law, some on civil law, some on former ecclesiastical law, and some are new and innovative laws for the contemporary world.

Book II: The responsibilities of the clergy and the laity

To correct any inadvertent misconceptions that only the clergy and those with religious vocations (see Chapter 2) were called to live lives of holiness and prayer, Vatican II emphasized the important role of the laity and all the Christian faithful. So Book II of the Code concerns the people of God — meaning *all* the baptized people, whether clergy or laity.

Baptism is the sacrament of initiation into the Church, the family of God. The 1983 Code of Canon Law relies heavily on Vatican II to remind members of the Church that all baptized people share in the common priesthood of Christ, which means all men and women are expected to sanctify the world, teach the Word, and give Christian witness and leadership. The distinction between the common priesthood of the baptized and the ministerial priesthood of the ordained is significant and substantial, but it doesn't make one better or holier than the other. The laity sanctifies the world by living in it and giving good example, whereas the clergy sanctify the members of the Church by serving their spiritual and sacramental needs in the Church.

Canon 226 reminds parents that they're the primary teachers of their children and that the schools and parishes can offer assistance but can't replace or duplicate what God intended parents to do. In addition to their duties of giving life, sustaining it with food and shelter, and providing education, parents are also reminded of their duties to give good example and ensure that their children learn and practice the Catholic faith.

Canon 208 emphasizes the genuine equality of dignity and action among all of Christ's faithful. This means that clergy aren't better than laity, and both have equal importance, although they have different functions. The following numbered listing of Canons 209 through 222, which deals with the obligations and rights of all the Christian faithful (all baptized people), is a general overview of what's in each code. So all the baptized . . .

209 Are bound to preserve their part in the Church at all times, even in their external actions.

210 Must make a wholehearted effort to lead a holy life according to each person's own condition and to promote the growth of the Church.

211 Must actively participate in the evangelization and missionary work of the Church (prayer, financial, or personal).

212 Have the right to make known to their pastors (priests and bishops) their spiritual needs; have the right and, at times, the duty to share their

views with pastors on matters concerning the good of the Church while respecting their faith and morals and showing respect for pastors.

213 Have the right to hear the Word of God and receive the sacraments when properly disposed and prepared.

214 Have the right to worship God according to their legitimate liturgical rite and to follow their own form of approved spirituality.

215 May freely establish and direct associations that serve charitable or pious purposes.

217 Have the right to a Christian education by virtue of Baptism.

219 Have the right to immunity from any kind of coercion in choosing a vocation (married life, single, religious, or ordained).

220 Have the right to a good reputation and to protect their privacy.

221 Have the right to make a claim and/or defend themselves, to due process within the Church courts.

222 Have the obligation to provide for the needs of the Church and are obliged to promote social justice.

The following listing provides a synopsis of Canons 225 through 231, which give a little different perspective — the obligations and rights of just the laity. People who are baptized but not ordained . . .

225 Have a special obligation to give witness to Christ and to their Catholic faith in the world where they live, work, and recreate.

226 If parents, have the most serious obligation and right, as the primary teachers of their children, to provide an education for their children — especially a Christian education. Married couples are to be witnesses to the world of Christian love and life.

227 As laity, have a freedom in secular affairs insofar as they conform to the Gospel and the teachings of the Church and don't propose their own opinions as official teachings of the Church.

228 If found suitable and capable, may be admitted by pastors to certain ecclesiastical offices.

229 Have a duty and right to acquire knowledge of the Catholic faith — especially the sacred sciences — and to proclaim and defend it.

230 May be given a temporary assignment as an extraordinary minister of the Word (sometimes called a *lector* or *reader*) or as an extraordinary minister of the Eucharist when the need warrants and with the consent of the pastor.

231 Have a right to an equitable and just remuneration to provide for their own needs and those of their families.

And Canons 273 through 289 list the obligations and rights of the clergy. So people who are both baptized and ordained . . .

273 Have a special obligation to show reverence and respect for the pope and their local bishop.

274 Can be given offices that require the power of governance and are obliged to obey and fulfill the lawful authority of their bishop.

275 Are to acknowledge and promote the mission of the laity.

276 Have a special obligation to seek holiness in their lives. To do so, they're to fulfill their pastoral obligations; invited to celebrate daily Mass; if priests or deacons, obliged to daily pray the Liturgy of the Hours; obliged to make an annual retreat; and urged to engage in regular mental prayer, go to confession often, and honor the Virgin Mary with special veneration.

277 If priests in the Western (Latin) Church, are obliged to observe perpetual celibacy.

278 Have the right of association with others in the sacred ministry but are to avoid and shun associations whose purposes or activities can't be reconciled with the clerical state or are opposed to Church teaching and discipline.

279 Are to continue their sacred studies after ordination.

280 Are highly recommended to have some manner of common life.

281 Deserve fair remuneration for their ecclesiastical ministry.

282 Are to live simple lives and avoid opulence and ostentatious living.

283 Have a right to annual holidays and vacations, as well as a weekly day off (30 days vacation per year and one 24-hour day off per week).

284 Are to wear suitable clerical garb and attire.

285 Are forbidden to assume public office.

287 Aren't to play an active role in political parties or trade unions unless their superiors judge it necessary for the welfare of the Church.

289 May only join the armed forces as chaplains with the express and explicit permission of their bishop or superior.

Book II finishes with details on the election of the pope, the role of his cardinal advisors, the function of the local bishop and local pastor, national conferences of bishops, the role of the assistant pastor, and such. After defining and delineating the hierarchical structure of the Church, Book II continues with the role of those who have a religious vocation, which is sometimes called a *consecrated life.* (See Chapter 2 for details on the differences between diocesan priests and religious order priests.)

Book II also describes the consecrated lives of men and women who become religious brothers or sisters, monks or nuns by embracing poverty, chastity, and obedience. (See Chapter 2 for more on brothers, sisters, monks, and nuns.)

- ✔ **Poverty:** The religious community pays for, owns, and shares everything. Members don't own anything privately or exclusively.

- ✔ **Chastity:** They live celibate lives and practice self-discipline and self-denial while seeking to live pure lives.

- ✔ **Obedience:** They surrender their own will just as they surrendered their possessions in poverty and their bodies in chastity; so in obedience, they seek to obey the will of God as demonstrated through their superiors.

Book II also contains codes for the Societies of Apostolic Life, Secular Institutes, and Personal Prelatures (such as Opus Dei) — communities that focus on communal prayer and apostolic work. Each offers members of the laity a modified form of community life that does not follow the canonical mandate of poverty, chastity, and obedience.

Book III: Teaching and preaching the Word

According to Canon 767 in Book III, preaching a *homily* (the sermon given after the Gospel at Mass) is exclusively reserved for bishops, priests, and deacons. Homilies are mandatory at every Sunday and holy day Mass. The local bishop may give a lay person temporary permission to preach (Canon 766), but the preaching can never be the homily, which always comes after the Gospel at Mass and can only be given by someone who is ordained. Preaching in church outside of Mass is permitted for serious reasons at the discretion of the pastor and bishop.

Canon 803 states that only schools authentically teaching the Catholic faith as defined by the Church and with the approval of Church authorities can use the word *Catholic* in their title or description. According to Canon 805, the local bishop has the right to name or approve religion teachers in Catholic colleges, universities, and high schools, and he has the right to demand that those who dissent from orthodox teaching be dismissed. Theology instructors in Catholic colleges and universities must obtain a certificate called a *mandatum* (Latin for *mandate*) from the local bishop authenticating their theology (Canon 812).

Book IV: Requirements for Mass and the sacraments

Book IV discusses the sanctifying office of the Church, which involves predominantly the seven sacraments including the Holy Mass. For each sacrament — Baptism, Confirmation, Penance, Holy Eucharist, Anointing of the Sick, Matrimony, and Holy Orders — the Code reiterates what the Church teaches on the theology of the sacrament. The *Catechism of the Catholic*

Church, the documents of Vatican II, and most of the Bible are the sources for explanation. Canon law also spells out what's needed for a valid (real) and licit (legal) sacrament. For example, wheat bread and grape wine are needed for a valid Mass. If the priest omits other requirements or violates canon law in another way, such as not wearing proper vestments, it's an illicit but valid Mass as long as he still uses valid words during the consecration and valid elements, wheat bread and grape wine.

Book IV is like the rulebook for the coach and the quarterback. Most of the canonical requirements for the sacraments are the duty and responsibility of the priest, bishop, or deacon; the person receiving the sacraments should merely prepare by being in the state of grace, which means being consciously free of all mortal sin (see Chapter 7) and having adequate preparation and catechesis. This means that the sacraments are not like getting fast food at the drive-in window. Spiritual preparation requires time for prayer and study of the Bible and the *Catechism of the Catholic Church,* so the person receiving the sacrament(s) knows what's about to happen, why, and what's then expected of them afterwards.

A large section of Book IV also deals with the serious impediments that make a marriage invalid. For example, the marriage is invalid if either or both the bride and groom never intend to have children or if either or both don't intend to enter a permanent and faithful union. The groom must be at least 16 and the bride at least 14 for a valid sacrament, but most states and countries require an older age just to get the license! If a person was previously married validly and then divorced but never obtained an *annulment* (what's commonly and *incorrectly* called a Catholic divorce), he can't validly marry again. An annulment is unlike a divorce in two ways:

✔ First, divorce is a civil law decree from the state whereas an annulment is a canon law decree from the Church. The state issues a marriage license, and the state issues a divorce decree. The Church, on the other hand, grants an annulment. The Church celebrates the Sacrament of Matrimony, and only the Church can issue a Decree of Nullity (otherwise known as an annulment).

✔ The second is that a civil divorce basically says that what was once a marriage is no longer a marriage. A previously married couple no longer has the legal obligations of husband and wife anymore. An annulment, on the other hand, basically says that the Sacrament of Matrimony never took place to begin with. Civil divorce ends a civil marriage, but a Church annulment declares that the Sacrament of Matrimony didn't occur from day one. Even though a couple gets married in a Catholic church by a priest or deacon and has every intention of entering into a valid sacrament, other factors can greatly obstruct the validity anyway even unknowingly and unintentionally.

Who is at fault, if anyone, isn't the issue. The matter at hand is whether a supposed valid marriage is in fact invalid for some serious reason. Both may have entered in good faith, and even the bishop or pope himself could have performed the ceremony, but if a major impediment was present at the time of the wedding, then the sacrament of marriage is invalid, and the man and woman are free to marry someone else validly for the first time. Aside from a bride or groom intentionally not wanting to enter a permanent, faithful, and fruitful union, another impediment would be if either person was incapable of assuming the duties and obligations of Christian marriage due to a severe addiction to drugs or alcohol or some serious psychological disorder, which was present but unknown to anyone at the time of the wedding.

Books V–VII: The Church court system

The rest of the Code of Canon Law deals with the ecclesiastical court system — procedures, penalties, proofs, sentences, appeals, and such.

Some of the punishments handed down by the ecclesiastical court system include suspension, excommunication, and interdict.

- **Suspension:** The Church forbids a cleric (priest, deacon, or bishop) to exercise his ordained ministry and to wear clerical garb. However, suspension doesn't deprive the cleric of receiving the sacraments.

- **Excommunication:** The most severe form of penalty, *excommunication,* which means being outside of the Church, is only used as a last resort, with the hope that the excommunicated person will repent and seek reconciliation. Excommunicated people are deprived of the sacraments, such as receiving the Holy Eucharist at Mass. The excommunicated are also forbidden from employment or holding any position of authority in a diocese or parish and are deprived of a Catholic burial.

  Some excommunications, however, are automatic (Canon 1314) and without the intervention of the Church *(latae sententiae),* and most often, Catholics know what it takes to be excommunicated. Much like being in the state of mortal sin (see Chapter 7), which also prohibits receiving the Holy Eucharist, carrying out the penalty of excommunication often rests with the conscience of the excommunicated individual.

- **Interdict:** This is a temporary penalty that can be applied to one or more persons. Under this punishment, the persons named can't receive the sacraments, but they aren't excommunicated, so they still can receive income, hold office, and so on. It is lifted when the person repents and seeks reconciliation.

Note that an interdict can be lifted quite easily, but usually only the bishop, the pope, or their delegates, depending on the offense, can remove an excommunication. For example, in the eyes of the Catholic Church, abortion is a mortal sin. The sin of abortion may incur an automatic excommunication (Canon 1398) for everyone involved — the mother and father of the aborted child, the doctor and nurse, and anyone whose cooperation was needed to perform the abortion.

In the eyes of the Church, abortion includes not only removing a fetus before birth, but the use of all abortifacients, including intrauterine devices and certain types of birth control pills that prevent implantation or stimulate uterine contractions to reject a fertilized egg. It also includes the use of drugs such as RU486, called the abortion pill, which provokes miscarriages by blocking progesterone in the first weeks of pregnancy.

The local bishop has the authority to remove most excommunications, but many bishops delegate this power to all their parish priests when it involves a penitent confessing the sin of abortion. This way, the person going to confession can simultaneously have the sin absolved and the excommunication lifted. This is to make it easier for people to go to confession and reconcile themselves with God and the Church, especially after a very emotional, personal, and serious matter, such as abortion.

Some excommunications, however, are so serious that only the pope or his delegate can remove the penalty. For example, if someone desecrates (shows irreverence) the Holy Eucharist, only the pope can remove that excommunication. Likewise, if a priest attempts to absolve someone guilty of breaking the Sixth Commandment with whom he himself participated in that sexual sin, his excommunication is automatic and reserved to Rome. So, too, a bishop who ordains a priest to the order of bishop without prior orders from the pope is automatically excommunicated, and only the pope can remove that excommunication, which applies equally to the ordaining bishop and the bishop being ordained.

Prior to 1983 when the revised Code of Canon Law was issued, the 1917 Code was in effect, and it explicitly mentioned membership in the Freemasons as an automatic excommunication for all Catholics (2335). The current law in the 1983 Code (1374) doesn't mention the Masons by name but still retains the excommunication for *belonging to any anti-Catholic organization.* Catholics who do join a Masonic Lodge, however, "are committing serious sin and forbidden to receive Holy Communion" (Congregation for the Doctrine of the Faith, Nov. 26, 1983). This ban also applies to membership in overtly anti-Catholic associations, such as the Communist Party, the Ku Klux Klan, and so on.

The following list includes some of the offenses that warrant excommunication according to the 1983 Code of Canon Law.

1364 Apostasy, heresy, schism

> *Apostasy* is the total rejection of the Christian faith.

> *Heresy* is the obstinate post-baptismal denial of some truth, which must be believed with divine and Catholic faith.

> *Schism* is the rejection of the authority and jurisdiction of the pope as head of the Church.

1367 Desecration of sacred species (Holy Communion)

1370 Physical attack on the pope

1378 Absolution of an accomplice in sin against the Sixth Commandment

1378 Pretended celebration of the Holy Eucharist (Mass) or conferral of sacramental absolution by one not a priest

1382 Unauthorized episcopal (bishop) consecration

1388 Direct violation of confessional seal by confessor

1388 Violation of confessional seal by interpreter and others

1398 Procuring of abortion

Playing by the Rules

While the 1983 Code of Canon Law has 1,752 laws, the Church has only six precepts, which are the Catholic Church's house rules — the basic recipe for spiritual health for each and every Catholic. Just as schoolchildren must at least attend school daily in order to remain in school and employees must show up for work each day to keep their paychecks coming, so, too, Catholics must do the minimum by following these six precepts. These simple precepts are, of course, in addition to the Ten Commandments, which apply to every Christian (Protestant, Catholic, and Orthodox) and Jew alike. But the precepts of the Church are only binding on Catholics. To be a good, practicing Catholic means obeying these rules and believing what the Church teaches.

- Attending Mass on all Sundays and holy days of obligation
- Receiving the Holy Eucharist during Easter season
- Confessing your sins at least once a year
- Fasting and abstaining on appointed days
- Observing the marriage laws of the Church
- Contributing to the support of the Church

Except for the Ten Commandments and the natural moral law, most Catholics aren't well versed in the 1983 *Code of Canon Law,* because so many laws (1,752) exist. But Catholics are aware of the six precepts of the Church, which are personal applications of the numerous canons from the Code.

Nowadays, the minimum requirements for the precepts are manageable — they're not nearly as burdensome as they were in the old, old days (back when monks were monks and nuns were nuns). Of course, personal piety may motivate some people to go beyond the minimum by, for example, praying the Rosary daily, going to confession once a week, or attending Mass once or twice during the week in addition to Sunday.

Being a Catholic means doing more than just showing up at Mass on Sunday. But, hey, the six precepts are easy to remember and easy to practice.

Attending Mass on all Sundays and holy days of obligation

Catholics must regularly and faithfully attend and participate at a Catholic Mass each and every Sunday and holy day of obligation. Missing Mass on one of these days is a mortal sin. (See Chapters 7 and 11 for more on mortal sin.) Only inclement weather and bad health, which would prevent you from leaving home at all, excuse you from the obligation of going to Mass that day.

Even on vacation, Catholics are obliged to attend Mass. Non-Catholic religious services are fine as long as Catholics don't attempt to substitute a non-Catholic worship service for the Mass. So, for example, if you attend a Lutheran Sunday service, you still have to go to Sunday Mass in addition if you're a Catholic. See Chapter 8 for more on the holy days of obligation.

Receiving the Holy Eucharist during Easter season

Catholics must receive the Holy Eucharist at least once during the Easter season, which for U.S. Catholics is from Ash Wednesday to Trinity Sunday.

In the Middle Ages, many Catholics, feeling personally unworthy, received the Eucharist only rarely even though the Church never endorsed that they only go occasionally. Pope St. Pius X (1903–14), however, felt that Catholics should receive Christ every time that they went to Mass as long as they were without the blemish of mortal sin. So Catholics were encouraged and prepared for more frequent reception, which is why this precept was created. Still, the Church requires that Catholics fast for an hour before receiving the Eucharist. This means that Catholics can't eat or drink anything besides water or necessary medication for at least an hour before receiving the Holy Eucharist.

Receiving Holy Eucharist once a year during the Easter season is the minimum requirement for Catholics, and receiving it twice a day — if you attend two Masses — is the maximum allowed.

Confessing your sins at least once a year

Confessing your sins once a year, applies only if the person is guilty and conscious of a mortal sin. Full consent of the will, full knowledge, and grave matter are all required elements for mortal sin. (See Chapters 7 and 11 for more on mortal sin.) Missing Sunday Mass without a valid excuse, such as really bad weather or serious illness, a sin of the flesh, and blasphemy by using God's name in vain are all mortal sins. These sins and all other mortal sins must be confessed before a Catholic can worthily receive the Holy Eucharist. The bare-minimum requirement is that those in a state of mortal sin must go to confession before receiving the Holy Eucharist. Otherwise, they've committed another mortal sin — the *sacrilege* of receiving Communion when in the state of mortal sin, sort of spiritual double jeopardy.

Before the Vatican II (see Chapter 8), most Catholics went to confession every week before going to Communion. Today, many in the Church feel that too many people go to Communion with mortal sin on their soul, or without fasting for an hour beforehand, or who aren't in full communion. (See Chapter 6 for details about being in communion with the Church.)

Fasting and abstaining on appointed days

Today, *abstaining* applies to all Catholics 14 and older and means that they must not eat meat on Ash Wednesday and all Fridays in Lent. (Meat is any beef, pork, chicken, or fowl.) *Fasting* applies to all Catholics ages 18 to 59 and means they must eat only one full meal on Ash Wednesday and Good Friday, which means no snacks between meals. However, two smaller meals, such as breakfast and lunch, can be eaten in addition to the one full meal (supper) as long as they don't equal the one full meal if combined.

Some Byzantine Catholics and many Orthodox Christians observe the *Great Fast,* meaning they don't eat any meat, egg, or dairy products during all 40 days of Lent, and they often fast every Friday — if not every day — of Lent (from midnight to noon) except on Sundays (to honor the Resurrection).

Before Vatican II, *every* Friday of the year — Lent or not — was a day of abstinence from meat. Today, in most countries, only Fridays in Lent are obligatory, but the Church highly recommends abstinence on Fridays during the rest of the year to show respect for the day Christ died and sacrificed his flesh on the cross. The Church also recommends that if Catholics don't abstain on Fridays outside of Lent, they should do some small form of penance or work of mercy, nevertheless.

Observing the marriage laws of the Church

Catholics must be married with two witnesses before a priest, bishop, or deacon in a Catholic Church at a Catholic wedding ceremony, unless a special *dispensation* (a special allowance in light of circumstances that warrant it) has been granted from the local bishop for the couple to be married by a non-Catholic minister in a non-Catholic ceremony at a non-Catholic church.

In addition, Catholics must take 9 to 12 months to prepare for their marriage. During this prep time, called the *Pre-Cana period,* the couple receives practical advice and instructions from the priest or deacon. Catholics can only marry someone who's never been married before, or the intended spouse must have an official annulment from a previous marriage. And both the bride and groom must intend to enter a permanent, faithful, and God-willing, fruitful union for it to be a valid sacrament. (See Chapter 7 for much more information about the Sacrament of Matrimony.)

Contributing to the support of the Church

Although *tithing,* giving 10 percent of your income to the parish, is mentioned in the Bible (Leviticus 27:30–34), it isn't mandatory in the Catholic Church. Most Catholics are encouraged to donate at least 5 percent of their income to the parish and 5 percent to their favorite charities. Statistically, though, Catholics are notoriously the lowest givers of all Christians, dedicating 1 percent of their incomes to the Church. Mainline Protestants give 2 percent, and Evangelical and Fundamentalist Christians give 5 to 10 percent.

But those who can't give much financial support can and often do donate an abundance of volunteer time to the parish by holding fundraisers and supporting other parish events and projects. Volunteers sometimes teach religious education programs for children, also known as the Confraternity of Christian Doctrine (CCD) classes and the Rite of Christian Initiation of Adults (RCIA) classes (convert classes for adults). Catholic children who can't attend a Catholic school learn about the Catholic faith through CCD classes, and non-Catholics who are interested in the Catholic faith attend RCIA classes, usually at a local parish. And those volunteers who are too old or infirm support the parish with their prayers. Giving of one's time and talent as well as giving of your treasure (financial contributions) are ways that Catholic Christians support their church, from the parish to the diocese.

In the eyes of the Church, nobody goes to heaven merely by earning their way through obedience, because salvation is a free gift from God, but following the laws of God (divine and natural laws) and the laws of his Church help a person be a better person, a better Christian, and a better Catholic. These rules and regulations help promote holiness just as following your doctor's advice and prescriptions help promote good health.

Chapter 10

Loving and Honoring: The Ten Commandments

*T*he Catholic Church sees the Ten Commandments as one of the four *pillars of faith,* along with the Creed (the Apostles' Creed and the Nicene Creed), seven sacraments, and the Our Father. They're called the *pillars of faith,* because they're the foundations upon which the Catholic Church is built, just as an altar would have four solid pillars to support itself. Each one pillar represents a major component to Catholicism and all four together establish the core of Catholic belief and practice. The Church treats the Ten Commandments as divine laws from God that the Church and pope can never change, add to, or subtract from.

The Church doesn't see the Ten Commandments as arbitrary rules and regulations from the man upstairs but as commandments for protection. Obey them and eternal happiness is yours. Disobey them and suffer the consequences.

The Ten Commandments have also been called the *Decalogue* (Greek) and the *Debarim* (Hebrew), which mean *the Ten Words.*

Demonstrating Love for God

The first three commandments focus on the individual's relationship with God. The main objectives are to honor: God, his name, and his day.

1: Honor God

The First Commandment is "I am the Lord thy God, thou shalt not have any strange gods before Me." This commandment forbids *idolatry,* the worship of false gods and goddesses, and it excludes *polytheism,* the belief in many gods, insisting instead on *monotheism,* the belief in one God. This commandment forbids the making of golden calves and temples to Isis and worshipping statues of Caesar. So the obvious and blatant ways to break this commandment are to

- ✔ Worship a false god, be it Hercules, Zena, or Satan
- ✔ Consciously and willingly deny the existence of God, as in the case of atheism or having no religion whatsoever

Yet the Church asserts that you can break the commandment in other ways, such as willingly and consciously being ignorant of what God has revealed in Sacred Scripture (the Bible) and Sacred Tradition (see Chapter 3), as well as believing in and/or using *astrology* (horoscopes), numerology, and *dianetics,* which refers to the Church of Scientology.

Another way to break this commandment is to become involved with *New Age spirituality,* which is an informal religion of no creed, no liturgy, no doctrine, and no church structure, leadership, or institution. Yet it blends ancient paganism with the occult, superstition, gnosticism, and so on. It's extremely different from the three monotheistic religions of Judaism, Christianity, and Islam.

Dabbling in witchcraft, sorcery, devil worship, white or black magic, voodoo, *spiritism,* communicating with the dead, *fortune telling,* which is also known as psychic reading, tarot cards, Ouija boards, lucky charms, and such are all violations of this commandment, too.

Sacrilege, the desecration of holy objects, and *simony,* trying to buy or sell spiritual favors or graces, are also ways in which you can break the First Commandment. The Church believes that all these things are forbidden by the first commandment, because they don't put the one, true God before all else — and many of them put credence in superstition.

The Catholic Church looks at the commandment — the letter of the law and the spirit of the law — and tries to apply it to daily life. Granted, in the 21st century, the Church doesn't see many people worshipping idols and man-made deities, which was the case in pagan Greece and Rome. But the church believes that the First Commandment is still broken day by day in many other ways.

Tuning out the distractions and putting God first

Today, the most common way that the First Commandment is broken is when you put someone or something before God. In other words, God isn't your highest priority. According to Catholicism, when career, fame, fortune, comfort, pleasure, family, or a friend, for example, is the most important object, value, and priority, you're violating the First Commandment.

Even though you're not denying the existence of God or showing contempt for God or things symbolizing the divine, the Church believes that you're showing disrespect by not making God your highest priority and most cherished relationship. When you're too busy to go to church every week or going to church becomes too inconvenient, and yet you have time to attend every soccer game for Susie, music recital for Johnny, and football game at your favorite college, then God's no longer *numero uno* in your life.

The Bible, Jesus Christ, and the Catholic Church say that we're to love God "with all our heart, all our soul, all our mind and with all our strength" (Matthew 22:37 and Luke 10:27). So no one and no thing can be number one in your heart except God.

Spending QT with God

To the Church, the First Commandment implies that if God is the most important person in your life, you'll want to honor him, spend quality time with him, and communicate with him daily through prayer. Prayer enables you to speak to God with your heart and mind — vocally or mentally — and neglecting to pray, or intentionally not praying, violates the First Commandment.

Honoring, not idolizing, Mary and the saints

According to the First Commandment, only God the Father, God the Son, and God the Holy Spirit are entitled to and deserve worship and adoration. Worshipping or adoring anyone or anything else is idolatry and forbidden. Yet Catholics are sometimes accused of idolatry for the prayer and honor they give to the saints — especially the highest honor and respect they give to Mary, the Mother of Jesus.

In Catholicism, the devotion to and veneration of Mary and the saints aren't considered idolatry, because devotion, honor, and veneration aren't considered the same as worship and adoration. The Fourth Commandment, "Honor thy father and mother," shows the faithful that honoring a human being, like mom or dad, is permissible — even commanded — because honor isn't adoration or worship. And in the Gospel, even Jesus showed honor to dead people, such as Abraham and Moses, speaking of them with great respect.

Catholics believe that if humans can and must honor their parents, then it's only logical to honor the faithful servants of God who lived holy lives on earth and are now in heaven before the throne of God.

11: Honor God's name

The Second Commandment, "Thou shalt not take the name of the Lord thy God in vain," tells the faithful to honor the name of God, which goes hand in hand with the First Commandment saying to honor the person of God by not worshipping anyone else. It makes sense that if you're to love God with all your heart, soul, mind, and strength, then you're naturally to respect the name of God with equal passion and vigor.

Imagine a man using his fiancée's name whenever he wants to curse. How can he say that he loves his girlfriend if he shows contempt for her very name? A person's name is part of who that person is, and respect for the name is respect for the person. Disrespect and contempt for the name is disrespect for the person.

So Catholics believe that using God's name — especially the name *Jesus Christ* — to swear and curse when, say, a car cuts you off in traffic, a bird leaves a little surprise on your new suit, or a stranger waves with his middle finger is disrespectful to God. It's using the sacred name of the Lord and Savior to show anger and hostility. It's ironic that many who claim to be followers of Christ show their anger and animosity by using his name. Think about it. When was the last time you heard someone say *Jesus Christ?* Was it in prayer or shouted from an open window?

Using God's name in a disrespectful manner is *blasphemy,* and it's the essence of the Second Commandment. Also, any act of disrespect to anything holy — be it a holy image, place, or person — is considered a *sacrilege,* and it's forbidden by the same commandment.

Respecting God and holy things

The Church believes that you're being irreligious when you show contempt for God, such as by desecrating a holy object or place. This action is called a *sacrilege.* When a house of worship — a church, temple, synagogue, or mosque — is vandalized, the Church maintains that the sin of sacrilege has been committed; a house of God was desecrated, and contempt was shown not solely for those who attend the house's services but also and preeminently for the person the place was built for.

You're also violating the Second Commandment if you make jokes, watch movies, or read books that are disrespectful to God or anything considered holy. So, for example, if you ridicule or laugh at a Jewish man for wearing a *yarmulke* (skull cap), a Muslim woman for wearing a *khimar* (head covering), a nun for wearing her religious habit, or a priest for wearing a *cassock* (a long, close-fitting garment, usually black), you're being sacrilegious. Human beings wear certain things out of religious tradition, or they perform certain rituals as an external way of showing their love for God. When others make fun of religious garb or religious practices, it's an insult to the one being remembered by them, God himself.

The Second Commandment also forbids false oaths and perjury. So to place your hand on the Holy Bible and swear to tell the whole truth and nothing but the truth "so help me God," and then tell a lie is considered perjury and a serious violation of this commandment. Also, when a couple plans to get married, they meet with a priest or deacon and fill out papers that ask questions, such as "Were you ever married before?" and "Do you intend to enter a permanent, faithful, and, God willing, fruitful union?" They're asked to sign this document, and by doing so, they're placing themselves under oath and saying that they've answered all the questions truthfully. Lying about any of the questions is considered a false oath — a mortal sin. (See Chapter 7, for more about mortal sin.)

III: Honor God's day

The Third Commandment is "Remember to keep holy the Sabbath day." The Jewish celebration of Sabbath *(Shabbat)* begins at sundown on Friday evening and lasts until sundown on Saturday. So, basically, Saturday is the Sabbath Day. It's the last day of the week, the seventh day, the day (according to the Book of Genesis) on which God rested after six days of creation. Even modern calendars have Saturday as the last day of the week and Sunday as the first day of the new week.

So why, then, do Catholic, Protestant, and Orthodox Christians go to church on Sunday, treating it as the Lord's Day instead of Saturday? In general, Catholicism and Christianity moved the celebration of the Lord's Day from the Saturday to Sunday, because Jesus Christ rose from the dead on Easter Sunday. In other words, Sunday has become the Christian Sabbath, the day of rest, to honor the day Christ rose from the dead. Jesus said in the Gospel that the Sabbath was made for man, not man for the Sabbath. So, Christians who wanted to honor their Risen Lord on the day of the week that he rose from the dead made Sunday their day of worship instead of the former day of Saturday, which the Hebrews had honored from the time of Moses.

The Day of the Lord is also considered the day of the family. Because God created the family, spending quality time as a family on the Day of Lord, in addition to going to church, is an excellent way to fulfill the commandment.

Catholics are also bound to attend a Catholic Mass on each and every Sunday or the Vigil Mass on Saturday of every weekend in the calendar year. To miss Mass on Sunday is considered a mortal sin unless the person has a legitimate excuse, such as serious illness.

Ever wonder why some Catholics go to Mass on Saturday evening instead of Sunday morning? Using the Hebrew method of time reckoning, after sundown on Saturday evening is actually the beginning of Sunday, so the Church allows parishes to offer a Saturday evening *Vigil Mass* to satisfy the Sunday obligation.

Just going to a Christian Sunday worship service isn't good enough. In order for Catholics to satisfy and fulfill the Third Commandment, they must attend a valid Catholic Mass. Going to another denomination for a Sunday worship service is nice, but Catholics must also attend Mass the evening before or sometime during the day on Sunday. The reason is that the Church maintains that only the Mass has the real, true, and substantial presence of Christ in the Holy Eucharist. Even if a Catholic doesn't receive Holy Communion, she still satisfies the Sunday obligation by attending and participating at Mass.

The Third Commandment also forbids doing any servile work — unnecessary hard labor — on the Lord's Day, because it's a day of rest. And Pope John Paul II wrote a document about Sunday, *Dies Domini* (Latin for *Day of the Lord*), in which he reminded Catholics of the serious obligation to attend Mass each and every weekend and to refrain from doing unnecessary manual work.

To meet this obligation, all Catholics would optimally have Sunday off, so they'd have the opportunity to go to church and spend time with family. But in reality, some people must work frequently on Sundays — doctors, nurses, pharmacists, police officers, firefighters, and so on. Pastors can transfer the obligation to another day, but only on an individual basis and only for serious reasons.

Loving Your Neighbor

The last seven of the Ten Commandments focus on the individual's relationship with others. The main objectives are to honor your parents, human life, human sexuality, the property of others, and the truth.

1V: Honor your parents

The Fourth Commandment, "Honor thy father and mother," obliges the faithful to show respect for their parents — as children *and* adults. Children must obey their parents, and adults must respect and see to the care of their parents, when they become old and infirm.

Therefore, the Catholic Church believes that adult children who abandon, abuse, or neglect their elderly parents are violating the Fourth Commandment as much as teenage children who refuse to show respect or obedience to their parents. Likewise, being ashamed or embarrassed of your parents is considered as much a sin as disobeying them when you're a child or harboring feelings of hatred or revenge for them even if they weren't the parents they should've been.

This commandment is meant to protect the dignity and integrity of the family, which consists of a father, a mother, and their children. However, some families are composed of one single parent because of the death or illness of the absent parent or because the absent parent was abusive or delinquent or because the parents never married in the first place. But Catholicism also teaches that this commandment frowns on the option of freely and willingly choosing to establish a single-parent family. Voluntary single parenthood is considered an abuse, because all things being equal, a child deserves both a loving mother and a loving father. Sadly, circumstances such as death, illness, and abuse force some people to become single parents, and they do a terrific job. Whether it's adopting a child or having your own, parenthood should be sought and tried within the context of the family, which means a husband and a wife to be the mother and the father, rather than just being a parent by yourself. Just as the Church discourages parenthood outside of marriage, she also condemns artificial insemination especially of donors not married to the potential mother. According to the Church, children deserve (if possible) to have both parents. The Church also believes that even if the children are adopted, parenthood means both genders. So two men or two women can't replace the divine plan that everyone deserves — a father and a mother.

The Catholic Church believes this commandment means more than just keeping order in the home and preventing the kids from establishing anarchy. It also entails and implies a respect and honor for everyone in legitimate positions of authority — be it civilian, military, or ecclesiastical (church related). Teachers, employers, police officers, and so on, have some degree of authority over others, and the Fourth Commandment requires that respect be shown to those given the responsibility of taking care of others. Whether you like or dislike the person who was elected president or prime minister, for example, the office demands some respect and dignity if the prime minister enters the room. To show contempt or disrespect is considered sinful.

In the same line of thinking, this commandment also involves respect and love for your country. Patriotism isn't the same as nationalism. The former is a healthy love and respect for your country, but the latter is blind, total, and unrestricted support for any and all legislation, policies, or activities of a nation. Nationalism is the extreme, whereas patriotism is the goal, because good patriots know when to challenge their political leaders, laws, and policies when they become unjust or immoral.

For Catholics, this commandment recognizes the natural right of the family and of the state to form society. The family is the primary and fundamental building block from which comes the civil union of many families into a local and national government. And the family is the basis for the faith community of the Church, which is the family of God and the union of all the natural families around the world.

V: Honor human life

In English, the Fifth Commandment is read as "Thou shalt not kill" (Exodus 20:13), but the Hebrew word *ratsach* (murder) was used rather than *nakah* (kill), so the better translation would be "Thou shalt not murder." And St. Jerome used the Latin word *occidere* (to murder) instead of *interficere* (to kill) when he translated the Hebrew into the *Latin Vulgate,* which was the first complete Christian Bible combining the Old and New Testaments in one volume and translated.

It's a subtle distinction but an important one to the Church. Killing an innocent person is considered murder. Killing an unjust aggressor to preserve your own life is still killing, but it isn't considered murder or immoral by any means. The use of deadly force is morally permitted *only* if it's the last resort, and the person isn't innocent — they must be guilty of a most serious offense or threatening to commit such horrible evil.

The Catholic Church believes that murder is the sin prohibited in the Fifth Commandment. Killing in self-defense has always been considered justifiable and morally permissible. This distinction is the reason that when God ordered the Israelites to kill sometimes in the Old Testament, it wasn't a violation of the Fifth Commandment. Only unjust killing (taking innocent life) or murder is forbidden. Likewise, police officers and soldiers may have to use deadly force in certain well-defined and restricted circumstances. Again, this is morally permitted. Yet the legitimate taking of life isn't casual, unlicensed, unrestricted, or uncontrolled. The Church sees it as only a last resort — rare rather than common.

In broader terms, the Church believes that the intentional taking of innocent life includes murder (homicide or manslaughter), abortion, euthanasia, suicide, and in most cases the death penalty, and even the old custom of dueling. The Church also condemns terrorism, violence, and any unjust war or physical abuse. Capital punishment where the death penalty is inflicted on someone guilty of a grisly murder is obviously not the same as the murder of an innocent person. The pope and the Catechism acknowledge the theoretical right of the state (civil government) to resort to this extreme measure, but its actual implementation must be morally done across the board. Due to the fact that it's not currently performed universally, uniformly and equitably, the Church claims that very few if any circumstances or situations today fulfill the moral criteria to allow the death penalty to be carried out. Because some countries outlaw it and others do not; some states and provinces allow it and others do not; location has plenty to do with capital punishment. How just is it to put criminals to death based on where the crime took place? Is life more or less sacred in one location than another? Also, several means of capital punishment are more humane than others. Does making it *painless* make it more possible? Finally, it's often the poor who get executed, but the rich and famous can hire expensive lawyers to appeal their cases. The poor people are given public defenders and don't have the money to make appeals. Based on these inequities of place, diversity of means, and the unfairness of economics as to who has access to aggressive attorneys and long appeal processes, the reality of the death penalty overrules the theory that some criminals can be morally executed as a last resort. Although not overtly condemning capital punishment, the Catechism does strongly discourage it. The other instances where innocent life is unjustly taken are always condemned as murder.

More subtle violations, according to the Church, include growing angry in your heart with your neighbor, harboring feelings of hatred or revenge, being criminally negligent, such as refusing to save someone's life when you're able to do so, and committing personal abuse, which is intentionally neglecting to take care of your own health and safety.

Abusing drugs and alcohol is considered breaking the Fifth Commandment, because it recklessly endangers the user's life and potentially endangers others if someone under the influence becomes violent and irrational. Drunk driving is considered a violation, because drunk drivers are jeopardizing their own life and the lives of others by using an auto under the influence.

Mutilation and torture of human or animal life is also considered breaking the Fifth Commandment. Using animals for medical and scientific research is permitted as long as no suffering or unnecessary death is involved. To boot, psychological or emotional abuse is considered forbidden, because such abuse attacks the victim with unjust consequences.

Because the natural moral law (see Chapter 9) tells anyone with the use of reason that the intentional, direct taking of innocent life is immoral and wrong, the Fifth Commandment is no secret nor is it a change from general human experience. In the Bible, Cain knew it was wrong to murder his brother Abel, even though it was centuries before Moses ever received all Ten Commandments. And the Nazis who were convicted of war crimes, such as genocide, were found guilty not by reason of the Fifth Commandment, but because of the natural moral law, which also outlaws such atrocities.

VI and IX: Honor human sexuality

The Sixth Commandment is "Thou shalt not commit adultery," and the ninth is "Thou shalt not covet thy neighbor's wife." Both deal with honoring human sexuality.

The Sixth Commandment forbids the actual, physical act of having immoral sexual activity, specifically adultery, which is sex with someone else's spouse or a spouse cheating on their partner. But this commandment also includes *fornication,* which is sex between unmarried people, prostitution, pornography, homosexual activity, masturbation, group sex, rape, incest, pedophilia, bestiality, and necrophilia, and the Ninth Commandment forbids the intentional desire and longing for immoral sexuality. To sin in the heart, Jesus says, is to lust after a woman or a man in your heart with the desire and will to have immoral sex with them. Committing the act of sex outside of marriage is sinful and wanting to do it is immoral as well, just as to hate your neighbor is like killing him in your heart. Just as human life is a gift from God and needs to be respected, defended, and protected, so, too, is human sexuality. Catholicism regards human sexuality as a divine gift, so it's considered sacred in the proper context — marriage.

Taking the cake: Marriage

The Church believes that sexual intercourse was ordained by God and designed exclusively for a husband and wife. Marriage is the best, most sacred, and most efficient union of man and woman, because God created marriage. It's a sign of the permanent, faithful, and hopefully fruitful covenant that's made on the day that the man and woman make their vows and exchange consent. Human sexual activity is designed to promote love (unity) and life (procreation). And whenever that formula is altered or divided, the Church believes that sin enters the equation.

Only sex between a husband and wife is considered moral, and even then, the couple must be mutually respectful of each other. If the sole objective is personal pleasure and nothing more, then even a husband or wife sins by reducing his or her partner to a sex object or just a means to self-gratification. For example, using pornography or any kind of sex toy is strictly forbidden in the eyes of the Church.

So married sex is considered holy and sacred when it focuses on the unity of the couple as husband and wife — two human people who deserve dignity, respect, communication, honesty, fidelity, and compassion. To the Church, human sexuality isn't an end but a means to an end — the greater unity between husband and wife and the possibility of new life.

It's all about a covenant — the glue that bonds

Catholic teachings on sexuality are based on the biblical notion of covenant: A man and woman enter a permanent, faithful, and hopefully fruitful covenant of marriage. So, too, marriage is often a metaphor that describes the covenant relationship between God and the Hebrew people and between Jesus Christ and his church. The sign of that marriage covenant between two people is licit sexual activity that honors and respects each as a human person and doesn't treat either one as a mere sex object or tool for personal use. Animals have sex out of instinct to perpetuate the species, but human beings have the use of reason and free will, which makes humankind "in the image and likeness of God" (Genesis 1:27). Unlike animals, humans can choose when, with whom, and why to have sex.

Planning a family the natural way

Catholicism doesn't teach that married couples *must* have as many children as biologically possible. It does, however, allow for Natural Family Planning (NFP), which is *not* the old, archaic, and unreliable rhythm method. So responsible parents can morally decide how large or small a family they can reasonably afford, raise, and maintain, as long as moral means are employed to do so.

Contraceptive sex, the Church says, divides the bond of love and life, unity and procreation — isolating the dimension of human sexuality that unites two people from the possible procreative level. Likewise, any form of human reproduction that results from anything other than sexual intercourse, such as surrogate mothers, sperm banks, in vitro fertilization, and human cloning, and all methods of artificial conception are equally sinful because they isolate and separate the God-intended bond of the unitive and procreative. Sex outside of marriage and conception outside of sex are considered violations of the unity within human sexuality. For more info about the Church's stand on these and other sticky issues, turn to Chapter 12.

Cheating and philandering don't cut it

The Church teaches that sex outside of and/or before marriage is considered sinful and immoral, but strictly speaking, *adultery* is having sex with someone else's spouse or cheating on your own spouse by having sex with someone else. Catholicism says that adultery is primarily a sin against justice because all married couples make a solemn oath, a sacred covenant, to be faithful to each other until death. So marital infidelity is an injustice as well as a selfish and irresponsible sin of the flesh. The Don Juans and Lolitas needn't apply.

Playing footsie with fire

Even though the hoi polloi may think nothing of experimenting with sex before marriage, the Church says that true love means wanting what's best for the other person — body and soul. Having sex before or outside of marriage, whether it's a one-night stand or a long-term shack up, isn't sanctioned or blessed by God and lacks respect for the people involved. True love and respect mean you'd never want to lure the one you love into a sinful situation any more than you'd intentionally lead that person into a scenario that would endanger his or her life or health. So having sex supposedly just to show your love is considered a lie.

Engaging in sexual intercourse without a life-long commitment blessed by God is also dishonest. Sex without a life-long commitment is a pretense of the most intimate union that only marriage can actually accomplish. Having sex before or outside of marriage is considered dishonest to the people involved, because they deserve only the best, and the best is the total gift of self — lifelong commitment, fidelity, and openness to the possibility that God may use this couple to bring a new human life into the world.

VII and X: Honor the property of others

The Seventh Commandment, "Thou shalt not steal," and the tenth commandment, "Thou shalt not covet thy neighbor's goods," focus on respecting and honoring the possessions of others.

The Seventh Commandment forbids the act of taking someone else's property, and the Tenth Commandment forbids the wanting to do it.

Explicitly, these two commandments condemn theft and the feelings of envy, greed, and jealousy in reaction to what other people have. The Catholic Church believes that, implicitly, these commandments also denounce cheating people of their money or property, depriving workers of their just wage, or not giving employers a full day's work for a full day's pay. Embezzlement, fraud, tax evasion, and vandalism are all considered extensions of violations of the Seventh Commandment. Showing disrespect for the private ownership of someone else's property — be it money or possessions — occurs when these sinful acts take place.

In addition, the Church believes that governments have no right to usurp private property and nationalize businesses, and they do have an obligation to protect private property and to help individuals and other nations in great need.

The Church maintains that personal property is a fundamental right, but it's not considered an absolute right. If a person owns more food than he needs, and someone comes along who is starving, the person with more food than he needs is obligated to share with the one who's starving. In the same way, governments and corporations have no right to deny the individual his inalienable right to private property. But although private property is a right, it's subservient to higher values, such as human life and national security.

VIII: Honor the truth

The Eighth Commandment, "Thou shalt not bear false witness against thy neighbor," condemns lying. Because God is regarded as the author of all truth, the Church believes that humans are obligated in the Eighth Commandment to honor the truth.

The most obvious way to fulfill this commandment is not to *lie* — intentionally deceive another by speaking a falsehood. Say, for example, you're trying to sell your car to someone, who asks whether the car was ever in an accident. If you give the potential buyer a snow job and say, "No," with the conscious intention of withholding the fact that your car was in a collision, you're telling a lie, which the church considers immoral and sinful.

Low blows and cheap shots

Lies come in many different forms, and sometimes even the truth can be sinful, depending on your intentions. For example:

✔ **Calumny** is telling a lie about someone with the purpose of ruining his reputation.

✔ **Detraction** is telling the truth about someone, usually something embarrassing and confidential, with the intent and purpose of ruining her reputation.

✔ **Slander** is verbally telling lies about someone.

✔ **Libel** is publishing a lie in print, such as in a book, magazine, or newspaper. People in the public eye are often victims of libel.

On the other hand, if someone in an *informal conversation* asks how old you are, and you say 39 when you're actually, say, 42, it's not considered a lie, because common convention is that 39 implies anything over that number when you ask a person their age who is much older than that. If you're asked in a formal setting, however, such as in a court of law or on a legal document or when filling out an application, then the accurate age is expected and anything else is lying. Verbally saying 39 in polite discourse is considered a figure of speech, whereas writing that number down on a credit card application, when you're actually younger or older is lying and immoral. Saying you're 39 is a figure of speech, just like saying that you're "hungry enough to eat a horse," even though you have no intention of ever consuming horse meat in your entire life.

Figures of speech, metaphors, hyperboles, fairy tales, and such aren't considered lies, because the listener isn't expecting the accurate facts or exclusive truth, and the speaker isn't intending to deceive but make a point.

Keep reading, because you haven't heard it all yet. *Mental reservation* is considered a means by which you can withhold the truth without telling a lie. The Church believes it can be used in very limited circumstances:

✔ When someone isn't entitled to know all the facts and seeks to know them for evil purposes.

✔ To protect the safety of self or others.

✔ To protect confidentiality of penitent and confessor, doctor and patient, or attorney and client.

Concealing the truth is different from distorting it, which would be a lie. Lying is the act of intentionally deceiving someone, when they're expecting the truth. It's not telling the truth. Concealing the truth is different, because not everyone is entitled to know all the facts. Withholding information by concealing the truth can be called *mental reservation,* because you intentionally hold back some facts and only tell enough *not* to lie. This process, however, isn't to be practiced carte blanche, because in most circumstances, the common expectation is to tell the truth.

The bottom line? Telling bedtime stories, jokes, writing fiction, using figures of speech, and using mental reservation are all permissible acts when done in the proper context. But intentionally lying is always considered sinful, even if the reasons may be noble. According to the Church, God created the human intellect to know the truth, just as he made the human will to seek the good. Intentionally distorting the truth is wrong, but in certain circumstances, withholding some facts is permitted if the person doing the asking isn't entitled to know all the facts or if those who ask intend to use them for evil purposes.

This line of thinking is why the Church considers it moral to keep certain secrets confidential. For example:

- ✔ Catholicism regards the secrecy of the confessional as absolute, and no priest can ever reveal who went to confession or what was confessed. This is what's known as the *Seal of the Confessional.* Yet a priest can't lie to protect the penitent, because the ends can never justify the means. He can and must simply remain silent rather than tell a falsehood.

- ✔ Doctor-patient and lawyer-client confidentiality is considered close to but not synonymous with, the Seal of Confession and priest-penitent secrecy. Whereas the priest can never divulge anything about the sacrament, physicians and attorneys may — in very extreme cases and circumstances — reveal aspects of what they know for the common good and to prevent greater evil. But, again, breaking this confidentiality is permissible only on the most serious and grave occasions.

- ✔ The government can have secrets to protect the national security of the country and all its citizens, but just like the individual, the government isn't allowed to tell a lie even to save lives. Governments can use mental reservation to keep strategic information from enemies.

Coming Out Even Steven

Certain differences exist between Catholicism and the way that some Protestants follow the Ten Commandments. You'll find that the wording and numbering of some commandments differs.

However, the Bible doesn't number the Ten Commandments; it merely states them in Exodus 20:1–17 and Deuteronomy 5:6–21. Both Roman Catholics and Lutherans use a numbering sequence devised by St. Augustine in the 5th century, because Martin Luther (1483–1546), a German theologian, had been an

Augustinian priest before he left the priesthood in favor of his new Lutheran religion. The Augustinians were followers of St. Augustine. (For more on St. Augustine, see Chapters 3 and 15.) Protestant denominations other than the Lutheran Church, however, use the sequence of commandments devised by English and Swiss reformers in the 16th century. Table 10-1 lists the two sequences. The differences stem from personal preference, opinion, and variations in translations. There are no theological reasons but merely the historical fact that Catholics and Lutherans have always numbered their Commandments this way and other Protestants have numbered them their way. It's like the reason why the British drive on the left side of the road and Americans drive on the right; a matter of custom, that's all.

Table 10-1	The Ten Commandments
Catholic/Lutheran	*Protestant*
1. I am the Lord thy God, thou shalt not have any strange gods before Me.	1. I am the Lord thy God which brought thee out of the land of Egypt. Thou shalt have no other gods before Me.
2. Thou shalt not take the name of the Lord thy God in vain.	2. Thou shalt not make unto thee any graven image.
3. Remember to keep holy the Sabbath day.	3. Thou shalt not take the name of the Lord thy God in vain.
4. Honor thy father and mother.	4. Remember the Sabbath Day.
5. Thou shalt not kill.	5. Honor thy father and mother.
6. Thou shalt not commit adultery.	6. Thou shalt not kill.
7. Thou shalt not steal.	7. Thou shalt not commit adultery.
8. Thou shalt not bear false witness against thy neighbor.	8. Thou shalt not steal.
9. Thou shalt not covet thy neighbor's wife.	9. Thou shalt not bear false witness against thy neighbor.
10. Thou shalt not covet thy neighbor's goods.	10. Thou shalt not covet thy neighbor's house nor his wife nor anything that belongs to him.

In the Catholic and Lutheran version, the First Commandment includes the prohibition of idolatry — adoring graven images. In other words, *no strange gods* implies *no graven images,* because the pagans used idols to worship their false deities. The Protestant version separates false worship (First Command) and graven images (Second Commandment).

In the Catholic and Lutheran version, one commandment forbids you to covet your neighbor's wife (Ninth Commandment) and another commandment forbids you to covet your neighbor's goods (Tenth Commandment). The Protestant version combines all forms of coveting into one commandment, the Tenth Commandment).

Note, too, that the Catholic and Lutheran numbering system lends to a connection between the Seventh and Tenth Commandments and between the Sixth and Ninth. The Seventh Commandment forbids stealing, which is the actual taking of another's property, whereas the Tenth Commandment forbids coveting that property — having an immoral and inordinate jealousy for what someone else has. Number 6 forbids adultery, which is the actual act of having sex with someone else's spouse or cheating on your own spouse, and the Ninth Commandment forbids coveting that spouse — lusting in the heart after another.

The Ten Commandments are indeed one of the pillars of Catholic faith, because they spell out what's considered sinful behavior by direct decree from God. The Ten Commandments condemn idolatry, blasphemy, sacrilege, murder, adultery, stealing, lying, and so on. Catholicism sees these ten rules as more than just the law of behavior. Like a chemical formula or a physician's prescription or a chef's recipe, if the Ten Commandments are followed diligently, then their outcome is certain. Obey the commandments, and you'll have eternal life.

Chapter 11

Being Good When Sinning Is So Easy

In This Chapter

▶ Practicing virtue in thought, word, and deed

▶ Striking a balance between deprivation and excess

▶ Avoiding the seven nasty no-nos

▶ Knowing what antidotes to apply

Catholic morality is more than just avoiding what's sinful. Just as peace is more than the mere absence of war and good health is more than the mere absence of disease and injury, holiness is more than the mere absence of sin and evil. It's not enough to say, "I've committed no sin today." A cat could say the same.

If a doctor gives you a prescription to cure a disease or infection, you must choose to follow the directions, such as "Take twice daily with plenty of water," to make it work. If you don't, you can't blame the doctor if you don't get better. Likewise, God gave humans the Ten Commandments — a prescription for protection from spiritual disease (sin), but it's up to the individual to consciously choose to follow the directions.

But a good doctor does more than just give a prescription to cure the infection. She also gives overall directions for good and sustained physical health, such as "Drink plenty of fluids and get plenty of sleep and exercise," as well as "Stay away from high-fat and high-cholesterol foods." Likewise, Catholics believe that God did more than give the Ten Commandments for protection from sin. He also gave overall directions for good and sustained spiritual health — specifically, what the good habits are and how to cultivate them and what the bad habits are and how to eliminate those.

Cultivating Good Habits

A *virtue* is a habit that perfects the powers of the soul and disposes you to do good. Catholics believe that divine grace is offered to the soul, because without God's help, humans can't do good on their own. Grace, which is God's intervention, bolsters a person's soul, providing the necessary oomph to do the right thing, that is, if the recipient recognizes its value. Catholics believe that virtues prepare and dispose people so that when the grace is offered, people readily recognize, accept, and cooperate with it. In other words, God's grace is necessary, but virtues make it easier to work with.

Traditionally, the cardinal virtues number four, but you don't have to be a cardinal in the Catholic Church to possess them. The root meaning of *cardinal* is *cardo,* which is Latin for *hinge.* These four virtues are the hinges on which the rest of the moral life swings:

- Prudence
- Justice
- Temperance
- Fortitude

The four cardinal virtues are also called *moral virtues* to distinguish them from the *theological virtues* of faith, hope, and love (charity), which are given to the soul at Baptism.

Taking virtuous actions doesn't make you a virtuous person. A virtuous person is able to do what's virtuous, because he's committed to doing the right thing for the right reason. Being and doing good merely because it's the right thing to do — instead of for profit, fame, or esteem — is the motivation for a virtuous person to do virtuous acts.

Prudence: Knowing what, when, and how

Too many people today carelessly blurt out statements that, although true, aren't spoken in charity and compassion but with cold, deliberate, and calculated harshness. That's where prudence can help.

Prudence is basically practical common sense. It's saying or doing the proper thing, at the proper time, and in the appropriate manner. It's also the ability to know and judge whether to say something or do nothing at all.

You don't need a high IQ to be prudent. Prudence, like wisdom, isn't measured by intelligence but by the willingness of a person to think, discern, and then act. For example, it's not prudent to ask a friend for the $500 he owes you, while you're both at a funeral parlor for the viewing of his deceased brother. You're entitled to the money, and he should repay you, but prudence is the good habit of knowing the right time and place to bring up the topic.

Or say your girlfriend has a smudge of mustard on her chin from lunch. It's not prudent to say, "Better wipe that off your face, 'cause you look like a disgusting pig." If you do, you won't have a girlfriend anymore. Instead, with prudence, you're able to make the judgment that in certain circumstances, you shouldn't speak to people with abrupt or coarse words or a harsh tone of voice. Knowing what to say, how to say it, and when to say it is prudence.

Likewise, prudence can help you find the right time to appropriately mention that a family member or friend has an eating disorder, for example. With prudence, you're not negligent, saying nothing at all, but neither are you abrupt or rude, saying, "Hey, you're anorexic!" or "Wow, you're fat!"

An alcoholic practices prudence when declining an invitation to lunch at a bar, even though the person doing the inviting assures the alcoholic that they won't sit at the bar but merely eat at a table. Prudence tells the alcoholic that it's too dangerous for her to enter a room where the aroma of booze permeates the air, where many old drinking buddies hang out, and where she has many memories of getting plastered. Prudence tells the alcoholic to decline or offer an alternative — a restaurant with no bar or, better yet, where no alcohol is served.

Prudence takes time and practice. In the olden days, when good manners were more important than income, portfolio, or net worth, noblemen and peasants alike strove to show respect for their fellow man through the practice of prudent speech. Today, manners come in two extremes: The politically correct fear of offending anyone and saying nothing controversial — even when someone is in danger, and alternatively, the shock-jocks who bluntly bludgeon you over the head with the raw, unadulterated truth, hoping to hurt your feelings and get a violent reaction rather than help you. Prudence, on the other hand, is in the middle of the two extremes. Prudent people speak the truth when needed and appropriate and in a way that doesn't offend, but they never lose their force and conviction.

Acting prudently requires mature deliberation, wise choice, and the right execution:

- ✔ **Mature deliberation:** Think carefully before acting or not acting. This condition involves contemplating past experience, examining the current situation and circumstances, and considering the possible results or outcome of the decision. Mature deliberation means that you're not content with just personal knowledge, either. Seek the good advice of others. It can be the opinions of well-respected, good, and morally upright people that you respect and admire. Consult with peers and colleagues, and research authoritative sources and documents. For Catholic Christians, it includes both the Bible and the *Catechism of the Catholic Church*. In any event, it means not just depending on your own personal experience and opinion but testing it and getting good advice.

> ✔ **Wise choice:** Determine which of the options is feasible and appropriate. Getting input is the first stage and deciding which course to take after examining all the possibilities is the second. This may not be the quickest or easiest route, but prudence enables you to judge the most beneficial path to take.

> ✔ **The right execution:** Don't delay but swiftly and thoroughly follow through on what you've decided to do. Procrastination and haste are the two foes to look out for. The right execution means that you've planned and prepared and now know what to do. It's not hesitation. It's following through.

Justice: Treating others fairly

Justice is the virtue that seeks to promote fair play. It's the desire and resolve to give each person his due. It demands that you reward goodness and punish evil. Justice can be one of three different types: commutative, distributive, and social.

Six or one-half dozen of the other

Commutative justice concerns the relationship between equals — between two people, such as a customer and a merchant. Commutative justice demands, for example, that the customer be asked to pay a fair price for a product and that the merchant be honest about the condition and history of the item, so the buyer can know if the price is indeed fair. So if a merchant tries to sell a coin that allegedly belonged to Abraham Lincoln, the consumer needs some proof to verify the claim. It's unfair to charge an enormous amount of money for something that can't be authenticated or, worse yet, isn't really as old or in as good condition as advertised.

Forgive thine enemies but do what justice demands

Christians are taught that they can and must forgive their enemies. And doing so was demonstrated when Pope John Paul II personally forgave Mehmet Ali Agca, the man who attempted to assassinate him in 1981.

Showing mercy and forgiveness, the pontiff also realized that justice demanded that the criminal be punished for his crime by spending time in jail — which he did. But later, the pope asked the Italian President to pardon the man, so he could return to Turkey during the Jubilee Year of 2000. The would-be assassin was pardoned and released, but when returned to Turkey, he was taken to a Turkish jail to resume a previous sentence for the murder of a newspaper editor.

Commutative justice is based on the principle *quid pro quo,* which is Latin for *this for that.* I'm willing to pay you the price that you ask for this item, and you're willing to sell it to me at that price." But the item must actually be what it's advertised to be. If the advertised price isn't correct or facts about the item are wrong, then commutative justice is violated.

Cheating the consumer *and* cheating the merchant are both ways of violating commutative justice.

Another situation in which commutative justice comes into play is when you're robbed. Commutative justice demands that the thief make restitution by giving back the stolen money or property or, if that's impossible, recompensing you in another way, such as giving you something equal in value or providing services. So when you were a kid and smashed your next-door neighbor's window, your mom or dad rightfully enforced commutative justice. And after apologizing to Mr. Wilson, you had to save your allowance until you could pay for the replacement window.

All for one and one for all

Distributive justice involves the relationship between one and many — between an individual and a group. This kind of justice is most obvious in the relationship between a citizen and her government. The city, state, and federal government are required by distributive justice to levy fair taxes to pay for services provided. Charging excess taxes is a violation of distributive justice. Likewise, not charging enough taxes to pay for services — resulting in cuts to essential services — is a violation. A flip-side violation is when a citizen refuses to pay her fair share of taxes and yet often benefits from the government's services.

Distributive justice means that taxpayers have a right to know where their money goes, who spends it, and on what. The government has a right to ask citizens to financially support police, ambulance, firefighter, national defense, and other social services.

Another example of how distributive justice comes into play would be among members of a private club. Suppose that Fred and Barney belong to the Loyal Order of Water Buffaloes. They pay their annual dues, and in return, they get a monthly newsletter, an annual membership card made of bedrock, and an invitation to the annual convention. Distributive justice demands that members pay their dues and that the board of directors is responsible for the monies collected, giving an accounting each year so that everyone knows where the loot went. If Mr. Slate skims some money off the top for personal use or if favoritism or nepotism creep in, this type of justice has been violated. All members should be treated fairly and equally.

Fair play from Dan to Beersheba

Social justice concerns the relationship of both individuals and groups between one another and everyone. The bottom line is the common good — the public welfare of all. Social justice is concerned with the environment, the economy, private property, civil rights, and church-state relations.

Although businesses have the right to make a profit by manufacturing and selling goods and services, for example, polluting the local water system just to make more profit is a violation of social justice. At the same time, environmental extremists violate social justice when they take the law into their own hands and perpetrate property damage or seek to close a business, which results in many lost jobs that families depend on for survival. It's better for both sides to cooperate and communicate how to balance the needs of the community and the needs of the business.

Note that the right to profit or the right to property isn't absolute. So if a community is suffering from a severe drought, for example, it obliges the company that has access to drinkable water to share with those who are dying of thirst.

Social justice demands that everyone be treated fairly and equally under the law. It also recognizes the inalienable right and duty of every human being to work and receive a fair and just wage for that work. This type of justice defends the right of workers to form unions, guilds, and societies. And it defends the right of managers to expect reasonable and fair requests that won't put them out of business or make them lose money rather than make it.

If the economy is in a slump and profits are eroding, it's not a good time for labor to ask for a raise. Likewise, when business is good, it's unfair for the corporate executives to get obscene perks, while the workers get no increase and no benefit from the good economy.

Treating all citizens — regardless of gender, color, ethnicity, or religion — with the same dignity and human rights is a mandate of social justice to all governments. Likewise, citizens are expected to support their governments and nations in return for their protection and services.

Temperance: Moderating pleasure

Feast or famine. Many people live between extremes — too much or too little. Some party hearty, and some are party poops. From Puritans to Hedonists, the practices of self-deprivation and self-indulgence run the gamut, but it doesn't have to be either/or. Having some fun, enjoying your leisure time, taking pleasure, and relaxing isn't sinful or boring, immoral or dull, illicit or juvenile. Really!

Christians can and ought to have fun without it degenerating into depravity and debauchery. That's where temperance comes in.

Temperance is the virtue by which a person uses balance. It's the good habit that allows a person to relax and have fun without crossing the line and committing sin.

The Catholic Church believes that human beings are permitted to participate in legitimate pleasures but that, often, society and culture lures people into excesses in the direction of either extreme. For example, enjoying a good meal is a good thing, but if you continually eat more than you need and become obese, that's gluttony. On the other hand, if you deprive yourself of food until your health suffers, all for the sake of looking good, well, that's vanity.

Temperance is nothing more than moderation and balance in using lawful pleasures. Temperance is having an alcoholic beverage without abusing it. Drinking to get drunk, or drinking and driving, is a violation of the virtue of temperance. So are eating, sleeping, or recreating to excess.

Temperance is the habit of using prudence and restraint and doesn't require total abstinence unless someone has a problem. For example, an alcoholic can never have one or two social drinks. An alcoholic must forever abstain from booze, but she can still have a good time at parties with soft drinks instead.

Practicing temperance isn't about Carrie Nation and the Women's Christian Temperance Union and a bunch of old ladies banging a drum and decrying the evils of gin and rum. Rather, practicing temperance means knowing when to say when. It's knowing your limits and keeping them. For example, a kiss and a hug don't have to end in passionate sex, and an argument doesn't have to deteriorate into a fistfight. Temperance is establishing, respecting, and enforcing boundaries. Self-control is the key. Having a good time without it becoming an occasion of sin or a sinful act is what temperance is all about.

Fortitude: Doing what's right come hell or high water

Fortitude isn't about physical strength or mental intelligence. It isn't about being macho or bullying people around. Instead, this cardinal virtue centers on strength of character.

Fortitude is the ability to persevere in times of trial and tribulation — the ability to hang in there when the going gets tough. It's courage to do the right thing no matter what the cost.

Like a knight in shining armor

Having fortitude, as well as the other cardinal virtues, was the supreme goal and desire of every knight during the Middle Ages. Being prudent, just, temperate, courageous, and chivalrous were the duties and objectives of every man of honor.

But the Church doesn't consider these virtues to be the exclusive possession of nobility. All men and women of every economic and social class are able to practice these virtues, and doing so creates good habits and combats the temptation to try bad habits.

It's not enough to be fair, use self-control, and be prudent and know what, when, and how to do something. The virtue of fortitude gives you the strength to fulfill your commitments to God, family, and friends. This virtue enables

- You to keep your promise and your word even when the world and everyone else is telling you to forget it.
- Teenagers to combat peer pressure, avoiding drugs and sex.
- Young adults to remain chaste, abstaining from sexual relations until marriage despite the social pressures to have premarital relations.
- People of conscience to speak up and out when injustice occurs at work or in society.

When practiced faithfully and consistently, fortitude empowers people to remain courageous and overcome even the fear of death in order to help others and/or do the right thing for the right reason.

The Seven Deadly Sins

As you may have guessed, along with cultivating good habits, some bad habits need to be avoided. The Church maintains that seven vices in particular lead to breaking one or more of the Ten Commandments. These particular bad habits are called the seven deadly sins because, according to Catholicism, they're *mortal sins* — sins that kill the life of sanctifying grace. The Church believes that if you commit a mortal sin, you forfeit heaven and opt for hell by your own free will and actions. (See Chapter 7 for more on mortal sin.)

A mortal sin is any act or thought of a human being that turns away from God (*aversio a Deo* in Latin) and which turns toward a created thing instead (*conversio ad creaturam* in Latin). In other words, mortal sin is the complete turning away from God and embracing something else in place. It's deadly to the life of grace, because it insults the honor of God and injures the soul of the sinner himself. Mortal sin is like a malignant tumor or a critical injury that's lethal to the spiritual life. Three conditions are necessary for mortal sin to exist:

✔ **Grave Matter:** The act itself *is* intrinsically evil and immoral. For example, murder, rape, incest, perjury, adultery, and so on are grave matter.

✔ **Full Knowledge:** The person must *know* that what they're doing or planning to do is evil and immoral. For example, someone steals a postage stamp, thinking that it's only worth 50 cents. She knows that it's sinful, but if she's unaware that the stamp is rare and actually worth a $1,000, she's not guilty of mortal sin but of venial sin.

✔ **Deliberate Consent:** The person must *freely choose* to commit the act or plan to do it. Someone forced against his will doesn't commit a mortal sin. For example, a man who is drugged and brainwashed to assassinate a leader hasn't done so of his own free will; therefore, he's not guilty of mortal sin.

Venial sins are any sins that only meet one or two of the conditions needed for a mortal sin but do not fulfill all three at the same time, or they're minor violations of the moral law, such as giving an obscene gesture to another driver while in traffic. Venial sin is less serious than mortal sin. Like a benign tumor or a minor infection, venial sin only weakens the soul with sickness but doesn't kill the grace within. Venial sins aren't deadly to the life of grace, but like minor infections in the body, if casually ignored and left untended, may deteriorate into a more serious condition. For example, someone who tells so-called *white lies* commits venial sin, but if he does it long enough, it's much easier for him to be tempted to tell a big lie later on that would in fact be a mortal sin, such as cheating on a test or on his income tax return.

The seven deadly sins are pride, envy, lust, anger, gluttony, greed, and sloth, and Pope Gregory the Great made up the list in the 6th century. Later, in the 14th century, Geoffrey Chaucer popularized them in his *Canterbury Tales*.

In this section, we cover the seven deadly sins. As a bonus, we tell you about the remedies. Yep, *remedies.* Some specific virtues, lesser known than the four cardinal virtues, have traditionally been linked with a particular deadly sin. These virtues (listed in Table 11-1) help to defeat their counterpart.

Table 11-1	The Seven Deadly Sins and the Virtues That Defeat Them
Deadly Sin	*Conquering Virtue*
Pride	Humility
Envy	Kindness or meekness
Lust	Chastity
Anger	Patience

(continued)

Table 11-1 *(continued)*	
Deadly Sin	**Conquering Virtue**
Gluttony	Periodic fasting and abstinence
Greed (avarice)	Generosity
Sloth (acedia)	Diligence

Pride goeth before the fall

Parents and teachers say to take pride in yourself, so why is pride considered a deadly sin? In the context they're talking about, it's not a sin. Parents and teachers are talking about healthy pride, such as taking joy from belonging to a family, a church, or a nation. Being proud to be an American, a Canadian, an Australian, and so on, isn't sinful.

The sin of *pride* is an inordinate love of self — a super-confidence and high esteem in your own abilities. It's also known as vanity. It exaggerates your abilities, gifts, and talents, and ignores your weaknesses, frailties, and imperfections.

In Catholicism, sinful pride is the deviation or distortion of the legitimate need of self-affirmation. Liking yourself isn't sinful. In fact, it's healthy and necessary, but when the self-perception no longer conforms to reality, and you begin to think that you're more important than you actually are, the sin of pride is rearing its ugly head.

The sin of pride gives you a fat head. You think you're better and more important than anyone else. It leads to resenting others whom you consider inferior, and you become impatient with others, because you think they're less perfect than you.

Pride is the key to all other sins, because after you believe that you're more important than you actually are, you compensate for it when others don't agree with your judgment. You rationalize your behavior and make excuses for lying, cheating, stealing, insulting, ignoring, and such, because no one understands you like *you* do. In your mind, you're underestimated by the world.

That's the extreme expression of pride. A subtler example is when you refuse to accept the authority of someone else over you, be it a parent, teacher, employer, pastor, bishop, or pope. Most resentment toward those in authority has nothing to do with the occasional instances of abuse of power in the course of human history. Rather, anti-authoritarianism is rooted in pride: "No one is going to tell me what to do." The refusal to obey others is a by-product of pride. Showing disrespect for those in authority is pride as well. The ego can't stomach someone else having more power, intelligence, influence, or authority, so it rebels against the lawful superiors.

Pride also prevents you from seeking, listening to, or applying advice from others. It fools the mind into thinking that it alone has or can discover all the answers without help from anyone. Do you ever wonder why it is that most men refuse to ask for directions when we're lost? Pride prevents us from admitting that we can't read a map or follow directions properly. We can't let our wives, girlfriends, or mothers know the truth, so we drive on and on, hoping that something familiar appears before it gets too dark or too late.

The Catholic Church teaches that humility is the best remedy for pride. It's not a false self-deprecation, where you beat yourself up verbally only so others can say otherwise. It's not denying the truth. If you have a good singing voice, for example, responding to a compliment with "Oh, no, I can't carry a tune," isn't humility. Catholicism regards humility as recognizing that the talent is really a gift from God and responding with, "Thank you — I've been blessed by the good Lord." Pride would say, "You're darn right I've got a good voice. It's about time you realized it."

In other words, although acknowledging your talents is good, humility should remind you that your talents come from God. Pride fools you into thinking that you're the source of your own greatness.

Envying what others have or enjoy

Envy, another deadly sin, is the resentment of another person's good fortune or joy. Catholicism distinguishes between two kinds of envy:

- ✔ **Material envy** is when you resent others who have more money, talent, strength, beauty, friends, and so on, than you do.

- ✔ **Spiritual envy** is resenting others who progress in holiness, preferring that they stay at or below your level instead of being joyful and happy that they're doing what they're supposed to be doing. Spiritual envy is far worse and more evil than material envy.

Note that some spiritual writers and moralists make a distinction between envy and jealousy. They maintain that envy is the resentment of what others have, such as possessions, talent, fame, and so on, whereas jealousy is the fear of losing what you already have. So a jealous husband fears that he may or will lose his wife to another man. If he happens to think Julia Roberts is the most beautiful woman in the world, then that same husband may also be envious of Julia Roberts' boyfriend. Jealousy is considered to be as much a sin as envy, because it resembles that deadly sin a whole bunch.

The devil's downfall

Many spiritual writers, such as St. John of the Cross, St. Teresa of Avila, and St. Catherine of Siena, considered pride to be a form of idolatry, making yourself divine. Instead of being made in the image and likeness of God, the prideful make God in their own image and likeness and then they become a god.

This was considered to be the sin of Lucifer. According to pious tradition, he was the most intelligent and beautiful of all the angels, but his pride wouldn't allow him to embrace humility, and he rebelled against God. So St. Michael the Archangel cast him into hell.

Jealousy among professional people is common, because they often fear losing their own status, position, notoriety, or esteem to rival colleagues. Jealous people are insecure, apprehensive, and fearful of peers taking what they have, surpassing them, or leaving them behind with less than they started out with. Likewise among students. A student ranked with the best grades in class is jealous when he fears losing that ranking to another student who's getting better grades day by day and is moving up the list faster and faster. On the other hand, a B student is envious when he resents a straight-A student.

The Church maintains that meekness or kindness can counter envy. For example, Genesis 37–47 tells the story of Joseph's brothers, who were envious of Joseph, because he was the favorite son of their father, Jacob. At one point, Jacob gave Joseph a multicolored coat, which pushed the brothers over the edge. They sold Joseph into slavery after almost deciding to kill him. But Joseph rose through the ranks from slave to personal advisor to pharaoh. Later, when he met his brothers again, instead of seeking revenge, Joseph showed them kindness and brought them and their father into Egypt. These sons of Jacob became the heads of the Twelve Tribes of Israel.

Lusting after fruit that's forbidden

The Catholic Church believes that it's normal and healthy to be attracted to and to appreciate the opposite sex. That's not lust, and it's not considered a sin.

Lust is looking at, imagining, and even treating others as mere sex objects to serve your own physical pleasures, rather than as individuals made in the image and likeness of God. Lust is having someone become something merely to please you, in fantasy or reality.

The Church says that lust depersonalizes the other person and the one having the lustful thoughts. It makes both parties nothing more than instruments of enjoyment instead of enabling them to focus on the unique gift of personhood. And it seeks to separate, divide, and isolate what God intended to be united — love and life, the unitive and procreative dimensions of marriage.

The pleasure that lustful thoughts provide is only a sign of the human condition and its wounded nature from original sin, which is *concupiscence,* the proclivity to sin, especially the tendency toward sins of the flesh. The fact that you're entertained by impure thoughts isn't sinful; rather, it's that you entertain them — you engage in the conscious and deliberate act of having lustful thoughts. The sin occurs when you initiate, consent to, and/or continue fantasizing about sexual activity with another person, because all sin involves a free act of the will. Spontaneous thoughts — especially during puberty and adolescence — are primarily involuntary and aren't considered sinful. Such thoughts become sinful when the person recognizes them and has the ability to dismiss and reject them as soon as possible, yet doesn't do so.

Chastity, the virtue that moderates sexual desire, is the best remedy for lust. Chastity falls under temperance and can help to keep physical pleasure in moderation.

Without chastity, men and women become like animals that copulate when in heat. Animals have sex driven by instinct, but men and women have the gift of reason and can choose when and with whom to be intimate. Desirous of chastity, men and women can freely abstain from sexual activity until the wedding night. If they allow lust to drive their actions, however, they fornicate and commit adultery. Cultivating and clinging to chastity separates them from the animals.

Anger to the point of seeking revenge

You have no control over what angers you, but you do have control over what you do after you become angry. The deadly sin of *anger* is the sudden outburst of emotion — namely hostility — and sustaining thoughts about the desire for revenge.

If someone sticks you with a needle or pin, for example, or slaps you in the face, your initial reaction is probably one of anger. You resent what was done to you. The sin of anger occurs when you react by swearing, cursing, shouting, ranting, or raving. (Don't confuse those last three reactions with the shouting, ranting, and raving that occur at a typical Italian meal. Everyone screams and yells at those.) Likewise, if you brood over injuries and insults others have heaped on you and begin to yearn for revenge, the Church asserts that you're committing the sin of anger. Inordinate, violent, and hateful anger is always a mortal sin. Bloodthirsty revenge also comes from anger.

But what if, say, someone robs you? In that case, wouldn't those feelings be merited? No. Being upset that someone robbed you is normal and righteous indignation, but seeking revenge and desiring to see the culprit suffer isn't. Instead, with the virtue of justice, you can desire for the police to catch the thief and for a court to sentence her to a fair punishment.

Patience, the virtue that allows you to adapt and endure evil without harboring any destructive feelings, is the best countermeasure for anger. When you give yourself the time and opportunity to cool off, anger dissipates and more practical concerns come to the front line.

Gluttony: Too much food or firewater

Gluttony is immoderate eating and/or drinking too much alcohol. Enjoying a delightful dinner isn't sinful, but intentionally overeating to the point where you literally get sick to your stomach is. So, too, having an alcoholic beverage now and then (provided that you don't suffer from alcoholism) is *not* sinful in the eyes of the Church. Responsible consumption of alcohol is allowed. Making a champagne toast to a bride and groom or having a mixed drink with friends at a dinner party is all fine and well, that is, as long as you aren't a recovering alcoholic. But drinking to the point of drunkenness *is* a sin. Abusing alcohol is sinful, and it doesn't necessarily mean only getting drunk. People who use alcohol to lessen the inhibitions of themselves or others are committing sin. Driving under the influence or while intoxicated is a mortal sin, because you endanger your own life and the lives of others. Underage drinking is also considered a serious sin.

Legitimate eating disorders, such as anorexia and bulimia, aren't gluttony. They're medical conditions that require treatment and care. The sin of gluttony is freely choosing to over-consume. Gluttony is voluntary and merely requires self-control and moderation.

During the last days of the Roman Empire, when decadence was at an all-time high, *vomitoriums* were erected for people to regurgitate after eating and drinking too much — only so they could eat and drink more — the epitome of gluttony.

Like lust, gluttony focuses on *pleasure* and finds it in food and drink, and lust finds it in sexual activity. Both enslave the soul to the body, even though the soul — being superior to the body — should be in charge. Gluttons don't eat out of necessity or for social reasons, but merely to consume and experience the pleasure of taste.

Gorging yourself on appetizers, several courses, desserts, and so on — with no concern for the possibility of getting sick or the reality that millions of people are starving around the world — is the ugliness and evil of gluttony. In addition, gluttony endangers your life by jeopardizing the health of your body.

Periodic *fasting,* restricting the amount of food you eat, and *abstinence,* avoiding meat or some favorite food, are the best defenses against gluttony. Unlike dieting where the goal is to lose weight, fasting and abstinence are purify the soul by controlling the desires of the body. Occasionally, giving up favorite foods and beverages promotes self-control and temperance. In addition, deciding ahead of time what and how much to eat and drink is considered prudent and helpful.

Greed: The desire for more, more, and still more

Greed is the inordinate love of and desire for earthly possessions. Things are cherished above people and relationships. Amassing a fortune and foolishly trying to accumulate the most stuff is greed, which is sometimes called *avarice.* Next to anger, envy, and lust, more crimes have been committed due to greed than any other deadly sin. "It's never enough. I've got to have more." That's the battle cry of greed.

Greed is also a sign of mistrust. "I doubt that God will take care of me, so I try to gather as much as possible now in case no more is left later." The Gospel relates the parable about such a greedy man. He had so much grain that he tore down his bin to hold more — only to die that very night (Luke 12:16–21). But you can't take it with you. That saying was true then, and it's true now. So, too, some time ago, a rich woman stipulated in her will that she be buried in her Rolls Royce. Where's she going to drive that thing?

Greed, the apex of selfishness, has ruined marriages, families, and friendships. *Generosity,* however, is the best weapon against greed. Freely giving some of your possessions away, especially to those less fortunate, is considered the perfect antithesis to greed and avarice. Generosity promotes detachment from material things that come and go. Things can be broken, stolen, destroyed, or lost. They can be replaced, but people can't.

Sloth: Lazy as a lotus-eater

Sloth (sometimes called *acedia*) is laziness — particularly when it concerns prayer and spiritual life. It centers on doing nothing or doing just trivial things. Sloth is always wanting to rest and relax, with no desire or intention of making a sacrifice or doing something for others. It's an aversion to work — physical, mental, and spiritual. Sloth inevitably leads to lukewarmness and tepidity and then deteriorates into disinterest, discouragement, and finally despair. Sloth breeds indifference, which prevents joy from ever being experienced.

The Church says that the evil habit of being inattentive at religious worship services — just being physically present but not consciously participating — or being careless in fulfilling your religious duties is also a sin of sloth. Other examples include never getting to Church before Mass starts; just sitting in church but not singing, praying, kneeling, or standing; never reading the Bible or the *Catechism of the Catholic Church;* and not praying before eating a meal or going to bed.

Proverbs 24:30–34 says a little something about sloth:

> I went by the field of the slothful,
> and by the vineyard of the man void of understanding;
> And, lo, it was all grown over with thorns,
> and nettles had covered the face thereof,
> and the stone wall thereof was broken down.
> Then I saw, and considered it well:
> I looked upon it, and received instruction.
> Yet a little sleep, a little slumber,
> a little folding of the hands to sleep:
> So shall thy poverty come as one that travelleth;
> and thy want as an armed man.

Spiritual laziness can only be overcome by practicing the virtue of *diligence,* which is the habit of keeping focused and paying attention to the work at hand — be it the work of employment or the work of God. Diligent prayer and diligent worship can make you more reverent. Diligence in all things ensures that you don't become idle and then start daydreaming, leaving reality for fantasy island.

Catholics, like all other human beings, are asked to practice virtue and avoid vice. Going even farther, religion and faith ask God's children to seek holiness and avoid all sin and evil at the same time. The motivation for believers is simple: the choice of heaven or hell — eternal happiness, joy, and peace, or eternal pain, misery, and damnation.

Chapter 12

The Church's Stand on Some Sticky Issues

Catholicism may appear at times to go against the grain, risk unpopularity, or even chance rejection and persecution of some of its beliefs and practices. Like all religions, it seeks to conform to the Almighty rather than going along with the hoi polloi. Moods change, tastes differ, and crowds can be fickle, ugly or just plain apathetic. Whether something is popular doesn't determine whether it's true or good. When most of the people thought the world was flat, it didn't make it so. Moral and spiritual leaders have an obligation to conform to a higher authority than their own. Even though they serve and minister to the common folk, they owe their obedience not to the *vox populi* (voice of the people) but to the *vox Dei* (voice of God).

Most religions have some controversial teachings, doctrines, disciplines, and policies that the outside world rejects or misunderstands. A few members may even dislike or oppose some doctrine or other, yet these positions remain part and parcel of the official religion, because at the very core is an obligation to speak the truth "in season and out of season . . . for the time will come when they will not endure sound doctrine but wanting to have their ears tickled" (2 Timothy 4:2–3). For this reason, the Catholic Church, like other faiths, stands by her convictions and teachings on artificial birth control, abortion, euthanasia, capital punishment, and the like. Some issues take plenty of explaining and research, so for the sake of brevity and simplicity, we chose a few controversial positions that can be described briefly.

Celibacy and the Male Priesthood

Even before the advent of clergy sex scandals, the issue of celibacy has intrigued non-Catholics. Some claim it contradicts nature and goes against biblical teachings on marriage and the ministry (Genesis 1:28 "be fruitful and multiply" and 1 Corinthians 9:5 "do we not have a right to take along a wife?"). Because of the vocations crisis and fewer 21st-century ordinations to the priesthood, many people are questioning celibacy and the restriction of ordination to males only. Married clergy and women priests, some contend, would alleviate the shortage of personnel and bring a fresh perspective to the vocation. Protestant Christians have had both for decades now and wonder when Catholics will catch up. Legitimate questions and valid points to be sure, but Catholicism has some good answers and replies, as we shall see.

To address these issues, we must differentiate celibacy from the male priesthood. They're two separate and distinct issues and entities, even though they overlap in practice. Celibacy is a discipline of the Church that isn't absolute; exceptions and modifications have been made through the centuries. But the male priesthood is a part of doctrine and divine law that can never be changed or altered by any pope or council.

Flying solo for life

Celibacy is the formal and solemn oath to never enter the married state. Celibate men and women willingly relinquish their natural right to marry in order to devote themselves completely and totally to God and his Church.

The Catholic Church doesn't teach (and never has taught) that *all* clergy must be celibate. From day one, Eastern Catholic Churches, such as the Byzantine, have consistently and perennially had the option of married clergy. Only in the United States is celibacy imposed and forced on the Byzantine Catholic clergy. (See the sidebar "Only in the United States" for details.)

Celibacy isn't necessary, essential, or obligatory in the Roman Catholic Church. It's a *discipline* of the church, not a doctrine. The East never made it mandatory. The West made it normative in A.D. 306 at the Council of Elvira and mandatory in 1074 by Pope Gregory VII and reaffirmed in 1139 at the Second Lateran Council. Although the Eastern Catholic and Orthodox Churches have always had an optional celibacy, both have a celibate episcopacy, meaning that only celibate priests can become bishops. So although they have a married clergy, the upper hierarchy remains celibate and to a degree quasi-monastic. (They live and pray like monks more than like parish priests.)

Only in the United States

At the turn of the last century, many Eastern European immigrants came to America and brought their clergy with them. Some influential and shortsighted Irish-American bishops feared (with no foundation) that a married priesthood among Eastern Catholics would cause tension and animosity among the Western (Latin) Roman Catholic clergy and laity. So they asked Rome if they could force the Byzantine clergy to mandate celibacy in North America even though it would remain optional in the rest of the world.

Before that, every single Ruthenian, Ukrainian, Melkite, Maronite, Coptic, and Romanian Catholic priest had the option of being celibate or married all over the world. Today, only the United States still pushes mandatory celibacy on the Eastern Catholic clergy.

A rolling stone gathers no moss

Celibacy is legitimate for both the East and the West, even though it's optional for the former and mandatory for the latter. But why the difference between the two? Well, politics and culture. Even before East split from West in 1054 and formed the Orthodox Church, the Eastern part of the Holy Roman Empire operated differently from the Western part. (See Appendix A in this book for more on the history of Catholicism.)

In the East, a close association existed between the secular and religious spheres, which was dramatically different from the situation in the West. After Rome fell in A.D. 476, no single, powerful, and influential secular ruler arose until Charlemagne was crowned Holy Roman Emperor in A.D. 800.

So from the fifth to eighth centuries, the most powerful and influential person in the West was the bishop of Rome. As pope and head of the worldwide Catholic Church, he became the icon of stability and power as Western Europe survived the fall of the ancient Roman Empire, the barbarian invasions, and the so-called Dark Ages.

Instability in the secular realm meant that the clergy, especially the bishops, took on more than just spiritual leadership, just as the pope wielded more than pastoral power in Rome and around the world. And the West found that celibacy among the clergy was beneficial and helpful because that meant no divided loyalties.

Kings, princes, barons, earls, dukes, counts, and other nobility married first to make political alliances and second to establish families. Mandatory celibacy prevented the clergy from getting involved in the intrigue of who marries whom. Mandatory celibacy ensured that the priests were preoccupied with Church work and had no ties or interests in local politics among the fighting factions, which were trying to establish the infant nation states.

Priests with families would've been vulnerable to the local nobility, because their extended families would've been under secular dominion. A celibate clergy made for a more independent clergy, free from earthly concerns and corruption, enabling them to serve the people and the hierarchy with full attention and loyalty.

Biblical background for celibacy

Some people think that celibacy goes against biblical teachings on marriage and the ministry (Genesis 1:28 and 1 Corinthians 9:5). But the Catholic Church actually uses the Bible as part of its reasoning for priestly celibacy.

Jesus Christ never married and was celibate, and the New Testament affirms the value of celibacy:

- **Matthew 19:12:** Some are incapable of marriage because they were born so; some, because they were made so by others; some, because they have renounced marriage for the sake of the kingdom of heaven. Whoever can accept this ought to accept it.

- **1 Corinthians 7:8:** To the unmarried and the widows I say that it is well for them to remain single as I do.

- **1 Corinthians 7:27–34, 38:** Are you free from a wife? Do not seek marriage. But if you marry, you do not sin, and if a girl marries she does not sin. Yet those who marry will have worldly troubles, and I would spare you that. I mean, brethren, the appointed time has grown very short; from now on, let those who have wives live as though they had none, and those who mourn as though they were not mourning, and those who rejoice as though they were not rejoicing, and those who buy as though they had no goods, and those who deal with the world as though they had no dealings with it. For the form of this world is passing away. I want you to be free from anxieties. The unmarried man is anxious about the affairs of the Lord, how to please the Lord; but the married man is anxious about worldly affairs, how to please his wife, and his interests are divided. . . . So that he who marries his betrothed does well; and he who refrains from marriage will do better.

According to Catholicism, it's erroneous to claim that celibacy is nonbiblical. Many significant people in the Bible were unmarried, and the preceding passages show that the New Testament and the Early Church didn't frown on or merely tolerate celibacy. They saw it as a gift — as much a gift as the gift of faith and the gift of a vocation to serve the Church.

Mandatory celibacy for the priesthood is a discipline of the Church, not a doctrine or a dogma. Theoretically, any pope could modify or dissolve mandatory celibacy at any time, but it's highly improbable, because it's been part of the Western Church's priesthood since the 4th century. (See the sidebar, "Footloose, free, and on the run," in this chapter.) Additionally, the Church teaches and affirms that celibacy isn't just a sacrifice; it's also a gift.

Is celibacy to blame for the priest shortage?

Because of the declining number of newly ordained Catholic priests, some people think that allowing married clergy would alleviate the shortage of personnel. But statistics show that even Protestant ministers and clergy — who *can* be married and, in many cases, can be women or men — are decreasing in numbers, too. The Church believes that relaxing or eliminating celibacy isn't the panacea that will answer the priest shortage in the West.

Socially and culturally, first-world nations, such as the United States, Canada, and most of Western Europe, are having smaller and smaller families. The birth rate has dropped to an all-time low, because many couples in these affluent countries are having only one or two children. People in Islamic countries, on the other hand, are having the large families that were the unofficial trademark of Catholicism. When a family had four to eight children, the odds were good that at least one or two of them may have a vocation to the priesthood or religious life. Big families aren't the only, or primary, source of priests and nuns, but they do bring possible vocations into the world.

But if a pope decides to change, modify, or end mandatory celibacy for the Western church, the Church would still maintain and follow the same tradition observed by the Eastern Catholic Church concerning married clergy. Among the married clergy in the Eastern Church, marriage must come before ordination, and if he's ordained unmarried, he must remain unmarried:

- Ending mandatory celibacy would only affect those yet to be ordained. Celibate priests who're already ordained wouldn't be allowed to marry.

- Seminarians would have to decide before ordination whether they wanted to be married. They'd have to find a wife prior to their ordination or remain celibate.

- Anyone having aspirations to be ordained a bishop would have to remain celibate.

- Catholic priests who were ordained celibate and then later left the active ministry to get married would *not* be allowed back into the active ministry as a married priest.

The pros and cons

Celibacy can be difficult for those who don't come from a large extended family. An only son might feel anxiety and tension when his elderly parents become sick and need attention, and no other adult children are available to care for them. And a priest who comes from a small family may feel lonely more often during the holidays. He sees married families in his parish sharing the joy of the season with one another, and yet he doesn't have many aunts and uncles, brothers and sisters, and nieces and nephews to visit.

Another sacrifice is not having a lifelong companion to support, encourage, advise, and, of course, correct you at times. Not having a baby to rock to sleep, a son to watch in his first little league baseball game, and a daughter to walk down the aisle on her wedding day are all sacrifices required by celibacy.

But at the same time, celibacy gives a priest the time and opportunity to love hundreds of women and children and to give 100 percent of his attention, effort, zeal, and talent, whereas a married man must balance family and work. A celibate priest doesn't have to make the painful decision of whether to respond to an emergency phone call at 3 a.m. or stay home with a seriously ill wife or child.

Celibacy can be distorted into being only a sacrifice ("I gave up a wife and children"), or it can be seen as the Church intended — as both a sacrifice and a gift. ("I freely gave up a wife and children so that I can love and serve my parishioners as if they're my children.")

Catholic priests use the title *Father,* because they're spiritually considered the father of many children through the sacraments. Catholic Christians are spiritually born in Baptism, fed in the Holy Eucharist, made mature in Confirmation, and healed during Penance and the Anointing of the Sick. The responsibilities of parents parallel that of the priest: Parents give birth to their children, feed them, heal them, and help them grow and mature. So the Church is considered the spiritual mother. Catholics call the Church the *Holy Mother Church,* and the priest is their spiritual father.

Pope John Paul II's letter *Pastores Dabo Vobis* (I Will Give You Shepherds) reminds Catholic priests that although they have no wife and children of their own, they're not alone. They do have a spouse — the Church. A priest is to treat the people of his parish (and every member of the Church, for that matter) as his beloved bride. The parishioners aren't to be treated as stockholders, employers, employees, servants, customers, or clients. They're to be treated as a beloved spouse. The priest marries the Church, because the Church is considered the Bride of Christ, and the priest is considered "another Christ" by virtue of the Sacrament of Holy Orders. So the priest must love the Church as Christ loves the Church. It's a spousal relationship and covenant of love.

When put in this context, celibacy is merely the means to making the reality more possible and more dynamic. Married clergy can do a superb and phenomenal job, no matter what their denomination or gender. But celibacy for the Catholic priesthood in the Latin tradition makes sense, and although it's not always easy, neither is married life.

Footloose, free, and on the run

Because of the necessity of a priest for major Catholic religious practices to occur (only a priest has the power to say Mass and hear confession), a celibate, all-male priesthood is far more practical. A single priest can move about unencumbered, without having to think about and see after the welfare of a family.

In the late 1800s, Catholic homesteaders would go for weeks and sometimes months without the benefits of Sunday Mass. Then a priest, traveling from town to city and back again, would arrive in say, Helena, Montana, to hear confessions and say Mass. Catholics would come from miles around, sometimes walking all the way and undergoing great hardship to get to confession and Mass.

Priests are obliged to act as pioneers between this world and the next, leading Christ's flock into heaven. To remain focused on their calling, they can't afford to get hung up in worldly (or political) changes. This is particularly true for missionary priests in a foreign country, as well as those priests in any country that's experiencing a change in government that may be hostile toward the Church. In these situations, which have occurred over and over again throughout history and continue to occur, the priests who aren't arrested, thrown in prison, executed (martyred), or compromised, are apt to hide and travel throughout the countryside and the byways of the city, saying Mass, hearing confession, baptizing, and so on, in secret and on the run like outlaws.

During England's Reformation, priests were drawn and quartered, and citizens found guilty of hiding a priest were executed. Such was the fate of St. Margaret Clitherow, martyred on March 25, 1586. And today, *Fides,* the Vatican's missionary news source, tallies the number of priests throughout the world who suffer martyrdom annually.

The sexual abuse issue

Celibate clergy aren't more likely or prone to sexual misconduct (homosexual or heterosexual) than any other group, despite the rhetoric that ensued soon after the blitz of pedophilia cases came to light in the United States awhile back. Catholic priests were the focus of much media attention — mostly because of the unconscionable actions of a very small minority of deviant clergy and a few bishops who merely transferred known sex offenders. But the actual numbers demonstrate that the overwhelming majority of sexual abuse by adults toward children occurs within a family — 76 percent by parents and 12 percent by other family members. Married men who are related to the minors in some way commit most of the sexual abuse. So far, 1,500 priests have been accused of molesting children. Yet that's only 2.5 (two and a half) percent of the 60,000 priests who have served in the United States since 1984. Even one case is one too many, of course, because abusing children is one of the most heinous evils any adult can commit. But note that this horrible behavior isn't limited or even primarily found in the celibate male clergy. It's an evil that afflicts a few pastors of all denominations, as well as parents, family members, teachers, coaches and many other walks of life.

We in no way think that takes away from the horror, shame, and diabolical evil of a few celibate priests committing the heinous crime and sin of child sex abuse. But it's important to also look at the whole picture — to see that the overwhelming majority of child abuse cases are committed by married laymen who are related to the kids and that the overwhelming majority of celibate priests aren't pedophiles and have never abused any boy, girl, man, or woman.

The evil of child abuse makes no distinction between Catholic or Protestant, Christian or Jewish, celibate or married, black or white, young or old. All ethnic, religious, and racial groups have had a few deviants and perverts in their ranks. But indiscriminately associating the Catholic priesthood and its discipline of celibacy with pedophilia doesn't make sense. Yes, sadly, some priests and bishops did abuse children, and more disturbing is that some bishops merely moved these weirdos from place to place instead of stopping them once and for all. Nonetheless, no credible or logical argument or data supports the notion that celibacy encouraged or promoted sexual misconduct among the clergy. And from now on, those found ought to be and will be removed from active ministry, suspended of their ordained faculties, and reported to the civil authorities.

No-woman's-land

With an apparent priest shortage and so many Protestant denominations embracing women ministers, some people wonder why the Catholic Church doesn't allow female priests. First of all, it's *not* because women aren't qualified or that they're somehow not worthy of this calling.

It's a *constitutive element* of the Sacrament of Holy Orders — any pope, council, or bishop can't change it. The same is true about the use of water for Baptism and bread and wine for Holy Eucharist. The elements of every Sacrament can't be changed, because Christ established it. This belief is shared by the Eastern Orthodox, who also don't ordain women for the very same reason. It has nothing to do with who's more worthy or suitable for Holy Orders in the same way that the ban on non-Catholics receiving Holy Communion has nothing to do with any moral or spiritual judgment on the persons involved. It has to do with Sacred Tradition, which is considered as divinely inspired as Sacred Scripture. (See Chapter 3 for details about Sacred Tradition.)

The reason the Roman Catholic and Eastern Orthodox Churches are unable to ordain women — be it to the diaconate, priesthood, or episcopacy — is actually threefold:

✔ The Church can't change what constitutes valid matter for any of the seven sacraments.

✔ Sacred Tradition, nearly 2,000 years old, has never had an instance of women priests.

✔ Jesus didn't ordain any women or call any of them to be apostles — thus excluding his mother even!

The Sacrament of Holy Orders

No pope, bishop, or council can change the constitutive elements of any of the seven sacraments, and a valid Sacrament of Holy Orders requires a baptized male to be ordained by a validly ordained bishop. Maleness is as essential to the Sacrament of Holy Orders as wheat bread and grape wine are to the Sacrament of the Holy Eucharist. So just as the pope can't change the requirements of valid matter for the Holy Eucharist, he can't change the requirements of valid matter for Holy Orders.

Sacred Tradition

Both the Catholic and Orthodox Churches believe that the revealed Word of God is both written (Sacred Scripture) and unwritten (Sacred Tradition). When the Bible is silent or ambiguous, Sacred Tradition authentically fills in the gaps. Sacred Tradition shows that women were never ordained, and Pope John Paul II's encyclical, *Ordinatio Sacerdotalis* (1994), clearly states that women can't be ordained. (For more on encyclicals and other papal documents, see Chapter 2.)

It's not considered a matter of injustice, because not all men are allowed to be ordained. Just having a personal vocation isn't enough. The local bishop must call the man. No man can demand or expect ordination, because it's a gift, not a right. Think of it like this: Just as it's not unjust for men not to be able to give birth, it's not unjust for women not to be ordained.

Jesus and his apostles

The Church points to the fact that Jesus was both God and man. From all eternity, he was divine with a divine nature, intellect, and will. But he was also born of a human mother and took on a human nature as well. In his divinity, Jesus was God and pure spirit, but in his humanity, he was a man. His gender was more than accidental, because the Church is his bride. And because the priest acts *in persona Christi* (in the person of Christ) as an *alter-Christus* (another Christ), then the priest reflects Christ to the entire Church whenever he celebrates any of the sacraments. The maleness of Christ was part of who he was, and therefore, Jesus only called men to be his apostles even though his mother would've been a far better choice. But if a woman were to be ordained, she couldn't be espoused to the Church, because the Church is considered *mother*. A mother needs a father to complement the equation.

Catholicism regards Jesus as the groom and the Church as his bride. The priest is another Christ who acts in the person of Christ. The male priest represents the male Christ, and the priest is in a spousal relationship with the Holy Mother Church. Women priests don't fit into that typology.

The changing roles of women

Women have come a long way since the early and medieval Church. Although they can't be ordained priests, women have equal rights to be sponsors at Baptism and Confirmation. In Matrimony, they're treated and regarded as 100 percent full, equal partners with their husbands. Women can serve on the parish council and finance committees. They can be readers at Mass, *extraordinary ministers* (laypersons who assist the priest at Mass to give out Holy Communion) if needed, and ushers. They can work in the parish office, teach religious ed, and so on, just like their male counterparts. And many parishes have women *pastoral associates* — usually nuns or religious sisters who help the pastor with many spiritual and pastoral duties. In addition, women can hold positions of influence and power even in the diocesan chancery. The Church has women who are canon lawyers, judges, and chancellors across the country. The Church has allowed local bishops and pastors the option to permit female altar servers at Mass. Now many parishes have both altar girls and altar boys.

Matters of Life and Death

The Catholic Church's stand on various life and death issues — abortion, euthanasia, the death penalty, and war — doesn't always go with the flow. To find out exactly what each stand is and the reasoning behind it, keep reading.

Abortion

The Catholic Church opposes and condemns any and all direct abortions. Even pregnancies that result from rape, incest, and present a danger to the life of the mother aren't reasons for abortion. Although the Catholic position on abortion may seem extreme to some, it coincides consistently and completely with Catholic morality, which is based on the natural moral law, the Bible, and the official teachings of the Magisterium. (For more on natural moral law, see Chapter 9; for more on the Magisterium, see Chapter 2.)

The ends can never justify the means. Catholics believe that willingly, knowingly, and deliberately committing evil is never justifiable — no matter how good the intention and no matter how noble the cause. This is a moral absolute for Catholics, and it can't be diluted or altered one iota. The Church believes that if in even one circumstance, someone is allowed to knowingly and willingly commit evil so that good may come from it, then Pandora's box is opened for anyone to claim he was merely doing a so-called necessary evil for the greater good in the long run. So the Church teaches that one innocent life can't be taken even if it would save hundreds, thousands, or millions.

The Catholic Church sees abortion as the termination of an innocent though unborn life, and therefore, it's always wrong, sinful, and immoral. The circumstances by which that life was conceived are considered irrelevant to the question, "Is this an innocent person?"

The Church teaches that human life is created and begins at the moment of conception. A half-human or pre-human isn't growing in the womb but a growing and living unborn whole child. At the moment of conception, when the father's sperm fertilizes the mother's egg, God infuses an immortal soul into this brand new member of the human race. The embryo may not survive the nine months of pregnancy, but nature — not man — should decide when life should be terminated. It's human DNA in the baby and distinct from mom or dad, too. That means that only a human being exists in the womb, nothing less.

Often, people say that the Catholic Church opts for the child over the mother. Not the case at all. The real teaching is that each and every innocent life must be protected, and intentionally ending the life of the mother or the unborn child is immoral.

So if a pregnant woman has a heart attack and needs emergency surgery, it's considered morally permissible to put her under anesthesia and operate, even though it's likely that she'll spontaneously abort the unborn fetus on her own as a consequence. The distinction is that her body is doing the act of ejecting the fetus as an effect of the primary action of the doctors who are trying to save both lives — the mother and the baby. If the baby dies naturally, the Church believes that no sin has been committed. But if the doctor or nurse directly kills the baby, that's considered murder, the taking of an innocent life.

Likewise, if a pregnant woman has a cancerous uterus, and it must be removed immediately or she and the baby will die, it's considered morally permissible for the uterus to be removed as long as the unborn child isn't directly killed. If the womb is diseased and threatening the life of the mother, the Church permits removing both the uterus and the child while the child is still alive. In this case, the unborn are often too young to survive outside the womb even with the best of prenatal care, and the baby dies a natural death. The sin of abortion occurs if the doctor or nurse intentionally causes the death of the unborn while still in the womb or on the way out. The Church sees a drastic difference between causing death and allowing the process of certain death to continue.

Letting nature take its course

St. Thomas Aquinas defined *life* as spontaneous, immanent activity. Once fertilization occurs, the embryo begins to grow. Cells divide, grow, multiply, and follow a predetermined pattern, but the process is also independent to a degree. Although the embryo needs the womb to survive for nourishment and shelter, the process of cell division, growth, and development occur inside from a life force within the embryo itself. Unlike a red or white blood cell that takes orders from the brain to go to one part of the body, the embryo isn't being told what to do by the mother's brain.

It's working on its own initiative, plan, and schedule. Mom is merely giving the unborn child the time, place, and support he needs to complete the process begun at conception. If that internal, spontaneous, automatic, and independent process stops on its own, then the mother's body will eject the dead embryo by itself, which is commonly known as a miscarriage. On the other hand, if that process is intentionally stopped by any outside force, it's an abortion, which Catholics consider immoral, because it's the intentional taking of an innocent life.

The same applies to ectopic pregnancies. This pathologic condition can warrant the immediate removal of the fallopian tube even though an embryo is attached or embedded to it. As long as the unborn is never directly killed, then the Church doesn't consider the procedure an abortion.

Killing an embryo while in the womb or removing an unviable fetus from the womb with the intent and purpose to end its life is considered an abortion. Treating a life-threatening, pathological condition that indirectly results in the unborn child dying naturally is considered a tragedy but not an abortion. So it's not a question of who lives or who dies. It's not a battle of mother versus child.

Even the horror and tragedy of rape or incest isn't considered cause to kill an innocent unborn life. If possible, the woman — who is also considered an innocent victim — can get treatment as soon as possible to try to *prevent* conception from occurring immediately after the rape or incest. Moral theologians and doctors say that it takes several hours to a day for the sperm to reach the egg, so the Church permits a female rape victim to be given a contraceptive *only* if ovulation or conception haven't yet taken place *and* the drug given isn't an *abortifacient* — a so-called contraceptive that doesn't prevent fertilization and conception but rather removes, destroys, or prevents implantation of the embryo. If she waits too long, usually more than 24 hours, though, conception may take place, and any procedure or treatment to eject the unviable human embryo is an abortion. The Church's stand is that even though she's an innocent victim of a horrible evil, the unborn child is also an innocent victim. No matter what the circumstances that led to the conception, once conceived, that child has an immortal soul and has a right to live as much as the mother. In the United States, 98 percent of abortions have nothing to do with rape or incest, and throughout much of the world, the greater percentage of abortions also have nothing to do with rape.

Mary was single and pregnant

The Gospel of Luke tells the story of an encounter between Mary, the mother of Jesus, and her cousin Elizabeth, the mother of John the Baptist. According to Luke 1:26–38, Mary first meets the Archangel Gabriel, who announces to Mary that she's to conceive and bear a son and name him Jesus. At the very moment that Mary gives her free consent, "Be it done unto me according to thy word," the Holy Spirit overshadows her, and she conceives right then and there. So Mary became pregnant before she married Joseph. That's why he plans to quietly divorce her rather than expose her to the Law. He erroneously concludes that Mary was unfaithful as his fiancée and got pregnant through another man. An angel in a dream tells Joseph not to be afraid and to take Mary as his wife, because it was by the power of the Holy Spirit that she conceived, not through any sexual contact with a man. Joseph's fears are alleviated, and he takes Mary as his wife.

The Archangel also informs Mary that her elderly cousin Elizabeth is pregnant, and so Mary travels "in haste" from Nazareth to Judah to help Elizabeth. When Mary enters the home, Elizabeth is, as the Archangel told Mary, in her sixth month of pregnancy, and Mary, coming in haste from Nazareth, is only a few days into her pregnancy.

The Gospel says that when Mary enters the room, Elizabeth's unborn baby (John the Baptist) leaps for joy in his mother's womb, because he knows that within Mary is the unborn Jesus. So in the Bible, a 6-month-old unborn child recognizes the presence of a 2- to 3-day-old unborn child. It's not inanimate tissue that stirs within Elizabeth, and it's not a blob of protoplasm that the unborn John the Baptist is getting excited about. So not only are the two pregnant mothers — one six months along and one only a few days along — greeting one another, but their unborn children are also very much alive and participating in the event. The unborn John heralds the arrival of the unborn Jesus.

Euthanasia

The same principles used to condemn abortion are also used to condemn euthanasia. Catholicism regards life as sacred, and taking any innocent life is immoral and sinful.

The Church believes that no one needs or ought to suffer a long, painful death, and that the sick must be treated and the dying must be comforted. The dying and those suffering enormous pain from disease or injury or can and should have as much painkiller medication as they can tolerate, as long as the medication isn't the cause of death. Modern medicine has created a plethora of chemicals to diminish or even remove pain, even if it means the patient loses consciousness. So giving someone morphine is permitted and encouraged, for example, but the dosage can't be large enough to be the direct cause of death.

The Church distinguishes between two types of euthanasia:

- **Active:** Any procedure or treatment that directly causes the death of a patient. Giving someone a lethal injection or drinking poison are examples. This type is always considered immoral and sinful because it's the direct taking of an innocent life. The reasoning is that because the ends can't justify the means, causing the death of someone — even someone you love and hate to see in pain and suffering — is still immoral. Better to make them comfortable and give them pain medication, water, air, and nutrition.

- **Passive:** Intentionally withholding life-sustaining treatment. If the treatment is sustaining life and stopping or removing it ends life, then doing so is considered passive euthanasia. For example, turning off a respirator that's being used by a patient whose lungs won't work on their own is passive euthanasia. Another example is omitting medicine that's needed to preserve life — such as not giving a diabetic insulin. Like active euthanasia, passive euthanasia is considered immoral and sinful, because its primary purpose is the death of an innocent person. The means are different, however. In active euthanasia, you're causing death by doing something to hasten death. In passive euthanasia you intend and cause death by not doing what's necessary to preserve or sustain life.

The Church also distinguishes between direct and indirect passive euthanasia:

- **Direct passive:** Intentionally causing death by withholding medicine or a procedure or stopping one that's begun. This type is always immoral.

- **Indirect passive:** Withholding treatment or medicine that may cause death, but death isn't the intent or direct cause of withholding it. This type isn't considered immoral. For example, an elderly man dying of cancer who's also diabetic can refuse (or his family can refuse) insulin injections as long as he's already started the dying process and will die of cancer or complications of it well before he'd die of diabetes. As long as the medicine or treatment being withheld isn't the direct cause of death, it can be refused. Likewise, say that a 98-year-old person in a nursing home is in bad health and bedridden, has cancer, and has begun the dying process (the organs are starting to shut down one by one). It's considered morally permissible to have a Do Not Resuscitate (DNR) order on the chart in case the patient has a heart attack because doing cardio-pulmonary resuscitation (CPR) would be fruitless or would only prolong death by cancer. The *Catechism of the Catholic Church* clarifies when medical treatment can be refused or stopped: "Discontinuing medical procedures that are burdensome, dangerous, extraordinary, or disproportionate to the expected outcome can be legitimate; it is the refusal of 'over-zealous' treatment. Here one does not will to cause death; one's inability to impede it is merely accepted." (2278)

The death penalty

The *Catechism of the Catholic Church* says, "the traditional teaching of the Church does not exclude recourse to the death penalty, *if this is the only possible way* of effectively defending human lives against the *unjust aggressor*" (2267). This assumes that the truly guilty party's identity and culpability have been firmly established. But the death penalty is not an absolute right of the state as would be the case in defending the right to life of the innocent. In that case, it's always immoral to intentionally take the life of an innocent person, such as in the case of abortion or euthanasia. The pope unequivocally says that in his encyclical letter *Evangelium Vitae* (Gospel of Life): "Therefore, by the authority which Christ conferred upon Peter and his Successors . . . I confirm that *the direct and voluntary killing of an innocent human being is always gravely immoral*" (57).

If the innocent can never be intentionally killed, then what about the guilty? The Catechism and the pope, quoting St. Thomas Aquinas, affirm that legitimate defense is not only a *right* but may even be a *duty* for someone responsible for another's life. Sadly, sometimes the only way to render an unjust aggressor incapable of causing harm may involve the use of deadly force, such as a policeman in the line of duty may use or a soldier in time of war would do. But the very significant restriction, according to the Catechism, is "if nonlethal means are sufficient to defend and protect people's safety from the aggressor, authority will limit itself to such means."

What does this all mean? It's consistent Church teaching that the state *possesses* the right to impose the death penalty, but there is no unlimited or unrestricted *use* of that right. According to the Catechism, because the state can effectively prevent crime by stopping the perpetrator without the use of deadly force, **"the cases in which the execution of the offender is an absolute necessity are very rare, if not practically non-existent."** This severe restriction on the application of the death penalty is rooted in the fact that punishment isn't meant to be revenge but the restoration of justice, deterrence, and possible rehabilitation. Conversion of the criminal is an aspect not often brought into the public debate on the death penalty.

What about terrorists? There is significant evidence, argumentation, and sound reasoning that says you can invoke the rules of a Just War. (The Just War Doctrine is discussed in the next section.) This would mean that you could try terrorists in a military tribunal as enemy combatants. The thinking is that a terrorist is at war with the civilian (and in most cases) noncombatant population. So those who planned and executed the attacks of September 11, 2001, aren't just criminals, they're war criminals.

The Just War Doctrine

Catholicism has a tradition of discerning a Just War Theory, which says that all things being equal, the state has a right to wage war — just like it has a right to use capital punishment. However, just like capital punishment, the right to wage war isn't an absolute right.

St. Thomas Aquinas (1226–74) developed a theory of St. Augustine (354–430) into the now-known Just War Theory. (For more on St. Thomas Aquinas, see Chapters 3, 8, and 14; for more on St. Augustine, see Chapters 3 and 15.) It's basis is the natural moral law, and it incorporates a moral evaluation before going to war (the reasons for it) and during it (the means used). Everything leading up to war and every act during it must fulfill the criteria listed due to the seriousness of the actions. Otherwise, it's judged to be an immoral war. So the Church's stand is that in theory war is justified at times, and a just war can be waged. And the Church believes that throughout history, some wars were morally right, but many wars could've and should've been avoided.

We believe it's actually more accurate to call the Just War Theory the *Just War Doctrine,* because theories are ideas not yet proven. The doctrine uses the natural moral law as a litmus test, so its premises and conclusions are sound and morally binding. The Just War Doctrine can be broken down into two components: *Ius ad bellum* (Latin for *right to war* or moral reasons that justify a country's going to war) and *Ius in bello* (Latin for *right in war* or moral conduct during war). These two components are further elaborated in this way:

- Before war:
  - Just cause *(ius ad bellum)*
  - Competent authority *(ius ad bellum)*
  - Comparative Justice *(ius ad bellum)*
  - Right intention *(ius ad bellum)*
  - Last resort *(ius ad bellum)*
  - Probability of success *(ius ad bellum)*
  - Proportionality *(ius ad bellum)*
- During war:
  - Proportionality *(ius in bello)*
  - Discrimination of noncombatants *(ius in bello)*

Just cause (before war)

For a war to be morally permissible, the reasons for going to war must be morally correct. One example of a just cause is to repel invading enemy forces, which are considered unjust aggressors. Imperial Japan's attack on Pearl Harbor was sufficient reason to go to war, because the enemy was in the process of making an attack on the United States.

Another moral and just cause for going to war is to rescue or assist an ally who was attacked by an unjust aggressor, as Great Britain did in World War II when Poland was invaded by Nazi Germany. Removing or repelling an invading aggressor are sufficient reasons to go to war. Gaining new territory, financial or political superiority, however, aren't good reasons.

Just causes for war are morally acceptable reasons to use this last resort to end a conflict. That means that alternative measures must have been already tried and failed. Foremost of necessary attempts of peaceful resolution is diplomacy. Political and economic pressure to prevent or avoid war are preferred as long as human rights aren't sacrificed as a consequence of the agreements made between nations

If citizens are captured, property is seized, land is occupied, or allies are being attacked or invaded, the Church believes that going to war is justified. Defending or protecting lives and territory is considered a just cause. But aggression, revenge, or economic, political, or territorial gain is considered an immoral, or unjust, cause.

Competent authority (before war)

Morally speaking, only legitimate, authentic, and authorized leaders can declare and involve the nation in war. Private citizens, corporations, special interest groups, associations, political parties, and so on, have no moral authority to declare war. Only presidents and congresses, prime ministers and parliaments, kings and queens — those who wield executive power — have the capacity to engage the entire nation in a war. The press and media may cover the war, but they don't declare it. And they don't sue for peace or have the authority to sign treaties. Individual soldiers, sailors, admirals or generals, have no authority to declare war either.

Comparative Justice (before war)

Are the values at stake worth the loss of life, the wounding of others, the risk of innocent victims and damage to property sufficiently obvious?

Right intention (before war)

Morally acceptable reasons for going to war are a just cause, such as the stopping of an unjust aggressor, or having the goal of restoring peace rather than seeking revenge, retaliation, or total destruction of the enemy (without any possibility of surrender).

Last resort (before war)

Morally speaking, all viable alternatives must be exhausted before resorting to war. This includes but isn't limited to diplomatic dialogue and debate, quarantine, blockade, sanctions, economics, negotiation, mediation, arbitration, political and public pressure, and sufficient warning. Going to war shouldn't be the first step but the last one. All peaceful attempts must be tried. However, a country can't allow the unjust aggressor who has invaded time to regroup and strike again.

Probability of success (before war)

A just war demands that the hope of winning the war is reasonable. Fighting just to make or prove a point or merely defending honor when enemy forces are vastly superior in number, ammunition, or resources is foolish. Sacrificing troops and endangering citizens unnecessarily is irresponsible. The Mutual Assured Destruction (MAD) policy of the former Union of Soviet Socialist Republics and the United States during the Cold War had no probability of success, because the goal and objective was to totally destroy the enemy, knowing that the enemy had the same capability, thus no winners and no survivors.

Proportionality (before war)

The evils and suffering that result from the war must be proportionately less or smaller than the evils or suffering, which would have ensued had there been no conflict. If more misery will result by going to war than deciding not to go, the moral choice is to wait, defer, or use other means. Part of proportionality includes the aftermath and cost of the war — in lives, injuries, property damage, and economic consequences.

Proportionality (during war)

A just war uses moral means during the execution of the war. Biological weapons are considered immoral, because they disproportionately harm more people and in more severity than is necessary for victory. Furthermore, germ and biological weapons of mass destruction are intrinsically evil, because there is little control over the chance of harming innocent noncombatants. Tactical nuclear weapons are only permissible if employed as a last resort, and there are no other means to deter the aggressor, and there is significant accuracy and control to target only valid sites. Conventional weapons, troops and tactics should first be tried.

Discrimination of noncombatants (during war)

The last criterion for a just war is that collateral damage must be kept to an absolute bare minimum. Military and strategic targets are the only morally permissible sites for attack. Civilian population centers and any place where noncombatants reside shouldn't be targeted. Terror bombing of civilians, for example, is immoral.

The old distinction between *military* and *civilian* no longer applies, because not all combatants wear uniforms. Guerilla warfare that uses both military and civilian forces is common, so now the distinction is made between *combatants* (those who carry and use firearms or weapons) and *noncombatants* (those who don't).

Planning Your Family Naturally

Catholicism does *not* teach that wives are to have as many children as biologically possible. Women aren't baby factories. So why, then, is the Church against artificial contraception? Keep reading to get a glimpse of the Church's reasoning and to find out about what the Church considers a morally permissible alternative — Natural Family Planning (NFP).

The moral argument against artificial contraception

Pope Paul VI issued his encyclical *Humanae Vitae* (1968), which articulates and reiterates the Church's moral opposition to the use of artificial contraception. The Catholic Church had always said that artificial contraception was immoral. In fact, until 1930, every Christian denomination in the world — Protestant, Catholic, and Orthodox — felt that artificial contraception was sinful. The Anglican Lambeth Conference in 1930, however, permitted contraception in limited cases. Soon afterward, most Protestant churches followed suit. Today, Catholicism and a few Evangelical and Fundamentalist churches, still maintain that the use of artificial contraception isn't part of God's plan.

For the Church, the worst aspect of birth control pills is that many of them aren't true contraceptives; they don't prevent the sperm and egg from conceiving. Instead, they work as an *abortifacient,* causing the uterus to eject a fertilized egg, which according to Catholicism, is now an embryo and a human person. Many women think that their birth control pills are really contraceptives, but they're actually abortifacients.

The Church also says that artificial contraception is morally wrong because it synthetically divides and separates what God intended to always be together. Morally, each and every sex act can occur only between husband and wife *and* must be directed toward two ends: love and life, that is, the intimate unity between the man and woman (love) and possibly procreating another human being (life). Married conjugal love — the intimacy between husband and wife — is the most profound union on earth at the natural level. The physical union of bodies in married sex represents the spiritual reality of two becoming one flesh, but that unity is also present to be open to the possibility of new life. Conception and pregnancy don't have to occur each time, but no man-made barriers should prevent what God may intend to happen. For example, if a middle-age woman, having gone through menopause and lost the natural ability to become pregnant, marries, then her marriage is just as valid in the eyes of the Church as those who are young enough to conceive.

When love and life — unity and procreation — are separated, then sex becomes an end in itself rather a means to an end. Birth control makes sex recreational, and removing what may be perceived as the "danger" of pregnancy means that couples no longer need to communicate about when and when not to have sex and whether they want or can afford another child. The communication and consideration, however, that's necessitated by the possibility of having a child actually strengthens the marriage. Without the necessity for consideration, communication, and cooperation, their ties to one another may weaken or not live up to their full potential.

Whether it's the pill, a condom, an intra-uterine device (IUD), or a sponge, any artificial method of contraception is deemed immoral, because the Church believes that it divides what God intended and may frustrate a divine plan to bring a new life into the world.

The natural alternative to contraception

The Catholic Church permits and encourages married couples to space births and plan how big or small their families will be. But if artificial contraception is out, what's in? Definitely not the archaic and undependable rhythm method. That's not what the Church means by Natural Family Planning (NFP).

Because no two women are exactly alike, no two menstrual cycles are exactly alike, either. But science does show that women are infertile more times during the month than they're fertile. Each woman has a cycle unique to each woman in which she goes from producing eggs to being infertile and vice versa. By using natural science — taking body temperature, checking body fluids, and using some computations — a woman can determine with 95 percent accuracy when to have sex and not get pregnant.

Unlike artificial methods, NFP doesn't require foreign objects to be inserted into the woman's body. This method is completely natural, organic, and 100 percent safe, with no chemical side effects, no recalls, and no toxic complications. And it's a *team* effort. When using the pill or a condom, one person takes responsibility for spacing the births and regulating conception. But *both* the husband *and* the wife practice NFP. This makes sense in the eyes of the Church, because *both* get married on the wedding day, and *both* are involved if a baby comes along.

Love and marriage go together

Catholic husbands and wives must pay attention to each other, showing consideration and real Christian love and charity in all aspects of the life that they share together, including the possibility of children. The Catholic Church maintains that sex isn't an absolute right but a gift and a privilege that must be used properly. Neither the Catholic wife nor the husband can demand sex from the other, but both are entitled to regular intimacy unless prevented by illness, disease or other significant obstacles.

Artificially contraceptive sex, on the other hand, denies the couple another opportunity for exhibiting love and extending their love to the possibility of another human being. And who could be better parents than a husband and wife who've learned how to love?

But the challenge is to suspend confidence in easy medical fixes and trust that God will send only enough children as that couple can support. A couple that can rise to that occasion, however, must have faith, and the faith and trust that they have in God will also transfer to one another and children, too. However, without the faith and trust that couples must build to keep a marriage together, it falls apart. Using artificial birth control and not having to worry about the possibility of pregnancy, spouses can cheat with less hassle. On the other hand, the possibility of pregnancy keeps many on their toes and less likely to treat a spouse as a mere sex object. Is it any accident that the increased use of artificial contraceptives has coincided with the increase in the rate of divorce, infidelity, and venereal disease?

The ramifications of using artificial birth control aren't confined to couples and families either; the results extend out to society as a whole. Until 1930, everyone in the United States assumed that the population of young people would outnumber the old and that an abundance of young workers would continue to support the government and its institutions, such as social security, enough to see after the numbers of old people retiring and needing care. But that balance has tipped. The percentage of elderly in the total population has grown due to continual advancements in medical technology, and due to contraceptive sex and abortion, the percentage of youth in the total population has decreased. Combined, these facts have lead to the economic concern that the smaller younger population has fewer resources and the elderly have more needs. According to the United Nations, the birth rate among first world industrialized nations has decreased so rapidly that one European nation has dropped to an all time low of 1.2 children per family. That's not enough to replace the current generation.

When practiced properly, NFP is as effective as any artificial birth control method. And it's not difficult to learn. Mother Theresa taught illiterate Indian women from the gutters how to effectively use NFP. In addition, no prescription and no expensive devices are involved, so it's easy on the budget. Birth control pills, on the other hand, are commodities bought and sold for profit. Pharmaceutical companies have a vested interest as well.

A woman is fertile during approximately seven to ten days per cycle and is infertile the rest of the time. During those periods of fertility, a couple seeking to space out their family can abstain from sex. For more information on this topic, check out The Couple-to-Couple League, whose Web site is www.ccli.org. This international, interfaith, nonprofit organization teaches Natural Family Planning (NFP).

The Catholic Church believes that these times challenge the couple to remain romantic without becoming sexual. All too often, our culture and society have exclusively united the two so that people can't imagine how someone can be romantic without ending up in bed. Yet men still court women before marrying them. Courtship means being affectionate, romantic, and loving without any sex, because it's saved for the wedding night. The Church says that the brief period of abstinence that's observed by those practicing NFP enables husbands and wives to see each other as more than objects of desire and still encourages them to be close, romantic, and loving toward one another in other, nonsexual ways. It demonstrates that one can be romantic without being sexual.

What if you can't conceive naturally?

What about the other side of the coin? What if a man and woman are using Natural Family Planning (NFP) to have a baby but find that they can't conceive? Infertility is one of the most painful and agonizing crosses some married couples have to carry. Just as contraceptive sex is immoral, because it divides love and life (unity and procreation), conception outside of normal sexual intercourse is considered immoral, too. The Church teaches that the ends can't justify the means, so immoral means can never be used even to promote the birth of another human being to two loving parents who desperately want a child. Children are a gift from God, and not an absolute right that people can demand. Moral means must be employed when married couples have sex and when they want to have children.

That said, fertility drugs aren't per se forbidden, but the warning is that they often lead to multiple births, which then prompts some physicians to play God and say to the mother, "It's unlikely that all will survive, so let's terminate the least likely to survive to increase the chances of the rest." So a selective abortion is done. Kill one to save two, three, or more. To the Church, the end doesn't justify the means. Evil can never be knowingly, willingly, and intentionally done no matter how great and good the final effect.

Despite the sadness of infertility, the Catholic Church maintains that modern science doesn't offer moral solutions — only immoral alternatives. Natural sex between husband and wife is the only morally accepted means to conceive and have children.

When conception occurs artificially, the Church claims that it isn't in God's plan, which is found naturally (in nature as opposed to man-made) As such, the following methods of artificially creating new life, are considered immoral.

- ✔ **Artificial insemination (AIH):** The husband's sperm is inserted into the wife with a device. And often, because the man's sperm count is low, some of the husband's sperm is mixed with donor sperm. The mixture is used, but it only takes one sperm to fertilize the egg, so it's possible that someone else is going to be the genetic father of the child.

- ✔ **In vitro fertilization (IVF)** and **embryo transfer (ET):** With in vitro fertilization, several eggs are fertilized with plenty of sperm in a test tube or petri dish. Every fertilized egg becomes an embryo — a human person with an immortal soul. The clinic picks the best-looking embryo(s) and transfers one or more into the womb of the mother and discards the rest, which Catholicism regards as an abortion. The Church believes that at the moment of conception, a human being is created and that freezing or throwing away a person — no matter how small and developing — is gravely immoral.

- ✔ **Donor sperm** and **donor eggs:** These are forbidden because, again, artificial means are used to achieve conception and even more importantly, one of the spouses is completely absent from the act of procreation since it is another person's egg or sperm being used and involves a third party into the birth. The donor isn't married to the husband and wife, and yet he or she is going to genetically create a new human person with one of them. This is the same reason why sperm banks and surrogate mothers are also considered immoral as they literally exclude the husband or the wife in the very act of procreating. Also, clinics often overfertilize and then select good embryos from not-so-good ones. The ones that are tossed out are human beings nevertheless.

- ✔ **Human cloning:** It attempts to replicate rather than procreate. Using genetic material from mom and/or dad, a healthy egg is wiped clean of DNA, only to have someone else's put inside. Human cloning is an attempt to play God — as if a mere mortal can create life, and Catholicism teaches that it's dangerous and wrong.

Views on Homosexuality

The Church respects and loves the homosexual the same as it does the heterosexual. Catholicism teaches that the homosexual must be treated with respect, compassion, and sensitivity. Every act or thought of hatred, violence, or persecution toward the homosexual is condemned.

Respecting the dignity of every person, however, doesn't mean giving approval to any and all behavior. The Church considers *any* and *all* sexual activity outside of marriage as sinful and immoral; for example, masturbation, fornication, adultery, pornography, and artificial contraception are all sinful. This applies equally to heterosexuals as well as homosexuals. (For more on the Church's view of homosexuality, see the *Catechism of the Catholic Church, #2357–2359* and #2396.)

The Church's prohibition of same-sex union is based on Genesis 1:27–28: "God created man in his own image, . . . male and female he created them. . . . and God said, 'Be fruitful and multiply'" and Genesis 2:24 "a man shall be joined to his wife, and they shall become one flesh." Jesus Himself uses these same quotations in Mark 10:6–9 when asked about marriage.

Catholics believe that marriage is the permanent, faithful, and God-willing fruitful union of a man and woman who have entered the covenant relationship of husband and wife. The Sacrament of Matrimony (see Chapter 7) is a sacred bond that imitates the love between Christ and his bride, the Church. (See Ephesians 5:32.) This has been the Church's consistent teaching as shown in the Catechism, the writing of St. Thomas Aquinas, and several papal letters, especially Pope John Paul II's *On the Christian Family in the Modern World* (1981). The Church believes that because God instituted marriage, neither the Church nor the secular state (civil government) has the authority to redefine or substantially change the nature of marriage. (For more, see the Vatican's 2003 statement *Considerations Regarding Proposals to Give Legal Recognition to Unions between Homosexual Persons.*)

Despite the decision of some other Christian churches to accept openly gay ministers, the Catholic Church doesn't follow the same path. Just as it does not consider the restriction of marriage to one of each gender as being discriminatory against homosexuals, neither does it see the limitation of holy orders to heterosexual males as being unfair.

The Church doesn't want and shouldn't ordain anyone who opposes official doctrine. A man who favors abortion is as unsuitable for the seminary as a man who favors artificial contraception or same-sex marriage or who denies the divinity of Christ or the perpetual virginity of Mary. So ordaining any man whose ideology or lifestyle conflicts with the faith and morals of the Church that he's expected to explain and defend is both hypocritical and impractical.

Part IV
Practicing Catholicism through Devotions

The 5th Wave   By Rich Tennant

Spiritually, I believe I can manifest many good things in my life. But right now, I'd settle for being able to manifest a cab.

In this part . . .

We discuss the external expression of faith and morals beyond the Mass and take a look at some Catholic devotions. Novenas, litanies, devotions to the Virgin Mary, and petitions to St. Anthony when your car keys are lost: All these are examples of devotions. You can also find out how the Catholic Church goes about recognizing a saint and discover some great Catholic traditions — adoring Jesus in the Holy Eucharist, using holy water and blessed candles, and taking part in a religious procession.

Chapter 13

Showing Your Love for God

In This Chapter

▶ Praying more than the minimum weekly requirement

▶ Taking your pick of the litanies

▶ Getting a grip on your rosary beads

▶ Looking at the more popular Catholic devotions

The Mass is the central and fundamental form of Catholic worship. It's the reenactment of the Last Supper, Calvary, and the Resurrection; God is worshipped, the Sacred Scriptures are read, and prayers are offered in adoration, thanksgiving, contrition, and petition. And the Mass doesn't just happen on Sunday, either. Each and every day all over the world, a Mass is being celebrated somewhere in a Catholic church. (See Chapter 8 for more on the Mass.)

So isn't that enough? Do you really need anything more? The answer is yes; it's enough, because Catholics believe that Christ himself instituted the Mass. In addition, though, devotions are a way of expressing your personal love for God.

Whether praying devotions privately at home, in a small group, or in church, Catholics believe that they act like spiritual vitamins to supplement the primary and main form of divine communication — the Mass. This chapter explains how Catholics show their love for God through devotions.

Devotions are optional — Catholics can take 'em or leave 'em — but attending Sunday Mass or the Saturday Vigil Mass is mandatory. That is, missing Sunday Mass, without a legitimate excuse, is a grave sin.

Going Beyond Your Basic Duty

Devotions refer to the wide variety of prayers, both long and short, such as the Rosary and novenas, as well as various religious practices that Catholics engage in, such as making a pilgrimage or a retreat. Devotions are generally less official than the Mass, and so many different devotions are available such that individuals can find the one(s) to suit them and their personal spirituality.

Just like some people think that the Second Vatican Council (see Chapter 8) threw out Latin (which it didn't), some people think that it got rid of or discouraged devotions. Not true. Vatican II didn't pooh-pooh devotions. What it did say was that the separation between the Sacred Liturgy — the Mass — and all forms of public and private devotion must be clear and distinct. No mix and match. Pope Paul VI wrote in his encyclical *Marialis Cultus* (1974) regarding devotion to Mary that, "[I]t is a mistake to recite the Rosary during Mass, though unfortunately this practice still persists here and there." But praying the Rosary before Mass as a preparation or after Mass as a thanksgiving is allowed and encouraged. Likewise, the Stations of the Cross, a traditional Lenten devotion, should never be celebrated during adoration of the Holy Eucharist or in the middle of Mass, but it can be said before or after Mass. Adoration of the Holy Eucharist should be separate from Mass to differentiate the two. Devotion to the Virgin Mary and the saints are also subordinate and auxiliary to the Mass as well. (See "The Way of the Cross" and "Praying the Rosary" sections, later in this chapter.) Of course, plenty of Masses honor the Virgin Mary and the saints. Even though the names of Mary and the saints are mentioned in the Mass, as in the Eucharistic Prayer (see Chapter 8), they're still secondary. References to God are primary, and Mary and the saints are only honored, but God alone is worshipped and adored.

Because devotions aren't *actual* liturgy, a variety of choices are available. Not only are they all optional, but also how they're done is even somewhat variable in that many have been adapted over time and place to accommodate the needs of the people.

Devotions are prayed alone or with others and usually, but not exclusively, in church. They're done outside of the Sacred Liturgy — in other words, not during Mass, except for the Litany of Saints on special occasions. They can, however, be said in any public setting, such as a cemetery or a prayer gathering.

Running the Gamut of Devotions

To get up close and personal with God, Catholics pray a wide variety of devotions. In this section, we cover some of the most popular ones.

Novenas (nine days of prayer)

A *novena* (from the Latin word *novem,* meaning *nine*) is a traditional prayer that's said for nine consecutive days. The practice is based on the concept that nine days passed from the day of Christ's Ascension into heaven, 40 days after Easter, until the coming of the Holy Spirit at Pentecost — 50 days after

Easter. Presumably, the apostles, based on Acts 1:14 - 2:1-4, accompanied by Mary, prayed during those nine days in the Upper Room, where the Last Supper took place. And the Church considers that event the first novena.

Novenas are merely short prayers to a particular saint, requesting that the saint pray to Jesus for the person. The prayers are often said nine days before the feast day of the particular saint so that the novena ends on the actual day that the saint is believed to have gone to heaven, which is called their *feast day*. The hope is that after praying for nine days, some special spiritual blessings will be given by God through the intercession of the particular saint that the novena is addressed to. (For more on the saints, see Chapter 15.)

Is saintly intercession non-Christian?

Often, non-Catholics say that the idea of saintly intercession is non-Christian, because only Christ should be our mediator. The Catholic response is that intercession isn't mediation.

Catholics believe that only Christ had a complete divine nature with a divine intellect and will and a complete human nature with a human intellect and will united to his one divine person. So Catholics believe that he's the only and best mediator between God and humans, between heaven and earth.

Catholics believe that intercession is subordinate and optional. Human beings *need* Christ to be their mediator, but the intercession of Mary and the saints isn't by necessity. Yet their help is still part of God's plan. But intercession, someone asking a favor to God on your behalf, is considered helpful nonetheless. God doesn't need to use these intercessors. But every individual is a member of the family of God, so he wills that the members of his family assist one another. One way of helping others is to pray for them — to ask for God's favor on behalf of someone else. If those on earth can and ought to help their neighbor with prayer, then those in heaven, Mary and the saints, can, too.

Think of it like this: Suppose you ask me to pray for your mom, who is having surgery tomorrow, and I say, "Absolutely not. You have your mother

pray directly to Jesus. She doesn't need my prayers." I might get a slap in the face — or a flat tire, if I'm lucky. Of course, you'd expect me to respond (and I'd naturally respond) with, "I would be happy to pray for your dear mother." When Christians ask another person to pray for them, they don't consider it taking away from the mediatorship of Christ, but Catholics believe that they're nevertheless seeking intercession. And Catholics believe that if people can ask a living person to pray for them and for loved ones, then why not ask one of the deceased — the saints? Unlike folks on earth, saints won't forget and aren't too busy to do it, and their prayers go straight to the Lord. Saintly intercession doesn't diminish the role of Christ the mediator any more than people asking a living person on earth for their prayers. The belief is that they still go to Christ, who then brings the needs and petitions to God the Father, and he listens to his Son.

The Bible says that at the wedding feast of Cana, Mary went to her son, Jesus, and interceded with him to help out the groom because they ran out of wine (John 2:1-11). Jesus then changed the water into wine. The Church maintains that Jesus — as God, in his divine intellect, being able to know all things — already knew that they ran out of wine. Yet he chose to allow his mother to intercede.

Novenas can also be prayed anytime for a special need, such as in desperate and seemingly hopeless cases. Whenever you find yourself or someone you care about in a desperate or seemingly hopeless situation, consider doing what some Catholics do — pray a novena to St. Peregrine, Patron of Cancer Patients or to St. Jude (see Chapter 18), Patron of Hopeless Cases, such as the *Prayer to St. Jude* that follows:

> Most holy apostle, St. Jude, faithful servant and friend of Jesus, the Church honors and invokes you universally, as the patron of hopeless cases, of things almost despaired of. Pray for me, I am so helpless and alone. Make use, I implore you, of that particular privilege given to you, to bring visible and speedy help where help is almost despaired of. Come to my assistance in this great need that I may receive the consolation and help of heaven in all my necessities, tribulations, and sufferings, particularly *(state your request)* and that I may praise God with you and all the elect forever. I promise, O blessed St. Jude, to be ever mindful of this great favor, to always honor you as my special and powerful patron, and to gratefully encourage devotion to you. Amen.

Loving litanies

The *Contemporary Litany of the Saints* incorporates some recent saints relevant to U.S. Catholics. A *litany,* from the Greek *lite,* meaning *prayer,* is a long prayer often prayed *antiphonally,* meaning one person recites the first part and the rest of the group responds. For example, the leader says, "Holy Mary, Mother of God," and the people respond, "Pray for us." The leader then says, "St. Michael," and the people respond, "Pray for us." And so on until the end of the litany. In the *Contemporary Litany of the Saints* that follows, the leader's text is in Roman type, but the responses are italicized; at the asterisk, the people respond, "Pray for us."

> Lord, have mercy, *Lord, have mercy.*
> Christ, have mercy, *Christ, have mercy.*
> Lord, have mercy, *Lord, have mercy.*
> Holy Mary, Mother of God, *pray for us.**0

St. Michael, *
Holy angels of God, *
St. John the Baptist, *
St. Joseph, *
St. Peter and St. Paul, *
St. Andrew, *
St. John, *
St. Mary Magdalene, *
St. Stephen, *
St. Ignatius of Antioch, *

St. Lawrence, *
St. Perpetua and St. Felicity, *
St. Agnes, *
St. Gregory, *
St. Augustine, *
St. Athanasius, *
St. Basil, *
St. Martin, *
St. Benedict, *
St. Francis and St. Dominic, *

St. Francis Xavier, *
St. John Vianney, *
St. Catherine of Siena, *
St. Teresa of Jesus, *
St. Frances Xavier Cabrini, *
St. John Neuman, *

St. Elizabeth Ann Seton, *
St. Katherine Drexel, *
All holy men and women, *.

> Lord, be merciful, *Lord, save your people.*
> From all evil, *Lord, save your people.*
> From every sin, *Lord, save your people.*
> From everlasting death, *Lord, save your people.*
> By your coming as man, *Lord, save your people.*
> By your death and rising to new life, *Lord, save your people.*
> By your gift of the Holy Spirit, *Lord, save your people.*
> Be merciful to us sinners, *Lord, save your people.*
> Guide and protect your holy Church, *Lord, save your people.*
> Keep the pope and all the clergy in faithful service to your Church, *Lord, save your people.*
> Jesus, Son of the living God, *Lord, save your people.*
> Christ, hear us, *Christ hear us.*
> Lord Jesus, hear our prayer, *Lord Jesus, hear our prayer.*
>
> Let us pray: *God of our ancestors who set their hearts on you, of those who fell asleep in peace, and of those who won the martyrs' violent crown: We are surrounded by these witnesses as by clouds of fragrant incense. In this age, we would be counted in this communion of all the saints; keep us always in their good and blessed company. In their midst, we make every prayer through Christ who is our Lord for ever and ever. Amen.*

The Litany of the Saints is the one litany that's actually allowed to be used during Mass on certain occasions. At the Easter Vigil, before the Baptism of catechumens, and at the Ordination Mass of a deacon, priest, or bishop, you may hear the chanting of the Litany of Saints. Otherwise, litanies are prayed outside of Mass as a private devotion or publicly after Mass on the feast day of the particular saint.

The *Litany of the Blessed Virgin Mary* reserves many special titles for her, such as *Mother of Christ, Mother of the Church,* and *Queen of heaven and earth,* but the Litany of Saints merely lists the names of the saints. In the *Litany of the Blessed Virgin Mary* that follows, the leader's text is in Roman type, but the responses are italicized; the asterisk means to say, "Pray for us."

> Lord, have mercy, *Christ, have mercy.*
> Lord, have mercy; Christ, hear us, *Christ, graciously hear us.*
> God, the Father of heaven, *have mercy on us.*
> God the Son, Redeemer of the world, *have mercy on us.*
> God the Holy Spirit, *have mercy on us.*
> Holy Trinity, one God, *have mercy on us.*
> Holy Mary, *pray for us.**

Holy Mother of God, *
Holy Virgin of virgins, *
Mother of Christ, *
Mother of the Church, *
Mother of divine grace, *
Mother most pure, *
Mother most chaste, *
Mother inviolate, *
Mother undefiled, *
Mother most amiable, *
Mother most admirable, *
Mother of good counsel, *
Mother of our Creator, *
Mother of our Savior, *
Virgin most prudent, *
Virgin most venerable, *
Virgin most renowned, *
Virgin most powerful, *
Virgin most merciful, *
Virgin most faithful, *
Mirror of justice, *
Seat of wisdom, *
Cause of our joy, *
Spiritual vessel, *
Vessel of honor, *
Singular vessel of devotion, *

Mystical rose, *
Tower of David, *
Tower of ivory, *
House of gold, *
Ark of the covenant, *
Gate of heaven, *
Morning star, *
Health of the sick, *
Refuge of sinners, *
Comforter of the afflicted, *
Help of Christians, *
Queen of angels, *
Queen of patriarchs, *
Queen of prophets, *
Queen of apostles, *
Queen of martyrs, *
Queen of confessors, *
Queen of virgins, *
Queen of all saints, *
Queen conceived without original sin, *
Queen assumed into heaven, *
Queen of the most holy Rosary, *
Queen of families, *
Queen of peace, *

Lamb of God, You take away the sins of the world; *spare us, O Lord.*
Lamb of God, You take away the sins of the world; *graciously hear us, O Lord.*
Lamb of God, You take away the sins of the world; *have mercy on us.*
Pray for us, O Holy Mother of God. *That we may be made worthy of the promises of Christ.*
Grant, we beg you, O Lord God, that we your servants may enjoy lasting health of mind and body, and by the glorious intercession of the Blessed Mary, ever Virgin, be delivered from present sorrow and enter into the joy of eternal happiness. Through Christ our Lord. Amen.

Looking at statues and icons

Catholics have been accused of being idol worshippers, because they use statues and *icons* — paintings on wood of the Byzantine tradition — in church and at home. But unlike the pagan Romans and Greeks, who actually worshipped false gods, Catholics use statues and icons the same way that others use photographs.

Most people have photos of their loved ones — living and deceased — in their wallets and purses, on their desks, and in their homes. The pictures are nothing more than reminders of those people. Neither the images nor the people are worshipped. Likewise, Catholic statues and icons are merely religious reminders of friends and servants of God whom Catholics admire for their holiness, loyalty, and obedience to God. Catholics don't worship a statue any more than they worship the saint it represents.

If the biblical injunction against graven images is taken out of context, then you could say that the Louvre shouldn't have any paintings in it, and you could say that the Statue of Liberty is idolatry. But, of course, no one worships inanimate reproductions or the people they represent. Similarly, the saints depicted on Catholic statues and icons are nothing more than reminders of the people whom Catholics believe were faithful to God. If you see a Catholic kneeling before a statue, they aren't worshipping it or the person it represents. Kneeling is merely a posture of prayer, and the Catholic is merely praying *to* God *through* the intercession of that particular saint.

Making pilgrimages

Like all devotions, pilgrimages are optional. Jews, Muslims, and Christians all make *pilgrimages,* religious journeys to visit a holy place. For Muslims, it's Mecca, and many Protestant and Orthodox Christians as well as Jews and Catholic Christians make pilgrimages to the Holy Land, visiting the sites mentioned in the Bible. While on the way and during the pilgrimage, people say prayers and hope to have a spiritual renewal. It's like a revival but at a more individual, personal, and low-key level.

The fact that Christian pilgrims were prohibited from access to the sacred shrines in the Middle Ages was one of the motivations for the Crusades. But the Crusades deteriorated into an opportunity for some ruthless and ambitious men to seize wealth, land, and power at the expense of many innocent men, women, and children— Jewish, Muslim, and Christian.

When the Holy Land was too dangerous (sound familiar?), St. Francis of Assisi (1182–1226) created the *Christmas crèche* (nativity scene) and the 14 Stations of the Cross, and he erected them in the church, so people could imagine they were at the actual place and still pray. To this day, Catholic churches still have the 14 stations on the walls of their churches and still display the nativity scene at Christmastime. (For more on St. Francis, see Chapter 18.)

Catholics like to visit the Holy Land to see where it's believed that Jesus was born (Bethlehem), rose from the dead (Nazareth), and crucified and resurrected (Jerusalem). They also make pilgrimages to Rome to see St. Peter's

Basilica, where it's believed that St. Peter is buried, and the Vatican, where the pope lives. Other favorite destinations are Lourdes, France, where Mary appeared to St. Bernadette in 1858; Fatima, Portugal, where she appeared to three children in 1917; and Guadalupe, Mexico, where she appeared to St. Juan Diego, an Aztec Indian, in 1531. (See Chapter 19 for more on these holy sites.)

Going on a retreat

Because most Catholics don't have the time or money to make a pilgrimage to many of the holy places, they often make an annual retreat instead. It can last a week (five to seven days) or be a weekend event at a retreat center. The retreat is a time away from work, school, family, and friends. No radio or TV, no newspapers or magazines, no computers or Internet. They're an opportunity for Catholics to get away from the stress and anxiety of the world and just spend time praying, meditating, reflecting, and renewing. Retreats and days of recollection also give Catholics a chance to go to confession, because priests are often available on-site for that purpose. Priests, deacons, and bishops are required by canon law to make a five-day retreat every year. Some of the different types of retreats that are offered are as follows:

- **Private retreats** are one on one, between a retreat director and the person.

- **Group retreats** include a number of people at the same time.

- **Silent retreats** are almost completely speechless. Nothing is said — even at meals — except the prayers and responses at Mass and the talks of the retreat master.

- **Preached and directed retreats** offer some interaction among the fellow retreatants.

- **Days of recollection** are like mini-retreats. They're only a day and often only take up the morning and/or afternoon. They occur more frequently than retreats, which are annual. Days of recollection often occur every month or at least quarterly.

Priests and nuns of various orders run retreat houses. In addition, many Catholic organizations sponsor retreats.

Wearing sacred gear

Catholics often wear special religious articles, such as medals and scapulars (see Figure 13-1), as a type of personal devotion. *Scapulars* — coming from the Latin *scapula,* meaning *shoulder* – are worn around the neck and have two pieces of cloth — one piece rests on the chest and the other on the back. These items aren't considered good luck charms, magical amulets, or the like. Catholics don't believe that medals and scapulars prevent sickness or stop you from sinning. And they're not a get-out-of-hell-free card. Catholics use them as mere reminders to stay close to God and to try to imitate the sanctity and holiness of the saints. They're just tangible symbols of the faith, such as a crucifix.

A Catholic can wear any one of several kinds of scapulars, the most famous being the Brown Scapular that's associated with the Carmelite Order of Priests and Nuns. It has a picture of Our Lady of Mount Carmel on one side and a picture of St. Simon Stock on the other. Other scapulars include the Black Scapular of the Servite Order, which has an image of Our Lady of Sorrows on it, the Blue Scapular of the Immaculate Conception, the Red Scapular of the Precious Blood, the Purple Scapular of St. Joseph, the White Scapular of the Dominican Order (St. Dominic), and the Green Scapular of Our Lady, Help of the Sick, just to mention a few.

Praying the Rosary

Before Christianity, Hindus strung beads and used them to help count their prayers. Buddhists, Taoists, and Muslims have also used prayer beads to assist them in their private devotions. Hebrews used to tie 150 knots on a string to represent the 150 Psalms of the Bible.

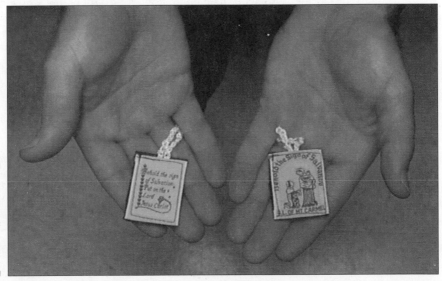

Figure 13-1: Scapulars are good reminders of prayer and faith.

According to pious Catholic tradition, in the 13th century, Mary, the Mother of God, appeared to St. Dominic de Guzman, gave him a rosary, and asked that instead of praying the Psalms on the beads or knots, the faithful pray the *Hail Mary, Our Father,* and the *Glory Be.* Fifteen decades made up the original Dominican Rosary, but it was later abbreviated. A *decade* refers to ten *Hail Marys* preceded by the *Our Father* and ending with a *Glory Be.* Today, most Catholics use the five-decade Rosary. (For more on St. Dominic, see Chapter 18.)

How to pray the Rosary

Want to know how to pray the Rosary? (Take a look at Figure 13-2 to help you follow along.)

1. **On the crucifix, pray the *Apostles' Creed.***

   I believe in God, the Father Almighty, Creator of Heaven and earth; and in Jesus Christ, His only Son, Our Lord, Who was conceived by the Holy Ghost, born of the Virgin Mary, suffered under Pontius Pilate, was crucified; died, and was buried. He descended into Hell; the third day He arose again from the dead; He ascended into Heaven, sitteth at the right hand of God, the Father Almighty; from thence He shall come to judge the living and the dead. I believe in the Holy Spirit, the holy Catholic Church, the communion of saints, the forgiveness of sins, the resurrection of the body, and life everlasting. Amen.

2. **On the next large bead, say the *Our Father.***

   Our Father, Who art in heaven, hallowed be Thy name; Thy kingdom come; Thy will be done on earth as it is in heaven. Give us this day our daily bread; and forgive us our trespasses as we forgive those who trespass against us; and lead us not into temptation, but deliver us from evil, Amen.

3. **On the following three small beads, pray three *Hail Marys.***

   Hail Mary, full of grace. The Lord is with thee. Blessed art thou among women, and blessed is the fruit of thy womb, Jesus. Holy Mary, Mother of God, pray for us sinners, now and at the hour of our death. Amen.

   The first part of the Hail Mary is taken word for word from the Bible. The Archangel Gabriel announces, "Hail, Mary, full of grace; the Lord is with thee," (Luke 1:28) and St. Elizabeth said to her cousin Mary, "Blessed art thou among women and blessed is the fruit of thy womb," (Luke 1:42).

4. **On the chain, pray the *Glory Be.***

   Glory be to the Father, to the Son, and to the Holy Spirit, as it was, is now, and ever shall be, world without end. Amen.

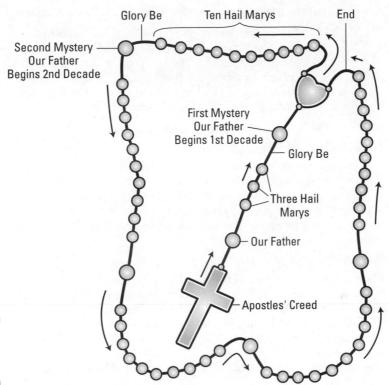

Glory Be   Ten Hail Marys   End

Second Mystery
Our Father
Begins 2nd Decade

First Mystery
Our Father
Begins 1st Decade

Glory Be

Three Hail
Marys

Our Father

Apostles' Creed

Figure 13-2:
How to pray
the Rosary.

5. **Then announce the first Mystery (Joyful, Luminous, Sorrowful, and Glorious).**

   (See "Meditating on the mysteries" section, later in this chapter, for an explanation of the mysteries of the Rosary.)

6. **On the large bead, pray the *Our Father.***

7. **On the ten beads after that, pray ten *Hail Marys.***

8. **On the chain, pray a *Glory Be.***

9. **Many Catholics add the Fatima Prayer after the *Glory Be* and before the next *Our Father.***

   O My Jesus, forgive us our sins, save us from the fires of hell and lead all souls to heaven, especially those in most need of Thy mercy. Amen.

   If you followed the preceding steps, you've just completed the first decade of the Rosary. Now, repeat Steps 5 through 9 four more times to finish the next four decades.

10. **Then, at the end of your Rosary, say the *Hail Holy Queen*.**

    Hail, Holy Queen, Mother of mercy, our life, our sweetness, and our hope. To thee do we cry, poor banished children of Eve, to thee do we send up our sighs, mourning and weeping in this valley of tears. Turn then, most gracious advocate, thine eyes of mercy toward us; and after this our exile show unto us the blessed fruit of thy womb Jesus, O clement, O loving, O sweet Virgin Mary.

    Pray for us, O holy Mother of God. *That we may be made worthy of the promises of Christ.*

    O God, whose only-begotten Son, by His life, death, and resurrection, has purchased for us the rewards of eternal salvation; grant we beseech Thee, that meditating upon these mysteries of the most holy Rosary of the Blessed Virgin Mary, we may imitate what they contain and obtain what they promise. Through the same Christ our Lord. Amen.

Meditating on the mysteries

While saying the prayers of the Rosary, Catholics meditate on what's called the *Joyful, Luminous, Sorrowful,* and *Glorious Mysteries of the Rosary.* But saying the mysteries is really no mystery at all, because each so-called mystery refers to a different passage in the life of Christ or Mary, his mother. Each *decade* (an *Our Father,* ten *Hail Marys,* and a *Glory Be*) recalls a different mystery.

The *Joyful Mysteries* are prayed on Mondays and Saturdays, and they remind the faithful of Christ's birth. Each decade corresponds with a different mystery. Starting with the Annunciation for the first decade, try meditating on these scenes with each decade that you say:

1. The Annunciation (Luke 1:26–38)

2. The Visitation (Luke 1:39–56)

3. The Nativity (Luke 2:1–21)

4. The Presentation (Luke 2:22–38)

5. The Finding of the Child Jesus in the Temple (Luke 2:41–52)

Pope John Paul II added on The *Mysteries of Light,* also known as the *Luminous Mysteries,* in 2002. Pray the Rosary and recall these Mysteries of Light on Thursdays:

1. The Baptism in the River Jordan (Matthew 3:13–16)

2. The Wedding Feast at Cana (John 2:1–11)

3. The Preaching of the coming of the Kingdom of God (Mark 1:14–15)

4. The Transfiguration (Matthew 17:1–8)

5. The Institution of the Holy Eucharist (Matthew 26)

The *Sorrowful Mysteries* are prayed on Tuesdays and Fridays, and they remind the faithful of his Passion and death:

1. The Agony of Jesus in the Garden (Matthew 26:36–56)

2. The Scourging at the Pillar (Matthew 27:26)

3. The Crowning with Thorns (Matthew 27:27–31)

4. The Carrying of the Cross (Matthew 27:32)

5. The Crucifixion (Matthew 27:33–56)

The *Glorious Mysteries* are prayed on Wednesdays and Sundays, and they remind the faithful of his Resurrection and the glories of heaven:

1. The Resurrection (John 20:1–29)

2. The Ascension (Luke 24:36–53)

3. The Descent of the Holy Spirit (Acts 2:1–41)

4. The Assumption of Mary, the Mother of God, into heaven

5. The Coronation of Mary in heaven

Both the divinity and humanity of Jesus are presented in these mysteries. Only God could be born of a virgin, rise from the dead, and ascend into heaven, and yet only a man could be born, get lost, be found, suffer, and die. Meditating on the Joyful, Luminous, Sorrowful, and Glorious Mysteries helps Catholics confirm that Jesus is both divine and human. Contemplating the time when Jesus was crowned with thorns, scourged with whips, and nailed to the cross — meditating on Jesus' Passion — convinces the prayerful that those sufferings are real and only a real man could feel such pain and agony. Yet reflecting on his Transfiguration, Resurrection, and Ascension reminds believers that only God can transfigure, rise from the dead, and ascend into heaven. By praying the Rosary, the faithful reaffirm that Jesus is true God and true man, one divine person with two natures — divine and human.

Just as Pope Paul VI did, Pope John Paul II reminds the faithful that the Rosary is *Christocentric* — it focuses on Christ and is more than a *Marian* (of Mary) devotion.

Saying the Divine Mercy Chaplet

The Rosary and the Divine Mercy Chaplet may be prayed at home, in church, alone or in a group. Our Lord presented the Divine Mercy Chaplet to St. Faustina Kowalska in a vision during the 1930s, but it didn't gain much notoriety until the late 20th century. The Divine Mercy Chaplet is said using rosary beads (see Figure 13-2), but it doesn't take as long as a Rosary, because the prayers are shorter.

1. **Begin the Divine Mercy Chaplet by saying the following three times in a row:**

   O Blood and Water, which gushed forth from the heart of Jesus, I trust in You.

2. **Then say an *Our Father,* the *Hail Mary,* and the *Apostles' Creed.***

   (See Steps 1 through 3 in the "How to pray the Rosary" section, earlier in this chapter, to pray the *Our Father, Hail Mary,* and *Apostles' Creed.*)

3. **Then, on the large bead before each decade, say**

   Eternal Father, I offer you the Body and Blood, Soul and Divinity of Your Dearly Beloved Son, Our Lord, Jesus Christ, in atonement for our sins and those of the whole world.

4. **Then, on the ten small beads of each decade, say**

   For the sake of His sorrowful Passion, have mercy on us and on the whole world.

5. **Conclude the chaplet by saying the following three times:**

   Holy God, Holy Mighty One, Holy Immortal One, have mercy on us and on the whole world.

The Way of the Cross

Another popular devotion is the Way of the Cross. All Catholic parishes have what's called the *Stations of the Cross* (see Figure 13-3), which are depictions of Christ's Passion and death. Often on Friday evenings during Lent, you can find a parish that's open with Catholics saying prayers in unison before each of the 14 stations that follow:

1. Jesus is condemned to death (Luke 23:24)

2. Jesus takes up his cross (John 19:17)

3. Jesus falls the first time (By inference from stations 2 and 5)

4. Jesus meets his sorrowful mother (By inference from John 19:25–27)

5. Simon of Cyrene helps carry the cross (Matthew 27:32)

6. Veronica wipes the face of Jesus (Not recorded in Scripture)

7. Jesus falls a second time (Not recorded in Scripture)

8. Jesus meets the holy women of Jerusalem (Luke 23:27–31)

9. Jesus falls the third time (Not recorded in Scripture)

10. Jesus is stripped of his garments (John 19:23)

11. Jesus is nailed to the cross (Mark 15:24)

12. Jesus dies on the cross (Mark 15:37)

13. His body is taken down and laid in the arms of his mother (Luke 23:53)

14. His body is placed in the tomb (Matthew 27:60)

Figure 13-3:
The Tenth Station: Jesus is stripped of his garments (John 19:23).

Courtesy of Esmeralda St. Clair

Chapter 14

Expressing Affection for Mary

In This Chapter

▶ Honoring Mary isn't the same as worship

▶ Asking for a mother's intercession

▶ Examining the logic behind the Marian perspective

▶ Appearing to the poor and guileless

You've heard about all those ladies — Our Lady of Lourdes, Our Lady of Fatima, Our Lady of Sorrows, Our Lady of Grace, Our Lady of Peace, and Our Lady of Mount Carmel, and Our Lady of Guadalupe. They're one and the same person — Mary. Catholics refer to Mary in many ways, which can be confusing at times. The same goes for the *Blessed Virgin Mary* (BVM for short), the *Virgin Mary, Our Lady,* and the plain and simple — Mary. No matter what the title, it refers to the Mother of Jesus, and she's what this chapter is all about.

No, Catholics Don't Worship Mary

Born of two saintly parents — St. Joachim and St. Ann — Mary is mentioned in the King James Bible 47 times. Regarding Mary, the Bible says that

✔ She came from Nazareth (Luke 1:26), and it was in Nazareth that the Archangel Gabriel appeared to her and *announced,* hence the term *Annunciation,* that she was to have a son and name him Jesus (Luke 1:31).

✔ She was engaged (Matthew 1:18 and Luke 1:27) to a carpenter (Matthew 13:55) named Joseph, whose ancestor was King David (Matthew 1:6–16)

And through the ages, more poems, hymns, statues (see Figure 14-1), icons, paintings, treatises, and sermons have been produced on this one woman than any other in all human history.

Figure 14-1:
A statue of
the Virgin
Mary.

To understand why Catholics are so affectionate and attached to her, you must look at the most primal of all emotions. The bond between a mother and her child is the strongest and most penetrating. Nine months in the womb is just one part of it. (Personally, we think that to consider Mary as just a baby factory is an insult to her, to motherhood, and to all women.) Motherhood is biological *and* emotional *and* intellectual. The flesh, the heart, and the mind are the center of human feelings and thoughts. A mother is more and gives more than her DNA and nine months in her womb. She's intimately bonded and connected with her child. And Catholic devotion to Mary is nothing more than a logical extension of a child's personal affection for his own mother.

Catholic theology teaches that Jesus Christ was human and divine — not 50/50 but true God and true Man. In other words, he was one divine person with two natures — human and divine. And his humanity wasn't overwhelmed or smothered by his divinity. So whatever he did or was in his human nature was as real and as much a part of him as whatever he did or was in his divine nature. So whether he was performing miracles from his divine nature or feeling and expressing emotions from his human nature, he was still one and the same person. That said, what human being doesn't have strong feelings of affection and love for his mother? So Catholics identify their own feelings for Mary with the feelings Jesus had for his mom. This is nothing but devotion, without the slightest hint of worship or adoration in it.

The quote du jour about Mary

"[S]he is full of grace, proclaimed to be entirely without sin. . . . God's grace fills her with everything good and makes her devoid of all evil. . . . God is with her, meaning that all she did or left undone is divine and the action of God in her. Moreover, God guarded and protected her from all that might be hurtful to her."

Guess where that quote is from? Martin Luther, the father of the Protestant Reformation and the founder of the Lutheran Church. (*Luther's Works,*

American edition, vol. 43, p. 40 , ed. H. Lehmann, Fortress, 1968)

In his *Commentary on the Magnificat,* Luther also said, "Men have crowded all her glory into a single phrase: The Mother of God. No one can say anything greater of her."

Martin Luther even said, "She is rightly called not only the mother of the man, but also the Mother of God. . . . it's certain that Mary is the Mother of the real and true God."

Some people also say that the word *Blessed* in the title *Blessed Virgin Mary* is idolatry (or Mariolatry, as some call it). But the term and concept is biblical. Mary tells her cousin Elizabeth, "All generations shall call me blessed." (Luke 1:48) In the Bible's original Greek, *blessed* was *markariousin.* For nearly 2,000 years, the adjective *blessed* has been used, and it's never taken away from the ultimate holiness of God — just as when Jesus himself used the word in his Sermon on the Mount (Matthew 5:3–12): "Blessed are the poor in spirit, theirs is the kingdom of heaven." *Blessed* isn't a word that's restricted to divinity, so using it with Mary is okay.

Another argument for discouraging devotion to Mary, also known as *Marian devotion,* is the claim that Jesus himself apparently rebuked his own mother and called her *woman* rather than mom. The Catholic response? The original text of the Gospel According to John was written in Greek, not the King's English of the King James Version of the Bible. At the wedding of Cana, when they ran out of wine, Mary told Jesus about it. The King James Bible has Jesus saying, "Woman, what have I to do with thee?" (John 2:4) But the original Greek reads *Ti emoi kai soi gynai,* which literally translates to "What [is it] to me and you, woman?" This is exactly the same translation in Latin: *Quid mihi et tibi est mulier.* The International Standard Version reads, "How does that concern us, woman?" And what does all this have to do with the price of eggs? As always, a quote can't be taken out of context. As soon as Jesus uttered the phrase, he proceeded to go and change the water into wine. Had it been a rebuke, he would've ignored the request altogether. By granting his mother's plea to help, he showed that he listened to her as a son but as God he performed the miracle.

Calling his mother *woman* must also be seen in context with the whole of Scripture. For example, at the cross, as Jesus was dying, some of his last words were to Mary and then to John, his beloved disciple: "Woman, behold your son" and "Behold your mother." Using the term *woman* (*gynai* in Greek) was meant as a compliment, because Eve, the wife of Adam, is referred to as the *woman.* (Genesis 2:23) So, too, the famous line between God and the serpent goes, "I will put enmity between you and the woman, between your offspring and hers." (Genesis 3:15) In fact, Mary is the New Eve, because her offspring was Jesus, the New Adam, and he conquered the devil by his death and Resurrection. So when seen in this light, the supposed insult turns out to be a term of endearment.

The Official Scoop on Mary

Official Catholic doctrine on Mary is called *Mariology,* just as doctrine on God is called *Theology,* from the Greek word *theos* for *God.* Keep on reading if you want to get a peek at some significant aspects of Mariology.

She's the Mother of God

The title *Mother of God* goes back to the year 431. At the Ecumenical Council of Ephesus, it was determined that Mary could be called the Mother of God (*Theotokos* in Greek) instead of just the Mother of Christ (*Christotokos*) as the theologian Nestorius contended. (For more on the Church councils, see Chapter 2.)

The thinking went thus: Granted, as a human being, Mary can't be the origin of a divine person. Only gods and goddesses can make other gods, but Mary is the Mother of Jesus. He wasn't born in parts, like building blocks, needing to be put together after his birth. One divine person lived in Mary's womb for nine months, and one divine person came forth and was born. Even though Mary didn't give Jesus his divine nature, she did bear the second person of the Holy Trinity for nine months in her womb, and one person was born on Christmas Day — whole, complete, and intact. So even though she was a creature and not the Creator, because she did give birth to the Son of God, and because she is the Mother of the Son of God, she can be called the Mother of God.

Looking at your own mother is another way to see the concept: Your mother didn't give you your immortal soul. That came from God. She gave you 50 percent of your genetic makeup, but she needed your dad to give you the other half, and they needed God to give you a soul. However, on Mother's Day, do you send her a card entitled, "To the woman who gave me half of my genetic code?" Or would you tell her that she didn't give you a soul — that she only gave you a body — so she's only half your mother? Of course not, that is, unless you want the wooden spoon across your hand. In your mind and your mother's mind, she may have only given you 50 percent of your DNA, but she gave birth to *you*. A whole and complete person was born — not two pieces. The body and soul were united at conception. A person grew and lived in the womb, and a whole and intact person was born from it.

The Bible verifies this logic: Mary, pregnant with Jesus for only a few days, visited her cousin Elizabeth, who was six months pregnant with John the Baptist. Elizabeth greeted Mary, "Who am I that the mother of my Lord should come to me?" (Luke 1:43) Elizabeth used the word *Lord* (*Kyrios* in Greek and *Adonai* in Hebrew), which was also used to refer to God — the Lord God — *Adonai Elohim* in Hebrew. Elizabeth called Mary *the Mother of the Lord,* and the Lord is God. Mary is the Mother of God, because she's the mother of the Lord. It doesn't mean that Mary was divine or that she was a goddess or had any divine attributes.

She's the Mother of the Church

Most titles for Mary are by way of metaphor. Calling her the Mother of God, for example, is a legitimate figure of speech, for even though she isn't the mother of divinity, she did give birth to a divine person. She is a real, biological mother, because she gave birth to Jesus, and he is the Son of God according to Christians.

Similarly, the title *Mother of the Church* can only be properly understood as a metaphor. When people say that necessity is the mother of invention, isn't that a metaphor? The same goes for Marian titles. (*Marian* is an adjective that refers to Mary.)

On top of that, consider this: Men and women are creatures, whereas God is the Creator. Mary was just a creature, but she gave birth and a human nature to the Son of God. The only way that Christians can call themselves brothers and sisters in Christ is by way of adoption. In other words, Jesus is, was, and always will be the Eternal Son of the Father. Christians are children of God and brothers and sisters in Christ by adoption. Similarly, if Christians are brothers and sisters in Christ by adoption, then by adoption, they also inherit the same mother. Mary is the Mother of Christ by nature, and she is the mother of Christians by adoption, because Christians are adopted children of God and adopted brethren of Christ. Make sense? You'll be given a quiz later.

Catholic dogma on the Assumption (discussed in the "What the Assumption was all about" section, later in this chapter), sees Mary's Assumption as a foreshadowing and precursor to the end of time, when the Church as a whole will be taken up into heaven. All the members of the Church will be raised from the dead by Christ and given a glorified body for eternity with God in heaven. (For more on dogma, see Chapter 3.)

In another way, Mary is the Mother of the Church, because she was at the foot of the cross on Calvary. The Bible says that as he was dying on the cross, Jesus turned toward his mother and said, "Woman, behold, your son," and he then turned to John the Beloved Disciple and said, "Behold, your mother." (John 19:26–27) The bestowal of Mary to John is symbolic insofar as John represents all disciples and all men and women.

Mary's presence at Pentecost, ten days after the Ascension of Christ into heaven and 50 days after his Resurrection, also establishes her role as Mother of the Church. Acts 1:14-2:4 says that Mary was with the apostles in the Upper Room — or probably, more accurately, they were with her. Until the Holy Spirit gave them strength and courage, they received encouragement from the Mother of Jesus as she and John were the only ones not to abandon Christ, while he died on the cross.

From the Catholic perspective, Mary becomes the Mother of the Church by adoption. This concept doesn't detract, diminish, or dilute the singular mediatorship of Christ, because he's still the one mediator between God and humans. Yet he also had a human mother, and she's connected to the Church, because she's connected to him and because he's connected to the Church. In other words, because people are God's children by adoption and that makes every one brothers and sisters in Christ by adoption also, every one therefore inherits the same mother of Christ as well by adoption.

She's the Mother of the Mystical Body of Christ

Mary is called the Mother of the Church, because she's the Mother of Christ, and the Church is the Mystical Body of Christ (I Corinthians 12:12–27, Romans 12:4–5, and Colossians 1:18). So the Mother of Christ can also be called the Mother of his Mystical Body.

Catholics believe that Christ founded the Church as a necessary institution to safeguard and protect Revelation by authentically interpreting the biblical texts. It's a necessary and organic community, called by St. Paul the Body of Christ (Colossians 1:24) and later called the Mystical Body of Christ by Pope Pius XII in his encyclical letter *Mysticis Corporis* (1943). This means that the Church is more than an external organization, structure, and institution, but also and more primarily, it's a union of all the members forming one body. The human body has many parts, which are different and have different functions. This is what St. Paul means by the *Body of Christ.* Every body has one head and the Church has one visible head on earth, the pope. But a head with no body isn't alive. The Church has a head but also a body made up of many members, laity and clergy. These individual members have different functions, just as your heart, lungs, kidneys, arms, legs, eyes, and ears have their respective function but all work in harmony for the good of the whole body. Pope Pius added the adjective *mystical* just to accentuate the idea that the Church isn't a physical body with organs and limbs, but it's mysteriously and spiritually organic.

St. Paul said that the universal body of Christian believers makes up the Church. They're considered the body or, as Pope Pius XII said, the "Mystical Body of Christ." St. Paul also said, "Now I rejoice in my sufferings for your sake, and in my flesh I am filling up what's lacking in the afflictions of Christ on behalf of his body, which is the Church," (Colossians 1:24). It's not that Jesus didn't suffer enough for us, but St. Paul is saying that God freely chose to allow individuals to unite their sufferings *with* the sufferings of Christ on the cross. To pick up one's cross (see Matthew 16:24) and endure evil for the sake of all is spiritually beneficial. For Catholics, suffering can be spiritually meaningful and redemptive. Catholicism believes that suffering — unavoidable suffering, such as the pain, anguish, and suffering that inevitably results from an incurable illness — can be offered up with prayer for the salvation of one's own soul and/or the souls in purgatory or for the living on earth. This is where the famous saying, "Offer it up," originates. Many Catholics who attended parochial grade school remember the nuns telling the kids that phrase often. Anytime an inconvenience, a disappointment, or more importantly, anytime unavoidable and unwarranted suffering — physical or emotional — inflicted a Catholic, she was encouraged to offer it up — to unite her suffering with Christ's as alluded to in Colossians 1:24.

The last word on the Immaculate Conception

The Immaculate Conception is one of the most Catholic, most mysterious, and most misunderstood Catholic dogmas. The Immaculate Conception has nothing to with the conceiving of Jesus within the womb of Mary — even though the Gospel reading at Mass that day is the account of the Annunciation, when the Archangel Gabriel told Mary that she was to be the Mother of Jesus. It's within the text of that Gospel that Catholicism gets the Immaculate Conception.

Catholics believe in the *Immaculate Conception,* which means that from the first moment of *her* conception in the womb of her mother, St. Ann, Mary was kept free from original sin by the power of divine grace. So the Immaculate Conception is about Mary's conception in her mother's womb. The *Incarnation,* on the other hand, refers to Jesus' conception in his mother's womb.

In the eyes of the Church, Adam and Eve's sin, called *original sin* (see Chapter 6), is transmitted to every subsequent generation. So just as you inherit the color of your eyes and hair from your parents, you also spiritually inherit original sin from them.

Baptism (see Chapter 6) is the means to remit original sin and replace it with sanctifying grace. But God gave Mary the singular grace and privilege of the Immaculate Conception to prevent original sin from being transmitted to Jesus, so she was literally full of grace. A glass full of water has no room for anything else, and a soul full of grace has no room for sin.

When the Archangel Gabriel addressed Mary in the first chapter of Luke's Gospel, he said, "Hail Mary, full of grace," (*kecharit men* in Greek, from the root word *charis,* meaning *grace*). She was full of grace because of the Immaculate Conception, a divine gift to her from God. She didn't earn or merit it. He freely gave it to her, so she could provide a worthy, spotless, and pure human nature for Jesus.

Because Jesus had no human father, his only human parent was Mary. She gave him his human nature, whereas he — as God — always possessed his divine nature. In order to give Jesus a completely untainted, spotless, and immaculate human nature so that he could be the Spotless Lamb of Sacrifice. (Catholics have many titles for Jesus, too.) Mary had to be kept free from original sin. She couldn't do so on her own, because she was a mere mortal. She needed a Savior and Messiah like everyone else. But God isn't limited to time and space. Mary enjoyed an effect of salvation before Jesus actually did the work of salvation. She was given the gift of being preserved from original sin well before her son Jesus was born let alone before he suffered and died, achieving salvation for the entire human race. Jesus, being divine and being God, retroactively applied the fruits of his salvific suffering and death from Mary's future to her past. He extended the benefits backward in time just as you who live now can have the same fruits of redemption applied to you from the past into your present. If what Jesus did 2,000 years ago can be applied to a newly baptized person today, then what he did can go in the other direction and be applied to his mother as she was being conceived.

It's like getting into a time travel machine (okay, we admit it — we're *Doctor Who* fans), going into the future, and finding that your son wants to become a physician but can't, because neither you nor your son has the money for medical school. So you go back in time and leave a few hundred dollars in a bank account in your child's name, so when you return to the future, you can withdraw it and all the accumulated interest to send Junior to med school.

Some people try to use an old, archaic argument that even the great theologian St. Thomas Aquinas didn't fully endorse the doctrine of the Immaculate Conception. (For more on St. Thomas, see Chapters 3 and 18.) The Catholic response? First of all, the dogma wasn't solemnly defined until 1854 by Pope Pius IX, and Aquinas lived in the 13th century — almost 600 years before. Second, basic human anatomy and physiology that's now taken for granted wasn't understood until the Renaissance — 250 years after Aquinas. During the Renaissance, people like Da Vinci began to paint and draw human bodies, often from cadavers and autopsies. But the biology known to Aquinas was primitive, and he relied heavily on Aristotle not only for philosophy but for other disciplines as well.

The medieval concept of human reproduction was that a vegetative soul existed before a human being did and that the vegetative soul developed into an animal soul and then God infused an immortal human soul, called *animation,* at which time the embryo was a human person. Based on this medieval science, it didn't make sense to Aquinas that God would preserve Mary from original sin at the moment of conception, because the human soul (it was thought) didn't yet exist to benefit from the divine gift. But Aquinas believed that after the immortal soul was infused, Mary could and did receive the grace of being free from original sin. So Aquinas believed in the Catholic doctrine that Mary was *born* without original sin, but he had serious reservations as to whether she was *conceived* without it.

If Aquinas had lived at the time of Da Vinci, if he could've seen a sonogram of an unborn fetus, or if he merely knew the common DNA science that grade schoolers know today, then he would've realized that *at conception* a human being is created and *animation* (God infusing the immortal soul) occurs. The embryo may resemble something animal-like, but genetically, the DNA is human from the moment of conception and remains so throughout gestation, birth, and life. These blueprints tell the cells what to do and how to grow, and no animal or vegetable will ever become anything else but an animal or vegetable. Only humans beget other humans and nothing else.

So the bottom line is that St. Thomas Aquinas really didn't deny the Immaculate Conception. He merely had trouble reconciling it with the extremely primitive physiology of his time. His contemporary St. Bonaventure, on the other hand, did accept the Immaculate Conception, but back in the 13th century, it wasn't a defined dogma as yet. It was taught, but no pope had given it the official nod yet. After Pius IX defined the dogma, however, the matter was no longer open for discussion.

Sacred Tradition reigns on the Assumption

The Assumption of Mary isn't in the Bible. An apocryphal account of the Assumption is in the *Transitus Beatae Mariae of Pseudo-Melito,* but it's not — and has never been — considered inspired text. The authenticity of this apocryphal Gospel is so dubious that the Church never thought of it as evidence for the Assumption, but the existence of it does show that the early Church did believe in the Assumption.

Because divine revelation consists of both the written Word of God (the Bible) and the unwritten Word of God (Sacred Tradition), then matters where the Bible is silent or ambiguous can usually be determined by what was taught via Sacred Tradition. The Bible is silent on Mary's death, but Sacred Tradition says that she was taken up (by God) into Heaven. The Church maintains, however, that a biblical allusion to the Assumption does exist in Revelation (Apocalypse) 12:1: "A great sign appeared in the sky, a woman clothed with the sun, with the moon under her feet, and on her head a crown of twelve stars."

In all 2,000 years of Church history, only two papal *ex cathedra* statements have been made. When the pope, exercising his authority as Supreme Teacher, makes an *ex cathedra* statement, he's *infallible* — the Holy Spirit prevents him from teaching error. In 1854, Pope Pius IX made the first *ex cathedra* statement — the Immaculate Conception. The other *ex cathedra* statement was made in 1950; Pope Pius XII defined the dogma of the Assumption of Mary, body and soul, into heaven. (See the next section, "What the Assumption was all about," for details. See Chapter 2 for details about *ex cathedra* statements and the pope's infallibility.)

She went to heaven body and soul

The Church professes that when Mary's time on earth came to an end, Mary died and her body was placed in a tomb, but her body didn't decay on earth. Instead, her son, Jesus Christ, assumed her into heaven, body and soul.

We want to make something clear. Only God can rise from the dead of his own divine power, and only God can ascend into heaven of his own divine power. So Jesus himself, being God, rose from the dead, but Lazarus was raised *by* Jesus. Likewise, Jesus himself ascended into heaven, but he also assumed his mother.

So why would he do such a thing? For many reasons.

One is that having affection for your mom is as human as it gets. In his humanity, Jesus had all the emotions that any man or woman would have. If you were Jesus, wouldn't you want to prevent any decay from touching the body of your mother? Wouldn't you want her to be with you in heaven? To portray Jesus as an emotionless man who had no filial love for his mom is to deny his humanity.

Also, the Immaculate Conception preserved Mary from original sin, so Mary would've also been free from the consequences of sin as well — namely, physical death, the separation of body and soul. That being the case, the Eastern Church uses the term *dormition* (falling asleep) rather than her death before the Assumption. But because she voluntarily joined with her son's suffering on the cross, Pope John Paul II said that the logical conclusion is that she also willingly followed him through her own death as well.

The more fundamental reason, however, that Jesus assumed his mother, body and soul, into heaven was to give people on earth encouragement. Sacred Tradition (see the sidebar "Sacred Tradition reigns on the Assumption" in this chapter) teaches that the Assumption was meant to give humans hope and consolation that what Jesus did for his mother in reward for her being a faithful disciple throughout her life, beginning with her response to the Archangel Gabriel, "Be it done unto me according to thy word." (Luke 1:38) He will also do this for humankind at the end of time. At his Second Coming, Jesus will raise the dead and take the righteous to heaven, and the reprobate will go to hell. So, in other words, Mary's Assumption was like a preview of coming attractions: She was the first human — but won't be the last — to be assumed by God into heaven. Someone had to be first, and why not the Mother of Christ?

Her never-ending virginity

Mary's virginity *before* the birth of Christ is a matter of Catholic dogma: No human father was associated with Jesus, because he was the Son of God as well as the son of Mary. Having a human mother gave him his humanity; having no human father but by the power of the Holy Spirit being conceived in his mother's womb gave him his divinity.

But what about *after* the birth of Christ? Did Mary have other children besides Jesus? Some people say that she did, because the New Testament speaks of the brothers and sisters of Jesus. Although it certainly wasn't necessary that Mary and Joseph not have any children of their own, Sacred Tradition says that they didn't. The way that Catholicism sees it, the doctrine of the Perpetual Virginity of Mary is no harder to believe than the miracle of the Virgin Birth, which most Christians accept. If Mary could remain a virgin before and during the birth of Christ her son, then it isn't any more difficult to believe that she could remain a virgin *after* his birth. (To find out more, see Chapter 4.)

Some people ask the Church to explain the reference to James, as the brother of Jesus in the Bible (Matthew 13:55). But the word used to mean *brother* in the Bible's original Greek was *adelphos,* which can also mean *relative, cousin,* or *kinsman* as well as *sibling.* In the Bible, referencing the father indicates close relations. Jesus is referred to as the son of Joseph and the son of Mary, but no one else in the Bible is ever called the son or daughter of Joseph or Mary. So many possible scenarios exist for understanding the term *brother of Jesus* but only one for understanding *son* or *daughter.* Why doesn't the Bible call James the brother of Jesus and the son of Mary or just the son of Mary? The reason is that Mary had only one son. She was a virgin before, during, and after the birth of Jesus.

Mark 15:40 mentions Mary the mother of James, but the belief is that she was another Mary — not the Mary who was the Mother of Jesus. The mother of James was in the distance looking on, while the Mother of Jesus was at the foot of the cross. (See Chapter 4 for more on the possibility that Jesus had siblings.)

Up Close and Personal with Mary

Devotions are traditional forms of prayer that aren't part of the Mass. They can be public or private, however, and express love for God and for neighbor, as personified in Mary and the saints.

Actually, we're not going to describe how to say the Rosary in this chapter. Don't get us wrong. We think it's a great devotion. It's just that we covered the Rosary in Chapter 13. No need to repeat ourselves, eh?

May crowning

May is the month of Mother's Day, and for Catholics it's the month for honoring two moms — their earthly one, who gave birth to them, and their spiritual mother, Mary.

Traditionally, Catholic parishes pick one day in May to host a devotion called a *May Crowning*. After the Ecumenical Council of Nicea II in 787, the public veneration of icons and images of Jesus, Mary, and the saints was no longer persecuted by some in the Church as though it were a form of idolatry. Consequently, the tradition of crowning a statue of Mary arose in recognition of her heavenly position as Queen of Heaven and Earth. This concept came from Revelation (Apocalypse) 12:1, which is the same as the image of Our Lady of Guadalupe, who, in 1531, appeared to St. Juan Diego in Guadalupe, Mexico. (See Chapter 1 and 19 for more on Our Lady of Guadalupe.)

Mary's queenship is analogous to her son's kingship. She's a queen, because her son is the King of Kings and Prince of Peace. You can think of it like this: The Queen Mother of England was given the title, honor, and respect of queen, because of her relationship first as the wife of the king and then as the mother of Queen Elizabeth II. So, too, the mother of the King of Kings is given the title and honor of being called *queen*.

Often for the occasion of the May crowning, roses and flowers galore adorn the Church. Typically, a young girl is chosen to place a crown of roses on a statue of Mary, which is sometimes carried in a *procession,* a dignified religious parade, around the inside or outside of the church, or perhaps around the neighborhood. People march reverently to symbolize that they're fellow pilgrims — travelers who walk with the Lord and the saints, hopefully on the path to Heaven. All those in attendance sing hymns and pray the Rosary.

First Saturdays

Traditionally, Catholics honor Mary on the first Saturday of every month. Why that particular day? Well, the first Friday of the month is when Catholics give honor to Jesus with the Sacred Heart of Jesus devotion. Because Mary is secondary to Christ, the Church deemed that he would come first and then close by would be his mother. So the devotion to the Sacred Heart of Jesus is first and then the devotion to the Immaculate Heart of Mary follows.

The focus on the heart is merely a romantic and metaphorical way of describing the love of Jesus and the love of Mary. It's just like sending hearts to loved ones on St. Valentine's Day even though you know that, biologically, the brain does the thinking and the heart merely does the pumping. Even in the 21st century, you hear the words "heartache" and winning someone's "heart," so the devotion to the Immaculate Heart of Mary is merely a recognition of her motherly heart, because she loves her spiritual children.

The First Saturday devotion is relatively new compared with the First Friday devotion to the Sacred Heart of Jesus. The devotion came about because of the belief that Mary appeared to mere children, Lucia, Jacinta, and Francisco, in Fatima, Portugal, in 1917 (see Chapter 19) and then again to Sister Lucia in 1925, asking for the faithful to honor her on the first Saturday of the month. Saturday is also special; it was on the first Holy Saturday that Mary didn't lose faith, even though she'd just buried her son, Jesus. Her love and faith in him got her through to his Resurrection on the next day.

Catholics believe that during her appearance in Fatima, Mary specifically asked that Catholics honor her Immaculate Heart on the five first Saturdays of five consecutive months by going to confession, receiving Holy Communion, praying five decades of the Rosary, and meditating for 15 minutes on the mysteries of the Rosary in reparation for sins. If done, she promised her maternal intercession and prayers at the hour of death when it's the devil's last chance to get the soul.

Marian shrines and apparitions

Catholics believe that a *shrine* is a holy place, usually where an apparition or other miracle took place, or where a saint lived, worked, or died. The shrine is typically where visitors learn about the holy person or place. Shrines are often connected to or located inside of a chapel or church where the faithful can pray and worship God, especially through the Holy Sacrifice of the Mass.

An *apparition* is an appearance of Jesus, Mary, or one of the saints. It's not a physical presence of the holy person but an appearance — an image being imprinted on the senses. This is the reason that not everyone sees or hears the apparitions or *locutions* (speeches). Those who do are called *visionaries*. Catholics aren't obligated to believe in any particular apparition, because apparitions aren't part of public revelation. The Church does, however, carefully investigate claims of alleged apparitions and then makes one of the following determinations:

✔ **It's a hoax.** Someone is pretending to see apparitions, when in reality, they're lies or staged illusions.

✔ **Natural causes can explain it.** Evidence of a supernatural occurrence is nonexistent. The visionaries may be prayerful and holy people, without any intent to deceive, but evidence of a miraculous apparition can't be found. For example, you see tears rolling down the cheeks of a statue of Mary. Then you look up and see that the old steamy water pipes near the ceiling are slowly dripping right onto the statue's face.

✔ **The phenomenon can't be explained one way or the other.** Any evidence of a supernatural occurrence is inconclusive — too many unanswered questions and not enough, if any, evidence.

✔ **The devil is at work.** It's a supernatural event all right but not of heavenly origin. Rather, it's an attempt by the devil to ridicule and mock the faith.

✔ **It's a supernatural event of heavenly origin.** The apparition or locution is credible and worthy of faithful pilgrims.

The Church condemns any and all hoaxes as well as any trick of the devil and repudiates any of natural explanation. It also only endorses authentic apparitions of supernatural and heavenly origin. If the evidence that surrounds a particular apparition is inconclusive either way, then pilgrims are neither discouraged nor encouraged.

Even if the Church determines that an apparition is worthy of belief, Catholics aren't obligated to believe it as they're obligated to believe the words of the *Apostles' Creed* (see Chapter 3) or Sacred Tradition. Catholics are free to believe or disbelieve apparitions, because they aren't considered revealed truth. But many saints and recent popes have given full support to all apparition places and shrines deemed legitimate and authentic.

Most accounts of apparitions are appearances of Mary to children and simple, humble people of faith. She asks them to pray to her son, pray for sinners, do penance, pray the Rosary daily for world peace, and live holy lives in obedience to God. Anytime weird messages or secrets are supposedly released, particularly if someone claims to know when the world will end, the Church says that you can be assured that it's not authentic. The reason, according to the Church, is that Jesus said, "But as for that day and hour, nobody knows it, neither the angels of heaven, nor the Son, no one but the Father alone," (Matthew 24:36). So why would his mom blab and spill the beans if Jesus wouldn't when asked?

See the following listing of some famous Marian shrines and/or apparition sites that the Church has sanctioned:

- **Our Lady of the Snows, Rome, Italy:** In A.D. 352, several prayerful folks had the same dream: Mary told them that she would indicate the site on which to build a church in her honor by a miraculous snowfall. Now known as St. Mary Major (*San Maria Maggiore* in Italian), it's one of the churches where the pope says Mass.

- **Our Lady of Walsingham, England:** In gratitude for a favor received through the intercession of Our Lady, a wealthy woman built a small chapel to honor her in 1061. It inspired many pilgrims, the weak and the powerful, the poor and the wealthy, until Henry VIII put a stop to it.

- **The Black Madonna of Czestochowa, Poland:** St. Luke painted Mary's portrait, which eventually made its way to Czestochowa, Poland, where it's been enshrined since 1382. (See Chapter 19 for more on this icon.)

- **Our Lady of Guadalupe, Mexico:** Our Lady appeared to St. Juan Diego in 1531, leaving her image on his cloak. Today, a famous basilica in Mexico City now hosts her picture. (See Chapters 1 and 19 to find out more about this apparition.) The image is often depicted as shown in Figure 14-2.

- **Our Lady of La Vang, Vietnam:** In 1798, a fierce persecution aimed at Catholics forced some to take refuge in the forest. Clustered together, praying the Rosary nightly, these Vietnamese faithful see a consoling apparition of the Mother of God. A church is later built on the spot.

- **Our Lady of the Miraculous Medal, Paris, France:** Our Lady appears to St. Catherine Laboure, a member of the order called the Sisters of Charity, in 1830. Communicating the exact design, Our Lady asks St. Catherine that a medal be struck in her honor.

- **Our Lady of La Salette, France:** Tending their cows in a pasture, a young girl named Melanie and a young boy named Maximin, both born into poverty, see a tall lady who never stops weeping in 1846. Our Lady tells them, in a nutshell, that folks need to straighten up their act and start praying or else. A beautiful Alpine shrine now marks the spot.

- **Our Lady of Lourdes, France:** In 1858, asking that a chapel be built and identifying herself as the Immaculate Conception, Our Lady appears to another poverty-stricken child of God, St. Bernadette, on 18 different occasions. Today's pilgrims bring containers to fill with miraculous Lourdes water. In 1943, 20th Century Fox produced Hollywood's version of the event; *The Song of Bernadette* won four Academy Awards. (See Chapter 19 for more on Lourdes, and Chapter 18 for more on St. Bernadette.)

- **Our Lady of Knock, Ireland:** Our Lady, St. Joseph, and St. John the Evangelist appear to 15 humble, hardworking Catholics of various ages in 1879. Many pilgrims experienced healings, and a shrine was built.

- **Our Lady of Fatima, Portugal:** In 1917, asking everybody to pray the Rosary daily for world peace, a beautiful lady clothed in white appears to three young children. (For more on Fatima, see Chapter 19.)

Figure 14-2:
The
traditional
depiction of
Our Lady of
Guadalupe.

Many people have claimed to see Mary, Joseph, the Child Jesus, saints, and the angels, but the local Church authorities have determined that most of them aren't credible or lack conclusive evidence. The number of alleged apparitions and locutions in recent times is greater than ever, but most don't withstand the test of time. One alleged visionary made bizarre statements, such as the pope had been kidnapped and was being held hostage, while an actor impersonated him. Any messages such as these are sure to get the thumbs down from the local bishop and definitely from the Holy See in Rome.

Sensationalism, emotionalism, and the overly zealous can convince people of the veracity of an alleged apparition even though the Church has repudiated it or made no decision whatsoever. Anytime that Scripture or Sacred Tradition is contradicted, or anytime that disobedience to the pope is encouraged — or dissent from the Magisterium or disrespect for the hierarchy — you can be sure that it's not an authentic apparition. Real apparitions occur to help boost but never to replace the Christian faith. (See Chapter 2 for more on the Magisterium.)

Chapter 15

Calling on the Canonized

When you visit London, you may see the larger-than-life bronze likeness of Sir Winston Churchill in Parliament Square that pays tribute to a man who many, both within and outside of the United Kingdom, regard as a hero. So, too, an imposing representation of Robert the Bruce in full armor atop his horse has weathered the elements over the years at Bannockburn; Scots can't help but feel a sense of pride. Likewise, visit any city or town, and 99 percent of the time, you can find a statue downtown of some national or local hero.

That same sense of pride and gratitude fills the hearts of Catholic Christians whenever they see a statue or picture of one of the saints. Catholicism honors and memorializes the saints as friends and faithful servants of God. They're considered heroes of the Church as much as Ben Franklin and Susan B. Anthony are heroes.

The honor given to the dead person is seen as appropriate, and no one's accused of idolatry for admiring or wanting to visit the memorials. In the same way, Catholics aren't idolizing the saints, which is a common misconception among non-Catholic Christians. This chapter fills you in on the role that the saints play in Catholicism. To read about the lives of a few well-known saints, see Chapter 18.

Having a Place in the Hearts of Catholics

Catholic devotion to the saints is nothing more than respect and admiration for the memory of the deceased heroes of the Church — men and women who Catholics believe chose to surrender their will and in some cases their very lives to serve God and his Church. So just as a society honors its dead who helped make the world a better place while they were alive, Catholics honor certain people — the apostles, the martyrs, St. Peter (the first pope), St. Paul (the first missionary), St. Elizabeth (the mother of John the Baptist and cousin of Mary), and St. Ann (the mother of Mary and grandmother of Jesus), for example.

In the Catholic Church, only after death can someone be called a saint, even though while alive the person lived a saintly, holy life. Mother Teresa of Calcutta, for example, who was revered around the world by people of every religion, couldn't be given the title of saint until after her death and only after a thorough investigation of her life *and* only after what the Church believes to be some undisputed miracles that took place through her intercession.

In the broader sense, everyone who's now in heaven is technically a saint. Saints are human beings who lived holy lives in obedience to God's will and are now in heaven for eternity. The classification or title of *saint,* however, is a spiritual pronouncement that the faithful can be morally certain that this particular person is indeed in heaven; prayers to and from the saint are considered efficacious.

Often, the saints are considered the exception whereas the Church wants to portray them as the norm — or at least as the norm that God would want. According to the Church, saints aren't born saints. Saints are born sinners in the state of original sin (see Chapter 6) and were sinners throughout their lives. They weren't perfect, sinless, and invulnerable. Unlike comic book superheroes, the saints don't come from another planet like Krypton, and they don't possess superhuman powers. Even though a few or more miracles took place in conjunction with the saint, it's always God doing the miracles through the saint, because saints have no special supernatural powers of their own.

Saints are ordinary people. They come from ordinary families — with parents and siblings like any other human being. They grew up, got sick, got better, and went to school. Some married, some remained single, and some entered religious life. Some were intelligent, some were average, and some were below average. Some were young and handsome, and some were old and not so pretty. The bottom line is that all saints are human. They weren't born with a halo around their head, and they didn't glow in the dark. What separated them from those who weren't given the title is that the former never gave up and never stopped trying to be and do better. The latter did give up and literally stopped trying to be and do better. The saints persevered. The others gave up. Saints were men and women who didn't have all the answers nor were they spared pain and suffering simply because they were holy people. On the contrary, the more faith that you possess doesn't mean that you suffer less. If you have faith, it means that you can persevere and endure much more for the sake of Christ, Who suffered and died for all humankind.

Sins and imperfections of some famous saints

St. Peter, the first pope, wasn't perfect or sinless. The Bible says that he denied Christ three times (John 18:17, 25, and 27), and he should've sought out an oral podiatrist for treatment, because he often opened his mouth and inserted his foot. He spoke before thinking, which is dangerous and foolish to do. Yet he became a saint.

One of the original twelve apostles, St. Thomas (nicknamed "doubting Thomas") doubted that Jesus rose from the dead, but he became a saint. James and John fell asleep while Jesus prayed in the Garden of Olives, even though he asked them to stay awake and pray with him. But they still became saints. St. Mary Magdalene, an alleged prostitute, repented and became a saint.

St. Augustine (354–430) was a playboy. He got drunk, flirted, visited prostitutes, gambled . . . you name it; he did it, except murder. And for 20 long years, his saintly mother, St. Monica, prayed for him, until one day, he and his illegitimate son Adeodatus embraced the Christian faith, repented of their sins, got baptized, and even entered the religious life. He later became a bishop and finally a saint and *doctor* of the Church — a title given to a saint of significant knowledge and/or whose writings demonstrate outstanding faith.

Contemporary *hagiography,* the study of the lives of the saints, differs from older versions in that it seeks to tell the whole truth. Previous biographies of the saints tended to sanitize their histories and leave out any imperfections. Occasionally, you'll run into a book on saints depicting them as being almost divinelike in their holiness and intelligence, and almost sinless and perfect. But the Church says that those kinds of people never existed. Saints eventually wind up in heaven, but while alive on earth, they make mistakes. Instead of making excuses, though, they chose to admit their shortcomings and cooperate with God's grace to overcome them.

So instead of seeing or portraying saints as superheroes, Catholicism wants to present them as just heroes — ordinary people who made it to heaven. The idea is that if they could do it, so can you. Mother Angelica (see Chapter 17), the founder of the Eternal Word Television Network (EWTN), often says to her TV viewers, "God calls us all to become great saints. Don't miss the opportunity."

Honoring God's Good Friends

Sometimes, Catholics appear to worship the dead, because Catholics put statues of the saints in their churches and homes, address prayers to them, and name churches after the saints, too. Worshipping the dead, however, would be idolatry and a serious sin, because the First Commandment forbids all worship of anyone or anything other than God. But Catholics don't worship the saints; they *honor* them. The images are merely reminders and nothing more.

Because the Fourth Commandment obligates the faithful to honor their parents, honoring the saints is the same type of respect. Catholics believe that worship can only be given to God, but honor can and should be given to certain human beings, such as parents and heroes of the faith. All the good guys and gals — the holy men and women — of the Bible are considered saints, which means that the Church regards them as being in heaven, honors their memory, and tries to encourage people to emulate their holiness.

The Church wants a saint's name to be used for Baptism or Confirmation. *Abraham, Sarah, Isaac, Noah, Rebecca, Mary, Elizabeth, Joseph, Matthew, Mark, Luke,* and *John,* for example, are all okay. These are all names of holy saints mentioned in the Bible and living in heaven. But picking a name, such as *Cain, Judas, Jezebel,* or *Herodias,* although biblical, isn't proper for Baptism or Confirmation, because those people are villains, not heroes. And secular names, such as *Corey* and *Morgan,* that don't originate in a saint's name are discouraged. For example, the name *John* is the origin of *Jack,* and *Kate* is short for *Katherine.* Unless a Christian name is chosen for the middle name, secular names are inappropriate. In many European and Latin American countries, the middle name is often the mother's maiden name. Sometimes, in the U.S. and Canada, the first name is secular and the middle name is Christian. Catholics should name their kids after a saint so that when their children are old enough to find out about the saint that they've been named after, the child will hopefully mimic that saint's behavior and lifestyle. Catholic moms and dads are delighted when their son or daughter tries to emulate a saint. Naming a child after a saint in Sacred Scripture or Church history used to be a hallmark of Christianity until the latter 20th century. Since then, strange and esoteric names have become prevalent.

It's All about Intercession

Praying to the saints is also often misunderstood. Traditionally, Catholicism has four kinds of prayer:

- **Adoration:** Praising God
- **Contrition:** Asking for God's forgiveness
- **Petition:** Asking God for a favor
- **Thanksgiving:** Showing God gratitude

We are family

In the Bible, a mother begged Jesus to drive a demon out of her daughter (Mark 7:25–30). The Church maintains that Jesus, being God and man, already knew that the daughter was plagued by a demon, so he didn't need the mother to tell him. But he allowed and permitted the mother to get involved and ask for help on behalf of her child.

Likewise, the Church believes that Jesus doesn't need the saints to tell him anything, but

he permits people to ask the saints to ask him for help. Why? Because humankind is all one family, all made in the image and likeness of God, all children of God, and all brothers and sisters in Christ, with Jesus being the brother. And the dead whose souls are with God are still part of the family of humankind and still connected to all on earth.

This may surprise you, but only adoration is restricted exclusively for God. Think of it like this: Just as people can say they're sorry to God when they sin, they can also say that they're sorry to another human person they've offended or hurt. Likewise, people can say, "Thank you!" to God or to another person. In the same way, making your petition known to a saint is asking the saint to pray for you. It isn't adoration, because the saint isn't worshipped. He's being asked for a favor: "Please pray for me!"

Often, the non-Catholic response is that Jesus Christ is the one and only mediator between God and humankind, so asking a saint for a favor is unnecessary, and no human being can duplicate, replace, or enhance what Christ the Mediator does. That's true from Catholicism's perspective, too. But the Church adds that when you read the Bible, you see people asking Jesus for favors on behalf of others. Whenever another person asks a favor on behalf of someone else, that's interceding on behalf of someone else's petition.

For example, some parents came to Jesus and said that their little girl was sick. These parents were interceding before Jesus on behalf of their daughter (Matthew 15:22, Mark 5:23 and 7:26, and Luke 8:41–42). And when the Roman centurion approached Christ and interceded on behalf of his servant (Matthew 8:5–6), Jesus healed the servant. He didn't say to the centurion or to the parents of the sick daughter, "You have come directly to me and have them ask me themselves to help them. They don't need your intercession." Instead, after those people made the request on behalf of another, the request was granted because they showed faith.

If a saint asks God for a favor on your behalf, it's called an *intercession*. The word comes from the Latin *intercedere,* which means to plead on another's behalf — to act as an advocate, especially for a favor for someone else. These intercessors are still using the one and only mediator, Jesus Christ, because they're going directly to him. Remember when you used to ask your Mom to approach your Dad about a request you had? That was using your mother as an intercessor.

So praying to Mary or a saint for their intercession is merely asking Mary or the saint to ask Jesus for help. Catholics believe that any reply, response, or answer comes from God, but the saint brought the concern to Jesus Christ. The bottom line? Just because Catholics ask the saints for prayers doesn't mean that Catholics worship the saints.

Some people ask, "Why even pray to Mary or a saint when you can go directly to God?" The answer is that Catholics never *have* to pray to any saint. They can always go directly to God. Catholicism doesn't say that saintly intercession is necessary or mandatory, but it's possible. The faithful can ask living people on earth to pray for them, and they can also ask the saints to pray for them.

The Church believes that the only time that prayers to and from the deceased have no effect is when the deceased are damned in hell. The Gospel parable of the rich man (traditionally known as *Dives,* which is Latin for *rich*) and the poor man, Lazarus, concludes with the former in hell and the latter in heaven (Luke 16:19–31). Dives asked "Father Abraham" if Lazarus could help him. Lazarus couldn't help, however, because the rich man was in hell. Catholicism teaches that the divide between heaven and hell can't be breached. The boundary between heaven and earth, however, is different, because we're still alive.

Recognizing a Saint

First of all, we want to make a clarification: The Catholic Church doesn't *make* saints like Hollywood makes movie stars. So, too, people can make chocolate chip cookies or Italian cannoli, but they can't make saints. However, the Church does *recognize* them.

Catholics say that saints are men and women who lived holy lives in obedience to God's will, and they became saints at the moment that they entered heaven. Getting to heaven involves faith, hope, and love — the three theological virtues given at Baptism. A person must have faith and hope in God and must love God in order to go to heaven.

The process for being declared a saint is ancient, traditional, and often mysterious. Everyone in heaven is a saint, but knowing whether a particular person is in heaven is a different matter. Evidence must be presented to persuade Church officials that the person in question in fact lived a virtuous life, had faith, and had the support and help of God. The Church also looks at miracles as evidence that God is working through that person. (See the "Bona fide miracles" sidebar in this chapter.)

A thorough investigation takes place, and after strict criteria are met, the case ends up on the pope's desk. He alone decides who's in and who's out. By that, we don't mean that the pope decides who *is* a saint. That's a judgment that only God can make. We mean that the pope, as the supreme head of the Church, has the authority to decide who is publicly *recognized* as a saint in churches all over the world and gets their name on the calendar; that is, they get a feast day. For more on feast days, see Chapter 8 and Appendix B.

Are you a saint?

Why not imagine yourself becoming a saint? Maybe you are, but you don't know it. (Saints are often very humble souls.) Just for now at least, imagine that you are. Pretend that you passed away at least five years ago and entered heaven after living an exemplary life on earth. Looking down, you see that your relatives, friends, and even the people who barely knew you are all abuzz, because they're convinced of your sanctity and recognize that you were especially virtuous during your lifetime, maybe even mystical. Now that you've passed away, they're nudging your pastor to present your cause to the bishop. Specific steps must be taken to declare that you're a saint, posthumously of course, in the Catholic Church:

1. **Servant of God:** As soon as your cause is opened for consideration, you're called a *Servant of God.*

2. **Venerable:** After the Vatican Congregation for the Causes of Saints determines that you did indeed live a life of heroic virtue, you're called *venerable. Heroic virtue* doesn't mean that you were perfect or sinless, but that you worked aggressively to improve yourself spiritually and that you never gave up trying to be better and grow in holiness.

3. **Blessed:** After the Church establishes one miracle, your cause is presented to the pope to see whether he deems you worthy of being called *blessed.* This step is called *beatification* and is the next-to-last step.

4. **Saint:** Another miracle and your cause is presented to the pope again for his judgment. If he determines that the evidence is clear and that contrary reports aren't credible, he may initiate the canonization procedure. If all goes well, you'll be publicly recognized as a saint.

From the Catholic viewpoint, you don't have to be canonized a saint to be a saint. Billions and billions of people are saints in heaven, but they just aren't publicly recognized as saints. Canonized saints are merely those who are known, proven, recognized, and publicly honored for their holiness. Your grandma or grandpa in heaven may not be canonized, but they're saints just as much as St. Peter, St. Paul, St. James, and St. John. They have no feast day, no statues of themselves in church, no holy card with their face on it, and no church named after them, but they're still saints. They're in heaven and at peace, so they aren't bummed that St. Dominic and St. Francis of Assisi have churches, schools, and religious orders named after them. Catholicism teaches that in heaven, jealousy, regrets, and disappointments are nonexistent.

The investigation

The first step to beatification and finally canonization begins with an investigation. Only people whose existence can be verified and whose lives can be examined are possible candidates for canonization. Legendary figures of the past don't make it if no proof exists that they walked this earth. Also, the living can't be declared venerable, blessed, or a saint, because those titles are reserved for souls in heaven.

The background check

Normally, from 5 to 50 years after death, a formal request is made to open the cause. This request is presented to the local bishop of the place where you died. The group making the request is called the *Actor Causae* and is usually composed of people from your former parish, diocese, religious community, or organization with whom you were associated, affiliated, or connected while you were alive.

Just being a nice guy or girl isn't enough. You must have demonstrated exemplary and heroic virtue — gone beyond what was expected and necessary and done far more to serve God, the Church, and your neighbor. You didn't have to be perfect or totally sinless. Catholics believe that no one but God is perfect. For example, the Bible tells of the good thief, St. Dismas, who hung on the cross next to Jesus on Good Friday. Jesus promised, "This day you will be with Me in Paradise." (Luke 23:43) St. Dismas was a sinner, but he repented and sought the divine mercy and forgiveness of God. However, as a candidate for beatification, you still must've lived an exemplary life. The purpose of the process isn't to get you into heaven, but to recognize that you're already on board and that you lived a life worthy to be imitated.

Usually, a number of people who lived and worked with you want to attest to your personal holiness and the effect that you had on many lives. One or two people aren't enough. The local bishop must decide if enough initial interest and evidence exists, and if the possibility of completing the process exists before he asks Rome to open your cause. If the arguments from the group are persuasive and the evidence compelling, the bishop asks Rome and the Congregation for the Causes of Saints for permission, and when given, he forms a special tribunal to investigate your cause.

Everyone is called to holiness

The Church believes that because every man and woman on earth is made in the image and likeness of God, and by Baptism they become adopted children of God, then all human beings are called to holiness. In the mid-1960s, the Second Vatican Council (see Chapter 8) spoke of the Universal Call to Holiness. But 30 years prior, St. Josemaría Escrivá, the founder of Opus Dei, taught that God wants all people, be they clergy or laity, male or female, children or adults, young or old, to live holy lives.

Escrivá often spoke of the sanctification of one's daily work, meaning that a person can transform his mundane and sometimes tedious chores into the Work of God (*Opus Dei* in Latin). Everyone can and should become a saint by sanctifying their daily work. He pointed out (as

did St. Francis de Sales, St. Thérèse of Lisieux, and other spiritual writers) that the holy family of Jesus, Mary, and Joseph spent most of their time doing ordinary work. St. Joseph worked as a carpenter, and it wasn't a cushy nine-to-five job. Mary spent 80 percent of her day cooking, shopping for groceries, cleaning, sewing, doing laundry, and other household chores. And until he turned 30, Jesus worked with Joseph so much that at one time in the Bible, he was called a carpenter (Mark 6:3). Escrivá taught that because Jesus, Mary, and Joseph didn't spend all their time in the Temple or on their knees in prayer, holiness isn't just doing holy things or going to holy places. Holiness is actually *being* holy and that means uniting yourself to God.

During this period, witnesses are called who can verify or refute your public life. Did you live a virtuous life or a scandalous one? Did you regularly practice your religion or were you lax? Did you treat others with love and respect or with contempt and disdain? Concrete examples of how you exhibited the theological virtues of faith, hope, and love — as well as the cardinal, or moral, virtues of prudence, justice, fortitude, and temperance — must be proven by oral testimony or written evidence. If sufficient witnesses and documentation are present, you're then called a Servant of God.

The full-scale investigation

Three levels of investigation occur:

✔ Informative inquiries into your life, reputation, and activities while you lived on earth

✔ Proof that no one has proclaimed or is already proclaiming and honoring you as a saint before it's been officially declared

✔ A thorough examination of your written and spoken (transcripts) works

Miracles aren't necessary at this point, but if it's believed that a miracle occurred during your life and/or after your death, it's noted in this first stage of the investigation.

Bona fide miracles

In March 1981, Maureen Digan of Roslindale, Massachusetts, traveled to St. Faustina's (1905–1938) tomb at the Shrine of The Divine Mercy outside of Krakow, Poland. From her early teens, Maureen suffered from an incurable illness known as Milroy's Disease, a form of lymphedema. It had already claimed one of her legs and doctors recommended amputating the other. At St. Faustina's tomb, Maureen prayed for St. Faustina's intercession and immediately felt the pain leave her and the swelling in her leg going down. Upon the doctors' examination, they stated that Maureen's incurable ailment had disappeared. After exhaustive examination by medical professionals, the Church declared the healing a miracle through St. Faustina's intercession.

In 1995, Fr. Ron Pytel of Baltimore, Maryland, knew that he had a problem. His doctors discovered a massive calcium build-up in his aortic valve. As a result, the left ventricle of his heart had become badly damaged, a condition that rarely heals, and if it does, it occurs over a span of many years. In June of 1995, Fr. Ron had surgery to replace the valve with an artificial one, but the damage to his heart was another problem. When he went for his first regular check-up two months later, the prognosis wasn't good. Dr. Nicholas Fortuin, a world-renowned cardiologist from Johns Hopkins in Baltimore, said that Fr. Ron's heart would never be normal and that the 48-year-old priest would likely never be able to return to his priestly duties. On October 5, 1995, the 58th anniversary of St. Faustina's death, Fr. Ron prayed for St. Faustina's intercession at a healing service. After venerating her relic, he collapsed on the floor and felt unable to move for about 15 minutes. During his next regular check-up, Fr. Ron's doctor could not explain the condition of the priest's heart: It had returned to normal. On November 16, 1999, a panel of doctors declared the healing scientifically unexplainable. Theologians from the Church's Congregation for the Causes of Saints dubbed the healing a miracle on December 7. Then one week later, a panel of cardinals and bishops gave their unanimous approval.

After the local diocesan investigation goes to Rome, the next step, called the *Apostolic Process*, is to translate the documentation into Italian, because the cardinals and other theological experts live in Italy, not in the country where the case originated. After the documentation is translated, a summary called the *Positio* is presented to the Congregation for the Causes of Saints. Nine theologians scrutinize the evidence and documentation. If a majority passes it, it then goes to a committee of cardinals and bishops who meet twice a month and work at the Congregation. If they approve, the Prefect of the Congregation gives permission for the title *venerable* to be associated with your name. If at least one miracle has been attributed to your intercession then the Prefect presents the case to the pope for his personal judgment. He alone decides whether you're declared *blessed* (beatification). The pope makes this declaration at a Mass celebrated in your honor.

If you were martyred for the faith — killed because of your religion or because you refused to renounce Christ or the Church — then no miracle is needed before beatification. If you died naturally and weren't martyred, then a miracle *after death* is required before beatification. If it can be proven that another miracle occurred after beatification, then the cause is presented to the pope again to consider canonization, at which time, you're finally called a saint! Again, he makes this declaration at a special Mass in Rome or in the country where you lived and died. Canonizing a saint is considered a function of *papal infallibility* (see Chapter 2), because it's vital that the faithful give public veneration and honor only to those who truly are in heaven.

Miracles matter

All miracles need to be documented and authenticated, so eyewitnesses alone are considered insufficient. Medical, scientific, psychiatric, and theological experts are consulted, and evidence is given to them for their professional opinion. If a scientific, medical, or psychological explanation exists for what had only appeared to be a miracle, then it isn't an authentic miracle. Only immediate, spontaneous, and inexplicable phenomena are up for consideration as authentic miracles. A group of Italian doctors *(Consulta Medica)* examine the healing miracles. Some of the doctors aren't Catholic and some are, but all are qualified and renowned physicians. They don't declare a healing a miracle, but instead say, "We can find no scientific or medical explanation for the cure."

Besides miraculous healings, the commission examines other phenomena:

- ✔ **Incorruptibility:** Long after the saint is dead, the body is found free of decay when exhumed from the grave. The Church considers St. Catherine of Siena to be an example. She died in 1380, and 600 years later without any embalming, her flesh hasn't decomposed.

- ✔ **Liquefaction:** The dried blood of the saint, long dead, miraculously liquefies on the feast day. The Church considers St. Januarius (*San Gennaro* in Italian; A.D. 275?–305), the patron saint of Naples, to be an example. According to the Church, a vial of his dried blood liquefies every year on September 19.

- ✔ **Odor of sanctity:** The body of the saint exudes a sweet aroma, like roses, rather than the usual pungent stench of decay. The Church considers St. Teresa of Avila (1515–82) to be just such an example. The Church believes her grave exuded a sweet odor for nine months after her death.

In addition, during the life of the saint, some miraculous things may have happened:

- ✔ **Levitation:** The saint floats in the air without the help of David Copperfield. An example is St. Joseph of Cupertino (1603–63), who, according to the Church, levitated often during prayer.

 ✔ **Bilocation:** The saint appears in two places at the same time. According to the Church, Padre Pio (1887–1968) was seen and heard in two places at the same time yet spanning great distances. (For more on Padre Pio, see Chapter 18.)

 ✔ **Stigmata:** The saint's body is marked with the five wounds of Christ on both hands, both feet, and on the side. These wounds often bleed during Mass and then stop. After death, the stigmata disappear. The Church believes that Padre Pio (1887–1968) and St. Francis of Assisi (1181–1226) were blessed with the stigmata. (To find out more about St. Francis, flip ahead to Chapter 18.)

The Church believes that most saints didn't have these rare experiences, but the experiences of those who did were proven to be authentic and inexplicable by modern science.

Beatification and canonization

The actual act of beatification, in which a person is declared *blessed,* or of *canonization,* which is officially recognizing a saint, usually takes place in St. Peter's Square outside the Vatican and St. Peter's Basilica. In 2001, almost half a million people attended Padre Pio's outdoor canonization Mass. When Monsignor Josemaría Escrivá was canonized four months later, 300,000 were present.

Sometimes, though, the pope beatifies and canonizes in the country where the person lived and died, as in the case of St. Juan Diego. He was an Aztec peasant, and the Church believes Mary, as Our Lady of Guadalupe, appeared to him in Mexico in 1531. In his case, 12,000 people were present in the Basilica in Mexico City, and 30,000 waited outside, watching on monitors.

Because the Mass is the highest form of worship for Catholics and the Holy Eucharist is the zenith of Catholicism, it makes perfect sense for the pope as supreme head of the universal Church to beatify or canonize a saint within the context of the Mass.

After the life history is read aloud, the pope chants the following in Latin. For a canonization, it's chanted as shown; for a beatification, the word *blessed* is substituted for *saint:*

> In honor of the Blessed Trinity, for the exaltation of the Catholic Faith and the growth of Christian life, with the authority of Our Lord Jesus Christ, of the Blessed Apostles Peter and Paul and Our Own, after lengthy reflection, having assiduously invoked God's assistance and taken into account the opinion of many brothers of ours in the episcopate, we declare and define [*Blessed Josemaría Escrivá* or *Blessed Pio* or *Blessed Juan Diego,* for

example] to be a saint, and we enroll him in the Catalogue of the saints, and we establish that in the whole Church he should be devoutly honored among the saints. In the name of the Father and of the Son and of the Holy Spirit. Amen.

During a beatification, right at this point, the person is recognized as *blessed*. During a canonization, at this point, the person is recognized as a saint. Then a huge, larger-than-life tapestry, showing an image of the blessed or the saint is unfolded for the faithful to look at and admire.

The Communion of Saints

Part of the Apostles' Creed says, "I believe in . . . the communion of saints." People sometimes ask us, "But what in the world does that mean? Is it holy people receiving Holy Communion?" Well, yes and no. The term *communion of saints* (*hagion koinonian* in Greek) is rich in meaning. It refers to the fellowship or community that exists between all the members of the Church. Three levels are traditionally identified:

- **The Church Triumphant:** Saints in heaven
- **The Church Militant:** Believers on earth
- **The Church Suffering:** Souls in purgatory

Catholicism teaches that death can't sever the ties that bind the members of the Church, because the soul is immortal and only the body can die. So Catholics believe that the ties and connections that link them together in life continue in death. The beloved dead are still connected to the living and still love the living as much as they still love the dead. Even though the body is dead, the immortal soul is very much still alive and in existence.

The Church believes that the communion of saints is most fully expressed and experienced during the Holy Sacrifice of the Mass — especially at the Consecration and at Holy Communion. The Church believes that heaven and earth are united at that time. The saints in heaven, the believers living on earth, and the souls in purgatory are all intimately connected and united at the Mass, because the power of Jesus Christ binds them in the first place.

Saints in heaven

The Catholic Church believes that the saints are ordinary and typical human beings — with faults and failures, talents and gifts, vices and virtues — who made it into heaven not by being perfect but by persevering. As the late

Mother Teresa of Calcutta often said, "We aren't called to be successful; rather God calls each of us to be faithful." Catholics believe this means that the saints were sinners who never gave up and never quit on God. They never stopped trying to do and be better.

In terms of the communion of saints, the *Church Triumphant* refers to all the saints who are now in heaven. And Catholicism teaches that just because the saints are in heaven, that doesn't mean they stop loving their family and friends who are still alive on earth.

Heaven is described in the Catechism as the communion of life and love with the Holy Trinity (God the Father, Son, and Holy Spirit), the Blessed Virgin Mary, and all the angels and saints. It's not just me getting to Paradise but much more. Heaven is our spiritual home and home is where the family lives, in this case, the family of God. Jesus said, "In my Father's house are many rooms; if it were not so, would I have told you that I go to prepare a place for you? And when I go and prepare a place for you, I will come again and will take you to myself, that where I am you may be also." (John 14:2-3)

Are angels among us?

Angels are pure spirits whereas men and women have bodies and souls. Angels were created before humankind, and some of them sinned and were cast into hell for all eternity. These fallen angels are known as devils and demons. Lucifer was an angel, but after his fall, he became known as Satan or the devil. Most of the angels remained obedient to God. St. Thomas Aquinas (see Chapter 18) described nine choirs or groupings of angels in his *Summa Theologica* based on Sacred Scripture (Colossians 1:16 and Romans 8:38) as well as Sacred Tradition. The following list presents them in order from highest to lowest:

- **Seraphim:** Isaiah 6:2
- **Cherubim:** Genesis 3:24
- **Thrones:** Colossians 1:16
- **Dominions:** Colossians 1:16
- **Virtues:** Ephesians 1:21
- **Powers:** 1 Peter 3:22
- **Principalities:** Romans 8:38
- **Archangels:** 1 Thessalonians 4:16
- **Angels:** Romans 8:38

Guardian angels are spirits God has commanded to watch over you and guard you. The belief in guardian angels is based on Matthew 18:10: "See that you do not despise one of these little ones; for I tell you that in heaven *their* angels always behold the face of my Father who is in heaven." Some angels, like the Archangels Michael, Gabriel, and Raphael, are mentioned in the Bible. Other angels like Uriel, Jophiel, Chamael, Zadkiel, and Jophkiel are only listed in what Catholicism calls the Apocrypha or what Protestantism calls the Pseudepigrapha. See Chapter 3 for more on the Apocrypha and the Pseudepigrapha.

Catholics believe that going to heaven is going home to your destiny, because you were created to know, love, and serve God in this world so as to be happy with Him in the next. But heaven is also a great family reunion where you're reunited with all your deceased loved ones who went to heaven before you. Imagine seeing grandparents, parents, children, brothers and sisters, cousins and in-laws, not to mention the famous people of history, such as Adam and Eve, Abraham and Moses, Mary and Joseph, and so on. The joy and happiness of being with those you love and those who love you is nothing, however, in comparison with the bliss and ecstasy that the soul experiences just seeing God face to face (called the *beatific vision*), because he's all truth, goodness, and holiness. Heaven is so fantastic, wonderful, and desirable, that human beings should want to go there more than wanting anything else in the universe. Catholics believe that everybody should be willing to do anything to get there, which means that loving and obeying God is a must.

According to the Catholic Church, when a human being — even a baby or small child — dies, the person doesn't become an angel but, rather, a saint. The Church believes that angels are separate beings from humans.

Believers on earth

The third tier of the communion of saints is the *Church Militant,* the believers on earth. And they're always united in a mystical fashion to the Church Triumphant, the saints in heaven, and the Church Suffering, the souls in purgatory.

Vatican II described the faithful alive on earth as a Pilgrim People. The Church believes that those still living on earth are on a pilgrimage from this land to the promised land of heaven. St. Augustine (354–430) remarked that the faithful are citizens of the Heavenly Jerusalem while temporarily traveling through the earthly Babylon.

In this case, the word *militant* isn't used in the sense that Catholics are at war with Protestants, Jews, or Muslims. The term *militant* refers to a *spiritual warfare* against sin and the devil. Catholics believe that their fellow man is their ally, not their enemy. The devil and sin are the real enemies. Confirmation makes the faithful Soldiers of Christ, who battle against greed, envy, anger, lust, pride, laziness, and gluttony, as well as prejudice, racism, anti-Semitism, hatred, violence, terrorism, abortion, euthanasia, pornography, physical/emotional/sexual abuse, child abuse, and so on. The Church believes that those sins are the enemies of God and of humankind, and therefore, the Church Militant does battle against vice and error through the weapons of grace and truth — not guns, tanks, and missiles. The spiritual battle is for souls — to rescue them from sin and evil.

Where is hell anyway?

Ancient man believed that hell was underground, in the center of the earth, where it was hot. This was based this on the erroneous notion that the earth was the center of the universe. When science proved that the sun was the center of the solar system, then what? Well, the Bible and Sacred Tradition never defined the exact location of hell. Because God created hell as a place to incarcerate the devil and all the bad angels who rebelled with him, and because angels are pure spirit and have no bodies which take up space, then hell isn't a physical place. It's as real as heaven or purgatory, but you can't travel to it anymore than a spaceship can reach heaven.

The essence of hell isn't a million degrees of heat from fire but the heat that comes from hatred and bitterness. Hell is a lonely and selfish place in that no matter who or how many souls it contains, no one cares about anyone else except himself. It's utter isolation as well as eternal torment, and that's why everyone should want to avoid it at all cost. Heaven, on the other hand, is a place of happiness and joy, because everyone there knows and loves each other, and most of all, because of what's called *beatific vision* — seeing God face to face for eternity. Being in the presence of the Supreme Being who is all truth and all goodness ought to be the desire of every person.

Souls in purgatory

Purgatory is an often-misunderstood Catholic doctrine. It isn't considered a spiritual jail or hell with parole. And Catholicism doesn't teach that everyone goes to purgatory. On the contrary, the Church believes that many people are purified or purged, hence the term *purgatory,* in this life. For example, the Church believes that many innocent persons who suffer from disease, poverty, or persecution are living their purgatory now, and when they die, they probably go straight to heaven. The same goes for people who live an exceptionally good and holy life — no need for purgatory. But the Church believes that most everyone else, although not bad enough to go to hell, *aren't* good enough to skate into heaven with no need for some introspection and purification.

The real doctrine consists of the conviction that God's mercy and justice must be kept intact and upheld. God's divine mercy refers to the fact that he forgives any sin as long as the sinner is truly repentant and sorry. God's justice, however, is that good is rewarded and evil punished. Catholics believe that purgatory evens the score and fulfills justice while accommodating mercy. They believe that *purgatory* isn't a place but a spiritual state of the soul in which it's purified before entering heaven. Known as the *Church Suffering,* the souls in purgatory are definitely and absolutely going to heaven, just not yet.

Think of it like this: Joe and Max were both born on the same day and both died on the same day. Joe was a gambler, boozer, and womanizer, and he was dishonest, lazy, and undependable. Max, on the other hand, spent his life obeying the Ten Commandments, practicing virtue, and loving God and neighbor. Just before dying, Joe repents of his old ways and accepts the Lord into his heart. Should Joe and Max both go to heaven at the same time? Catholicism teaches no. The Church believes that Jesus' death allows everyone the possibility of heaven, and his mercy grants forgiveness, but his justice demands that good be rewarded and evil punished — in this life or the next. If one man struggles all his life to be good while another lives a life of selfishness, greed, and comfort, both can't walk through the pearly gates side by side.

Purgatory is more than the temporal punishment for sin. It's also the cleansing from the attachment to sin. _Purgatory_ purifies the soul before the soul's grand entrance into heaven.

It may help to think of the purgatory in terms of a major operation to save a life. Say a doctor performs surgery on someone's heart or brain and removes a cancerous tumor. The surgery achieves the main objective, but the wound needs to heal, and the incision needs to be cleaned and rebandaged. Purgatory is like that secondary part of recovery — the healing, cleaning, and bandaging. The belief is that the evil of sin is revealed to the person so she can totally and absolutely reject even the most venial and smallest of sins.

Hankerin' for heaven

Dante Alighieri (1265–1321) wrote a famous poem, _La Divina Commedia_ (The Divine Comedy), made up of three shorter poems, the _Inferno_ (hell), _Purgatorio_ (purgatory), and _Paradiso_ (heaven). Dante described purgatory as a suburb of hell — close enough to smell the stench and feel the heat but still far enough away for hope. And he described those in hell as never getting out of the torment they deserved for their evil.

Although not a theological work – and never meant as theology — Dante's poem greatly influenced the Medieval and Renaissance mindset. Many people felt that what Dante described was what purgatory really was — hell with parole or a suburb of hell.

According to the Church, however, purgatory is more like a suburb of heaven. It's close enough to hear the laughter and singing, smell the sweetness in the air, and feel the warmth nearby, but far enough away to remind everyone that they haven't yet arrived.

Or, as some people would like to think of it, it's like being stuck in traffic on the day before Thanksgiving. You know for certain that you're on your way home, but you just don't know when. And it's the not-knowing part that causes the anxiety and purgative pain.

Often, after committing a sin, people later regret it and are remorseful. Catholics confess their sins and believe that God forgives them in the Sacrament of Penance. However, many times people still have pleasant memories of those sins. They're sorry and regret doing them, but they have some enjoyable and pleasurable memories — some leftover attachment to the sins. Catholicism teaches that the souls in purgatory want to be in purgatory, because they *know* that they have some leftover attachment to sin that they want to be removed.

Does purgatory make any more sense to you now than it did before you read this chapter? No? Keep on reading. We'll try again. Pretend that you went to an ear, nose, and throat doctor, and he said that you have allergies, and one of them is to dust mites. Now, dust mites can't be seen, so people usually aren't too concerned or worried about them until they see them under an electron microscope, which reveals how ugly and harmful these critters are. After you see them, you never look at dust the same way again, and you never want to get anywhere near those mites, because you have an idea how nasty they really are. Anyway, you can think of purgatory like a spiritual electron microscope that shows all that nasty sin — mortal and venial —revealing how dangerous and harmful any sin is to the soul. Purgatory allows people to recognize that even one small sin is repugnant and offensive to an all-loving and all-good God. It may last a few minutes, a few months, or many years, because only the undefiled and pure can enter heaven. Actually, time, as mere mortals know it, doesn't exist in purgatory, because departed souls have no bodies, so any mention of minutes, days, months, or years in purgatory is merely analogous.

The word *purgatory* isn't in the Bible, but neither is the word *Bible*. However, praying for the dead is mentioned in the Second Book of Maccabees (12:43–46):

> He then took up a collection among all his soldiers, amounting to two thousand silver drachmas, which he sent to Jerusalem to provide for an expiatory sacrifice. In doing this he acted in a very excellent and noble way, inasmuch as he had the resurrection of the dead in view; for if he weren't expecting the fallen to rise again, it would have been useless and foolish to pray for them in death. But if he did this with a view to the splendid reward that awaits those who had gone to rest in godliness, it was a holy and pious thought. Thus he made atonement for the dead that they might be freed from this sin.

The belief is that if the dead were in hell, no prayers could help them, and if they were in heaven, they wouldn't need any prayers. So a place must exist in between heaven and hell where the souls who aren't completely prepared or ready to enter heaven go after death.

Catholics don't see purgatory as a place of pain and torment. Instead, it's considered a place of expectant joy, although suffering occurs from the temporary distance. Imagine being in a room with a door that has no handle or knob on your side. You can hear the joy and merriment on the other side, smell the good food, and hear the music and laughter, but you can't see any faces or distinguish voices or aromas. You're close but yet far enough away to feel the pain of not being on the other side. Yet you know that you aren't ready yet. Your clothes are dirty and wrinkled, your hair's a mess, and you need to shave and brush your teeth. Why all this preparation? Catholics believe that God and heaven are worth it.

A Saint for Every Day of the Year

The Catholic Church assigns one date out of the year for each and every canonized saint — known as the saint's *feast day.* The saints are remembered on their individual feast days with special mention, prayers, and possibly a scripture reading. Usually, it's the day that the person died. That's the day that the Church believes the person went to heaven, so it's the saint's heavenly birthday. The number of canonized saints, however, is greater than the number of days in a calendar year. So two or more saints often share the same feast day. Because overlap often occurs, and the Church isn't sure of the date of death of some saints, other calendar dates are sometimes chosen — such as the day that the saint was canonized.

Relics of the saints

The relics of the saints fall into one of the following three categories:

- **First class:** Actual body part

- **Second class:** Article of clothing or personal artifact

- **Third class:** Item, such as a holy card or a piece of cloth, touched to a first-class relic

These relics aren't good luck charms or magical items but merely mementos of holy people. The relic is venerated, not adored, because it represents its original owner. Just like fans of Elvis want memorabilia of the King, and those who admire Winston Churchill want items that he owned or used, Catholics often show respect and devotion to relics of the saints, because they're friends of God in heaven with him. These relics have no power of their own but are used to bless people — especially the sick so that through the intercession of that particular saint, God's healing may occur. Some may think it macabre to have small bits of a saint's bone encased in glass and metal for public veneration, but what about keeping a lock of hair of a loved one even after death? The relic of a saint's body is only recognition that this same body was united to a soul who's now in heaven.

Some saints' feasts are only celebrated in the particular saint's town or country. Others are internationally celebrated.

For example, St. Patrick's Day, March 17, is celebrated in Ireland, because St. Patrick is the patron saint of the entire nation. St. Patrick's Day is also celebrated in many areas of the United States due to the Irish immigrants who crossed the Atlantic. Many U.S. dioceses have cathedrals dedicated to St. Patrick, or he's the patron saint of the diocese, such as in Harrisburg and Erie, Pennsylvania. Celebrating the Feast of St. Patrick is a big occasion and a *solemnity,* a full-blown liturgical feast, in such places. In other places, such as Italy, Spain, France, Poland, and Germany, it isn't celebrated with the same fanfare.

Another example is St. Joseph's Day, March 19, which is celebrated in Canada and Europe with more hoopla than in the United States. He's the patron of the universal Church and the head of the *holy family,* which refers to Jesus, Mary, and Joseph during the first 30 years of Jesus' life. Mediterranean people remember him in particular with special foods and festivities, and his day is also a full solemnity all over the world. If his feast day falls on a Friday in Lent, then abstinence from meat and any fasting are dispensed to give the day full recognition. The reason is obvious due to the belief about Joseph's role in the early life of Jesus: As the husband of Mary and foster father of Jesus, he took care of Mary and Jesus.

On some feast days, such as the Feasts of St. Patrick, St. Joseph, St. Januarius (September 19), and St. Gerard Majella (October 16), Catholics process through the streets and host festivals with plenty of pomp and circumstance. And with some feasts, such as the Feasts of St. Ann (July 26), the Archangels St. Michael, St. Gabriel, and St. Raphael (September 29), and St. Thérèse of Lisieux (October 1), parishes often have a special Mass and may even have a nine-day novena, which usually concludes on the day of the feast itself. For more on St. Patrick, go to Chapter 1; for more on St. Thérèse, see Chapter 18.

In addition, on the feast days of the founders of religious orders, such as August 8 (St. Dominic), October 4 (St. Francis of Assisi), July 11 (St. Benedict), and July 31 (St. Ignatius of Loyola), the religious orders that they founded — the Dominicans, Franciscans, Benedictines, and Jesuits, respectively — usually honor the feast of their founder with a healthy mix of praying and partying.

You can find saints for different places and saints for different occasions. The idea isn't to replace or diminish the role of Christ as the one sole mediator but to show how the family of faith continues to remain a part of each member in different ways.

Chapter 16

Catholic Traditions

You've seen Catholics with ashes on the foreheads on Ash Wednesday, the beginning of Lent. Does it look odd to you? These ashes may look strange, but it's traditions like this one that maintain Catholic identity. But Catholics don't practice their traditions for the sake of identity. Rather, these faith traditions all have religious significance and meaning.

In this chapter, we cover the traditions that are predominantly Catholic in nature and origin. Many of these traditions have their origins in the mostly Catholic countries of Western Europe.

Adoring the Blessed Sacrament

To understand what adoring the Blessed Sacrament is all about, you first need to understand Catholicism's perspective on the Holy Eucharist. So we're going to take a roundabout way of getting to the tradition itself. Bear with us.

Catholicism has three perspectives on the Holy Eucharist:

✔ **Sacrifice:** The same sacrifice of Jesus' death on the cross for the remission of sins occurs during Mass at the Consecration in the form of the Holy Eucharist. This is called a *sacrifice,* because Jesus, the Son of God, is being offered by the priest to God the Father.

✔ **Sacred Banquet:** After the Consecration of the Mass, wherein what was wine and bread became the *real* body and blood of Christ, the faithful walk up to the altar to receive the Holy Eucharist. Entering a person's body, soul, mind, and heart all at once, Jesus — really, truly, and substantially — in the Holy Eucharist is placed on the tongue or in the hand. This is called a *sacred banquet* because the Holy Eucharist is food and nourishment for the soul.

✔ **Blessed Sacrament:** Catholics believe that this is Christ himself — his real, true body and blood, soul and divinity, and substantial presence under the appearances of a wafer of bread. Some Christian religions regard it as a symbolic, spiritual, or moral presence, but Catholic Christianity and Eastern Orthodoxy staunchly hold to his Real Presence in the Eucharist. So the Eucharist, whether in the tabernacle (see Figure 16-1) or in the monstrance on the altar, warrants the same adoration and worship given only to God. This is called the *Blessed Sacrament,* because of all the seven sacraments, this one not only gives divine grace, but it's also God himself.

You can read more about the Holy Eucharist in Chapters 6 and 7. That said, we can explain what adoring the Blessed Sacrament is all about.

Figure 16-1:
The Blessed Sacrament exposed in the monstrance on the left and within the tabernacle on the right.

Courtesy of St. Louis de Montfort Church, Fishers, Indiana.

The Holy Eucharist, also known as the *Blessed Sacrament,* is placed in a monstrance (see Figure 16-1) and left on the altar for public adoration and worship — 24/7 in some churches. Catholics consider it a great privilege and blessing to be able to adore the Blessed Sacrament, however, Jesus must never be left exposed in the monstrance without anyone in attendance. So those parishes that offer adoration 24/7, which is called *Perpetual Adoration,* also maintain a list of individual parishioners who commit about one *holy hour* — usually the same hour each week — to private adoration, saying prayers, such as the Rosary or the Divine Mercy Chaplet, silently in the company of Jesus.

The Eucharist should never be exposed at home. Adoration of the Blessed Sacrament can only take place in a church, a chapel, or an oratory, but adoration and Benediction can't take place during Mass.

Benediction

A formal service, Benediction takes place while adoring the Blessed Sacrament and can only occur if a priest or a deacon leads it. Sacred Scripture is read, a homily may be preached, the Rosary may be said, and silent prayer is offered. At the end, the priest, his shoulders enveloped in a special stole called a *humeral veil,* blesses the faithful kneeling in attendance with Jesus exposed in the monstrance, making the sign of the cross.

The history of the 40-hour devotion in a nutshell

The 40-hour devotion originated in Europe and was known as *Quarant' Ore* in Italian, which simply means *40 hours.* St. Anthony Maria Zaccaria started the first 40 hours in Milan in 1527. He wanted to renew and reaffirm the belief in the Real Presence and the practice of giving adoration and worship to the Holy Eucharist, because it's no longer merely bread in the form of a wafer. It only looks and tastes like bread, but Jesus is now present in the Eucharist — the substantial body and blood, soul and divinity of Christ.

St. Philip Neri (1515–95) brought the practice to Rome after Martin Luther initiated the Protestant Reformation. At the time, clergy and laity alike were getting confused about what the Church really taught. Even a few priests who celebrated Mass daily began to doubt that they had the power to actually change bread and wine into the body and blood of Christ.

St. John Neumann, Archbishop of Philadelphia (1811–60), an immigrant from Bohemia, brought the tradition to the United States. Once a year, each and every Philadelphia parish had a 40-hour devotion on a regularly scheduled basis.

During Mass, a priest wears a *chasuble,* a colored outer garment, but during Benediction, the priest wears the humeral veil over a *cope,* the gold or white full-length liturgical cape worn for Eucharistic devotions. By covering his hands with the humeral veil, the priest or deacon symbolizes that the blessing being given isn't his own as a sacred and ordained minister (as at the end of Mass), but the blessing of Christ himself present in the Holy Eucharist contained in the monstrance. Bells are normally rung three times as the blessing is given with the Blessed Sacrament.

Candles surround the monstrance that holds the Blessed Sacrament resting on the altar. That same Blessed Sacrament is incensed. As a sign that the people are now in the presence of divinity, incense is burned in a container and waved in front of the monstrance. Benediction also consists of the singing of certain hymns (often in Latin) and litanies, such as the *Divine Praises,* that follow:

Blessed be God.
Blessed be his holy name.
Blessed be Jesus Christ, true God and true man.
Blessed be the name of Jesus.
Blessed be his most Sacred Heart.
Blessed be his most Precious Blood.
Blessed be Jesus in the most Holy Sacrament of the Altar.
Blessed be the Holy Spirit, the Paraclete.
Blessed be the great Mother of God, Mary most holy.
Blessed be her holy and Immaculate Conception.
Blessed be her glorious Assumption.
Blessed be the name of Mary, Virgin and Mother.
Blessed be Saint Joseph, her most chaste spouse.
Blessed be God in his angels and in his saints.

The 40-hour devotion

The term *40 Hours* refers to the traditional three days — from Sunday afternoon to Tuesday evening — during which many Catholic parishes display the Blessed Sacrament in a gold monstrance on the altar. The number of hours represents the time that the faithful believe Jesus was absent from the world. Beginning from his death on Good Friday at around 3 p.m. to his Resurrection on Easter morning at about 7 a.m., that's 40 hours. Displaying the Holy Eucharist is meant to promote adoration and worship of Jesus in his hidden but Real Presence in the Blessed Sacrament.

Consecrated hosts that are left over after Mass are kept in a tabernacle (locked container) so that the priest, deacon, or extraordinary minister can bring Holy Communion to the sick *and* so that the faithful can come to church outside the time of Mass and just pray before the Holy Eucharist, which is inside it.

The 40-hour devotion gives Catholics a chance to just worship the Real Presence and nothing else. At Mass, the emphasis is on the sacrifice and the sacred meal, but during the 40 hours and other Eucharistic devotions, the emphasis is on the Blessed Sacrament. Yet Catholics believe that all three focus on the same reality — Jesus Christ.

The 40-hour devotion begins after the last Mass on Sunday. Usually, a consecrated host from that Mass is placed in the monstrance and put in the center of the altar after the faithful have received Holy Communion. The priest says the final prayer, but no final blessing is given and no closing hymn is sung. The priest, deacon, and altar servers kneel down before the Blessed Sacrament, and incense is burned. (Psalm 141: "Like burning incense, let my prayer rise before You.") Six candles, three on each side, are traditionally placed to the left and right of the monstrance. (Some people have connected the six days of creation in the book of Genesis with the use of six candles, but no hard evidence is at hand.) Parishioners come and go throughout the day to spend anywhere from 30 minutes to an hour or more, just praying before the Blessed Sacrament on the altar. This amount of time represents the request that Jesus made during his agony in the Garden of Olives: Before his Crucifixion and death on Good Friday, he asked, "Could you not spend one hour in prayer with Me?" (Mark 14:37)

The goal is to have the church open all night and all day for 40 continuous hours to represent the time that Jesus spent in the grave. But this goal can only be met if safety and security needs are met to protect the church and any faithful making a visit. Parishioners sign up to commit themselves for an hour or half-hour around the clock, never leaving Jesus unattended. It's easier to get that many people to make a commitment in a large parish of a thousand families than in a small parish of, say, only 200 families. Some parishes ask different Catholic organizations, such as the Knights of Columbus, the Council of Catholic Women, the St. Vincent de Paul Society, and the Parish Council, to commit their members for time slots. And some have asked ushers, extraordinary ministers (laypersons who assist the priest with Holy Communion at Mass), altar servers, and so on, to take turns.

Today, many parishes are forced to repose the Blessed Sacrament (put the Holy Eucharist back into the tabernacle) each evening of the 40-hour devotion after a prayer service — usually a combination of *Vespers* (evening prayer that includes the Psalms and other Scripture readings) and a sermon from a visiting priest or deacon. Then the Blessed Sacrament is exposed again after morning Mass on the next day. It doesn't add up to 40 hours, but the traditional three days are still a part of the process.

On the final evening, after the prayers and sermon, the pastor, priests, deacons, religious sisters, and parishioners process before the Blessed Sacrament around the church. They march in front of the monstrance in the Roman tradition of having the most important person at the end of the line — in this case, Jesus himself. The act of processing reminds the faithful of the joyful procession of Jesus into Jerusalem on Palm Sunday, the Sunday before Easter. It also symbolizes the return entrance of the same Son of God at the end of time when the Second Coming of Christ takes place. Finally, the pomp and and pageantry of processing with the singing of hymns, the burning of incense, and the solemnity of the moment also reaffirms the belief that this is no mere wafer of bread being paraded around. Rather, it is believed to be the actual and real body and blood, soul and divinity of Christ. When the Blessed Sacrament passes the faithful kneeling in the pews, they bless themselves with the sign of the cross. (See the "Benediction" section, earlier in this chapter.) They kneel in adoration of their Lord and God present in the monstrance.

Following the elaborate procession outside around the church or inside around the four inner walls and through the aisles of the church, the priest or deacon places the Blessed Sacrament in the monstrance back on the altar and incenses it again. Benediction then follows. (See the "Benediction" section, earlier in this chapter.)

Following the procession, the priest or deacon again incenses the monstrance and then picks it up and blesses the entire congregation while holding it. When the Blessed Sacrament passes the faithful kneeling in the pews, they bless themselves with the sign of the cross. (See the "Benediction" section, earlier in this chapter.)

In many parishes during 40 hours, the pastor typically invites a guest preacher to speak all three nights: Sunday, Monday, and Tuesday. This priest or deacon is often from another parish (to give the parishioners a break from hearing their own clergy) and can be newly ordained, newly transferred, or a classmate or friend of the pastor or neighboring cleric. On the third evening, a formal dinner is served with appetizers beforehand for all the priests, deacons and their wives, and religious sisters of the local area where the parish resides. In some dioceses, all the priests and deacons of the entire diocese are invited to the dinner. It's a time of fellowship, commaraderie, and fraternity.

Religious Processions

Public processions are as ancient as civilization itself. Kings, Caesars, and armies processed in triumphant victory after a successful battle or on the anniversary of the coronation of the monarch. The Ark of the Covenant — believed to contain the tablets of the Ten Commandments (often called the *Debarim,* Hebrew for the *Ten Words*) — was often carried in procession by the

Israelites to protect them in battle and to rejoice in victory. When the troops came home from World War II, the Allies celebrated with parades everywhere, which in essence were processions, because people moved from one place to another.

So what's the difference between a parade and a procession? A parade is spectator oriented; the crowd views the person(s) of honor. A procession requires active participation; most of the people involved are actually walking and going to the same destination. When a head of state dies, for example, a formal funeral procession travels down the main boulevard. Even when a common person dies, a funeral procession of cars is often lead by a police escort from the church or funeral parlor to the cemetery.

In medieval times, the faithful had processions in which they prayed while moving from one church to the next, and they often asked God for rain during a drought, good weather during a storm, and safety in time of famine, plague, or war.

Church processions remind the faithful that they're pilgrims — people on a journey. The ultimate hope and goal is to get to heaven someday. A procession symbolizes that the faithful haven't arrived yet, but God-willing, they're on the way and hopefully going the right way.

Besides the procession of the Blessed Sacrament at the end of a 40-hour devotion (see the "The 40-hour devotion" section, earlier in this chapter), some other processions are part of Catholic tradition.

- ✔ **Palm Sunday:** During this procession, the priest and people march around the church or from the outside of the church, through the doors, up the main aisle, and eventually, into the pews to represent the procession that they believe Jesus experienced on the first Palm Sunday.

- ✔ **Good Friday:** Processions occur in Rome and Jerusalem on this solemn day. The pope in Rome and the patriarch of Jerusalem in the Holy Land walk with a congregation to symbolize the walk that they believe Jesus was forced to endure while carrying the cross that he was then crucified on.

- ✔ **Corpus Christi:** On the Feast of the Body and Blood of Christ (called *Corpus Christi* in Latin for the *body of Christ*), a traditional procession takes place with the Blessed Sacrament in the monstrance. After Mass has just ended, the priest or deacon with all the faithful process from inside the church to outside and may stop at three different outdoor temporary and removable altars, pausing to read Scripture, pray silently, and offer Benediction with the Blessed Sacrament. Finally, they return to the church for more hymns, incense, and the last Benediction. In 1246, St. Juliana of Mont Cornillon (1192–1258) first promoted this feast, and in 1264, Pope Urban VI extended it to the universal Church, so as to bolster and reaffirm the belief in the Real Presence. (See Chapter 8 for more on the Real Presence.)

✔ The Byzantine Divine Liturgy has two small processions:

- **The little entrance:** The Book of Gospels is carried around the altar by the priest or deacon. It symbolizes the entrance of Jesus (the Word) into the world by his holy birth.

- **The great entrance:** The holy gifts of bread and wine are carried by the priest to the altar, while the choir sings the Cherubic Hymn. It symbolizes the entrance of Jesus on Palm Sunday into Jerusalem.

Meatless Fridays

Another Catholic tradition is abstaining from meat on Fridays during Lent. Practicing abstinence or abstaining, in the general sense, means voluntarily doing without food, drink, or some other pleasure. But for Catholics, it's a specified requirement: Catholics must abstain from meat on Ash Wednesday and every Friday of Lent and fast on Ash Wednesday and Good Friday.

✔ **Abstaining:** Refraining from eating all meat, if you're 14 years old on up. Yep, chicken is *still* meat — white meat but meat nonethless. Fish is the typical substitute, but vegetarians and anyone else can eat any non-meat product, such as fruits, vegetables, pasta, and so on. Only the flesh meat of warm-blooded animals is off limits on days of abstinence.

✔ **Fasting:** If you're required to fast, then you can only eat one full meal for the whole day. However, you can have two small meals in addition to the full meal, but they can't equal the main meal when combined. Snacking isn't allowed, either. Fasting only applies to Catholics who are 18 through 59 years old. (See Chapter 9 for more on the laws of fasting and abstinence.)

According to an urban legend, the pope, cardinals, and bishops initiated abstinence from meat on Friday to promote the pope's fishing business. Nah! That legend has no foundation in fact. St. Peter, the first pope, was a fisherman, and Jesus said to the apostles, "I will make you fishers of men." (Matthew 4:19) Yet subsequent popes have had no financial or economic interest in the fishing business despite this bizarre rumor.

The tradition goes back to the first century, when Christians abstained from eating meat on Fridays to honor Jesus' death on the cross on Good Friday. Because Jesus sacrificed his flesh for the salvation of humankind, the flesh of warm-blooded animals wasn't consumed on Friday.

The practice of abstaining from certain foods and fasting actually goes back to Old Testament times. The Bible says that God told the Hebrews through Moses how to prepare for celebrating *Yom Kippur*, the Day of Atonement. Although fasting isn't mentioned, the Bible does say for this day, "You shall afflict your souls" (Leviticus 16:31; 23:27–32; Numbers 29:7), and from antiquity, rabbis have interpreted this to mean fasting. The New Testament also mentions the practice, saying "It has been decided by the Holy Spirit . . . to abstain from meat sacrificed to idols, from blood, from meats of strangled animals." (Acts 15:28–29)

Before Vatican II (see Chapter 8), Catholics weren't allowed to eat meat on any Friday of the year, and they also had to fast all the weekdays of Lent. But sick people, pregnant or nursing mothers, and those who worked in hard labor jobs, as well as those in the military during wartime, were dispensed. Going back even farther into Catholic history, Catholics weren't allowed to eat meat, eggs, cheese, or dairy products all during Lent. Since Vatican II, however, the obligation is to abstain from meat on Ash Wednesday and every Friday of Lent and to fast on Ash Wednesday and Good Friday.

Even though the U.S. bishops received a *dispensation* (relaxation of rule for legitimate reason) from Rome to refrain from abstinence on every Friday and not just during Lent, Catholics are strongly encouraged to do some form of penance, mortification, work of charity, or exercises of piety on all Fridays outside of Lent — to show respect and honor for the Lord. This isn't often mentioned when the revised rules are explained, but it's mentioned in canons 1252–1253 of the 1983 Code of Canon Law. Recently, many bishops and pastors have been suggesting that Catholics abstain from meat on every Friday of the year in reparation for the sin of abortion and to pray for the defense of the sanctity of human life in all its stages and conditions.

The Corporal and Spiritual Works of Mercy

One of the ways for Catholics to replace abstinence on every Friday outside of Lent is by performing one of the seven *Corporal Works of Mercy,* which are based on Christ's sermon on the Last Judgment (Matthew 25:35–36):

1. Feeding the hungry

2. Giving drink to the thirsty

3. Clothing the naked

4. Sheltering the homeless

5. Visiting the sick

6. Visiting the imprisoned

7. Burying the dead

In contrast to the Corporal Works of Mercy, which attend to a person's physical needs, the seven *Spiritual Works of Mercy* that follow, respond to a person's spiritual needs:

1. Admonishing the sinner

2. Instructing the ignorant

3. Counseling the doubtful

4. Comforting the sorrowful

5. Bearing wrongs patiently

6. Forgiving injuries

7. Praying for the living and the dead

Using Sacramentals

Don't get confused. Sacramentals may be used in the course of administering and receiving a sacrament, but sacramentals do *not* refer to the seven sacraments: Baptism, Penance, Holy Eucharist, Confirmation, Holy Orders, Matrimony, and the Anointing of the Sick. We're talking apples and oranges. Christ instituted the seven sacraments (see Chapters 6 and 7) himself, and they're unchangeable and permanent. Sacramentals, on the other hand, were created by the Church and can therefore be changed or revised. New ones can be made and old ones suppressed.

After a priest, bishop, or deacon blesses an object, it becomes a *sacramental,* which means that when it's used in conjunction with prayer, it invokes God's blessing. Blessed objects — rosary beads, scapulars, medals, statues, icons, bibles, crosses, and crucifixes — are sacramentals. Almost anything can be blessed, but the Catholic who possesses the blessed item can't sell it or use it except in a holy manner. Normally, the priest or deacon makes the sign of the cross with his right hand over the object and sprinkles holy water on it while saying a prayer of blessing. By the way, holy water is a sacramental, too. Water that's been blessed by a priest, bishop, or deacon is then *holy* water, the most common sacramental, and it's used every day by Catholics around the world. (For more on holy water, see Chapter 5; for more on blessing objects, see Chapter 1.)

Sacramentals aren't good luck charms, talismans, or magic objects. For Catholics, they're merely reminders of the supernatural gifts God gives — such as grace, which is invisible. These visible and tangible sacramentals remind Catholics of all that the senses can't perceive.

Ashes on Ash Wednesday

Marking the beginning of Lent, this tradition is a poignant reminder that our bodies will die someday and turn to dust. "Ashes to ashes, dust to dust" is said at the cemetery when the body is ready for burial, so ashes on Ash Wednesday, the first day of Lent, are religious reminders, just like holy water and palms on Palm Sunday. Ashes remind us of our mortality and the need for repentance. The words spoken as the ashes are imposed on the forehead are: Remember man that thou art dust and unto dust thou shalt return. (Genesis 3:19) (For more on Lent, see Chapter 8.)

Blessed palms

These palm leaves, distributed to the congregation at Mass on Palm Sunday, the Sunday before Easter, commemorate the palms the crowd threw at the feet of Jesus as he processed through Jerusalem (Mark 11:1–11). Interestingly, in the Byzantine tradition, they use pussy willows rather than palms, merely because it was too difficult if not impossible to get palms in the old days before UPS and Federal Express in cold regions, such as Russia and Eastern Europe.

Blessing of throats

On the Feast of St. Blaise (February 3), Catholics may walk up the aisle to have their throats blessed after Mass. The priest holds two blessed candles in criss-cross fashion around the throat of the each individual, while praying: "Through the intercession of St. Blaise, Bishop and Martyr, may you be delivered from every ailment of the throat and from every other evil, in the name of the Father, and of the Son and of the Holy Spirit. Amen."

St. Blaise, a bishop and martyr of the fourth century, was a physician before becoming a priest and then a bishop. During a resurgence of Roman persecutions, a small boy, choking on a fish bone, was brought to St. Blaise, who was awaiting a martyr's death in prison. Because no one knew the Heimlich maneuver back then, praying was all that could be done. After St. Blaise blessed the boy, the fish bone popped out of his mouth miraculously, and the boy's life was saved.

Exorcism

Authentic demonic possession is quite rare. Demonic possession is mentioned several times in the New Testament, telling the story of how Jesus exorcised demons (Matthew 4:24). The Church maintains that demons are former heavenly angels who were cast into hell because they rebelled against God. The supernatural gifts that they had in heaven, however, went with these devils into hell. So devils can manipulate people and things in supernatural ways. Demons may attack in one of several ways:

- **Possession:** Assaulting a person from within, the devil takes control of the individual in some ways.

- **Obsession:** The devil attacks the individual from the outside.

- **Infestation:** A building or dwelling of some sort is taken over by Satan.

An *exorcist,* a priest with the faculty to drive out demons, may be called on to perform an *exorcism,* a prayer that asks God's blessing, using holy water and blessed salt to ward off evil and to protect from diabolical assaults. But before the local bishop authorizes an exorcism, which is also a sacramental, competent psychiatrists and medical doctors are asked for their professional evaluation of the victim. If medical science can't explain or treat the person and the evidence of the diabolical is present, then an exorcism might be permitted. Diabolical phenomena may be any of the following:

- The possessed individual speaks in languages that he never knew

- Unnatural voices emanate from the possessed individual

- The body of the possessed *levitates* (rises up off the floor or ground)

- Objects or furniture levitates

- The presence of foul odors

But exorcism is only a last resort, because the majority of reported incidents are considered natural phenomenon. The bottom line, however, is that the devil can only influence the body and the physical world, and he has no power whatsoever over the soul, especially free will. The devil can't force someone to sin against their will. The best defense against most supernatural evil is faith in God and prayer. Whenever Catholics feel anxious that some form of evil is at work, they typically pray to St. Michael, because he's the one who defeated Lucifer and cast him into hell for rebelling against God. (Revelation or Apocalypse 12:7) The *Prayer to St. Michael the Archangel* follows:

> St. Michael the Archangel, defend us in battle, be our protection against the wickedness and snares of the devil; may God rebuke him, we humbly

pray and do thou, O Prince of the heavenly host, by the power of God, thrust into hell Satan and all evil spirits who wander through the world for the ruin of souls. Amen.

Bells

When a bell that's destined for the bell tower is blessed, it's sometimes called the *baptism* of the bell. Actually, only human beings are baptized through the Sacrament of Baptism, but bells are sort of baptized in that the bishop anoints the bell with Chrism Oil, and traditionally, a name is given to each bell just as a name is given to a baptized person.

Since the time of Charlemagne, churches, especially cathedrals, were expected to have bells that would ring out whenever Mass was being celebrated and at the hours of prayer — 6 a.m., 9 a.m., 12 noon, 3 p.m., 6 p.m., 9 p.m., 12 midnight and 3 a.m. The hours of prayer coincide with the *Liturgy of the Hours* (also known as the *Breviary* or *Divine Office*), which is the official prayer of the Church after the Mass. It's basically a praying of the psalms with some other biblical readings and done several times during the day. Bells would be rung so that the monks of the monastery could come in from the fields where they were working and enter the chapel for Morning or Evening Prayer. Bells would also be rung to announce the death or the election of a new pope, the death or ascension of a new king or queen, and so on. Traditionally, when the church bells ring at noon and at six o'clock, the *Angelus,* which originated in the 14th century, is prayed. One person may lead and the rest of the people respond say the italicized words, and all say the *Hail Mary.* To say the *Angelus,* read the following:

> The Angel of the Lord declared unto Mary.
> *And she conceived by the Holy Spirit.*
> Hail Mary, full of grace. The Lord is with thee. Blessed art thou among women, and blessed is the fruit of thy womb, Jesus.
> *Holy Mary, Mother of God, pray for us sinners, now and at the hour of our death. Amen.*
> Behold the handmaid of the Lord.
> *Be it done unto me according to thy word.* (Say another *Hail Mary* here.)
> And the Word was made Flesh.
> *And dwelt among us.* (Repeat the *Hail Mary* here.)
> Pray for us, O holy Mother of God.
> *That we may be made worthy of the promises of Christ.*
> Let us pray: *Pour forth, we beseech Thee, O Lord, Thy grace into our hearts, that we to whom the Incarnation of Christ Thy Son was made known by the message of an angel, may by His Passion and Cross be brought to the glory of His Resurrection. Through the same Christ Our Lord. Amen.*

Part V
The Part of Tens

The 5th Wave   By Rich Tennant

"Sorry, but I don't understand your 'Ecclesiastical Latin'. Could you repeat that using 'Classical' pronunciation?"

In this part . . .

We talk about ten famous Catholics, ten people who have died and are now regarded as saints, and ten popular places that many Catholics want to visit sometime in their life.

Chapter 17

Ten Famous Catholics

In This Chapter

▶ Finding out about some famous Catholic leaders

▶ Converting to Catholicism and then writing about it

*I*n this chapter, you get to see our picks for the ten most-famous Catholics, beginning with the most famous. But take heed: Just being *baptized* Catholic doesn't mean a person is a *good* Catholic. The Catholic Church believes that a good Catholic is one who regularly and faithfully practices his faith every day of his life. A person who dissents from official Catholic teaching on faith and morals, who never or only irregularly attends Mass, or who has a scandalous, immoral lifestyle is *not* considered a practicing — or a good — Catholic.

Mother Teresa of Calcutta (1910–1997)

Agnes Gonxha Bojaxhiu was born August 26, 1910, of Albanian ancestry. She was baptized August 27 in Skopje, in Macedonia and was later known to the world as Mother Teresa of Calcutta.

She joined the Sisters of Loreto in 1928, was trained in Dublin, Ireland, and took her final vows in 1937. Known as Sister Teresa at the time, she was named headmistress of a middle-class girls' school in Calcutta, India, after some years of teaching history and geography. Later, on a train ride to Darjeeling on September 10, 1946, she said that she had a strong intuition and message from the Lord to work among the poorest of the poor in the world. So contrary to myth, it wasn't an emotional reaction to seeing starving and dying people in the gutter that prompted her to leave the Sisters of Loreto and form the Missionaries of Charity. It was that train ride — where she said that Jesus spoke to her heart and called her to go and serve his poor brothers and sisters.

In 1948, Pope Pius XII gave her permission to form her own religious community as she asked to work among the poorest of the poor. Staunchly Catholic, she openly taught and defended Church doctrine on abortion, contraception, and euthanasia, as well as on social justice and *preferential option for the poor* — Catholic social teaching that says believers and society have a special duty to help the poor, because they lack the resources to help themselves. She founded modest hospitals, clinics, schools, and centers to care for lepers in India and AIDS patients in the United States. She addressed the United Nations, the U.S. Congress, and the President of the United States, and boldly defended the life of the unborn and promoted adoption and Natural Family Planning as the only moral alternatives to abortion.

Mother Teresa and her sisters spent an hour each day before the Blessed Sacrament. When asked why, she replied, "How else can we recognize Christ in the poor if we do not first see and know him in the Holy Eucharist?"

Probably the most famous Catholic of the 20th century, this nun, who earned the Nobel Peace Prize (1979) and was only the fourth person in the world to be named honorary citizen of the United States (1996), traveled the world spreading the message of love for the poor — especially the poorest of the poor. Regarded as a modern-day St. Francis of Assisi, Mother Teresa is respected by peoples of all faiths, religions, cultures, and political persuasions. Whether a person was an "untouchable" leper in India or someone dying of AIDS in North America, she saw Christ in those who suffer. She was a true servant of charity to them.

Mother Teresa died on September 5, 1997, the same day as Princess Diana's funeral in England.

Pope John Paul II (1920–   )

We think the second most well-known Catholic of the modern era is Pope John Paul II, the 264th pope and first non-Italian pope in more than 450 years (see Figure 17-1).

He was born Karol Josef Wojtyla on May 18, 1920, in Wadowice, Poland, the son of Karol Wojtyla and Emilia Kaczorowska. His mother died nine years later, followed by his brother, Edmund Wojtyla, a doctor, in 1932, and then his father, a noncommissioned army officer, in 1941.

The Nazi invasion and occupation of Poland in 1939 forced Karol to work in a stone quarry from 1940 to 1944 and then in a chemical factory, to prevent his deportation to Germany. In 1942, he felt called to the priesthood and joined the clandestine underground seminary of Adam Stefan Cardinal Sapieha, Archbishop of Kraków. He was ordained a priest on November 1, 1946. He was sent to Rome, and he earned a doctorate in theology from the Dominican seminary of the Angelicum in 1948.

Figure 17-1:
Pope John
Paul II.

For the next ten years, he taught as a professor of theology at Catholic colleges and universities in Poland. On July 4, 1958, Pope Pius XII ordained and consecrated him an Auxiliary Bishop of Kraków. In 1964, Pope Paul VI promoted him to Archbishop of Kraków and then made him a cardinal three years later. He was present at Rome for the Second Vatican Council, which met from 1962 to 1965.

Pope Paul VI died in August 1978, and Albino Cardinal Luciani was elected his successor and took the name John Paul to honor Paul VI and John XXIII, the two popes of Vatican II. But John Paul I only lived a month. So on October 16, 1978, Karol Cardinal Wojtyla was elected bishop of Rome and took the name John Paul II.

Since then, Pope John Paul II has written 78 encyclicals, exhortations, letters, and instructions to the Catholic world; beatified 1,282 and canonized 456 saints; and created 201 cardinals. In addition, 16,000,000 pilgrims have participated in his weekly audiences on Wednesdays. And in nearly 100 trips, he has visited more than 123 countries, spoken to more than 846 heads of state, and covered more than 730,000 miles of the globe. Busy man.

At 5:19 p.m. on May 13, 1981, a would-be assassin, Mehmet Ali Agca, shot Pope John Paul II and nearly killed him. Following a six-hour operation and 77 days in the hospital, the pope returned a year later from the assassination attempt to give thanks to Our Lady of Fatima in Portugal, whom he attributed to saving his life. Fluent in several languages, he also took seriously the desires of the Second Vatican Council to revise the Code of Canon Law, which hadn't been done since 1917, and to revise the Universal Catechism, which hadn't been done since the Council of Trent in the 16th century. The 1983 Code of Canon

Law and the 1992 Catechism of the Catholic Church stand along with his encyclicals as a lasting monument to his commitment to truth and justice.

Fond of young people, Pope John Paul II conducts an international World Youth Day. Despite his age and health, crowds of nearly 3,000,000 attended the event in Rome in 2000, and 800,000 from 173 countries gathered in Toronto two years later.

Archbishop Fulton J. Sheen (1895–1979)

Born on May 8, 1895, in El Paso, Illinois, the son of Newton Morris and Delia (Fulton) Sheen was baptized Peter John (P.J.) Sheen but later took the maiden name of his mother and was thereafter known as Fulton J. (John) Sheen (see Figure 17-2).

Ordained in Peoria on September 20, 1919, he did graduate work at Catholic University of America and then post-graduate studies (PhD) at the University of Louvain, Belgium (1923). He also attended the Sorbonne in Paris and the Angelicum University in Rome, where he earned a doctorate in theology (1924).

He was made an assistant pastor for one year in Peoria at St. Patrick's Parish. Eight months later, Bishop Edmund M. Dunne of Peoria said he'd been testing the young priest to see whether his success had gone to his head. "I wanted to see if you were obedient," the bishop said. Fulton was then transferred to Catholic University to teach from 1926 to 1950.

His eloquent preaching and erudite speaking prompted the National Council of Catholic Men to sponsor a Catholic Hour Sunday evening radio broadcast on NBC in 1930. When it aired, 118 NBC radio affiliates as well as short-wave transmitters ensured that 4,000,000 people across America heard a Catholic preacher for the first time. Fulton believed this was his opportunity to intellectually show the errors and weaknesses of Communism.

Pope Pius XI made him a monsignor in 1934, and then he was ordained and consecrated an auxiliary bishop for the Archdiocese of New York in 1951. Later that same year, he was asked to host a weekly television series, entitled *Life is Worth Living*. The program ran for five seasons from February 12, 1952, to April 8, 1957, first on the Dumont Network and then on ABC. And at one point, it beat *The Milton Berle Show* as number one in the ratings. He showed and exhibited a classy, edified, yet also patriotic and pastoral approach, which helped to erode some deep-seated and hateful anti-Catholic bias prevalent since the days of colonial America.

Figure 17-2:
Archbishop
Fulton J.
Sheen.

© Bettmann/CORBIS

In 1950, Fulton was named national director of the Society for the Propogation of the Faith, the Catholic Church's primary mission organization. Sixteen years later, he was promoted to Bishop of Rochester (1966–1969). But he remains most famous and influential for his radio and television programs and the numerous talks, lectures, retreats, and conferences he gave around the world.

Many famous celebrities, musicians, and politicians owe their conversion to Catholicism to Fulton J. Sheen. He died at the age of 84, on December 9, 1979.

Mother Angelica (1923–   )

Rita Frances Rizzo was born in Canton, Ohio, on April 20, 1923, the daughter of John Rizzo and Mae Helen Gianfrancisco. Six years later, her parents divorced, and Rita and her mom were on their own. She entered the Franciscan Sisters (Poor Clares) of Perpetual Adoration in Cleveland, Ohio, on August 15, 1944, as Sister Mary Angelica of the Annunciation.

Sister Mary Angelica eventually ended up in Birmingham, Alabama, the heart of the Baptist Bible Belt. Rome allowed her — despite her young age — to become an Abbess of a new monastery, and Our Lady of the Holy Angels opened on May 20, 1962, just ten months from its groundbreaking. (Upon becoming Abbess, she received the title of respect of "Reverend Mother" or just "Mother" for short.) Her own mother entered the community and took the name of Sister Mary David.

In 1973, she inaugurated a Catholic book and pamphlet apostolate to spread the faith. But the big stuff was yet to come. In 1981, Mother Angelica decided to go into television. And on August 15, 1981, the Eternal Word Television Network (EWTN) was launched. She reached 1,000,000 homes in less than two years and in 1990 went 24 hours a day. Today, two decades later, through EWTN's own satellite, cable, radio, and short-wave broadcasting, 79 million people are being reached across 81 countries. (EWTN is even on the Internet at www.ewtn.com.) EWTN has become the world's largest and most-watched Catholic network, and Mother Angelica is still very much a part of it.

Mother Angelica had many injuries due to an accident with a floor-buffing machine. The accident occurred when she was a *novice* (new nun in training who hasn't yet made vows) in 1946. On January 28, 1998, while she was praying the rosary with an Italian lady she didn't know, she was miraculously cured — her legs and back no longer needed braces or crutches.

One year later, on December 19, 1999, she had her new monastery and temple consecrated: The Shrine of the Most Blessed Sacrament in Hanceville, Alabama, which is one hour north of Birmingham and Irondale; the television studio and Internet services are located on-site. Built by the generosity of a handful of millionaires, this house of God rivals any in Europe. The seven-foot monstrance is the jewel of the crown containing the Holy Eucharist, which is exposed for public adoration outside of Mass.

John F. Kennedy (1917–1963)

The 35th President of the United States of America, John Fitzgerald Kennedy was the first Roman Catholic to hold the highest office in the land (see Figure 17-3).

Born in Brookline, Massachusetts, on May 29, 1917, to Joseph P. Kennedy and Rose Fitzgerald Kennedy, he was one of nine children in this affluent and influential family. His father was the head of the Securities and Exchange Commission (SEC) and later became the Ambassador to Great Britain.

John graduated from Harvard in 1940 and a year later enlisted in the U.S. Navy before the attack on Pearl Harbor and the declaration of war. The boat he commanded (PT-109) in the Pacific theater was attacked and sunk by the Japanese. He saved his crew but seriously injured his back. He was discharged in 1945 and ran as a Democrat for the U.S. Congress in 1946. He was re-elected twice.

On September 12, 1953, he married Jacqueline Bouvier, who gave him three children (Caroline, 1957; John, Jr., 1960; and a son who died in infancy). He became a Massachusetts senator in 1953. Seven years later, he ran against Vice President Richard M. Nixon and won the presidency in 1960.

Figure 17-3:
John
Fitzgerald
Kennedy.

© CORBIS

During the campaign, his Catholicism was thrown into his face as a possible impediment to being an effective president — as though he'd have dual or torn loyalties between the U.S. Constitution and the pope as supreme head of the Catholic Church. Cartoons ran in the papers depicting JFK in a boat with Jesuit sailors coming from Rome to invade America. Anti-Catholic prejudice reared its ugly head in editorials and articles across the nation. But he dispelled the irrational anxieties by assuring the public of his commitment to upholding and defending the Constitution — maintaining that it didn't, couldn't, and wouldn't conflict with his personal religious beliefs. The public finally accepted the fact that Catholics could be patriotic Americans and good Catholics at the same time.

Historians are still debating whether John F. Kennedy was a devout or practicing Catholic. What's known is that he was the first Catholic to be elected president and that his Catholicism received positive press coverage during his term in office: He and Jackie and the kids went to Sunday Mass, bishops and cardinals frequented the White House, and an elaborate, solemn, and sad Catholic requiem Mass was said for his funeral following his assassination in November 1963.

Alfred E. Smith (1873–1944)

Born on the East Side of New York City in 1873 to poor parents and Irish immigrant grandparents, Alfred Emanuel Smith was the first Catholic politician to be nominated as a presidential candidate. He was the Democratic Governor of New York twice and worked hard for political reforms. His Catholicism, however, and his opposition to Prohibition cost him the election to Herbert

Hoover in 1928. Each year, the Archdiocese of New York sponsors the Alfred E. Smith Memorial Foundation Dinner where politicians from both sides of the aisle and ecclesiastics alike get together.

Father Edward Flanagan (1886–1948)

Born in Roscommon, Ireland, in 1886, Edward Flanagan came to America in 1904. He was ordained a priest in 1912 after attending Mount Saint Mary's College in Emmitsburg, Maryland, and St. Joseph's Seminary in Dunwoodie, New York, and finally finishing his studies in Rome and Innsbruck, Austria. Sent to Omaha, Nebraska, as a newly ordained priest, he found the extreme poverty among the orphans in Omaha heart-wrenching. The situation motivated him to found Boys' Town in 1917 for homeless boys, which today takes care of both boys and girls who are underprivileged. In 1938, Spencer Tracy won an Academy Award for portraying Father Flanagan in MGM's *Boys Town.*

John Ronald Reuel Tolkien (1892–1973)

J.R.R. Tolkien, author of *Lord of the Rings* and *The Hobbit,* was born in South Africa in 1892, but after his father died four years later, he and his mother and younger brother, Hilary, moved to England. There, his aunt and mother converted to Catholicism, which annoyed both sides of the family. Ronald, as he was known then, and his brother, however, embraced the Roman Catholic religion. A contemporary of C.S. Lewis, the author of the *Chronicles of Narnia* and the *Screwtape Letters,* Tolkien learned to use fantasy writing to strategically but subtly convey Catholic values while retaining imagination and excitement in reading.

Gilbert Keith Chesterton (1874–1936)

Born in London in 1874, G. K. Chesterton was baptized in the Church of England (Anglican). Ironically, he wrote his famous *Father Brown* mysteries (1910) before joining the Roman Catholic Church in 1922. Those mysteries tell of a quiet, unassuming priest who solves mysteries like Sherlock Holmes, Lord Peter Whimsey, or Hercule Poirot. Another irony is that he didn't learn to read until he was 8 years old but would later prove to be a prolific and scholarly author of 17 nonfiction and 9 fiction books and numerous essays and poems. His book *Orthodoxy* remains a classic for *apologists* — people who defend Catholicism through the use of logic, reason, and debate — and for literary critics alike.

Christopher Columbus (1451–1506)

The European discoverer of America in 1492 may be the bane of politically correct historians, but no one can deny that his insistence on bringing Franciscan and Dominican missionaries with him to the New World was pivotal to the spread of Catholicism among the natives in North, Central, and South America.

Born in Genoa in 1451, Cristoforo Columbo (his name in Italian) became a superior sailor from his youth and always dreamed of making a voyage to find a shortcut to the Far East, because Marco Polo's land route to China was becoming more and more dangerous and expensive. He knew the world wasn't flat, and so did most educated, literate people of his time. King Ferdinand and Queen Isabella of Spain eventually funded the expedition to secure Spain's wealth (Ferdinand's goal) and to evangelize and spread the Catholic faith (Isabella's dream).

Before setting sail on the Nina, Pinta, and Santa Maria, Columbus went to confession and Mass, and he received Holy Communion. His flagship had a chapel, where Mass was offered daily. Today, the chapel's altar is in Boalsburg, Pennsylvania, at the Christopher Columbus Museum. Earlier, however, the altar had become part of the Columbus (*Colon* in Spanish) Castle in Spain. But Mathilde DeLagarde Boal, the wife of Colonel Theodore Boal, inherited it from her aunt, Victoria Colón, a descendant of Columbus, in 1908. Then a year later, the altar was shipped to Pennsylvania, where it remains today on display just a stone's throw away from Penn State University. (David Boal, the great-great grandfather of Theodore Boal, founded Boalsburg, Pennsylvania.)

Keep in mind that 1492 was still the Middle Ages. The Reformation didn't occur for another 15 years. And the sociological dimension to exploration and colonization wasn't comprehensible to that mindset. Unlike Cortez, Columbus didn't see Native Americans as slaves or enemies but as potential converts to and allies of Catholic Spain.

Chapter 18

Ten Popular Catholic Saints

In This Chapter

▶ Discovering some saints who bore Christ's wounds

▶ Finding out about a few martyrs

The saints are near and dear to Catholic hearts. Catholics respect and honor the saints and consider them to be the heroes of the Church. The Church emphasizes that they were ordinary people, from ordinary families, and they were totally human. They weren't born with a halo around their heads, and they didn't always wear a smile, either. What separated them from those who weren't given the title of *saint* was that they didn't despair; they kept right on honing their souls for heaven come hell or high water.

In this chapter, we share some tidbits about the lives of ten such ordinary people who became ten popular saints. We've listed them in chronological order, too.

St. Peter (Died around A.D. 64)

The brother of Andrew, son of Jona, and the Prince of the Apostles, St. Peter was originally called Simon. A fisherman by trade, he and his brother were from Bethsaida, a town on Lake Genesareth — the same hometown of St. Philip the Apostle.

Biblical scholars believe that he was married, because the Gospel speaks of the cure of his mother-in-law (Matthew 8:14; Luke 4:38). But whether he was a widower at the time that he met Jesus, no one knows for sure. Scholars believe it's likely that his wife was no longer alive, because after the Crucifixion, Resurrection, and Ascension of Christ, Peter, as head of the Church, had a busy schedule and itinerary. He also never mentioned his wife in his epistle. All these facts lead many biblical scholars to conjecture that the first pope was a widower.

According to the Bible, Andrew introduced his brother, Peter, to Jesus and told him, "We have found the Messiah!" When Peter hesitated to follow Jesus full time, Jesus came after him and said, "I will make you fishers of men."

The faithful believe it was his confession of faith that made Peter stand out in the crowd, even among the twelve apostles. Matthew 16 tells the story: Jesus posed the question, "Who do people say that I am?" The other eleven merely reiterated what they'd heard others say: "John the Baptist, Elijah or one of the Prophets." But when asked directly, "But who do you say that I am?" only Peter responded, "You are the Christ, the Son of the living God." His answer received the full approval of Jesus and he was made the chief shepherd of the Church and head of the Apostles. Matthew 16:17–19 says:

"Blessed art thou, Simon Bar-Jona: for flesh and blood hath not revealed it unto thee, but my Father who is in heaven. And I say also unto thee, that thou art Peter *(Petros),* and upon this rock *(petra)* I will build my church; and the gates of hell shall not prevail against it. And I will give unto thee the keys of the kingdom of heaven: and whatsoever thou shalt bind on earth shall be bound in heaven: and whatsoever thou shalt loose on earth shall be loosed in heaven."

The Greek language, in which the Gospel was first written, uses the word *Petros* as the proper first name of a man and the word *petra* to refer to a rock. *Peter* means *rock,* but in Greek, as in most other languages except English, nouns have gender. *Petra* is the word for rock, and it's feminine, so you wouldn't call a man *petra* no matter how "strong as a rock" he may be. We believe that had Jesus used *petra* instead of *petros* for Peter, the other apostles and disciples would never have let Peter live it down, because using a feminine ending would've been inappropriate. (You know how sailors and fishermen can use colorful language.)

A significant aspect of this passage is that Jesus said he would build *his Church,* so Catholics believe that the Church doesn't belong to Peter or the pope but to Christ. That's why one of the pope's titles is the Vicar (Ambassador) of Christ. Note, too, the punchline at the end: "Whatsoever you shall bind on earth shall be bound in heaven: and whatsoever you shall loose on earth shall be loosed in heaven." That's a pretty extensive piece of authority: whatsoever. And the second-person singular, *you,* was used in Greek — not the plural — so Catholics believe the full, supreme, immediate and universal authority was only given to Peter and not to the other apostles. That's why the successor of Peter, the pope, has more authority in the Church than the successors to the apostles — the bishops.

According to pious tradition, Peter was crucified upside down, because he felt unworthy to die exactly as Jesus did on Good Friday. That same tradition has it that Peter was fleeing the initial persecutions in Rome when he saw an apparition of Jesus on the road going toward Rome. This was after the Resurrection and Ascension, mind you. Peter asked, "*Quo vadis Domine?*"

which is Latin for, *"Where are you going Lord?"* When Jesus replied that he was going to Rome to be crucified again, Peter realized it was a sign that he should turn around and go back to Rome to take care of the infant Church, even if it meant he'd suffer martyrdom, and he did.

St. Jude (Died during first century A.D.)

Brother of St. James the Less and believed to be a relative of Jesus, Jude is also known as Jude Thaddaeus, Patron Saint of Hopeless Cases. One reason is that it's almost hopeless finding much information about him. In fact, he's often called St. Jude the Obscure. But another reason is that he was invoked for hopeless cases could be that his name is so close to Judas — who the faithful believe betrayed Christ.

It's conjectured that his father was Cleophas, who was murdered for his support of Jesus, and that his mother was Mary Cleophas, who was mentioned at the cross in the Gospel (John 19:25).

He was allegedly clubbed to death as his form of martyrdom. (See Chapter 13 to read a popular novena to St. Jude.)

St. Benedict (480–543)

Benedict of Nursia, the founder of Western monasticism, was the son of a Roman nobleman and the twin brother of St. Scholastica, foundress of the Benedictine nuns. He grew up and studied in Rome until the age of 14, when he decided to leave the city for a quieter life of prayer and work.

He developed a structure for monastic life called a *Rule,* which is a set of laws, customs, and practices for all members of a religious community that continues to this day and is the basis for many religious communities. Living a simple life of poverty, chastity, and obedience in community with others and devoting oneself to sanctity and holiness is the main objective of Benedictine life. Known for their hard work and their love of the Sacred Liturgy and Sacred Scripture and dedicated to study and learning, the Benedictines were role models for many religious communities that came later, such as the Dominicans. The Benedictine monks were the ones who fled the morally decaying cities of the disintegrating Roman Empire, and after the Barbarians invaded and occupied the land, those same monks preserved culture, language, heritage, art, and learning. They kept most of the secular and religious manuscripts and writings of that era and eventually taught the domesticated barbarians after they had settled in and tired of pillaging.

The famous Benedictine Monasteries of Monte Cassino and of Subiaco, Italy, date back to the time of Benedict and still house members to this day. A hallmark of Benedictine life, besides work and prayer, is the vow of stability: Unlike diocesan priests who get transferred frequently, after a man joins a Benedictine monastery, he usually stays on-site for the rest of his life unless special circumstances require him to join another abbey.

St. Dominic de Guzman (1170–1221)

St. Dominic was a contemporary of St. Francis of Assisi. The faithful believe that when St. Dominic's mother, Joanna of Aza, the wife of Felix de Guzman, was pregnant, she had a vision of a dog carrying a torch in his mouth, which symbolized her unborn son who would grow up to become a *hound of the Lord.* The name Dominic was thus given to him, because in Latin *Dominicanis* can be *Domini + canis* (*dog* or *hound of the Lord*).

With the Rosary, Dominic was able to preach successfully against the Albigensian heresy. He promoted Marian devotion, the practice of praying the Rosary, around Western Europe. The Albigensian heresy denied the human nature of Christ and only believed in his divine nature, whereas Catholicism teaches that he had both a fully human and a fully divine nature united in one divine person. People who followed Albigensianism couldn't accept a god who would suffer and die for humankind's sins. Catholics believe through pious tradition that Mary gave the Rosary to Dominic and that he conquered Albigensianism not by preaching alone but with the help of the Rosary.

His order of friar preachers, the Dominicans, along with their brother Franciscans re-energized the Church in the 13th century and brought clarity of thought and substantial learning to more people than ever before. The motto of St. Dominic was *veritas,* which is Latin for *truth.*

St. Albert the Great, St. Thomas Aquinas, St. Catherine of Siena, St. Vincent Ferrer, Pope St. Pius V, St. Martin de Porres, St. Raymond Peñafort and St. Rose of Lima were all Dominicans.

St. Francis of Assisi (1181–1226)

The son of a wealthy cloth merchant, Pietro Bernadone, Francis was one of seven children. Today, people would say that he grew up with a silver spoon in his mouth.

Even though he was baptized Giovanni, his father later changed his name to Francesco (Italian for *Francis* or *Frank*). He was handsome, courteous, witty, strong, intelligent, but very zealous. He liked to play hard and fight hard like most of his contemporaries. Local squabbles between towns, principalities, dukedoms, and so on were rampant in Italy at this time in the 12th century, because the country didn't unify until the end of the 19th century, under the leadership of Garibaldi.

Francis was a playboy of sorts but wasn't a nasty or immoral one. After spending a year in captivity with the rival Perugians, who fought their neighbors the Assisians, Francis decided that he was going to cool his jets for a while. One day, he met a poor leper on the road who at first repulsed him by his stench and ugliness. Remorseful, Francis turned around, got off his horse, embraced the beggar and gave him clothes and money. The man immediately disappeared, and Francis believed it was Christ visiting him as a beggar. He then went to Rome to visit the tomb of St. Peter where he gave all his worldly possessions — money, clothes, and belongings — to the poor and put on the rags of a poor man himself. Lady Poverty was to be his bride.

His dad wasn't happy for the embarrassment he caused, so he dragged, beat, and locked up Francis so he would come to his senses. Then his mother helped him escape to a bishop friend of his, but his father soon found him. Because he was on church property, however, Signor Bernadone couldn't violate the sanctuary and force his son home. Francis took what little clothing he had from home still on his person and threw it at his father and said: "Hitherto I have called you my father on earth; henceforth I desire to say only 'Our Father who art in Heaven.'"

In 1221, he started his own religious community called the Order of Friars Minor (OFM), which today, is known as the Franciscans. They took vows of poverty, chastity and obedience, but unlike the Augustinian and Benedictine Monks who lived in monasteries outside the villages and towns, St. Francis and his friars were not monks but mendicants, which means that they begged for their food, clothes, and shelter. What they collected they shared among themselves and the poor. They worked among the poor in the urban areas.

Catholics believe that in 1224, St. Francis of Assisi was blessed with the extraordinary gift of the *stigmata,* the five wounds of Christ imprinted on his own body.

St. Francis of Assisi loved the poor and animals, but most of all, he loved God and his Church. He wanted everyone to know and experience the deep love of Jesus that he felt in his own heart. He is credited with the creation of two Catholic devotions, the Stations of the Cross (see Chapter 16) and the Christmas crèche.

St. Clare, the foundress of the Poor Clares and the female counterpart to St. Francis of Assisi, St. Anthony of Padua, St. Bernardine of Siena, St. Bonaventure, St. Lawrence of Brindisi, St. Joseph of Cupertino, and St. Maximilian Kolbe, who was killed in Auschwitz by the Nazis during World War II, were all Franciscans.

St. Thomas Aquinas (1225–1274)

The greatest intellect the Catholic Church has ever known was born of a wealthy aristocratic family, the son of Landulph, Count of Aquino, and Theodora, Countess of Teano. Thomas' parents sent him at the age of five, which was customary, to the Benedictine Abbey of Monte Cassino. It was hoped that if he didn't show talents suited for becoming a knight or noble-man, he could at least rise to the rank of abbot or bishop and thus add to his family's prestige and influence.

Ten years later, Thomas on the other hand, wanted to join the new mendicant order, which was similar to the Franciscans in that it didn't go to the distant monasteries but worked in the urban areas instead. The new order he was interested in was the Order of Friars Preachers, O.P., known as Dominicans.

His family had other ideas, putting him under house arrest for two years in an effort to dissuade his Dominican vocation. He didn't budge. While captive, he read and studied assiduously and learned metaphysics, Sacred Scripture, and the *Sentences of Peter Lombard.* They finally relented, and at the age of 17, he was put under the tutelage of St. Albert the Great, the pride of the Dominican intelligentsia. Albert was the first to bridge the gap between alchemy and chemistry, from superstition to science. Thomas learned much from his academic master.

Thomas Aquinas is best known for two things: one is his monumental theological and philosophical work, the *Summa Theologica,* which covers almost every principal doctrine and dogma of his era. What St. Augustine and St. Bonaventure were able to do with the philosophy of Plato regarding Catholic Theology, St. Thomas Aquinas was able to do with Aristotle. The *Catechism of the Catholic Church* has numerous references to the Summa some 800 years later. He's also well known for the hymns and prayers he composed for Corpus Christi at the request of the pope. St. Thomas also wrote *Pange Lingua, Adoro te Devote, O Salutaris Hostia*, and *Tantum Ergo,* which is often sung at Benediction. (See Chapter 16 for more on Benediction.) He died while on the way as a *peritus* (expert) to the Second Council of Lyons.

For more on St. Thomas Aquinas, see Chapters 3, 8, 9, 14, and Appendix A.

St. Ignatius of Loyola (1491–1556)

Son of Don Beltrán Yañez de Oñez y Loyola and Marina Saenz de Lieona y Balda, Ignatius was born in 1491 and grew up to become a soldier. Military life suited him. He liked the regimen and discipline, and it gave him a sense of accomplishment, because he was serving and defending the homeland and his monarch.

After a cannon ball injury to his leg compelled him to a long recuperation, he asked for reading materials to pass the time. All that was available was a book on the lives of the saints. One day, he realized that instead of fighting for earthly kings and princes, he should become a Soldier of Christ and win souls away from the real enemy, the devil, and bring them back to the true King of Kings, Almighty God. He saw how the military discipline could be used to discipline the soul rather than just the body.

He developed a method of spirituality, *Ignatian Spiritual Exercises,* named after him, which focused using the fullest amount of imagination during meditation. People were asked to pick a scene from the Bible and imagine they weren't spectators, like in the audience of a play, but actual bystanders or participants in the biblical scene being contemplated. For example:

Say you're at the wedding feast of Cana (John 2:1–11). You feel a cool breeze blow across the left side of your face. You can smell the aroma of lamb being roasted in an open pit. The sun is out, and people are laughing and talking as they often do at wedding receptions. Then you hear the words being whispered around the table, "They have no more wine," just as you take a sip from your goblet and realize that it's almost empty. Now, try to imagine the rest of the story on your own.

This use of the imagination helped the faithful appreciate the reality of the scriptural text. It also enabled them to transcend what they merely knew cognitively from memory and to use previous sense experiences to pretend but also to learn and experience the event.

At 46 years old, Ignatius was ordained a priest, and so he's often invoked as the Patron Saint of Delayed or Second Career Vocations. In 1534, he formed the Society of Jesus, which would later be known as the Jesuits. Feared, admired, scorned, and often misunderstood, the Jesuits became a powerful and influential religious community for two reasons.

- ✔ **Their fourth vow of total obedience to the Roman pontiff.** Other orders took the vow of obedience but sometimes loyalty to the order came before obedience to the hierarchy. Ignatius preferred that his priests be at the total disposal of the pope to go wherever he sent them and to do whatever task he gave them.

- ✔ **Their professional expertise and background.** Most Jesuits have one or more doctorates or the equivalent and study more before ordination as opposed to their diocesan or other religious community colleagues.

St. Francis Xavier, St. Edmund Campion, St. Aloysius Gonzaga, St. Peter Canisius, St. Robert Bellarmine, and St. Isaac Jogues were Jesuits.

St. Bernadette Soubirous (1844–1879)

Bernadette was born on January 7, 1844, in Lourdes, France. Her parents, Francis and Louise Soubirous, were extremely poor but loved their daughter very much. She suffered from severe asthma, which kept her behind a few years in school.

The faithful believe that on February 11, 1858, she saw an apparition of Mary in a cave on the banks of the Gave River near Lourdes. The woman didn't identify herself but asked Bernadette to faithfully come to the grotto as it was called and to pray the Rosary for the conversion of sinners so that they might turn away from their evil ways and come back to God.

Initially, the townsfolk thought she was insane. But on February 25, the woman asked Bernadette to dig in the soil until a spring of water would appear. She did as the woman asked, and the spring did appear.

It's believed that the water had immediate miraculous properties, and the skeptic populace of Lourdes flocked to the grotto to get some of this healing water. The blind could see, the lame could walk, the deaf could hear, the sick regained their health, and so on.

The faithful believe that on March 25, 1858, the woman announced to Bernadette that she was the *Immaculate Conception*. Ironically, the dogma of the Immaculate Conception had only been defined by Pope Pius IX four years earlier (1854), and scholars maintain that an intellectually challenged peasant girl from the rinky-dink town of Lourdes couldn't have heard about such a term let alone understand it.

The public authorities, which were anti-Catholic and anti-clerical, closed the grotto only to have the Emperor Louis Napoleon III order it reopened. His son had taken ill and his wife, the Empress Eugenie of France, obtained some Lourdes water, which the faithful believe cured his imperial royal highness.

Bernadette didn't live a normal life after that, and in 1866 she entered the convent of the Sisters of Notre Dame in Nevers where she spent the rest of her short life. Thirteen years later, she was found to have an illness similar to tuberculosis, which produced excruciating and chronic pain, but she said the healing waters of Lourdes were not for her.

She died in 1879, but today, her body remains *incorrupt* (free of decay despite the lack of embalming or mummification treatments). The Shrine at Lourdes is an international place of prayer, and some miraculous healings are still being attributed to those waters from the grotto where Catholics believe Mary appeared to Bernadette.

St. Thérèse of Lisieux (1873–1897)

Francoise-Marie Thérèse, the youngest of the five daughters, was born on January 2, 1873. At the age of four, her mother died and left her father with five girls to raise on his own. The eldest, 13-year-old Marie, helped much. The second oldest, Pauline, later joined the Carmelite order of nuns and was then followed by her sister Marie. Thérèse wanted to join her sisters as a Carmelite when she was but 14 years old. The order normally made the girls wait until they were 16 before entering the convent or monastery, but Thérèse was adamant. She accompanied her father to a general papal audience of His Holiness Pope Leo XIII and surprised everyone by throwing herself before the pontiff, begging to become a Carmelite. The wise pope replied, "If the good God wills, you will enter." When she returned home, the local bishop allowed her to enter early. On April 9, 1888, at the age of 15, Thérèse entered the Carmelite monastery of Lisieux and joined her two sisters.

On September 8, 1890, she took her final vows. She showed remarkable spiritual insights for someone so young, but it was due to her childlike (not childish) relationship with Jesus. Her superiors asked her to keep memoirs of her thoughts and experiences.

In 1896, at the age of 23, she coughed up blood and was diagnosed with tuberculosis. She lived only one more year, and it was a long year in which she endured intense, painful, and bitter physical suffering. Yet it's said that she did so lovingly, to join Jesus Christ on the cross. She offered up her pain and suffering for souls that might be lost, so they could come back to God. Her *little way* consisted of, in her own words, of "doing little things often, doing them well, and doing them with love." She died on September 30, 1897.

Despite the fact that she lived such a short and cloistered life, having never left her monastery let alone her native France, she was later named Patroness of the Foreign Missions. The reason was that during World War I, many soldiers who were wounded in battle and recuperating in hospitals — as well as those who were in the trenches awaiting their possible death — read her autobiography, and it changed their hearts. Many who had grown cold or lukewarm in their Catholic faith wanted to imitate St. Thérèse of Lisieux, who was also known as the *Little Flower,* and become a little child of God.

St. Pio of Pietrelcina (1887–1968)

Padre Pio was born on May 25, 1887, in Pietrelcina, Italy. Because he showed evidence of having a priestly vocation early in his youth, his father went to the United States to make enough money so Francesco (his baptismal name) could attend school and seminary. At the age of 15, he took the vows and habit of the Friars Minor Capuchin and assumed the name of Pio in honor of Pope St. Pius V, patron of his hometown. On August 10, 1910, he was ordained a priest. Catholics believe that less than a month later, on September 7, he received the stigmata, just like St. Francis of Assisi.

During World War I, he served as Chaplain in the Italian Medical Corps. After the war, news spread about his stigmata, which stirred up some influential enemies who were jealous and envious of this simple, prayerful, and mystical man. Because of the false accusations that were made and sent to Rome, he was suspended in 1931 from saying public Mass or from hearing confessions. Two years later, Pope Pius XI reversed the suspension and said, "I have not been badly disposed toward Padre Pio, but I have been badly informed."

In 1940, he convinced three physicians to come to San Giovanni Rotundo to help him erect a hospital, *Casa Sollievo della Sofferenza* (House for the Relief of Suffering). It took until 1956 to finally build the hospital due to World War II and slow donations, but it eventually came to pass.

Catholics believe that he was able to read souls, meaning that when people came to him for confession, he could immediately tell if they were lying, holding back sins or truly repentant. One man reportedly came in and only confessed that he was unkind from time to time and Padre Pio interjected, "Don't forget when you were unkind to Jesus by missing Mass three times this month either."

He became so well loved all over the region and indeed all over the world that three days after his death on September 23, 1968, over a 100,000 people gathered at San Giovanni Rotundo to pray for his departed soul.

Chapter 19

Ten Popular Catholic Places

In This Chapter

▶ Seeing some miraculous shrines near and far

▶ Discovering Catholic history, art, and architecture

Although some religions require or strongly exhort their members to visit their holy and sacred places, the Catholic Church doesn't. Catholics are simply *encouraged* to make *pilgrimages* — religious journeys to holy places. This chapter covers our picks for the top ten places that Catholics like to visit sometime in their lives, starting with the most popular at the top of the list.

The Basilica de Guadalupe

The Basilica de Guadalupe in Mexico City, Mexico, is the number one pilgrimage site for Catholics — second only to the Eternal City of Rome. This basilica contains the miraculous image of Our Lady of Guadalupe that Catholics believe was imprinted by Mary on the cloak of an Aztec Indian, 57-year-old St. Juan Diego, on December 12, 1531.

Walking north of Mexico City in the Tepayac hill country, Juan Diego saw the Virgin Mary, but she had the appearance of an Aztec woman, not a European, and she was pregnant. She directed St. Juan Diego to go to the local bishop and tell him that she wanted a church built in her honor.

After waiting several hours to see the Spanish-born aristocratic Bishop Fray Juan de Zumarraga, St. Juan Diego was granted an audience. The respectful yet incredulous Bishop told St. Juan Diego that he needed a sign from heaven that this was indeed God's will to build a church in that location. St. Juan Diego told Mary what the bishop had requested, and she told him to gather roses from a bush that appeared out of nowhere. These Castilian roses weren't indigenous to Mexico, and certainly not in cold December, but they were popular in Spain. It just so happened that the bishop's hobby was gardening, and he'd been an official rose expert back in Spain before being sent to Mexico.

Juan Diego carried the roses in his *tilma* (cloak) to the bishop, opened his garment, and the bishop fell to his knees. Not only were the roses beautiful and rare, but also, a gorgeous image of Our Lady of Guadalupe was on the tilma. She was like the scriptural passage that describes a woman who is "clothed with the sun and upon her head a crown of twelve stars with the moon under her feet and she was with child." (Revelation 12:1–12)

To this day, science can't explain how that image got onto the tilma. It's not painted, dyed, sewn, printed, sealed, or the product of any man-made process, nor is it a natural phenomenon. It remains on display in the Basilica Church in Mexico City where Pope John Paul II canonized Juan Diego in 2002. Millions of people from South, Central and North America, Europe, Africa and Asia visit this holy place.

San Giovanni Rotondo, Italy

Forty miles from Foggia, Italy, a town called San Giovanni Rotondo is the resting place of St. Pio of Pietrelcina, affectionately known as Padre Pio. (Pietrelcina is the town where Padre Pio was born.) He was a humble, simple but holy Capuchin monk, a type of Franciscan. (We provide a brief bio of his life in Chapter 18 if you're interested.)

While he was alive, thousands came to him for confession and his priestly blessing. Since his death, tens and hundreds of thousands have made pilgrimages to this town to see where Padre Pio celebrated Mass, heard confessions, and to see the church where he's buried. Most of all, they want to see where they believe he received the *stigmata* — the five wounds of Christ. The Church of Our Lady of Grace is where all this happened and where people visit every day. *Casa Sollievo della Sofferenza* (House for the Relief of Suffering) is the hospital founded by him in the same town and visited by many pilgrims as well. In every store, restaurant, and home in San Giovanni, you can see pictures and statues of Padre Pio, their local saint whom they love and admire to this day.

At the *National Padre Pio Center* is in Barto, Pennsylvania, not far from Reading, Pennsylvania, you can see a replica of the chapel in San Giovanni. One of the bloodstained gloves that Padre Pio wore while he had the stigmata is on display in the chapel.

The Basilica of Czestochowa, Poland

Pious tradition maintains that St. John, the Beloved Disciple, painted an icon of the Virgin Mary (see Figure 19-1) sometime after Christ's Crucifixion on the cross. The faithful believe that Jesus entrusted his mother to John's care before his death (John 19:26–27). And pious tradition also has it that St. Helena, the founder of the True Cross (see Appendix A) in the fourth century and the mother of Emperor Constantine, was the one who discovered this painting.

No matter where the icon originally came from or who painted it, the fact remains that it has been one of great spiritual treasures of Poland. Somehow during the Muslim invasions, the image made its way to Poland through Russia. Polish Prince St. Ladislaus, in the 15th century, kept it safe in his castle until the Tartar invaders threatened to overrun Poland. Intending to move it to his hometown of Opala, Prince Ladislaus stopped overnight in Jasna Gora near Czestochowa.

According to the tradition, the next morning, the horses refused to move while the image was in the carriage. The Prince took this as a sign from God that the icon should stay there. So he entrusted the icon hereafter known as the Madonna of Czestochowa to the Pauline Fathers who cared for the spiritual needs of Czestochowa and Jasna Gora.

Today, the Black Madonna resides in a magnificent basilica in Czestochowa. Some say her face is black from attempts to destroy her, claiming that the heretical Hussites set it on fire but it would not burn. Others maintain that it is from the pigmentation in the paint, which was affected by the dark smoke from the hundreds of candles burning in front of it for centuries.

Figure 19-1:
Many believe that the disciple John created this painting of Mary, called the Black Madonna of Czesto-chowa.

© Nicolas Sapieha/Art Resource, NY

On one occasion, it's said that a Tartar soldier drew his sword and struck it twice, hence the two gashes to this day on her right cheek. The story continues that when he made a third attempt to strike the icon with his sword, before he could complete the swing of his arm, he yelled in pain and dropped dead of a massive heart attack.

Millions of pilgrims visit the town and Basilica of Czestochowa where the icon remains on display. Providentially, the painting survived the diabolical Nazi invasion and occupation and then the Communist takeover until Poland became independent again.

A replica of the icon adorns the National Shrine of Our Lady of Czestochowa in Doylestown, Pennsylvania, not far from Philadelphia.

The Basilica of Lourdes, France

St. Bernadette (see Chapter 18) was a young girl in Lourdes, France, and Catholics believe that Mary appeared to her in 1858 — from February 11 to July 16. Mary instructed St. Bernadette to dig with her hands in the soil and uncover a miraculous spring of water. To this day, the spring has been the catalyst for hundreds of thousands of inexplicable, immediate, and total cures.

The original basilica, built above the grotto in 1876, eventually became over-crowded, and in 1958, a concrete church, accommodating 20,000, was built. Today, four to six million pilgrims visit each year, and approximately 200 million have come since 1860.

We think it's moving to see and participate in the praying of the Rosary in all languages, which occurs on-site each night complete with a candlelight procession.

Fatima, Portugal

Catholics believe that Mary appeared to three small shepherd children, Lucia, Jacinta, and Francisco, in Fatima, Portugal, in 1917. She visited the children six times on the 13th of the month from May to October, asking them to pray the Rosary and to do so for the conversion of sinners so that they might repent of their sins and seek God's mercy and forgiveness. She said many souls were lost, because no one prayed for them, and they lived evil lives.

The faithful believe that during her apparitions to the children in Fatima, she also predicted World War II and the expansion of Communism, especially the Soviet Union's evil empire, which enslaved most of Eastern Europe throughout the Cold War. She asked that the pope and bishops of the world consecrate Russia to her Immaculate Heart and that the faithful receive Holy Communion on the First Saturday of the month.

In May of 1982, one year after an assassination attempt nearly killed him, Pope John Paul II asked the world's bishops to join him in consecrating Russia to the Immaculate Heart of Mary in thanksgiving for saving his life on May 13, 1981. Seven years after the consecration, the Berlin Wall fell, and in 1991, the Soviet Union collapsed and ceased to exist. Russia survived. Many attribute the end of the Cold War to political forces like Ronald Reagan and Mikhail Gorbachev. Some Catholics attribute it to the spiritual influence of Pope John Paul II and the intercession of Our Lady of Fatima.

On the last day of the apparitions in Fatima, October 13, 1917, what's known as *the Miracle of the Sun* occurred. Avelino de Almeida, the Editor-in-Chief of *O Seculo,* the anticlerical daily of Lisbon, was among the 70,000 people who witnessed the event. He wrote this the day after in his paper:

> From the road, where the carriages were crowded together and where hundreds of persons had stayed for want of sufficient courage to advance across the muddy ground, we saw the huge crowd turn towards the sun which appeared at its zenith, clear of the clouds. It resembled a flatplate of silver, and it was possible to stare at it without the least discomfort. It did not burn the eyes. It did not blind. We would say that it produced an eclipse. Then a tremendous cry rang out, and the crowd nearest us was heard to shout: "Miracle! Miracle! . . . Marvel! . . . Marvel!"

It had rained earlier, and the ground was wet as was the clothing of the crowd. When the sun in the sky began to shrink and expand and then rotate and spin as if it were going to impact the earth, most thought that it was the end of the world. It wasn't. And when it was over, their clothes were dry. Astronomers to this day can't explain what happened.

Jacinta and Francisco died shortly afterward, but the oldest of the three children entered a cloistered convent of the Carmelite order. Sr. Lucia is still in the cloister today. Pope John Paul II beatified Jacinta and Francisco on May 13, 2000.

Jacinta and Francisco are buried in a beautiful basilica, which is a short walk from the apparition site. Weather permitting, today's pilgrims pray the Rosary every evening where Our Lady of Fatima appeared. Pilgrims may also attend one of the outdoor Masses that are held on-site.

Rome

Just as Jews want to visit Jerusalem and Muslims want to visit Mecca, Catholics have an equal passion and desire to see Rome at some point in their lives. Since the conversion of the Roman Empire in the mid fourth century, the Eternal City, as it's often called since it was founded in 753 B.C., has been the center of Catholicism. The first pope, St. Peter, and the great missionary and apostle St. Paul were both martyred in this city between A.D. 64 and 67.

During early Church history (see Appendix A for details), Christian men, women, and children suffered 300 years of violent and aggressive persecution; many martyrs are buried in the catacombs underneath modern-day Rome. The city is a place of remembrance and memorial for those who died just because they were Christian.

In ancient Rome, the Christians buried their dead, especially the remains of martyrs, in underground cemeteries called *catacombs.* The Roman tradition was to burn the dead body whereas Christians, believing in the resurrection of the body at the end of the world, wouldn't burn their dead but bury them as was Jesus after his death and subsequent Resurrection.

Five catacombs are open to the public in Rome, and many Catholic pilgrims come to honor the dead who died in the early days of the Church for their Christian faith:

- St. Agnes on Via Nomentana
- St. Priscilla on Via Salaria
- St. Domitilla on Via Delle Sette Chiese
- St. Sebastian on Via Appia Antica
- St. Callixtus on Via Appia Antica

Rome is also predominantly a city of churches, about 900 of them if not more. Of these, seven are basilicas, four of which are called *patriarchal basilicas:*

- St. Peter *(San Pietro in Vaticano)*, shown in Figure 19-2.
- St. John Lateran *(San Giovanni in Laterano)*
- St. Mary Major *(Santa Maria Maggiore)*
- St. Paul Outside the Walls *(San Paolo fuori le mura)*

All basilicas have a special chair or throne for the pope to sit on whenever he celebrates Mass in that church, and only the pope may use it — no one else, not even a bishop or cardinal. A set of holy doors in each basilica is only opened during the Holy Year, which occurs every 25 years, and pilgrims pass through.

Figure 19-2:
The Basilica
of St. Peter
in the
Vatican.

- **Major basilicas** are often large churches that were imperial or aristocratic palaces during the pagan era of Rome. The emperor gave the palaces to the Catholic Church in compensation for all the lives, land, property, and money confiscated from the Christians during the Roman persecutions.

- **Minor basilicas** are those outside of Rome specially designated by the pope, such as the basilicas in Lourdes and Czestochowa.

The Cathedral of Notre Dame

Not the home of the Fighting Irish in South Bend, Indiana, but the original Notre Dame (see Figure 19-3) in Paris, France, is another popular Catholic place to visit. King Louis VII of France wanted a gorgeous cathedral for the eldest daughter of the Church (what France is often called), and he asked Bishop Maurice de Sully to oversee the project. The cornerstone was laid in 1163, and it took until 1250 to finally complete the magnificent cathedral.

Figure 19-3: The Cathedral of Notre Dame.

Kings and Queens have had their coronations in this cathedral; heads of state, such as General de Gaulle, have had their funeral Mass on-site; and several popes have celebrated Mass in this building over the centuries. It has become the prototype of Gothic cathedrals by which others, such as Chartres, Rheims, or Amiens, are compared.

Notre Dame is so large that its enormity can only be appreciated looking at it from across the bridge that covers the Seine. It's not the largest church in the world, however. That honor goes to St. Peter's Basilica in Rome. This famous cathedral became the focus of Victor Hugo's novel *Notre Dame de Paris,* which is now commonly known as *The Hunchback of Notre Dame.*

The National Shrine of the Immaculate Conception

You don't need to go to Europe to see large and beautiful churches. Many Catholics visit the National Shrine of the Immaculate Conception every day in Washington, D.C. (Take a look at Figure 19-4.)

Figure 19-4:
The National Shrine of the Immaculate Conception.

Since 1847, the Patroness of the United States of America has been Our Lady of the Immaculate Conception. On August 15, 1913, the Feast of the Assumption of Mary, Bishop Thomas J. Shahan, Rector of the Catholic University of America in Washington, D.C., had a papal audience with Pope St. Pius X and asked for permission to build a national shrine in the United States in honor of Mary. The pope not only gave his permission and blessing but also a personal check for $400 to start the contribution campaign. James Cardinal Gibbons, Archbishop of Baltimore, blessed the cornerstone on September 23, 1920, but the Depression and World War II slowed progress.

In 1953, the nation's bishops pledged their support to finish the Great Upper Church, which is the main body of the shrine; it's called the Upper Church to distinguish it from the basement or lower church, which is much smaller. The largest Roman Catholic Church in the Western Hemisphere and the eighth largest in the world, the shrine was completed on November 20, 1959.

Adjacent to the National Shrine of the Immaculate Conception is Catholic University of America (CUA). Founded in 1887, it's the only American college accredited to grant ecclesiastical degrees in theology, philosophy, and canon law, and it's the only national university of the Catholic Church in the United

States. If you want to visit the National Shrine via the Washington, D.C. subway system (Metro), you need to take the red line and get off at the Catholic University (Brookland-CUA) stop.

The Minor Basilica of Saint Anne de Beaupré

The oldest pilgrimage site in North America is the Minor Basilica of St. Anne de Beaupré in Quebec, Canada. The original church was built in 1658, followed by two more. The first basilica was erected in 1876, but a fire destroyed it in 1922. A second basilica and the fourth church were consecrated in 1976.

The Church is built in honor of St. Anne, the mother of Mary and grand-mother of Jesus Christ. The French settlers who came to Canada had a strong devotion to St. Anne, so it was natural for them to name it after her. It's the pride and joy of both French Canadians and English Canadians alike.

Numerous miraculous healings have been associated with pilgrimages to this fantastic shrine. Every year, over 1,000,000 people visit this holy place. They often recite the following prayer while visiting the basilica:

> Good St. Anne, I have come to honor you and to call upon you in this blessed Shrine of Beaupré. Here, pilgrims have often felt some of the fruits of your goodness, power, and intercession. Like every true pilgrim, I also have favors to ask of you. I know that you will be as good to me as you have been, in the past, to thousands of others who have come to implore you in this Shrine. St. Anne, you know the grace of which I stand most in need at the present moment, the special favor for which I have undertaken this pilgrimage. Hear my prayer. I entrust to your care, all of my material and spiritual needs. I commend my family, my country, the Church, and the whole world to you. Keep me faithful to Christ and His Church and one day, escort me into the Father's Eternal Home. Amen.

The Shrine of the Most Blessed Sacrament

Mother Angelica (see Chapter 17), who founded the Eternal Word Television Network (EWTN) in Irondale, Alabama, also built the Shrine of the Most Blessed Sacrament in Hanceville, Alabama.

Mother Angelica says that while on a pilgrimage in Bogota, Columbia, she saw a statue of the Child Jesus come alive and speak to her: "Build me a temple, and I will help those who help you." She says that she was puzzled, because Catholics aren't accustomed to using the word *temple.* The words *church, cathedral, basilica,* and *shrine* are familiar and used often, but not *temple.* Later, Mother Angelica, visiting St. Peter's Basilica in Rome, saw the word *temple* chiseled in the marble. She says that she knew then that it had to be big and awesome.

It took 200 workers — 99 percent non-Catholic — to build the temple in five years with donations from five millionaire families, who demand anonymity. Not one penny of the contributions collected for the EWTN network went to the project, which is calculated to have cost somewhere between 25 and 30 million dollars.

"Nothing but the best for Jesus," was Mother Angelica's motto. "If the President of the United States has the White House and the Queen of England has Buckingham Palace, then Our Lord and Savior, Jesus Christ, present in the Blessed Sacrament, deserves the very best for His house." The Shrine of the Most Blessed Sacrament may be in Hanceville, Alabama, but the materials used to build it came from all over the world. The ceramic tile came from South America, the stones from Canada, and the bronze from Madrid, Spain. The floors, columns, and pillars are made of marble from Italy. And a rare red Jasper marble came from Turkey that was used for the red crosses in the floor. The wood for the pews, doors, and confessionals is cedar imported from Paraguay. Spanish workers came to build the doors. The stained glass windows were imported from Munich, Germany. The most striking and moving feature, however, is the seven-foot monstrance containing the Blessed Sacrament.

Since the Mass of Consecration opened the shrine to the general public, hundreds of thousands of pilgrims — many of whom are non-Catholic — have visited this 380-acre place of prayer.

Part VI

Appendixes

The 5th Wave — By Rich Tennant

That one was reeeally close! A little lower and to the left!

In this part . . .

You can discover when it all happened by looking at Appendix A — a *very* abridged and condensed history of the Catholic Church. This part contains — in a nutshell — 2,000 years of development, life and death, joy and sorrow, intrigue and inspiration, vice and virtue, sin and grace. And then at the end, we threw some miscellaneous information into Appendix B just for your reference: A listing of all the popes and a liturgical calendar that contains all the solemnities, feasts, and memorials for the entire year.

Appendix A

A Brief History of Catholicism

. . . .

Ah, history lessons. To some, they're as exciting as a Stephen King novel (and often as gruesome). To others, they're as boring as a tax form. We're of the former variety. If you are too, you're definitely in the right spot.

Ancient Times (A.D. 33–741)

This section looks at the history of the Catholic Church from the time of Jesus through the fall of the Roman Empire — the first through eighth centuries.

Non-Christian Rome (A.D. 33–312)

Present-day Israel was known as Palestine at the time of Jesus, and even though it had a king (Herod), it was a puppet monarchy, because the real civil power ruling the Holy Land was the Roman Empire. Caesar Tiberius appointed Pontius Pilate the procurator (governor) of Judea, and he was the real political power in Jerusalem.

Yet Palestine wasn't considered a conquered territory of Rome — rather, an unwilling and impotent ally. And the Jews were initially exempt from the normal Roman requirement of worshipping the Imperial gods, even though divine attributes were ascribed to Caesar himself, beginning with Augustus.

As long as the Christians were seen as a fringe group of the Jews, they enjoyed the same protection and tolerance under Roman rule. (Scholars believe that in the Roman mind, at least, this involved a theological disagreement between mainline Jews and the small minority of Christian Jews, and until it became political, Pilate was initially hesitant to execute Jesus.)

The early Christians

The faithful believed that after Jesus was crucified and died, he rose from the dead. His followers became known as Christians. Mostly Jews who had come to accept Jesus as the Messiah, they wanted to maintain their Jewish traditions and keep practicing the Hebrew faith. They went to Temple and Synagogue, observed Sabbath and Passover, obeyed the dietary laws (kosher), and yet gathered every Sunday, the day of the Resurrection, to hear what Jesus preached and to celebrate the Mass. (See Chapter 8 for more on the Mass.)

The Acts of the Apostles, the New Testament book that immediately follows the Four Gospels (Matthew, Mark, Luke, and John), describes how in the beginning at least, Jerusalem's religious establishment tolerated the early Christians as a fringe element of Judaism.

How Christianity split into its own religion

Two factors led to the formal split and independence of Christianity as a separate religion:

✔ The growing number of Gentile converts to Christianity eventually eclipsed the original Jewish roots. Even though Jesus and the 12 apostles were practicing Jews when he first called them to follow him, the travels of St. Paul and the other disciples into non-Jewish lands proved to be a strong catalyst. More and more Greek and Roman cultural influences were adapted into Christianity, and fewer and fewer Jewish customs and traditions endured. By the end of the first century, the majority of Christians weren't Jewish converts to Christianity.

✔ The destruction of the Temple in Jerusalem in A.D. 70 was the Waterloo for Jewish-Christian relations. Six years earlier, Nero blamed the Christians for the burning of Rome, using them as the scapegoat. Now Jewish zealots — inspired and instigated by some of the radical Pharisees — pursued the removal of the Gentile Romans and attempted to launch a war against the empire. In response, the Romans burned the ancient and historical Temple, sacred to every Jew (and Christian, for that matter) under the orders of General Vespasian. It was his son, Titus, who wanted to teach the Jewish revolutionaries a harsh lesson and punish them for defying his father, Vespasian. He had the temple burned to the ground, and 97,000 survivors were sold into slavery.

This dark day in Jewish history resulted in the final and formal expulsion of the Christians from Judaism. No longer a fringe element or an equal co-partner, Christianity was a distinct and separate religion.

But Christians weren't liked in Rome or Jerusalem. The Romans considered worshipping an executed criminal (Jesus) dangerous to the political stability of the empire. And Jews claimed that worshipping Jesus as the Son of God was blasphemy and heresy. It shook the foundations of their Hebrew faith and belief in one God. So both sides had a grudge against the new religion, and both pagan Rome and Hebrew Jerusalem alike persecuted Christians.

Shifts and changes that affected the early Church

During the Diaspora, the Jews were expelled from Palestine. During the Babylonian exile, two-thirds of all Jews were forced to leave their land to prevent them from becoming a political and military rival — especially Greek-speaking Jews (known as Hellenistic Jews). Saul, who later became Paul after his conversion, was a Hellenistic Jew and later became one of the greatest missionaries of the Gospel of Christ and the Christian religion.

Some Christians were Gentile, and some were Jewish. This resulted in some problems at first — especially with dietary laws and circumcision. Most of the original Christians were first Jews who faithfully observed the Law of Moses. Their men were circumcised, and they ate only kosher food. But when pagan Greeks and Romans began accepting that Jesus Christ was the Messiah and the Son of God, the question arose whether they should follow the path of the apostles, who were first Jews before becoming Christians. Some said, "Yes," and others said, "No." The apostles were also divided.

Jesus left no explicit instructions on this issue, so this stuff was ironed out at the first general council of the Church, the Council of Jerusalem. The council decided that Jewish regulations were no longer applicable. It was no longer mandatory for Christian converts to first embrace Judaism. After the decision was made that those who were never Jewish didn't need to embrace Judaism or the Law of Moses before embracing Christianity, the ties with the old religion of Abraham, Isaac, and Jacob were finally severed. From that time on, the Christian faith was no longer tied to Judaism.

After the fall of Jerusalem, the destruction of the Temple, and the missionary expeditions of St. Peter and St. Paul to Rome, the Church moved from Jerusalem to the Eternal City — the permanent center of the Church.

The Roman persecutions

The Roman persecutions of the Christians were as fierce and as genocidal as the Nazi Holocaust against the Jews during World War II, but the Roman persecutions lasted almost 300 years. Historians designate three periods of persecution: The first period lasted from A.D. 64 to 112, the second period is from A.D. 112 to 186, and the third is from A.D. 189 to 312.

The first period

The first period of Roman persecutions began in A.D. 64 during the reign of Nero (A.D. 54–68), who blamed the Christians for the burning of Rome. (Many historians believe *he* initiated the burning of Rome to rebuild the city against the opposition of the local Roman aristocracy.) The period continued through the reign of Domitian (81–96) and finished with the reign of Emperor Trajan (98–117).

Prejudice survives on lies, and the falsehoods spread about Christians brought the persecutions to a fever pitch. Christians were accused of having human sacrifices, which the civilized Romans considered barbaric. Actually, they were taking out of context the Christian doctrine of the Real Presence in the Holy Eucharist: The faithful believed that they were eating and drinking the body and blood, soul and divinity of Christ. When distorted, it caused many people to fear and despise the alleged cannibals. People got so superstitious that any calamity or misfortune was seen as either a punishment from the gods or just the consequences of having Christians around the empire. In fact, whenever a flood, earthquake, or fire came about, the easiest solution was to blame the Christians.

Tertullian, a Christian apologist of antiquity, wrote,

> If the Tiber River rises above its banks, if the Nile does not overflow, if the skies are not clear, if the earth quakes, if famine or pestilence come, the cry goes out from Rome, "The Christians to the lions."

The second period

The second period of Roman persecutions continued with Trajan through the Philosopher Emperor Marcus Aurelius (161–180) and ended with Commodus (180–192) — the emperor alluded to in the movie *Gladiator* (2000; Universal Pictures), which, by the way, is a remake of the movie *Fall of the Roman Empire* (1964; Samuel Bronston). This period had less tyrannic and despotic emperors than the first period, but the persecutions were still promoted.

During this period, Pliny the Younger wrote to Emperor Trajan, asking what to do about the Christians who appeared to be good citizens of Rome yet were technically traitors, since they refused to worship Caesar. The emperor's reply?

- Christianity was still a capital crime, and those legally accused and convicted were to be executed for treason.

- Those who renounced their Christian religion were to be set free.

- Roman Magistrates weren't to seek out and hunt Christians, nor were they to act on anonymous tips. An almost "don't ask, don't tell" policy prevailed. However, this left the decision to arrest and torture Christians to the local authorities, as Rome considered it a menial task to rid the empire of Christians.

Most of the animosity toward Christians during this time was mob mentality. When a large group of Romans got together and had too much wine, they went out Christian-bashing.

The third period

The final period of persecutions was the most virulent, violent, and atrocious.

The successor to Commodus, Septimus Severus (193–211) changed the tone from letting local yokels beat up the Christians to reinstating full-fledged, across-the-board imperial persecutions. Four emperors later, Maximus Thrax (235–238) had it out for the bishops and started a campaign to arrest and execute popes and bishops, hoping to destroy Christianity by hitting its leaders. Three emperors later, Decius (249–251) inaugurated the bloodiest of persecutions. Not just persecuting formal, baptized Christians but anyone even suspected of being a Christian was treated as a traitor and potential terrorist, even though no threats whatsoever came from Christians against the emperor, the Empire, or anything Roman. They merely wanted to worship their own god. And under Diocletian (284–405), Emperor of the Eastern Empire (the Roman Empire split in half in 286), the most pervasive and intense persecution took place. Entire families, men, women children, elderly, infirm, and so on were tortured and put to death. He literally hated all Christians and Christianity and swore he'd rid the world of this cancer.

Famous martyrs of the Roman persecutions

Many were martyred during the Roman persecutions. *Martyr* is actually a Greek word for *witness.* These faithful Christians tried to avoid persecution, but if hours of torture and a horrible death resulted from witnessing to the faith, they accepted it.

St. Stephen was the first deacon of the Church and the first Christian martyr (also called the Proto-martyr). He was stoned to death for being a Christian (Acts 7:58). Saul of Tarsus was present at the event and later became St. Paul the Apostle. Emperor Nero had him beheaded. (Because St. Paul was a Roman citizen, unlike St. Peter and the other apostles, Paul couldn't be crucified, but he could be beheaded.) Peter was crucified upside down at his own request, because he felt unworthy to die in the same manner as Jesus.

All the apostles were martyred except St. John, known as the Beloved Disciple. His persecutors tried to burn him alive in boiling oil, but he survived. So he was exiled to the island of Patmos, where he wrote the Book of Revelation. He died of old age in A.D. 100.

We list some other famous martyrs as follows:

- St. **Agnes** was killed by a sword to the throat after attempts to burn her alive were unsuccessful.

- St. **Agatha,** the patroness of breast disease, had her breasts cut off.

- St. **Lucy**'s eyes were plucked out. (She's the patroness of eye diseases and ailments and patroness of Sicily).

- St. **Sebastian** was martyred by arrows.

- St. **Lawrence** was roasted alive on a hot gridiron.

- St. **Cecilia** was decapitated after attempts to suffocate her were unsuccessful.

- St. **Polycarp, St. Perpetua, St. Felicity, St. Thecla, St. Boris, St. Gleb, St. Sabbas,** and many others were martyred in many ways. Some were fed to wild animals and some skinned alive. Others were burned, poisoned, stoned, crushed, speared, whipped, drowned, and crucified.

Dreaming of Jesus

St. Helena was the mother of the Roman Emperor Constantine. She eventually led an expedition to the Holy Land to find the remains of the *True Cross,* the cross Jesus was crucified on.

Constantine himself even converted to Christianity, albeit on his deathbed. But his gradual conversion actually began before that — after a victory at the Molvian Bridge. He was convinced he achieved that victory, because he obeyed a dream in which he was instructed to emblazon the *Chi* (X) *Rho* (P) the first two Greek letters of the name of Christ — *Chr* istos) on all the shields of his soldiers. He said that the Lord spoke to him in the dream and said: "*in hoc signo vinces,*" which is Latin for *in this sign you will conquer.*

Christian Rome (A.D. 313–475)

"The blood of martyrs became the seed of Christians," said Tertullian, a Christian apologist of ancient times.

Three hundred years of relentless and violent persecutions ended when the Roman Emperor Constantine issued his famous Edict of Milan in A.D. 313, which legalized Christianity. Being that it was no longer a capital crime, Christians were able to come out in the open for the first time.

Christianity as the state religion

Although the edict allowed Christians to freely practice their faith, it wasn't until A.D. 380 that Christianity became the official state religion. At that point, the tables were turned: Paganism was outlawed, and the once-outlawed Christianity was the official religion of the Roman Empire.

The consequences of this new alliance of church and state were many. The Church obtained financial, material, and legal advantages from the state. Buildings, particularly the former pagan temples, land, estates, and properties, as well as money, were donated in compensation for the losses incurred during the 300 years of Roman persecutions.

In the old days of the underground Church, Christians literally worshipped underground in the *catacombs* — the ancient Christian burial spots. Pagan Romans burned their dead. Christians buried their dead because of the belief in the resurrection of the body at the end of the world.

To this day, many of the ancient basilicas in Rome and throughout Italy resemble pagan temples in their architecture, because that's what most of them were before being transformed into Christian houses of worship. Altars that sacrificed animals to the pagan gods of Rome became altars for the Holy Sacrifice of the Mass.

The state-church alliance produced some negative fallout. The emperors, especially in the Eastern (Byzantine) half of the empire, felt that they had a divine right to oversee Church affairs, settle doctrinal disputes, choose bishops, and enforce orthodoxy (correct belief). The concept that Caesar (or any secular ruler, emperor, or king) had a right and the authority to oversee the Church is called *Caesaro-papism,* a combination of the words Caesar and papal meaning *belonging to the pope*. This would appear time and time again between the Byzantine Emperors and later by the Holy Roman Emperors. On a more positive note, a clear example where imperial interference had a beneficial effect happened in 325 when the emperor told the pope (the bishop of Rome) and the other four Patriarchs (in Jerusalem, Antioch, Alexandria, and Constantinople) that he wanted a general council convened to end the Arian controversy. The hierarchy agreed. The Council of Nicea met, deposed Arius, condemned his heretical teaching, and formulated the Nicene Creed, which is said to this day at every Sunday Mass and Divine Liturgy. (See Chapter 4 for more on Arius and Arianism and see Chapter 3 for the Nicene Creed.) Despite the fact that it was the emperor who instigated the council as a secular ruler, nevertheless, the pope, the patriarchs and the bishops gave their full consent and used their authority as Church leaders and teachers to define what would be formal doctrine for the universal Church.

The development of the Christian Patriarchs

Five predominant centers of Christianity arose during this period: Jerusalem, Antioch, Alexandria, Rome, and Constantinople, and each place had a spiritual leader, a bishop, who was called a *patriarch* from the Latin *pater* meaning *father*. So these five towns and their surrounding area came to be known as Patriarchates.

The five Patriarchs who oversaw the Church in this era were given the highest honor and respect. The bishop of Rome became the Patriarch of the West, and the Patriarch of Constantinople was the spiritual leader of the East. Despite these patriarchates, the fundamental and final authority still rested with the Successor of Peter — another title for the pope.

Rome had been the center of the Roman Empire from the founding of the city in 753 B.C. So even when the empire split in A.D. 286 between East and West (Constantinople and Rome), Rome and its bishop (the pope) remained the supreme head of the universal Church. The day-to-day running, however — especially the selection of bishops and the appointment of ecclesiastical honors — was left to the individual and respective Patriarchs, because they knew their clergy and people best, being closer to the scene.

But professional rivalry emerged between Rome and Constantinople. Rome had been around since 753 B.C., but Constantinople was relatively new, created from the city of Byzantium (present-day Istanbul) in A.D. 324. The western emperors declined in power and prestige during the barbarian invasions (A.D. 378–570), while the papacy emerged as the stable center of a chaotic world. In the East, the emperors took on a more Oriental role of being total and absolute despots with little if any power showing among the aristocracy. The West had the long-standing tradition of the Roman Senate, which was run by the nobility and often came at odds with Caesar. The Eastern emperor used his upper class to fill the imperial court and to advise but not share authority.

This shift presented many advantages. First, conversions came along the lines of communication through Roman cities and roads. The *Pax Romana* (the Peace of Rome) that began with Caesar Augustus allowed the free flow of ideas, merchandise, people, communication, and religion. Also, with the decline of the traditional pagan religions, Christianity had appeal — specifically, to women, children, and slaves. Christianity preached that all were created equal in the sight of God. This was radical and freeing for the oppressed, and many converts came from these classes. In addition, Christianity also preached morality, and its citizens lived their lives according to high moral standards.

The Greek influence on the Christian Church

The Greek philosophers Plato, Socrates, and Aristotle had an enormous impact on Catholic theology. Twelve years after the Edict of Milan (A.D. 313), the Eastern emperor called for the Ecumenical Council in Nicea (A.D. 325) to end the Arian controversy. The debate focused on two Greek words referring to the nature of Christ and his relationship with God the Father. The heretical Arius, whose followers were called Arians, used the term *homoiousios,* meaning Jesus and the Father had similar but separate natures. Whereas the orthodox and catholic side used the word *homoousios,* which meant that they shared the same divine nature. (The word *orthodox* with a small *o,* means correct or right believer, but *Orthodox* with the capital letter *O* refers to the Eastern Orthodox Churches, such as the Greek, Russian, and Serbian Orthodox Churches.)

In addition, the Greek Church Fathers, such as St. Athanasius, St. Gregory Nanzianzen, St. Gregory of Nyssa, St. Basil, St. John Chrysostom, and St. John Damascene preserved the true faith from heresy and also greatly influenced the way that the Church does theology. Using philosophical terms and logical reasoning, they explained the revealed faith in a rational and coherent manner. This was considered the great gift of the Greeks in addition to their art and music, icons, and sense of mystery.

The Catholic Church gave the title *Church Father* to men who lived holy lives before A.D. 800, provided that their doctrines were orthodox, conforming to the official Magisterium.

The Western Church Fathers, St. Ambrose, St. Augustine, St. Jerome, and Pope St. Gregory the Great also relied heavily on Greek philosophy to help explain theological principles used to develop and understand Catholic doctrine.

✔ **St. Ambrose** (A.D. 340–397), the Bishop of Milan, coined the phrase *ubi Petrus ibi Ecclesia,* which is Latin for *where there is Peter, there is the Church.* This represents a fundamental doctrine that authentic Catholicism is found in the ministry of Peter, the Successors of St. Peter who are more commonly known as the popes. Any time a theological debate or controversy ensued and opposing sides and/or factions arose, the safe recourse is to side with the pope according to Catholic teaching. So when Pope St. Leo sent a letter to the Council of Chalcedon (A.D. 451) defending the doctrine of the Hypostatic Union (see Chapter 4), the bishops declared, "Peter has spoken through Leo!"

✔ **St. Augustine** (A.D. 354–430) was converted through St. Ambrose. Augustine's mother, St. Monica prayed for 33 years that her pagan, playboy son would convert to Christianity and be baptized into the Catholic faith. St. Ambrose was his mentor who taught him religion and baptized him in A.D. 387. Augustine wrote his spiritual journey and autobiography, *The Confessions,* in A.D. 397, and it remains a classic even today.

✔ **St. Jerome** (A.D. 340–420) is best known for being the first person to compile and translate the entire Christian Bible from the various Hebrew, Aramaic, and Greek manuscripts into a one-volume book in one language, Latin. Latin was the official language of the Roman Empire and the *lingua franca* (international language) of Jerome's time, and it was the common tongue (*vulgar* from *vulgus* meaning common people) of the average citizen who could read and write, hence this first complete Bible was called the Vulgate. It took him from A.D. 382–405 to translate it.

The fall of Rome and more barbarian invasions (A.D. 476–570)

One of the important developments in this period of time was an establishment of religious life, especially monasticism. *Monks* were men of prayer who left the secular world to commit themselves to a life of *ora et labora* (Latin for *prayer and work*), the motto of St. Benedict, the father of Western monasticism.

Monasteries were large houses that held anywhere from 10 to 50 or more residents with individual austere rooms called *cells* connected to several community rooms with the chapel as the focal point. Everything was done and shared in common, from food to work to leisure and even prayer. The only private things were sleep and sanitary habits.

Monks took solemn vows of poverty, chastity, and obedience. No wives, no children, and material wealth went to the monastery to be shared by all under the stewardship of the abbot, who was in charge and had the rank of bishop. This pooling of resources when aristocrats and middle-class Romans entered monastic life enabled poor men to join as well and truly be considered and treated as equal and full members of the community.

St. Patrick and his monks

St. Patrick (A.D. 387–493), the son of a Roman officer in Britain, was captured and enslaved by Irish pirates at 16 years of age. Six years later, he escaped. He was ordained a priest and later consecrated bishop before, ironically, Pope Celestine I sent him as a missionary in A.D. 433 to Ireland to convert the nation to the Catholic faith. (See Chapter 1 for more on St. Patrick.) The monks he brought with him and the natives he converted became the cornerstone for evangelization of most of the British Isles. They're also responsible for introducing the practice of private (auricular) confession (see Chapter 7) in the 6th and 7th centuries. Up to that time, the Sacrament of Penance was celebrated publicly, meaning that penitents confessed their sins openly before everyone in the congregation in the presence of the bishop or priest. The Irish monks adapted it so that people could go to a confessor in private and have their sins absolved with full anonymity and confidentiality.

The monks chose to leave the hectic and worldly cities of Imperial Rome, which saved them during the barbarian invasions. The cities were plundered, but the countryside was basically left untouched. The Goths, Huns, Franks, Lombards, Vandals, Angles, Saxons, Jutes, Mongols, Burgundians, Ostrogoths, Visigoths, Suevi, and so on, invaded the frontier of the Roman Empire, which had grown too vast, too thin, and too undermanned. (More Germanic and Gaulic tribes filled the ranks of the Roman Army than that of Roman blood from the Italian Peninsula.)

The most famous barbarian, Attila the Hun, made his way right up to the city gates of Rome in A.D. 452. Emperor Valentinian III asked Pope St. Leo the Great to do something, and he did: He went out to meet Attila with 100 priests, monks, and bishops, chanting in Latin, burning incense, and carrying crosses, crucifixes, and holy images of Jesus and Mary.

This entourage went before the fiercest and most ruthless of all barbarian invaders. Only Ghengis Khan possibly rivaled Attila's ferocity, and his very name instilled fear in the hearts of many. Thousands of Hun troops contrasted this little procession of a hundred clerics with an elderly white-haired, white-robed pope leading them. And Attila became afraid for the first time in his career.

He knew that everyone else feared him and trembled at his name, and he knew that he had superior troops. Yet seeing this saintly man and hearing that he was called the Vicar of Christ on earth and that even angels were under his authority, Attila feared not the power of man but the unseen power of God. He figured that only someone with confidence in more powerful weapons or in more troops than he had would dare come to him in this fashion. He feared that the pope was unafraid, because he could call down the heavenly armies of angels to fight for the Church, and men couldn't defeat spirits. So Attila agreed not to sack Rome, and he turned back. But Odoacer sacked Rome in A.D. 476, deposing the last Western emperor, Romulus Augustulus.

After the collapse of the Roman Empire, the Teutonic kings and overlords realized that governing all the people and all the territory would be extremely difficult. No more Roman Senate, no more legal system, and no more local authorities — just the authority of the conquering king. Yet the bishops survived the fall. The pagan kings dealt with the Christian bishops, and that contact with them gradually introduced the faith to the barbarian invaders.

The bishops depended on the monks to help. During the barbarian invasions, the cities were destroyed, but the monasteries — outside the cities — survived. The monks went out and preached to them about Jesus and the Catholic Church, and many converts were made — especially after a successful conversion of a king or tribal chief.

The invaders got urbanized and suburbanized, as well as civilized. They stopped pillaging and abandoned a nomadic life for a more stable one. This was the genesis of the European nations of Spain, France, Germany, and England. The Church had adopted the Roman Imperial model for governing by creating parishes, dioceses, archdioceses, and metropolitan areas, and that same structure helped the tribes form the civil boundaries and cultures of the Franks, the Lombards, the Saxons, and so on.

And guess where the Franks, Lombards, Anglo-Saxons, and so on, learned to read and write? For that matter, guess who preserved Latin and Greek as a spoken and written language — who protected the books and writings of philosophy and law, poetry and literature, geometry and grammar to allow culture to flourish again? The monks.

The monks not only preserved Greco-Roman literature, law, philosophy, and art, but also agriculture. Nomadic barbarians weren't natural farmers. They knew nothing of raising livestock, planting, harvesting, and such, but the monks did these things as part of their life — the *labora* part of the *ora et labora* (prayer and work). The monks taught the barbarians how to grow food; how to build bridges, aqueducts, and sewers; and how to make and interpret laws, because the monks retained all the Greek and Roman history and learning from being destroyed as it had been in the cities. The knowledge wasn't lost but shared.

Pope St. Gregory the Great to Charles Martel (590–741)

St. Benedict of Narsia (A.D. 480–547) is known as the Father of Western monasticism, because he established the first monastery in Europe at Subiaco, Italy.

He also founded the famous monastery of Monte Cassino, Italy, where a crucial battle took place during World War II in 1944. His religious order of monks is the Order of St. Benedict, or more commonly, the Benedictines. Their motto is *ora et labora* (pray and work), which is the focus of monastic life in the Western Church.

Pope St. Gregory the Great (A.D. 540–604) was a Roman-born nobleman, the son of a Senator, who became a Benedictine monk in A.D. 575. The people and clergy of Rome were so impressed with his personal holiness, wisdom, and knowledge that when Pope Pelagius II died in A.D. 590, Gregory was elected to succeed him by *acclamation* — unanimous consent. Before becoming a monk, he had been Prefect of Rome (A.D. 572–574), which was a political leadership role, and he was just 30 years old at the time. That experience helped him later on as pope (A.D. 590–604) when the political and military leadership of Rome disintegrated and left the city abandoned. He rallied the citizens by coordinating and personally participating in a monumental project to care for victims of the plague and the starving who literally overran the city of Rome, which more or less had no civil government left. Gregory's position as pope and the only visible leader in Rome further enhanced the power, prestige, and influence of the papacy.

Gregorian Chant, religious chants sung in Latin, gets its name from Pope St. Gregory due to his love of music and the Sacred Liturgy. In A.D. 596, he sent St. Augustine of Canterbury with 40 other missionaries to England to convert the Angles, Jutes, and Saxons, who were the Teutonic invaders of Britain, which had been a Roman outpost from A.D. 43–410.

Charles Martel (A.D. 688–741) is another key person in Catholic Church history. Muhammad, born in Mecca, A.D. 570, became the founder and prophet of Islam at the age of 40 (A.D. 610) and died in Medina in A.D. 632. By A.D. 711, Muslim forces occupied Spain after they had successfully conquered the Visigoths who had controlled it since A.D. 419. Charles Martel was the illegitimate son of Pepin II and also the grandfather of Charlemagne. He won a decisive and pivotal victory over Abd-er-Rahman and the Moors (Spanish Muslims of this period) at the Battle of Poitiers in 732. This was the most crucial victory for all Christendom, because it determined whether Islam or Christianity would be the predominant religion in Europe for centuries to come.

The Middle Ages (A.D. 800–1500)

This section looks at the history of the Catholic Church from the time of Charlemagne to the dawn of the Protestant Reformation — the ninth to fifteenth centuries A.D.

Christendom: One big, mighty kingdom

The strength of the ancient Roman Empire was its unification of many different peoples of various languages and cultures — unity within diversity. One emperor ruled many citizens from many places, and one law was enforced, applied, and interpreted all over the vast empire. But when Rome fell after different groups of barbarians invaded and occupied the empire, the unity dissolved and only diversity remained, bringing chaos.

Yet one single vestige of unity survived both the moral and military decline of the Roman Empire, and that was the Catholic Church, which had one head (the pope in Rome), one set of laws (canon law), and the same seven sacraments all over the world. And unity existed between the pope and the bishops, between the priests/deacons and their respective bishop, and between the people of the parish and their pastor.

After the barbarians settled down, settled in, and became truly civilized, thanks to the monks, the local barbarian chiefs, princes, and kings fought among themselves instead of unifying.

The rise of the Holy Roman Empire

Clovis, King of the Franks (A.D. 466–511), became the predominant ruler after he unified the semi-autonomous Frankish tribes into one large force and defeated the last Roman General, Syagrius, in 486. In 493, he married the Burgundian princess Clotilda and thus unified Franks and Burgundians. And he also converted to the Catholic faith along with all his soldiers on Christmas Day 496 in order to marry Clotilda, because she was a devout Christian.

Clovis established the first successful dynasty (known as the *Merovingian*) to arise from the ashes of the Roman Empire. This dynasty occupied the area the Romans called *Gaul,* which is mostly modern-day France, Belgium, and Luxembourg. He also saw the advantage of having one ruler and one religion, so he not only personally embraced Christianity but also demanded it of all his soldiers and subjects, who up to this point in time had been basically pagan.

Clovis' children and grandchildren weren't strong or competent monarchs as he was, so his unified kingdom eventually began to disintegrate. The Merovingians were replaced by another dynasty, the *Carolingian,* in 751 when Pepin the Short (714–768) deposed the last Merovingian king, Childeric III. Pepin's father was Charles Martel, who won the Battle of Poitiers in 732.

With Pepin the Short and the Carolingian Dynasty now in place, the scene was set for the arrival of Charlemagne, his son. Charles (742–814) was his baptismal name, but history knows him as Charles the Great (*Carolus Magnus* in Latin and *Charlemagne* in French).

Pope Leo III bestowed on Charlegmagne the same title that Charlegmagne's father held of *Patricius Romanorum,* which meant he had a special duty to protect the people and lands of Rome. On Christmas Day 800, Pope Leo crowned Charlemagne Holy Roman Emperor. Pope Leo's intent was that one ruler, the Holy Roman Emperor, would be the secular ruler over the known world. But by having the emperor crowned by the pope in Rome, the Church achieved the superiority it needed: The one who installed could also depose. So later, in the 11th century, when the Holy Roman Emperor Henry IV tried to control who was made bishop in his realm, he was deposed and excommunicated by Pope Gregory VII, also known as Hildebrand.

Under Charlemagne, one standard liturgical language also united the people of the Holy Roman Empire. Latin was the *lingua franca* (common language) for the Catholic Church and the government as well. This made sense, because the other languages spoken at the time were still primitive (they didn't have an extensive vocabulary), and many of them were never written — only spoken. In other words, unlike Greek and Latin, which were around much longer and had precise laws of grammar, declension, conjugation, and such, primitive French, Spanish, and Italian were just beginning to evolve. Universal standard definitions and translations were needed so that everyone was on the same page. And making Latin the language of worship solidified the empire, because people could travel anywhere and still experience the same exact Mass, no matter what country they were in or from.

Splitsville: The east/west schism

The Eastern Roman Empire, known as Byzantium, didn't take too kindly to having a Holy Roman Emperor or empire arise, because it was clear that the pope wanted to make the Carolingians the sole rulers of the entire old Roman Empire — East and West. This would make the emperor of Byzantium and the patriarch, who was always closely aligned with him, virtually redundant. Ever since the old Roman Empire was divided in A.D. 286 and the establishment of the imperial town of Constantinople by the Emperor Constantine (A.D. 306–337), the Eastern part of the Roman Empire survived despite the barbarian invasions in the West. After Rome fell in A.D. 476, Byzantium was the only vestige of the Empire. With the pope in Rome crowning Charlemagne, King of the Franks, as Holy Roman Emperor, it was seen from the Byzantine viewpoint as a slap to the Eastern Emperor and Empire itself. From then on, relations between the East and the West deteriorated until a formal split occurred in 1054 when the schism took place. The Eastern Church became the Greek Orthodox Church by severing all ties with Rome and the Roman Catholic Church — from the pope to the Holy Roman Emperor on down. Over the centuries, the Eastern Church and Western Church became more distant and isolated for the following reasons:

- **Geography:** The West encompassed Western Europe and the northern and western areas of the Mediterranean and the East took up Asia Minor, the Middle East, and Northern Africa.

- ✔ **Ignorance:** The Byzantine Church knew less and less Latin and even less Latin tradition, and vice versa. So most patriarchs in Constantinople couldn't read any Latin, and most popes in Rome couldn't read any Greek. Byzantines in the East used leavened bread in their Divine Liturgy to symbolize the Risen Christ, and Latins in the West used unleavened bread as was used by Jesus at the Last Supper.

- ✔ **Different theologies:** Both were valid, but each had its own perspective. The West (Latin) was more practical and, although fully believing in the divinity of Christ, put emphasis on his humanity when depicting Jesus in art — especially by making realistic crucifixes. The East (Byzantine) was more theoretical and, although fully believing in the humanity of Christ, focused on his divinity, which was much more mysterious.

- ✔ **Personalities and politics:** Michael Cerularius, Patriarch of Constantinople, and Pope St. Leo IX weren't friends, and each one mistrusted the other. Cerularius crossed the line when he wrote in a letter that the Latin use of unleavened bread was Jewish but not Christian. He was denying the validity of the Holy Eucharist in the Western Church. Leo countered by saying that the patriarchs had always been puppets of the Byzantine emperors.

In the end, Pope Leo and Patriarch Michael excommunicated each other and their respective churches. But more than 900 years later, in 1965, Pope Paul VI and Patriarch Athenagoras I of Constantinople removed the mutual excommunications.

In any event, the schism that divided Christendom right down the middle exists to this day. Although both sides accept the validity of each one's orders and sacraments, no inter-Communion exists between the Roman Catholic and the Eastern Orthodox. That means that normally speaking, Catholics aren't allowed to receive Holy Communion in Orthodox Churches, and conversely, Orthodox shouldn't receive Holy Communion in Catholic Churches. As we explain in Chapter 8, sharing the same belief in the Real Presence isn't enough to receive Holy Communion; one must also be *in communion,* that is, united doctrinally, jurisdictionally, and morally to everyone else who is sharing in Communion.

The Crusades

The intention of the Crusades was initially honorable. It was a response to a plea for help from the Byzantine Empire, still a sister church at the time.

In 1095, the Byzantine Emperor, Alexius Comnenus, sent ambassadors to Pope Urban II in Rome, asking for help to defend Christianity from an imminent attack. The Saracens (Arab Muslims during the time of the Crusades) had overrun the Holy Land, and Christians were no longer free to move about and visit their holy pilgrimage sites. A crusade to free the Holy Land was under way before you knew it.

The pope also saw the Crusades as a way to diffuse and dissolve internal fighting and battles being waged by the Christian monarchs for territory and power. (Clear and defined nation states didn't exist as of yet.) He wanted to unite them under one banner, Christianity, for one purpose, to free the Holy Land for pilgrims, against one common enemy, Islamic extremism and expansionism.

The Crusades totaled eight in number:

1. (1095–1101) During the first Crusade, the Crusaders captured Jerusalem in 1100. It was initiated by a group of poor German and French peasants under the leadership of Peter and Walter Penniless. Defeated by the Turks, they were later joined by nobility so that after a month's siege, they won the Holy City (Jerusalem). After this Crusade, nine French noblemen formed the Knights Templar as a military-religious order to serve the Church by freeing the Holy Land. Being an Order meant that they weren't subject to the authority of the local king or even the emperor. This autonomy along with their bravery, courage, and strategic and tactical skills made them successful in battle and wealthy in spoils. Eventually, Pope Clement V suppressed them after Philip IV (the Fair) trumped up false charges of heresy against them.

2. (1145–47) Emperor Conrad II and Louis VII of France headed the second Crusade after the Saracen reconquest of Edessa in 1144. This Crusade was promoted in Europe by the preaching of St. Bernard of Clairvaux (1090–1153).

3. (1188–92) Emperor Frederick I, Philip II of France, and Richard I of England (alias Richard the Lion Hearted) conducted the third Crusade after the capture of Jerusalem by Saladin in 1187. On the return to England, King Richard was captured by Leopold V of Austria and held for ransom by Emperor Henry VI. That left the rule of England to his brother, Prince John of Robin Hood fame until Richard's release in 1194.

4. (1204) The Saracens took Constantinople. The Marquis of Montferrat (France) led the fourth Crusade. In 1195, Byzantine Emperor Isaac Angelus II was overthrown and imprisoned by his brother Alexius III. Isaac's son, Alexius IV, was married to the sister of the German King Philip of Swabia and was attempting to gain support to claim the Byzantine throne by overthrowing his uncle (Alexius III). They asked the Crusaders to come to their aid. The destination of the Crusade was Egypt. Venice provided the fleet of ships for a sum of 85,000 marks. Only one third of the force reached Venice by October 1202, and the Crusaders were unable to raise the money. To pay their bill, they agreed to recover the town of Zara, Croatia, which had rebelled against Venetian rule and allied itself with Hungary in 1186. Pope Innocent III declared an excommunication if any Crusader attacked a Christian city, but the Crusaders did it anyway to pay the Venetians for their fleet. The Crusade

further deteriorated afterwards when they went to Constantinople to help Alexius IV overthrow his uncle. They occupied the town, and Isaac II and his son Alexius IV were installed as co-emperors for a short time until their own people deposed them. Riots broke out and anti-Western violence ensued as the local population resented the presence of Crusader troops. The Crusaders responded by sacking the city of Constantinople in 1204. The Byzantines recovered their capital in 1261.

5. (1217) Duke Leopold VI of Austria and Andrew of Hungary led the fifth Crusade, conquering Damietta in the Nile Delta. Internal squabbling, however, between French and Italian troops and the Knights Templar eroded their victory, and in 1221, the city was surrendered back to the Saracens.

6. (1228–29) Emperor Frederick II took part in the sixth Crusade, and Thibaud de Champagne and Richard of Cornwall joined in 1239. The pope excommunicated Frederick for his delay before going on the Crusade, which resulted in him not having a large army to command. He decided to negotiate with the Sultan rather than fight him and diplomatically won a ten-year truce and Christian control of Jerusalem, Bethlehem, and Nazareth.

7. (1249–52) St. Louis IX of France led the seventh Crusade after Jerusalem was annexed by the Sultan of Egypt. Frederick was captured, was held for ransom, and then released.

8. (1270) St. Louis of France led the troops again and died in Tunisia from an illness and not in battle. This last crusade with its defeat in Tunis signaled the end of the Crusades. By this time, petty fighting, national rivalry, political intrigue, and troubles at home dissuaded Christian monarchs to continue and convinced the pope to no longer invoke them.

The infamous Children's Crusade occurred in 1212. On their own, thousands of children wanted to free the Holy Land, but ruthless and evil men took advantage of them and sold many into slavery to some *Moors* (Muslims that inhabited Spain). Many of the children died of hunger and exhaustion on the way.

Deemed a total failure, the Crusades didn't free the Holy Land from Islamic rule, and injustice, debauchery, greed, envy, animosity, petty infighting, and prejudice erupted on both sides during these holy wars. For example, Latin Christians were invited by their Eastern brethren to free the Holy Land, and yet Crusaders attacked Byzantine territory, seizing it for themselves. Christian kings and princes often fought on the way to a crusade. Jealousy and envy prevented them from working together successfully. In addition, brutality and the absence of mercy — or even human decency — crossed over religious boundaries. Christians and Muslims alike slaughtered helpless, innocent women and children. Both sides acted atrociously. It wasn't that the religions of Christianity and Islam were at war; rather, some members of those religions abused faith as a catalyst for territorial, economic, and political purposes on both sides.

That said, had the Crusades not occurred, many historians believe that the Islamic military forces would've taken the opportunity to prepare for a massive assault on Europe, and no unified leadership or defense would have prevented it. The Crusades did contain the expansion. They also reopened trade routes to the Far East. (The trade routes had been closed for several centuries due to the strength and spread of Islam in Arabia and the Middle East.)

To Catholics, the Crusades are a poignant reminder that the ends never justify the means. The Catholic belief is that no matter how lofty the goal or noble the purpose, only moral means can be used. Otherwise, it's an immoral enterprise. In other words, although the goal of defending and freeing the oppressed was good and noble, the Crusades should've stopped when many of the Europeans started making a profit on it and when Christians and Muslims alike resorted to barbaric tactics.

The Golden Age

During the late Middle Ages, the Catholic Church flourished — especially under Pope Innocent III. The Church was at its zenith both spiritually *and* politically. In fact, never again would these two spheres be united so strongly in the Church.

Monastery men on the move

Two new orders developed at this time — the Dominicans and Franciscans. They were known as *mendicant* orders, because they didn't own any property and relied on alms. They weren't cloistered like the Benedictines or Trappists. Rather, they became itinerant preachers, going from town to town preaching the Gospel. So instead of people going to the monastery for religion, the monastery now came to them. These orders became very successful. Some tidbits about their founders follow:

- **St. Dominic,** founder of the Dominicans, was born in Spain in 1170. He was devoted to the task of preaching. A few zealous priests joined him, and they decided to live a common life. From this little group grew an order whose main purpose was preaching the Gospel. They became known as the Order of Preachers (OP) or more commonly as the Dominicans. By going from town to town, they were able to combat ignorance that led to *heresy* (false teachings in matters of faith and morals). They were so successful that they became the most brilliant professors at the University of Paris. St. Dominic also founded a female branch of Dominican Nuns.

✔ **St. Francis of Assisi,** founder of the Franciscans, was born in Italy in 1182. St. Francis said he received a calling from the Lord to rebuild his Church. And so he did with the establishment of the Order of Friars Minor (OFM) or more commonly referred to as the Franciscans. With St. Clare, he helped establish the female counterpart known as the Poor Clares. Like the Dominicans, the Franciscans went from town to town preaching, teaching, and celebrating the sacraments. Later, this order established universities and went to the New World to preach the Gospel. (See Chapter 18 for more on Saints Dominic and Francis.)

Gothic architecture, grand art, and great literature

The building of the great cathedrals occurred during this period in history. The architecture was gothic, and the new style allowed for high vaulted ceilings and large stained glass windows.

Books were rare during this time, because the printing press hadn't been invented yet. Manuscripts were penned by hand and were very expensive, so the general public was predominantly illiterate. Stained glass windows became a picture-bible for the peasants.

Every important city wanted a bigger cathedral than the others. Building these houses of God took centuries and kept people employed when a war or insurrection wasn't taking place. Today, travelers to France and Germany can still visit these awesome testimonies of faith.

This period in history also saw a rise of towns, guilds, and societies. (Guilds often sponsored a chapel, window, or side altar in a cathedral, by the way.) Great artists also flourished during this period. Giotto di Bondone (1266?–1337) painted with perspective and drew realistic and lifelike scenes of men, women, and nature.

This was also a time of great literature: Dante Alighieri of Florence (1265–1321) wrote the greatest of all Christian poems, the *Divine Comedy,* which is a story of an imaginary journey through hell, purgatory, and heaven; Geoffrey Chaucer of England (1343–1400) wrote the *Canterbury Tales,* which are vignettes of pilgrims on their way to a shrine.

Intellectual pursuit

Universities developed in the Middle Ages. First, they were attached to the cathedrals and staffed for the education of clergy. Later, they branched out into the secular sciences. Bologna developed a school of law; Paris, philosophy, rhetoric, and theology; and Salerno, a school of medicine. Oxford, Cambridge, St. Andrews, Glasgow, Prague, and Dublin universities all began at this time, too.

With great schools came great teachers, such as Peter Lombard, St. Albert the Great, Hugh of Saint Victor, Alexander of Hales, and John Duns Scotus — just to name a few. The two most notable and influential intellects and scholars were St. Thomas Aquinas and St. Bonaventure. The former was a member of the Dominican order (the Order of Preachers), and the latter was a Franciscan (the Order of Friars Minor).

St. Thomas Aquinas

St. Thomas Aquinas (1225–1274) was the son of a wealthy count and countess. His brothers had physical strength and looks, which made them eligible bachelors to marry nobility and live the life of a knight. Thomas was no Arnold Schwarzeneger, but he could've run circles around Einstein, Newton, or Stephen Hawking. His father figured that if Junior couldn't be a soldier or a knight or marry into greater wealth and status, then he could at least climb the ecclesiastical ladder. Thomas wanted to study, teach, and preach the Catholic faith, but he had no ambition for hierarchical advancement whatsoever. (See Chapters 3 and 18 for more on St. Thomas.)

Until St. Thomas Aquinas came around, the greatest theologian was St. Augustine (A.D. 354–430), who relied heavily on Plato for his philosophical foundation. But Thomas opted for the newly rediscovered works of Aristotle, who deviated slightly from Plato:

- **Plato** saw man as a soul imprisoned in a body and therefore did not completely trust what your five senses tell you. (He used the example of optical illusion for deception by the eye.)

- **Aristotle,** on the other hand, saw man as an essential union of body and soul, and therefore, the senses were very important in his philosophy as a source of knowledge. For him, it wasn't the senses that deceived but your judgment as to what they tell you.

Aristotle's inter-connection between body and soul, the material world and the spiritual world, made things click for Thomas. This is why the seven sacraments made perfect sense to him, because each one has an external component directed to one or more of the five senses. The tangible external signs, such as water, oil, bread and wine, and so on, symbolize the unseen invisible grace. Thomas employed this methodology in his great works, the *Summa Contra Gentiles* and the *Summa Theologica,* where he explained the doctrines of the Catholic faith.

St. Bonaventure

A colleague and contemporary of St. Thomas Aquinas, St. Bonaventure (1221–1274) belonged to the Franciscan order. An intellectual genius, St. Bonaventure wrote a commentary on the *Sentences of Peter Lombard,* which basically explained the principal doctrines of the Catholic faith. Whereas Thomas relied on Aristotle, Bonaventure used Augustine and Plato — without ever trashing or repudiating Aristotle. He also spent much time in the internal workings of the Franciscan order after being elected Minister General.

The downward spiral

If the 13th century was a golden one for the Church, the 14th and 15th centuries were tarnished ones.

The unstable and dangerous climate of Rome

Whereas Pope Innocent III (1198–1216) epitomized the zenith of papal power and influence, Pope Boniface VIII (1294–1303) personified one of the most complicated, mysterious, and at times contradictory pontificates of the Church.

King Philip IV of France and Boniface became bitter enemies early on. It worsened over time, and in 1303, Philip sent mercenaries to arrest and bully Boniface into resigning. He was beaten and humiliated at Anagni but refused to quit. The local citizens arose to his defense and rescued him. He intended to excommunicate Philip but died before it could be enacted.

After his death, Pope Benedict XI was elected but proved too weak and conciliatory to tangle with Philip. His nine-month reign evenly split the College of Cardinals between those who hated the French for what Philip did to Boniface and French sympathizers who wanted to reconcile and move on. (For more on the College of Cardinals, see Chapter 2.)

Pope Clement V (1305–1314) followed Benedict as pope. The papal coronation took place in Lyons, and Clement never set foot in Rome. Four years into his pontificate, Clement moved to his French palace at Avignon, allegedly to escape the dangerous mobs in Rome, because he was French and easily influenced by the King Philip of France who offered to protect him.

After Pope Clement arrived in Avignon, the popes remained there for 70 years — the same amount of time that the Jews were held captive in Babylon; hence the term *Babylonian Captivity of the Popes.*

Philip ensured his prestige by pressuring Clement to appoint more French cardinals than Italian ones. This way, when he died, the majority (two-thirds) would elect another Frenchman, which they did again and again.

Seventy years passed with seven popes in Avignon, while the people in Rome endured no resident bishop. Enough was enough said St. Catherine of Siena, (1347–1380) who made her way to France and in an audience with Pope Gregory XI (1370–1378) pleaded with him to return to Rome where the pope as bishop of Rome belongs. He listened and moved the papacy back to the Eternal City.

Two popes at the same time means double trouble

Pope Gregory XI died in 1378, and the conclave (see Chapter 2) that met to choose his successor was ready to pick another Frenchman so that he could move back to France. But Italian mobs in Rome had other ideas. The Italians became so animated about the non-Italian pope thing that they pried the roof off the conclave at the Vatican and shouted at the cardinals, many of whom were French, "Give us a Roman pope, or at any rate, an Italian." The conclave quickly elected the oldest, most feeble Italian cardinal — 60-year-old Urban VI. The plan was to choose someone not expected to last too long (a guy with one foot in the grave, so to speak), return to France, and then, after the old pope died, have another conclave but this time in France. But as soon as he was elected, Urban perked up and showed his real mettle. After he was made pope, his health improved, and he began the necessary reforms of the hierarchy to curb abuse and corruption.

You can imagine how the French felt when it was made obvious that the pope would not return to France and that he intended to make reforms. Instead of going back to France, the French cardinals fled to Fondi in the Kingdom of Naples to decide their next move. They realized Urban would be around for a while *and* would also clean house. The French cardinals cried foul and said that the election of Urban VI was invalid. They claimed they were under pressure and duress to elect an Italian or suffer the angry mob. So with King Philip's blessing, five months after the election of Urban VI in Rome, the *Avignon conclave* (all the French cardinals) met in 1378 at the Cathedral of Fondi and elected the *antipope* (the term used for an invalidly elected pope) Clement VII in Naples. Born in Geneva, he was neither French nor Italian (so he seemed like a good compromise) but spent most of his priesthood in France anyway. Eight months later he fled to Avignon.

At that point, a full-blown schism (division in the church) existed. Some Catholics obeyed and followed the Roman Pope Urban, and other Catholics followed the Avignon Pope Clement instead. When Urban died in 1389, the cardinals elected Boniface XI to succeed him. Five years later, Clement died, and the schism could've ended, but the French cardinals elected another antipope — Benedict XIII. So two men still claimed to be pope at the same time.

Better make that three

Having two men claiming to be pope simultaneously got so frustrating that scholars and secular rulers got in on the act and called for a General Council of the Church. The problem was that only a pope could call a council and only a pope could approve or reject its decrees. And neither the Avignon Pope Benedict nor the Roman Pope Boniface wanted to resign or step down.

In 1409, an illicit Council did meet in Pisa with neither pope present and without either's sanction. The cardinals who attended deposed both popes and elected a third one, Alexander V. Talk about going from the frying pan into the fire. Suddenly, three different popes claimed the throne of St. Peter: The Roman pope, the Avignon pope, and the Pisan pope. Each one denounced the other, and most of the faithful were genuinely confused as to who the real pope was.

The Pisan Pope Alexander V only survived 11 months, and his successor was John XXIII. (Because he's not recognized as a legitimate pope, when Angelo Roncalli was elected pope in 1958, he took the name and number John XXIII.)

A solution to the too-many-popes issue

The Holy Roman Emperor Sigismund demanded a General Council at Constance. The 16th Council of the Church met from 1414–1418. All cardinals and bishops had to attend, and 18,000 clerics took part as well. The agenda included finding a solution to the Great Schism, and one was found. Martin V was chosen to be the one and only pope, and the others were asked to resign or else. The Council also denounced and condemned the writings of John Wyclif (English) and Jan Hus (Bohemian) as heretical. Hus was turned over to secular authorities and burned at the stake in 1415. Wyclif had died in 1384.

Roman Pope Gregory XII, considered the true pope, voluntarily resigned after formally approving of the Council of Constance. (Without papal approval, this council would've become as lame as the Council of Pisa.) But Avignon's Benedict XIII refused to resign and was deposed publicly. Pisan's John XXIII tried to escape, but he was caught and deposed. Martin V (1417–1431) was then the only claimant and only recognized pope — the Bishop of Rome and Supreme Roman Pontiff.

The Church survived, but the wounds and scars ran deep and came back to haunt it later. The crisis of the Great Schism greatly weakened the political power of the papacy and sowed the seeds for anti-papal arguments during the Reformation.

The Black Death

As if the Babylonian Captivity (Avignon papacy) and the Great Schism (three popes at once) weren't enough, another fly in the ointment was the Black Death — the bubonic plague — killing 25 million people in five years. That's more than one-third of all Europe.

The bubonic plague was called the Black Death because of red spots on the body that eventually turned black as the flesh rotted. Hey, inquiring minds want to know. An outbreak of the plague erupted in China in the 1330s. In October 1347, several Italian merchant ships docked in Sicily, unknowingly infected with the plague.

The Black Death lasted from 1347 to 1352. The largest percentage of casualties came from the lower clergy, because parish priests were needed to give the Sacrament of the Anointing of the Sick (then known as Extreme Unction), and they obviously got infected. In fact, so many priests died from the plague that an extreme vocations crisis arose. In desperation, many bishops and religious superiors accepted unworthy, incompetent, or inadequately trained candidates for Holy Orders. This led to the introduction of many ignorant, superstitious, unstable, untrustworthy clerics running around Europe.

In the aftermath of the plague, amid immense devastation in Europe, abuses proliferated in the Church due to the poorly trained, immoral, and unreliable clergy filling in for all the good and holy ones who died from the plague. And although the standards for becoming a priest dropped in reaction to the enormous loss of clergy from the Black Death, the upper clergy (bishops, cardinals, and popes) fared no better. Their plague wasn't from a flea hiding on a rat but from their own hearts. Nepotism, greed, lust, avarice, envy, sloth — you name it, they did it. Not all the hierarchy, of course — not even the majority. But even one case was too many.

A case in point: The Borgia and Medici families vied for the papacy and used any method possible to get a relative made pope. Alexander VI (1492–1503) was a Borgia, and he sired several illegitimate children. His decadence was without rival. Between him, Pope Innocent VIII (1484–1492), and Pope Leo X (1513–1521), who was a member of the Medici family, the papacy reached its all time low. (See Chapter 2 for more on some notorious popes.)

The seeds were being sown for reform.

The Reformation to the Modern Era (1517–Today)

This section looks at the history of the Catholic Church from the time of the Reformation through the modern era — the 16th to 20th centuries.

The growing need for reform

During the Middle Ages, Greek philosophy (as epitomized by Plato and Aristotle) was used to help develop a Christian one (as seen in Augustine, Aquinas, and Bonaventure) in its own right. That would in turn become the partner with sacred theology. The Latin language was obviously known and used but mostly in religious and legal context. The liberal arts and religious sciences were the main staples of university education, and Christendom was the term given to a unified Christian culture, religion and empire that predominated Medieval Western and Central Europe.

At the end of the 15th century, however, people witnessed the gradual disintegration of that unity. They saw the appearance of modern nations and languages, the discovery of the New World by Columbus in 1492 and a revival of classical art, architecture, and literature. Greek and Roman classics from Homer, Sophocles, Virgil, Ovid, Horace, and Cicero eclipsed the former staples of Plato and Aristotle. Humanism arose as a system of thought that bridged the two worlds of heavenly faith and earthly wisdom; between the sacred and the secular. At least that was its original intent. This classical resurgence would become the impetus of what would be called the Renaissance.

The Renaissance was born in Florence, which gave the world poets Dante Alighieri and Francesco Petrarch, artists Michelangelo Buonarroti and Leonardo da Vinci, and thinkers Vittorino da Feltre and Giovanni Boccaccio. And that city is also associated with such famous names as Medici, Machiavelli, and Borgia. From Italy, the ideals of the Renaissance flowed, crossing the Alps into France, Germany, and finally, England.

The Church encouraged the Renaissance and became a great patron of the sciences, literature, and art. However, a great deal of *secularism* (worldliness) crept in, and people lost much of their respect for their spiritual leaders. Many abuses in the Church weren't dealt with in a timely manner. Ignorant clergy and a greedy episcopacy eventually gave rise to *reformers,* people determined to bring about reform. Unfortunately, some of it wasn't really reform but revolt, which led to division.

St. Francis of Assisi was a reformer in his time — the Middle Ages. The key difference between him and Martin Luther is that Francis reformed *within* the Church structure and Luther, as well as others such as Calvin, Zwingli, and Hus, sought to reform *outside* the Church structure, which eventually led to a division within and break from the Catholic Church. On the opposite side of the fence, St. Vincent Ferrer, St. John of the Cross, St. Teresa of Avila, St. Bernadine of Siena, and St. John Capistran chose the path of reform inside that same Church.

Corruption in the Church

Pope Julius II (1503–13) decided to rebuild St. Peter's Basilica, which was in desperate need of repair. He communicated to the faithful that anyone who went to confession and Holy Communion and then donated according to their means (called almsgiving) toward the restoration of the historic Church could receive a plenary indulgence if all the conditions were met. A *plenary indulgence* is a total remission of the temporal punishment due to sins already forgiven in confession. Simply put, it's an application of God's divine mercy to remove the effects of past sin. An indulgence isn't forgiveness itself nor is it absolution; it presupposes both before it can happen. Sin can have two consequences, *eternal* punishment (hell) and *temporal* punishment (purgatory). Unrepentant and unforgiven mortal sins result in eternal punishment. Forgiven sins are free from eternal punishment, but they retain a temporal punishment. It's God's mercy that forgives sin, but it's God's justice that rewards good and punishes evil.

Think of it this way. If a surgeon operates on you to remove a malignant tumor, which could kill you, she'll make an incision on your body. After removing the deadly tumor, she stitches you up. You're healed of the life-threatening cancer but the wound of the incision still needs to heal and in time the stitches must be removed. Sin is like a spiritual disease, and mortal sin is like a malignant tumor, which must be removed as soon as possible. Indulgences are merely like removing the stitches over an already healed wound.

These are the conditions for obtaining the plenary indulgence:

- ✔ Perform the prescribed prayers or works of charity.

- ✔ Go to Confession and Holy Communion seven days before or after.

- ✔ Be free from all attachment to sin, even venial.

That last condition is the punch line: No one can *buy* an indulgence. An evil person who had just, say, killed someone, robbed a bank, or committed adultery couldn't obtain an indulgence to escape Divine Justice. Instead, to gain the indulgence, the person had to be in the state of grace — not conscious of any mortal sins — and *free of all attachment to sin*, even venial ones. By attachment, we mean any fond memories of past but forgiven sins. So no amount of money would automatically guarantee someone an indulgence. If someone who had sorrow for their sins, confessed them, and had been absolved and then performed a charitable work, such as giving alms or some other act of mercy, then they could be eligible for an indulgence.

The problem was that a few avaricious and greedy bishops and priests, along with some like-minded princes, literally sold indulgences, which was a violation of canon law then and now and is also a mortal sin called *simony*. Telling people, "If you donate some silver pieces for this project, you can use the indulgence to get grandma out of purgatory," is a mortal sin. Indulgences don't work that way, but some unscrupulous people saw an opportunity to exploit others, and they did. Pope Julius' successor, Leo X (son of Lorenzo de Medici), was just such an unscrupulous man. And in Germany, this practice was encouraged, and preachers went from town to town to encourage the rebuilding of St. Peter's.

In addition, due to ignorant clergy (a result of the priest shortage after the Plague), Pope Julius II's original message became distorted, and it began to look like the Church was indeed selling spiritual favors for money.

The rise of the middle class

Before the Reformation, the last three significant events of the Middle Ages were

- ✔ **The Black Death** killed 25 million people (two-thirds of Europe) and wiped out a good portion of the clergy. This led to the ordination of many ill-prepared, badly trained, and incompetent men who infected the faithful with superstition and bad theology and left the Church ill equipped with proper personnel.

- ✔ **The Babylonian Captivity** (also known as the *Avignon papacy*) took the pope out of Rome for 70 years and left the Church unshepherded and discouraged.

- ✔ **The Great Schism** left the Church confused and bewildered, because three men claimed to be pope at the same time.

Those factors were combined with the fact that, economically, Europe was moving away from a feudal system and entering a commercial mercantile system. This change created a middle class that hadn't existed before.

Before the creation of the middle class, a poor peasant class contrasted a rich aristocracy. But with the addition of a middle class, the economic breakdown went thus:

- ✔ The Church and the nobility owned the land.

- ✔ The poor had nothing but worked the land for hire.

- ✔ The middle class had money but no land.

To obtain land, the middle class would have to get it from properties owned by the Church or by the nobility, which was an unlikely choice because the nobility had armies. A line of thinking developed that if the Church disappeared — or at least the Church's possession of land — then the new middle class could obtain property for the first time.

Now add in the politics of the time: The English, French, Spanish, Germans, and so on, all had their own kings and queens, princes and counts, barons, dukes and earls, but they were all subservient to the emperor. But if the emperor was eliminated, the local nobility could seize control and not have someone higher to answer to. So the nobles favored a break from the emperor.

But the emperor had troops, so how could they legally separate from him? Well, what if the German princes severed their ties with the emperor who was aligned with the pope? By dissolving their connection with the pope, these princes could simultaneously cut their bond with the emperor. If another religion other than that of the pope's came about, then the bonds of authority would loosen. A split from the Church of Rome was most opportune for some German princes who wanted to separate from the emperor. Likewise, a few bishops who would never become cardinals or popes saw a chance to seize the day and be their own authority by also severing ties with the Holy See. So they were in favor.

The economic and political forces in favor of a revolution eclipsed any chance of an internal reform as had happened in the past. Now the forces were moving toward revolt instead — from papal and imperial authority.

When the peasants saw their bishops opposing papal authority and the nobility revolting against imperial power, they saw their chance to rebel against the aristocracy. However, they had no money and no army, so the short-lived Peasants' Revolt (1525) ended in disaster and death.

The reformers

The corruption of some of the clergy and hierarchy was inexcusable, which aroused the righteous anger of the reformers. What follows is the Catholic perspective on the Reformers and their ideas and actions.

Martin Luther

Martin Luther (1483–1546), an Augustinian priest, challenged John Tetzel, another Catholic priest, for selling indulgences.

On October 31, 1517, Luther nailed his 95 Theses to the door of a Wittenberg church, a kind of university bulletin board. This was no revolutionary act, however, because all announcements and news items — be they public debates or requests for bake sale items — were tacked to the door of the church where people could look at them every day when they entered.

Although Luther had many valid points and good intentions, some other factors also contributed to his predicament on the eve of the Reformation:

- ✔ His fear of thunder and lightning compelled him to make a promise to the Virgin Mary during a storm one day: If she helped him survive the storm, he'd in turn become a monk. He kept his word, but promises like that are the worst reasons to enter religious life.

- ✔ He was always concerned about the salvation of his soul. Discouraged with himself and his inability to lead the kind of life required of a monk, he came to the conclusion that it's impossible for anyone to be good. And that conclusion led to his famous words "Only by faith alone can man be saved. Good works are useless." And those famous words became the doctrine that he taught at the University of Wittenberg.

St. Augustine (354–430), whose religious order Luther joined, was a foe of Pelagius, a heretic who claimed that humans could earn their way to heaven and that humans were in no need of God's assistance. This heresy was condemned, and the Church solemnly taught that every good work depended on divine grace; alone, humans could do nothing but sin, but with grace, they could do great things. *Pelagianism,* on the other hand, taught that humans could save themselves. Augustine rightly condemned Pelagius' idea that good works alone, without faith, could make a person holy. Luther, an Augustinian, went to the other end of the spectrum, however, saying that faith alone without works was all a person needed.

The Bible only uses the phrase *faith alone* once, "Man is justified by works and not by faith alone." (James 2:24) It doesn't say that works alone save humankind, but St. James says, "Faith by itself, if it has no works, is dead." (James 2:17) Ironically, St. Paul says, "For we hold that a man is justified by faith apart from works of the law." (Romans 3:28) He doesn't use the phrase *faith alone.* Only James does. Catholicism teaches that it's by grace alone that we are saved and that *both faith and works* are necessary for salvation.

Going back to the plenary indulgence controversy, the Church believes it wasn't the concept or the practice but the abuse that needed to be corrected. The Church believes that Luther was justified in his denunciation of the abuse but considers his subsequent reaction to indulgences in general went too far and in a sense threw the baby out with the bath water, so to speak.

The Church believes that Luther had zeal for the faith but that he erroneously associated *infallibility,* freedom from error, with *impeccability,* freedom from sin. Immoral priests, bishops, or even popes are inexcusable. No doubt about it. Yet their personal sins don't affect the truthfulness of their teaching or the validity of their sacraments. Think of it this way: If Jack the Ripper told you that 2 + 2 = 4, it's still a true statement no matter how evil or sinful he may be. Likewise, sadly, some immoral popes and bishops have existed, but their personal sanctity or lack thereof has nothing to do with the truth they teach. Similarly, it's Catholic teaching that the validity of the sacraments is not contingent on the moral state of the sacred minister (deacon, priest, or bishop), because the people of God have a right to valid sacraments for their own well being. This is called *ex opere operato* in Latin, which translates to *from the work performed,* and simply means that the sacraments give grace regardless of the spiritual state of the priest celebrating them.

Anyway, Gutenberg's invention of the moveable type printing press (his first book was the Latin Vulgate Bible in 1455) revolutionized religious and political debate. With mass printings, pamphlets could now be disseminated to more people quickly and thus influence public opinion greatly. Martin Luther was keenly adept at using this technological innovation, which greatly helped to spread his Reformation ideas across Europe. It's incorrect, however, to infer that the Catholic Church was against the printing of the Bible in the native (vernacular) tongue or in large quantities for public use. On the contrary, it was the pope who asked St. Jerome to translate the Hebrew, Greek, and Aramaic manuscripts of Sacred Scripture into the common language of the day (Latin) and for the first time ever combine all the books of the Bible into one large volume. This made the use and spread of the Word of God much easier. Venerable Bede was the first to translate the Latin Bible into English at the end of the 7th century, and St. Cyril translated the Latin into Old Slovanic in the 9th century, proving that there was no Church prohibition against Bibles in the native language. Yes, most Bibles were chained in the churches, but not to keep them *from* the people but to keep them *for* the people, just like banks chain pens and the phone company chains the directory in their booths.

Luther found an ally in Elector Frederick who poised himself for conflict and battle with the Emperor (first Maximilian then Charles V). For Frederick, Luther and the Reformation was a catalyst to separate from the empire and begin an autonomous German kingdom. For Luther, Frederick was safe passage and a guarantee that he could dissent from papal teaching and authority. Luther's followers and subsequent Reformers became known as Protestants, because they were *protesting* against the Church of Rome. After the formal split from Catholicism, adherents of Luther's theology would be known as Lutherans.

Henry VIII

At first, Henry VIII, King of England, opposed Luther and the Protestant Reformation, but when his wife, Catherine of Aragon, couldn't give him a male heir, he wanted an annulment, so he could marry Anne Boleyn. (Catherine did, however, give him a daughter, Mary I, who would later be Queen after Edward VI succeeded Henry.)

The pope refused to grant the annulment, however, no matter how much money or how many threats were sent. So in 1533, Henry declared himself Supreme Head of the Church in England and dissolved the allegiance that the clergy in England had to Rome. He broke from Rome, starting the Anglican Church, and divorced Catherine to marry Anne. But Anne couldn't give him a son either. However, she did give him a daughter, Elizabeth I, the half-sister of Mary. The king had her executed. The English hierarchy and aristocracy went along with Henry's split from Rome except for a few loyal Catholics, such as St. John Fisher, the Bishop of Rochester, and St. Thomas Moore, the Chancellor of England. The movie *A Man For All Seasons* (1966; Columbia Pictures), based on the play by Robert Bolt, depicts the life and martyrdom of St. Thomas More, who sacrificed his life rather than compromise his Catholic faith and accept Henry as the Supreme Head of the Church in England.

Henry VIII went through a total of six wives and fathered one sickly son, Edward VI, and two daughters, Mary and Elizabeth. Edward finally took his father's throne, but his reign was short due to his bad health. Mary Tudor, the daughter of Henry VIII and his first wife Catherine, a staunch Catholic, took the throne after Henry. Her Catholicism and marriage to Spanish royalty made her unpopular with the nobility. After Henry broke from Rome, he seized all the lands owned by the Church, dissolved the monasteries, and sold their property or gave it away to his court and other aristocrats. It's no wonder that the nobility didn't want a restoration of Catholicism under Queen Mary.

Mary's half-sister, Elizabeth, followed Mary to the throne, re-impressing her dominion with the Anglican faith during her long reign from 1558 to 1603.

John Calvin

John Calvin, an austere Catholic layman of Switzerland, followed the ideals of Luther and established a new Calvinist church in Geneva in 1541. Calvinism frowned on most forms of entertainment and pleasure, because they were presumed sinful. Being successful in business and having good health were signs of being one of the Elect or Predestined. Calvin believed in an absolute *predestination,* that is, that a soul was damned for eternity in hell or was saved for heaven solely by an act of God's will. His theology could be expressed in the acronym TULIP:

- ✔ **T**otal depravity: Man can't save himself. Man isn't intrinsically evil but he has no power to do good.

- ✔ **U**nconditional election: God chooses to save some people independently and without regarding human merit.

- ✔ **L**imited atonement: Christ's sacrifice on the cross is for the purpose of saving the elect.

- ✔ **I**rresistible grace: When God chooses to save someone, they infallibly are saved.

- ✔ **P**erseverance of the saints: Those people God chooses can't lose their salvation.

These ideas disseminated into parts of France, where followers were called *Huguenots.* Scotland also took a form of Calvin's new religion, with the aide of John Knox, which developed into the Presbyterian Church.

The good and bad effects

Martin Luther taught that Scripture alone *(sola scriptura)* and faith alone *(sola fide)* were the cornerstones of Christian religion and that the Church wasn't a necessary institution for the believer's salvation. This teaching had a domino effect, with others dissenting from Catholic doctrine and starting their own religions.

But Luther and the Protestant Reformation did compel the Catholic Church to spell out its teachings on grace, salvation, and the sacraments more clearly. It also prompted internal reforms, such as the establishment of seminaries to give unified and thorough priestly training. Rather than just being put on the defensive, the Reformation instigated an internal re-evaluation, not of doctrine or worship, but a serious commitment to rid the Church of abuse and to delineate exactly and precisely what differentiated Catholic Christianity from Protestant Christianity.

The Catholic Church's response: The Counter Reformation

In 1545, the Church called the general Council of Trent, which lasted more than 18 years due to wars and other interruptions, such as the death of a pope. During this age, known as the Counter Reformation, men and women who were considered outstanding in their holiness combated the attacks. The following people, for example, were a fruit of the Counter Reformation, and they did more than just respond to the Protestant Reformation. They also brought authentic renewal into the Catholic Church:

- ✔ **St. Charles Borromeo** reformed the clergy with the institution of seminaries and rectories.

- ✔ **St. Ignatius of Loyola** created a spiritual army to win back souls to Christ and to the Catholic faith. His religious order is the Society of Jesus (abbreviated S.J.), but they're more commonly known as *Jesuits*.

- ✔ **St. Teresa of Avila** and **St. John of the Cross** reformed religious life, going back to the original spirit of their founders.

- ✔ **St. Philip Neri** gave the diocesan clergy a new sense of personal piety and priestly spirituality.

- ✔ **Pope St. Pius V** reformed the clergy by stopping abuses; unified the Sacred Liturgy (the same style of celebration of the Mass and sacraments everywhere) for the entire Western Church and the reformed *liturgical calendar* — the Church year.

Using the printing press now to its own advantage, the Church was able to counterattack its opponents, mass-producing its catechisms, canon law, the Catholic Bible, and the lives of the saints so that many new religious communities could evangelize through their schools and parishes. Parts of Germany, Switzerland, and France that had become Protestant then returned back to the Catholic religion.

The Catholic monarchs of Spain, Ferdinand and Isabella, colonized the New World, and religious orders, such as the Franciscans, Dominicans and Jesuits, went to that vast new area, evangelizing native peoples and establishing churches, missions, and schools.

The Society of Jesus (the Jesuits) gave rise to some of the best colleges and universities in the world. A Jesuit priest often received a doctoral degree in a secular science, such as math, chemistry, biology, or law, along with his religious background of philosophy and theology. Jesuits were considered the best answer to the Reformation by using positive means to show the advantages, logical rationale, beauty, and history of Catholicism without having to resort to bitter or personal attacks against their Protestant counterparts. Jesuit missionaries preached and taught where no European had gone before: Japan, China, India, and the New World.

The Counter Reformation also gave rise to a new style of art and architecture, known as Baroque. And whereas the new Protestant faith emphasized the written Word of Scripture, Catholicism continued its ancient tradition of appealing to the symbolism used by the sacraments. Sacraments were tangible signs to the physical body (via the human senses) of the invisible work and presence of divine grace.

As it progressed, Protestant worship became more simple, less mystical, and exclusively biblical, with as little ritual as possible. The more ritual present, the greater the danger of *popery* (Catholicism) creeping in, and that isn't the stuff that you burn in a dish to make the house smell nice. *Popery* meant anything having to do with the pope and Catholicism. So formal rituals, incense and holy water, Latin prayers, and elaborate vestments became identifiable with Catholicism and so-called popery. Where Catholicism tried to unite the physical and spiritual realms of the body and soul through the use of sacraments and ritual, Protestantism sought a streamlined method of focus on the Sacred Scripture alone as the compass of faith.

The Age of Reason

The latter half of the 16th century through the middle of the 18th century brought even more changes to the world's way of thinking — and to the Catholic Church.

Science and religion

People often remark that Galileo (1564–1642) was ahead of his time and that the Catholic Church held back science for centuries. Actually, quite the opposite is true.

First of all, modern science and the scientific method of experimentation and observation came from Catholic monks, such as St. Albert the Great and Gregor Mendel. Albert, for example, bridged the gap between alchemy and chemistry. Otherwise, science wouldn't have been taught in the medieval universities, but it was. It may have been primitive, but it was still science.

And Galileo Galilei (1564–1642) wasn't the first person to propose a *heliocentric solar system:* The sun is the center of the solar system, and the earth is but another planet in orbit around the sun. The Polish monk and astronomer Nicolaus Copernicus (1473–1543) disproved the erroneous *Ptolemeic system:* The earth is the center, and the sun and other planets revolve in orbit around it.

Galileo wasn't arrested, excommunicated, or mistreated for his scientific theory. He *was* ridiculed, however, because back then, his theories lacked overwhelming and conclusive evidence. Only later, advances in astronomy and telescopes would bring the needed proof.

To say that Galileo was imprisoned to keep him quiet on his heliocentric ideas is false. He was under house arrest (comfortable, mind you) only because he crossed the line over science into religion by boldly asserting that the Bible was in error when it said that the sun rose and set. He maintained that the sun was stationary and that it was the earth that moved. His science was correct, but the Church believes his biblical theology was wrong. Those figures of speech — *the sun sets* and *the sun rises* or even just *sunrise* and *sunset* — are still used today in the 21st century even though everyone believes in a heliocentric, not a geocentric, universe. The Bible contains many types of literature, genres, and forms of speech, such as analogy, metaphor, and simile. Had Galileo stuck to science, he would've been okay, but he chose to publicly attack what the Church believes is the inerrancy of Sacred Scripture. That's what got him into hot water.

Faith and reason

During the middle of the 18th century, lukewarm attitudes became evident in the French Church. Religious practices and morals were in decline. Then came the view that the Church wasn't necessary and that the human mind didn't need any guidance from divine grace. Reason alone was sufficient, and faith was nonsensical. This way of thinking was called *rationalism.*

Philosophy and empirical science sought truths that the human mind could attain. Theology wasn't treated as a science but as a superstition. The rationalists saw religion as a myth. And they had no respect for divine revelation. The Church, however, taught that revelation was the divine communication of truths that human minds could never achieve — or at least not everyone in the same way. And only faith could embrace revelation.

Yet the Church believed that faith and reason could coexist — because the Church believed that God created both. Catholic theologians didn't see philosophers or scientists as the enemy. Theologians believed that theological truths known by revelation and accepted on faith didn't contradict philosophical truths known by reason or scientific truths known by observation and experimentation. Instead, they saw it all as looking at the same universe from different perspectives.

The rationalists were confident in the world, human nature, and its power. Voltaire was the famous philosopher who incorporated rationalist ideas. Through the development of his philosophy, the Enlightenment movement became an anti-Christian war machine. Jean-Baptiste Rousseau, another philosopher of the period, claimed that the world could be saved through education instead of Jesus Christ.

The Age of Revolution

The 18th century witnessed the dawn of the Industrial Revolution in England. The American and French Revolutions also occurred during this time. Many new ideas and concepts were being introduced into philosophy, religion, and society, and these ideals were embodied in a movement called the Enlightenment. The age of revolution had begun.

The French Revolution's effect on the Church

Freemasons, rationalists, and philosophers supported the extremes of the Enlightenment, laying the cornerstone for the French Revolution. In addition, many of the French aristocracy and some corrupt monarchs had oppressed the common people for too long. Unfortunately, the Church in France had become too closely bound with the state. (Formerly called the Eldest Daughter of the Church because of the alliance between the Franks and Catholicism in the fifth century.) A pronounced division existed between the upper clergy, bishops and cardinals, and the lower clergy, priests.

In 1789, the atmosphere began to change in France. Church land was taken over by the government with the understanding that the state would take care of the clergy. The following year, all monasteries and convents were suppressed. The Civil Constitution of the Clergy was enacted and one-third of the dioceses were done away with.

In 1793, the Reign of Terror began, resulting in the execution of many, often innocent, people during the French Revolution. King Louis XVI was deposed and put to death. Hatred for the Church reached the point of insanity. Poulenc's *Dialogues of the Carmelites* (1957), a famous opera, highlights the ill effects of the French Revolution. Based on a true story, the opera portrays cloistered Carmelite nuns who refused to take the new oath and submit to the laws of suppression. It finally led them to the guillotine. This was all too common in France during that time. The Cathedral of Notre Dame in Paris, a bastion of French Catholicism, was reduced to a barracks for animals, and a statue of the goddess of reason replaced the one of Virgin Mary.

Napoleon came to power in France and saw that the French people were basically Catholic at heart. He tried to swoon these people to his side by making pseudo and bogus overtures to the Catholic Church. In 1801, he signed a concordat (Vatican treaty) with Pope Pius VII giving back Church property seized during the French Revolution and the infamous Reign of Terror. He went so far as to have the pope come to Paris and crown him emperor in the Cathedral of Notre Dame. With audacious pride, he grabbed the crown from the aged pope and literally crowned himself and then his Empress Josephine.

Yet the Revolution drastically changed Catholicism forever — not only in France but also throughout Europe. The people of France were able to declare themselves non-Catholic or non-Christian. By the creation of a civil state, divorce became acceptable. Anti-clericalism and atheism later flourished in a country that was called the Eldest Daughter of the Church.

After an unsuccessful campaign in Russia, Napoleon was defeated in 1814 and exiled to Elba. He returned to Paris a year later (1815) for a short reign of 100 days until his defeat by the British Duke of Wellington. He was exiled to the island of St. Helena until his death from cancer in 1821. After Napoleon's defeat and exile, two factions occupied France. The Liberals wanted to perpetuate the ideals of the French Revolution. The Conservatives wanted a restoration of the monarchy and Catholicism. However, the Catholic Church in France never fully recovered from the devastation that the Revolution created. Seeds of indifference to the true faith were sewn, and they blossomed and flourished into the 20th century after World War II.

The restoration of the monarchy and Church to France

The 19th century saw the restoration of the monarchy to France. Catholic schools, convents, monasteries, and seminaries were reopened. Great attention was given to clerical formation. As a result of the new freedom, the Church enjoyed a sense of renewed optimism. New religious communities were established and new parishes and new dioceses were created. A revival in devotion commenced, and the Church believes that two great spiritual events occurred:

- In 1858, the Blessed Virgin Mary appeared 18 times to a poor peasant girl named Bernadette Soubirous in Lourdes. Even to this date, hundreds of thousands of people flock to Lourdes for spiritual renewal or a miracle. (See Chapters 18 and 19 for more on St. Bernadette and Lourdes, respectively.)

- The little town of Ars, France, became the home of one the holiest parish priests, St. John Vianney (1786–1859). He didn't belong to any religious order, like the Dominicans or Franciscans. Rather, he was a diocesan priest (see Chapter 2), the first diocesan priest to be canonized. Today, he's the patron saint of all parish priests. His work and evangelization became a hallmark to be studied and copied by every priest. (See Chapter 7 for more on St. John Vianney.)

The Oxford Movement in England

In England, with the Act of Emancipation in 1829, the Catholic Church was allowed freedom of worship — something that had been denied since the Reign of Henry VIII. As a result, a great renaissance in the faith occurred. Religious communities were able to come from Italy and preach, teach, and commence devotions.

At this time, a great revival also occurred in the Anglican Church, the official Church of England. It was known as the Oxford Movement (1833–1845), and it attempted to recapture many Catholic doctrines and tried to introduce many of the customs, traditions, rituals, pageantry, and color of the Catholic Church. Up until then, the Anglican Church had leaned toward the Puritan style. Few vestments, little use of liturgical colors, statues, candles, and so on. In other words, the Oxford Movement attempted to Romanize belief and worship, while retaining their Anglican identity.

One of the great supporters of this movement was John Henry Newman. An Anglican minister and professor at Oxford, he became influenced by the Catholic Church and later converted to Catholicism. He then became a cardinal and joined the Oratory of St. Philip Neri.

A revival of Catholicism was beginning in England.

Catholicism in the New World

In the New World, the Catholic Church was firmly planted in French Canada and Spanish Central and South America, but in the Protestant colonies of England that would eventually become the United States, the Catholic Church grew slowly despite anti-Catholic prejudice and bias.

In 1792, Fr. John Carroll became the first bishop of the United States in Baltimore, Maryland, which had been colonized by Lord Calvert, a Catholic. From this colony, the Catholic faith spread by a priest who celebrated Mass secretly in Catholic homes during this time of persecution. Fr. Farmer provided for the spiritual and sacramental needs of Catholics already living in the colonies up to New York. By his hard work and effort, many converts were made and by 1808, a new diocese was established in New York, Philadelphia, and Boston.

The conversion of St. Elizabeth Ann Bailey Seton, a wealthy Episcopalian, to Catholicism saw the establishment of a new religious community devoted to education — the Sisters of Charity. The Episcopalian Church is the American — post revolution — version of the Anglican Church in England. In 1791, the first seminary and Catholic college was established. The French order of St. Sulpice staffed St. Mary's Seminary in Baltimore, and the Society of Jesus staffed Georgetown University. The early 19th century saw an increase in many orders dedicated to education, such as the Christian Brothers, Brothers of the Holy Cross, the Religious Sisters of Mercy, Sisters of St. Joseph, Chestnut Hill, Sisters of St. Francis, and the Xaverian Brothers.

Nuns and brothers of the immigrants' own nationality followed the different waves of immigration. These nuns and brothers were able to speak the immigrants' own language, making it possible for their children to enter into the life of the New World without losing their faith. The New World was a new continent on which to reestablish the Catholic Church.

But during the 19th century, with the increase of immigration from Catholic countries of eastern, southern, and central Europe, as well as Ireland, bigotry against Catholics increased. In New York, the Know Nothing party was established, and it provoked riots and the burning of Catholic churches. In Boston, convents were burned down. So, too, the Ku Klux Klan, which became very powerful in the 1920s, included Catholics and Catholic churches on their list of targets, along with Jews and Blacks.

However, by the end of the 19th century, the Church was firmly planted and rooted in the American soil. And in the early part of the 20th century, the United States wasn't considered missionary territory anymore.

The Modern Era

Roughly at the same time as the First Vatican Council (1869–1870), which defined the doctrine of Papal Infallibility (see Chapter 2), the Italian unification process took shape under Victor Emmanuel, threatening the Papal States. The Carolingian Frankish King Pepin the Short, father of Charlemagne, gave the Papal States *(Patrimonium Petri)* to the pope for his secular rule (754–1870). The temporal powers of the pope were being threatened under this unification of Italy especially since Rome was the center of the Papal States and the future capital of a unified Italy. Though the pope eventually lost his temporal power in 1870, he would later be recognized as the head of state of the smallest independent nation of the world (0.44 square miles). To accomplish this, Vatican City and the Republic of Italy signed the Lateran Treaty in 1929.

In the late 19th century, Europe was undergoing many changes. Areas that were parts of empires became separate countries. This era defined France, Germany, and Italy as countries. Germany formed a nation and saw the pope as a threat to its unification. Otto von Bismarck (1815–1898) passed laws that persecuted the Catholic Church in Germany called the *kulturkampf* (conflict of cultures). This led to a vast emigration of German Catholics to the United States fleeing persecution in the fatherland.

It was in this setting that Leo XIII (1878–1903) became pope. The Industrial Revolution was also in full swing in England, Germany, and the United States at this time. The common rights of workers were threatened and denied. As a result, Pope Leo wrote the magnificent papal encyclical *Rerum Novarum* on the sanctity of human work, dignity of workers, and the justice that's owed to them. He condemned all sorts of radical stances, such as extreme capitalism and atheistic communism, while defending the rights of private property and the right to form guilds or trade unions. This social encyclical gave the impetus for Catholic unions in the United States.

Pope St. Pius X (1903–1914) followed the reign of Leo XIII. He was known as the pope of the children. He extended the right to receive Holy Communion to all Catholic children who had reached the age of reason — 7 years old. Also, he composed a syllabus of errors. In it he condemned certain tenets of *modernism,* a heresy that denied aspects of the faith and accepted all sorts of progressivism to the point that it damaged the integrity of the faith. To be a modernist didn't mean that you were a modern thinker and able to communicate to your contemporaries. Rather, to get its message across, modernism used falsehoods to prove its point. If anything, modernism was nothing more than elaborate academic skepticism run rampant.

The turmoil of two world wars and the Church's stand against communism and fascism

World War I (1914–18), the war that was supposed to end all wars, was truly bloody. In the end, the Austrian Hungarian Empire was divided up. People in the old empire who hated Austria saw that the Church was in line with the old regime, and therefore, the Church was persecuted in these areas. Bismarck and his Germany were defeated, going into deep economic depression. Many lives were lost on both sides.

In 1917, three little children in Fatima, Portugal (see Chapter 19), saw an apparition of the Blessed Virgin Mary. She told the children that unless people reformed, turned away from their evil ways, and came back to her Son Jesus, a great war would rage. Mary also requested that the world be consecrated to her Immaculate Heart by the bishops of the world in union with the pope. People didn't heed her warning, and World War II resulted.

Combined with a worldwide depression in 1929, fascism gained power. Europe was in turmoil. In Spain, the anti-Catholic communists combated royalists in a terrible civil war. Like the French Revolution, many Catholic priests and sisters were martyred. However, under General Franco (1892–1975), the communists were defeated in 1939. Though the Church was able to flourish, Spain remained under his dictatorship until the 1970s.

Italy, ruled by the House of Savoy after its unification in 1870, came under the influence of the Fascist Dictator Mussolini (1883–1945) in 1928. Later, he teamed up with Adolf Hitler (1889–1945) during World War II (1939–1945). However, it was in Nazi Germany that fascism reached the depth of depravity and evil.

The Church was unanimously against the evils of communism on the one hand and fascism on the other. With the onslaught of World War II, Pope Pius XII (1939–1958) diplomatically tried to help those affected by the diabolical evil of Adolf Hitler. Though maligned terribly by some in the secular press today, Pius XII actively worked for the safety of the Jewish people. Shortly after his election as pope (March 2, 1939), the Nazi newspaper, *Berliner Morganpost* blasted: "The election of Cardinal Pacelli (as Pius XII) is not accepted with favor in Germany, because he was always opposed to Nazism."

At one point during the war, the Vatican, considered neutral territory by the Geneva Conference, hid and cared for up to 3,500 Jews. Through its nuncios (ambassadors), the Church falsified documents to aid Jews by providing fictitious baptismal certificates to appear as Catholic Christians. As a result, many priests, nuns, Catholic laymen lost their lives rescuing and sheltering their brother and sister Jews. Recently released Vatican records indicate that the Catholic Church operated an underground railroad that rescued 800,000 European Jews from the Holocaust. In 1942, the New York Times editorial (December 25) read:

> The voice of Pius XII is a lonely voice in the silence and darkness enveloping Europe this Christmas. . . . He is about the only ruler left on the Continent of Europe who dares to raise his voice at all.

Finally, in 1958, Prime Minister Golda Meir sent a moving eulogy at the death of Pope Pius XII:

> We share in the grief of humanity. . . . When fearful martyrdom came to our people, the voice of the pope was raised for its victims. The life of our times was enriched by a voice speaking out about great moral truths above the tumult of daily conflict. We mourn a great servant of peace.

The most eloquent testimony to the real Pius XII who did all he could to help save Jews during World War II is the conversion of the chief Rabbi of Rome, Israele Anton Zolli, to Roman Catholicism in 1945 in appreciation. He even took the baptismal name Eugenio, because it was Pius XII's baptismal name. Many complain 50 years later that Pius may have, could have, and should have done more to stop or impede the Holocaust. Hindsight is wonderful half a century after the fact. More recently uncovered documents from former Warsaw Pact nations after the collapse of the Soviet Union show that Hitler had planned to capture Pius XII and install his own antipope with residence in Belgium should the pope become too much of a nuisance. Whether Pius was aware of this plan, we may never know.

The Church's rocky road in Eastern Europe

Czarist Russia fell to the Communists in 1917 during World War I (1914–1918). As a result, a godless government came into being that later proved to be a nemesis for the Orthodox Church, as well as the Catholic Church in Eastern Europe.

After World War II, many of the Eastern countries were occupied by the U.S.S.R. This godless state actively persecuted the Church and anyone who belonged to it. Bishops couldn't be appointed to their diocese. Seminaries were illegal. The Catholic faith stayed alive in Eastern Europe because of the underground Church.

Let the sun shine in

Not all was gloom and doom after World War II. The Catholic Church greatly expanded in the United States. From 1910 to 1930, the population of the United States grew tremendously. This was a result from a vast emigration from Southern and Eastern Europe, which were mainly Catholic countries. As a result, by the 1950s, these emigrant groups grew financially, politically, and socially. The 1950s saw a rise in vocations to the priesthood and religious life. Churches, seminaries, schools, colleges, universities, hospitals, and other institutions grew tremendously.

With the death of Pius XII, a new era in the Church began with the reign of Pope John XXIII (1958–1963). Some of the man-made customs that crept into the Church since the Council of Trent were now archaic and needed reform. He called for a new council, the Second Vatican Council (1962–1965), also known as Vatican II. One year into the Council, John XXIII died. Paul VI (1963–1978) was elected after him and concluded the council. The council didn't define any new doctrines nor did it substantially alter any either. It didn't abolish any Catholic traditions or devotions but asked that they be kept in proper perspective to the revealed truths of the faith and subservient to the Sacred Liturgy of the Church. Vatican II didn't create new teaching but explained the ancient faith in new ways to address new issues and concerns. (See Chapter 8 for more on Vatican II.)

Paul VI wrote many *encyclicals* (letters from the pope addressed to the world), his most famous one being entitled, *Humanae Vitae* or *On Human Life*. It challenged modern-day society who had given in to the contraceptive mentality. He predicted in 1968 that if people didn't respect human life from the beginning, they will not respect it in the end. He claimed that artificial contraception would lead to an increase in abortions, divorce, broken families, and other social troubles. Twenty-five years later on the anniversary of the encyclical, Pope John Paul II wrote another encyclical, entitled *Gospel of Life*. In it, he states that the warnings of Paul VI have come true. (See Chapter 12 for more on the controversial issues addressed by the Church.)

After Paul VI died on August 6, 1978, and John Paul I was elected his successor 20 days later. He chose to take the names of his two most immediate predecessors, John XXIII and Paul VI, the two popes of the Second Vatican Council. Unfortunately, he only lived one month as pope and died mysteriously in his sleep on September 28, 1978. Rumors abound the circumstances of his untimely demise but nothing credible has ever been established or demonstrated.

On October 16, 1978, Karol Cardinal Wojtyla was elected pope and became Pope John Paul II. (See Chapter 17 for details on his life.) During his pontificate, the Berlin Wall fell, the Soviet Union collapsed, and much of the world went to war in the Persian Gulf. Though the Church faces new problems at the beginning of the 21st century, the encouraging words of John Paul II as he began his reign re-echo, "Be not afraid."

Appendix B

Fun Facts for the Faithful

· ·

All the Popes

Beginning with St. Peter, this complete listing of all the popes, with the years that they filled this high office alongside in parentheses, is a helpful reference tool, especially when you read Chapter 2 and Appendix A on Church history. You may want to paperclip or bookmark this page to save you from flipping through the pages to find it.

1. St. Peter (32–67)

2. St. Linus (67–76)

3. St. Anacletus (Cletus) (76–88)

4. St. Clement I (88–97)

5. St. Evaristus (97–105)

6. St. Alexander I (105–115)

7. St. Sixtus I (115–125)

8. St. Telesphorus (125–136)

9. St. Hyginus (136–140)

10. St. Pius I (140–155)

11. St. Anicetus (155–166)

12. St. Soter (166–175)

13. St. Eleutherius (175–189)

14. St. Victor I (189–199)

15. St. Zephyrinus (199–217)

16. St. Callistus I (217–22)

17. St. Urban I (222–30)

18. St. Pontain (230–35)

19. St. Anterus (235–36)

20. St. Fabian (236–50)

21. St. Cornelius (251–53)

22. St. Lucius I (253–54)

23. St. Stephen I (254–257)

24. St. Sixtus II (257–258)

25. St. Dionysius (260–268)

26. St. Felix I (269–274)

27. St. Eutychian (275–283)

28. St. Caius (283–296)

29. St. Marcellinus (296–304)

30. St. Marcellus I (308–309)

31. St. Eusebius (309 or 310)

32. St. Miltiades (311–14)

33. St. Sylvester I (314–35)

34. St. Marcus (336)

35. St. Julius I (337–52)

36. Liberius (352–66)

37. St. Damasus I (366–83)

38. St. Siricius (384–99)

39. St. Anastasius I (399–401)

40. St. Innocent I (401–17)

41. St. Zosimus (417–18)

42. St. Boniface I (418–22)

43. St. Celestine I (422–32)

44. St. Sixtus III (432–40)

45. St. Leo I (the Great) (440–61)

46. St. Hilarius (461–68)

47. St. Simplicius (468–83)

48. St. Felix III (II) (483–92)

49. St. Gelasius I (492–96)

50. Anastasius II (496–98)

51. St. Symmachus (498–514)

52. St. Hormisdas (514–23)

53. St. John I (523–26)

54. St. Felix IV (III) (526–30)

55. Boniface II (530–32)

56. John II (533–35)

57. St. Agapetus I (535–36)

58. St. Silverius (536–37)

59. Vigilius (537–55)

60. Pelagius I (556–61)

61. John III (561–74)

62. Benedict I (575–79)

63. Pelagius II (579–90)

64. St. Gregory I (the Great) (590–604)

65. Sabinian (604–606)

66. Boniface III (607)

67. St. Boniface IV (608–15)

68. St. Deusdedit (Adeodatus I) (615–18)

69. Boniface V (619–25)

70. Honorius I (625–38)

71. Severinus (640)

72. John IV (640–42)

73. Theodore I (642–49)

74. St. Martin I (649–55)

75. St. Eugene I (655–57)

76. St. Vitalian (657–72)

77. Adeodatus (II) (672–76)

78. Donus (676–78)

79. St. Agatho (678–81)

80. St. Leo II (682–83)

81. St. Benedict II (684–85)

82. John V (685–86)

83. Conon (686–87)

84. St. Sergius I (687–701)

85. John VI (701–05)

86. John VII (705–07)

87. Sisinnius (708)

88. Constantine (708–15)

89. St. Gregory II (715–31)

90. St. Gregory III (731–41)

91. St. Zachary (741–52)

92. Stephen II (752)

93. Stephen III (752–57)

94. St. Paul I (757–67)

95. Stephen IV (767–72)

96. Adrian I (772–95)

97. St. Leo III (795–816)

98. Stephen V (816–17)

99. St. Paschal I (817–24)

100. Eugene II (824–27)

101. Valentine (827)

102. Gregory IV (827–44)

103. Sergius II (844–47)

104. St. Leo IV (847–55)

105. Benedict III (855–58)

106. St. Nicholas I the Great (858–67)

107. Adrian II (867–72)

108. John VIII (872–82)

109. Marinus I (882–84)

110. St. Adrian III (884–85)

111. Stephen VI (885–91)

112. Formosus (891–96)

113. Boniface VI (896)

114. Stephen VII (896–97)

115. Romanus (897)

116. Theodore II (897)

117. John IX (898–900)

118. Benedict IV (900–03)

119. Leo V (903)

120. Sergius III (904–11)

121. Anastasius III (911–13)

122. Lando (913–14)

123. John X (914–28)

124. Leo VI (928)

125. Stephen VIII (929–31)

126. John XI (931–35)

127. Leo VII (936–39)

128. Stephen IX (939–42)

129. Marinus II (942–46)

130. Agapetus II (946–55)

131. John XII (955–63)

132. Leo VIII (963–64)

133. Benedict V (964)

134. John XIII (965–72)

135. Benedict VI (973–74)

136. Benedict VII (974–83)

137. John XIV (983–84)

138. John XV (985–96)

139. Gregory V (996–99)

140. Sylvester II (999–1003)

141. John XVII (1003)

142. John XVIII (1003–09)

143. Sergius IV (1009–12)

144. Benedict VIII (1012–24)

145. John XIX (1024–32)

146. Benedict IX (1032–45)

147. Sylvester III (1045)

148. Benedict IX (1045)

149. Gregory VI (1045–46)

150. Clement II (1046–47)

151. Benedict IX (1047–48)

152. Damasus II (1048)

153. St. Leo IX (1049–54)

154. Victor II (1055–57)

155. Stephen X (1057–58)

156. Nicholas II (1058–61)

157. Alexander II (1061–73)

158. St. Gregory VII (1073–85)

159. Blessed Victor III (1086–87)

160. Blessed Urban II (1088–99)

161. Paschal II (1099–1118)

162. Gelasius II (1118–19)

163. Callistus (1119–24)

164. Honorius II (1124–30)

165. Innocent II (1130–43)

166. Celestine II (1143–44)

167. Lucius II (1144–45)

168. Blessed Eugene III (1145–53)

169. Anastasius IV (1153–54)

170. Adrian IV (1154–59)

171. Alexander III (1159–81)

172. Lucius III (1181–85)

173. Urban III (1185–87)

174. Gregory VIII (1187)

175. Clement III (1187–91)

176. Celestine III (1191–98)

177. Innocent III (1198–1216)

178. Honorius III (1216–27)

179. Gregory IX (1227–41)

180. Celestine IV (1241)

181. Innocent IV (1243–54)

182. Alexander IV (1254–61)

183. Urban IV (1261–64)

184. Clement IV (1265–68)

185. Blessed Gregory X (1271–76)

186. Blessed Innocent V (1276)

187. Adrian V (1276)

188. John XXI (1276–77)

189. Nicholas III (1277–80)

190. Martin IV (1281–85)

191. Honorius IV (1285–87)

192. Nicholas IV (1288–92)

193. St. Celestine V (1294)

194. Boniface VIII (1294–1303)

195. Blessed Benedict XI (1303–04)

196. Clement V (1305–14)

197. John XXII (1316–34)

198. Benedict XII (1334–42)

199. Clement VI (1342–52)

200. Innocent VI (1352–62)

201. Blessed Urban V (1362–70)

202. Gregory XI (1370–78)

203. Urban VI (1378–89)

204. Boniface IX (1389–1404)

205. Innocent VII (1404–06)

206. Gregory XII (1406–15)

207. Martin V (1417–31)

208. Eugene IV (1431–47)

209. Nicholas V (1447–55)

210. Callistus III (1455–58)

211. Pius II (1458–64)

212. Paul II (1464–71)

213. Sixtus IV (1471–84)

214. Innocent VIII (1484–92)

215. Alexander VI (1492–1503)

216. Pius III (1503)

217. Julius II (1503–13)

218. Leo X (1513–21)

219. Adrian VI (1522–23)

220. Clement VII (1523–34)

221. Paul III (1534–49)

222. Julius III (1550–55)

223. Marcellus II (1555)

224. Paul IV (1555–59)

225. Pius IV (1559–65)

226. St. Pius V (1566–72)

227. Gregory XIII (1572–85)

228. Sixtus V (1585–90)

229. Urban VII (1590)

230. Gregory XIV (1590–91)

231. Innocent IX (1591)

232. Clement VIII (1592–1605)

233. Leo XI (1605)

234. Paul V (1605–21)

235. Gregory XV (1621–23)

236. Urban VIII (1623–44)

237. Innocent X (1644–55)

238. Alexander VII (1655–67)

239. Clement IX (1667–69)

240. Clement X (1670–76)

241. Blessed Innocent XI (1676–89)

242. Alexander VIII (1689–91)

243. Innocent XII (1691–1700)

244. Clement XI (1700–21)

245. Innocent XIII (1721–24)

246. Benedict XIII (1724–30)

247. Clement XII (1730–40)

248. Benedict XIV (1740–58)

249. Clement XIII (1758–69)

250. Clement XIV (1769–74)

251. Pius VI (1775–99)

252. Pius VII (1800–23)

253. Leo XII (1823–29)

254. Pius VIII (1829–30)

255. Gregory XVI (1831–46)

256. Blessed Pius IX (1846–78)

257. Leo XIII (1878–1903)

258. St. Pius X (1903–14)

259. Benedict XV (1914–22)

260. Pius XI (1922–39)

261. Pius XII (1939–58)

262. Blessed John XXIII (1958–63)

263. Paul VI (1963–78)

264. John Paul I (1978)

265. John Paul II (1978–)

Solemnities, Feasts, and Memorials for the Year

Like sorting through tabular material? If not, divert thine eyes quickly to another part of the book. If so, you're gonna love what's next. The following listing tells you all about the solemnities, the feasts, and the memorials that take place throughout the calendar year. For more information on solemnities, feasts, and memorials, see Chapter 8.

1/1: Solemnity of Mary, Mother of God (Solemnity)

1/2: SS. Basil the Great and Gregory Nazianzen (Memorial)

1/3: Most Holy Name of Jesus

1/4: St. Elizabeth Ann Seton (Memorial)

1/5: St. John Neumann (Memorial)

1/6: Epiphany (Solemnity)

1/7: St. Raymond of Penyafort

1/13: St. Hilary

1/17: St. Anthony (Memorial)

1/20: St. Fabian and St. Sebastian

1/21: St. Agnes (Memorial)

1/22: St. Vincent

1/24: St. Francis de Sales (Memorial)

1/25: The conversion of St. Paul (Feast)

1/26: SS. Timothy and Titus (Memorial)

1/27: St. Angela Merici

1/28: St. Thomas Aquinas (Memorial)

1/31: St. John Bosco (Memorial)

Sunday after January 6: Baptism of Our Lord (Feast)

2/2: Presentation of Our Lord (Feast)

2/3: St. Blase and St. Ansgar

2/5: St. Agatha (Memorial)

2/6: SS. Paul Miki and companions (Memorial)

2/8: St. Jerome Emiliani, St. Josephine Bakhita

2/10: St. Scholastica (Memorial)

2/11: Our Lady of Lourdes

2/14: St. Cyril and St. Methodius (Memorial)

2/17: Seven Founders of Servites

2/21: St. Peter Damian

2/22: Chair of St. Peter, Apostle (Feast)

2/23: St. Polycarp (Memorial)

3/3: St. Katherine Drexel

3/4: St. Casimir

3/7: SS. Perpetua and Felicity (Memorial)

3/8: St. John of God

3/9: St. Frances of Rome

3/17: St. Patrick

3/18: St. Cyril of Jerusalem

3/19: St. Joseph, Husband of Mary (Solemnity)

3/23: St. Turibius de Mongrovejo

3/25: Annunciation (Solemnity)

4/2: St. Francis of Paola

4/4: St. Isidore

4/5: St. Vincent Ferrer

4/7: St. John Baptist de la Salle

4/11: St. Stanislaus

4/13: St. Martin I

4/21: St. Anselm

4/23: St. George, St. Adalbert

4/24: St. Fidelis of Sigmaringen

4/25: St. Mark, Evangelist (Feast)

4/28: St. Peter Chanel, St. Louis Mary de Montfort

4/29: St. Catherine of Siena (Memorial)

4/30: Pope St. Pius V

5/1: St. Joseph the Worker

5/2: St. Athanasius (Memorial)

5/3: SS. Philip and James, Apostles (Feast)

5/12: SS. Nereus, Achilleus, and Pancras

5/13: Our Lady of Fatima

5/14: St. Matthias, Apostle (Feast)

5/15: St. Isidore

5/18: St. John I

5/20: St. Bernardine of Siena

5/21: St. Christopher Magallanes and Companions

5/22: St. Rita of Cascia

5/25: St. Bede, Pope St. Gregory VII, and

St. Mary Magdalene de Pazzi

5/26: St. Philip Neri (Memorial)

5/27: St. Augustine of Canterbury

5/31: Visitation (Feast)

1st Sunday after Pentecost: Holy Trinity (Solemnity)

Sunday after Holy Trinity: Corpus Christi (Solemnity)

Friday following 2nd Sunday after Pentecost: Sacred Heart (Solemnity)

Saturday following 2nd Sunday after Pentecost: Immaculate Heart of Mary

6/1: St. Justin (Memorial)

6/2: SS. Marcellinus and Peter

6/3: St. Charles Lwanga and companions (Memorial)

6/5: St. Boniface (Memorial)

6/6: St. Norbert

6/9: St. Ephrem

6/11: St. Barnabas, Apostle (Memorial)

6/13: St. Anthony of Padua (Memorial)

6/19: St. Romuald

6/21: St. Aloysius Gonzaga (Memorial)

6/22: St. Paulinus of Nola, SS. John Fisher and Thomas More

6/24: Birth of John the Baptist (Solemnity)

6/26: St. Josemaría Escrivá

6/27: St. Cyril of Alexandria

6/28: St. Irenaeus (Memorial)

6/29: SS. Peter and Paul, Apostles (Solemnity)

6/30: First Martyrs of the Church of Rome

7/1: Bl. Junipero Serra

7/3: St. Thomas, Apostle (Feast)

7/4: St. Elizabeth of Portugal

7/5: St. Anthony Zaccaria

7/6: St. Maria Goretti

7/9: St. Augustine Zhao Rong and Companions

7/11: St. Benedict (Memorial)

7/13: St. Henry

7/14: St. Camillus de Lellis, Bl. Kateri Tekakwitha

7/15: St. Bonaventure (Memorial)

7/16: Our Lady of Mount Carmel

7/20: St. Apollinarus

7/21: St. Lawrence of Brindisi

7/22: St. Mary Magdalene (Memorial)

7/23: St. Bridget

7/24: St. Sharbel Makhluf

7/25: St. James, Apostle (Feast)

7/26: SS. Joachim and Ann (Memorial)

7/29: St. Martha (Memorial)

7/30: St. Peter Chrysologus

7/31: St. Ignatius of Loyola (Memorial)

8/1: St. Alphonsus Liguori (Memorial)

8/2: St. Eusebius of Vercelli, St. Peter Julian Eymard

8/4: St. John Vianney (Memorial)

8/5: Dedication of St. Mary Major

8/6: Transfiguration (Feast)

8/7: Pope St. Sixtus II and companions, St. Cajetan

8/8: St. Dominic (Memorial)

8/9: St. Theresiae Benedicta of the Cross

8/10: St. Lawrence (Feast)

8/11: St. Clare (Memorial)

8/13: St. Pontian and St. Hippolytus

8/14: St. Maximilian Kolbe

8/15: Assumption (Solemnity)

8/16: St. Stephen of Hungary

8/18: St. Jane Frances de Chantal

8/19: St. John Eudes

8/20: St. Bernard (Memorial)

8/21: Pope St. Pius X (Memorial)

8/22: Queenship of Mary (Memorial)

8/23: St. Rose of Lima

8/24: St. Bartholomew, Apostle (Feast)

8/25: St. Louis of France and St. Joseph Calasanz

8/27: St. Monica (Memorial)

8/28: St. Augustine (Memorial)

8/29: Beheading of John the Baptist (Memorial)

9/3: Pope St. Gregory the Great (Memorial)

9/8: Birth of Mary (Feast)

9/9: St. Peter Claver (Memorial)

9/12: Most Holy Name of the Blessed Virgin Mary

9/13: St. John Chrysostom (Memorial)

9/14: Triumph of The Cross (Feast)

9/15: Our Lady of Sorrows (Memorial)

9/16: SS. Cornelius and Cyprian (Memorial)

9/17: St. Robert Bellarmine

9/19: St. Januarius

9/20: St. Andrew Kim Taegon, St. Paul Chong Hasang and companions

9/21: St. Matthew, Apostle and Evangelist (Feast)

9/23: St. Pio of Pietrelcina

9/26: SS. Cosmas and Damian

9/27: St. Vincent de Paul (Memorial)

9/28: St. Wenceslaus, St. Lawrence Ruiz and Companions

9/29: SS. Michael, Gabriel, and Raphael, Archangels (Feast)

9/30: St. Jerome (Memorial)

10/1: St. Thérèse of Lisieux (Memorial)

10/2: Guardian Angels (Memorial)

10/4: St. Francis of Assisi (Memorial)

10/6: St. Bruno

10/7: Our Lady of the Rosary (Memorial)

10/9: SS. Denis and companions, St. John Leonardi

10/14: Pope St. Callistus I

10/15: St. Teresa of Avila (Memorial)

10/16: St. Hedwig and St. Margaret Mary Alacoque

10/17: St. Ignatius of Antioch (Memorial)

10/18: St. Luke, Evangelist (Feast)

10/19: SS. Isaac Jogues, John de Brebeuf, and companions (Memorial)

10/20: St. Paul of the Cross

10/23: St. John of Capistrano

10/24: St. Anthony of Claret

10/28: SS. Simon and Jude, Apostles (Feast)

11/1: All Saints (Solemnity)

11/2: All Souls (Feast)

11/3: St. Martin de Porres

11/4: St. Charles Borromeo (Memorial)

11/9: Dedication of Saint John Lateran (Feast)

11/10: Pope St. Leo the Great (Memorial)

11/11: St. Martin of Tours (Memorial)

11/12: St. Josaphat (Memorial)

11/13: St. Frances Xavier Cabrini (Memorial)

11/15: St. Albert the Great

11/16: St. Margaret of Scotland, St. Gertrude

11/17: St. Elizabeth of Hungary (Memorial)

11/18: Dedication of the churches of SS. Peter and Paul, Apostles

11/21: Presentation of Mary (Memorial)

11/22: St. Cecilia (Memorial)

11/23: Pope St. Clement I, St. Columban & Bl. Miguel Pro

11/24: St. Andrew Dung-Lac and Companions (Memorial)

11/25: St. Catherine of Alexandria

11/30: St. Andrew, Apostle (Feast)

Last Sunday in Ordinary Time: Christ the King (Solemnity)

12/3: St. Francis Xavier (Memorial)

12/4: St. John Damascene

12/6: St. Nicholas

12/7: St. Ambrose (Memorial)

12/8: Immaculate Conception (Solemnity)

12/9: St. Juan Diego

12/11: Pope St. Damasus I

12/12: Our Lady of Guadalupe (Feast)

12/13: St. Lucy (Memorial)

12/14: St. John of the Cross (Memorial)

12/21: St. Peter Canisius

12/23: St. John of Kanty

12/25: Christmas (Solemnity)

12/26: St. Stephen (Feast)

12/27: St. John, Apostle and Evangelist (Feast)

12/28: Holy Innocents (Feast)

12/29: St. Thomas Becket

12/31: Pope St. Sylvester I

Sunday within the octave of Christmas or if no Sunday falls within the octave, or December 30: Holy Family (Feast)

Index

• I •

• R •